Ethnography in Today's World

HANEY FOUNDATION SERIES

A volume in the Haney Foundation Series, established in 1961 with the generous support of Dr. John Louis Haney

Ethnography in Today's World

Color Full Before Color Blind

Roger Sanjek

PENN

UNIVERSITY OF PENNSYLVANIA PRESS

PHILADELPHIA

Published by
University of Pennsylvania Press
Philadelphia, Pennsylvania 19104-4112
www.upenn.edu/pennpress

Printed in the United States of America on acid-free paper
10 9 8 7 6 5 4 3 2 1

Library of Congress Cataloging-in-Publication Data
Sanjek, Roger, 1944–
Ethnography in today's world : color full before color blind / Roger Sanjek.—1st ed.
p. cm. — (Haney foundation series)
Includes bibliographical references and index.
ISBN 978-0-8122-4545-5 (hardcover : alk. paper)
1. Ethnology—United States—Methodology. 2. Ethnology—Methodology.
3. Anthropology—United States—Methodology. 4. Anthropology—Methodology.
I. Title.
GN345.S255 2014
305.800973—dc23

2013019444

For my teachers: Anne Schwerner, Robert Stigler, Marvin Harris, Lambros Comitas, Jaap van Velsen, George C. Bond, Allen Johnson

Contents

Preface

This book might have been titled *For Ethnography!* or, alternatively, *Ethnography for What?* Throughout, it aims to affirm the value of ethnography in engaging contemporary issues of race, migration, political activism, and an urbanizing globe. It includes as well essays examining this distinctive anthropological fieldwork method—ethnography, or participant observation—which its practitioners use to understand particular groups and places. And last, it asserts that ethnography is inescapably lodged in the social worlds of those who use it: first, as they decide what to study; then, how to do it; and finally, how to engage various publics with their findings.

The essays, now revised, were originally composed during the last decade of the twentieth century and the first decade of the twenty-first. They build upon and extend ideas and arguments contained in my books *Fieldnotes: The Makings of Anthropology* (1990), *The Future of Us All: Race and Neighborhood Politics in New York City* (1998), and *Gray Panthers* (2009). They also reflect the journey of an anthropologist who entered the field when it was undergoing tumultuous change in the 1960s, who moved from fieldwork abroad in Brazil and Ghana to long-term engagements in his own society, and who, after weathering theoretical storms in ensuing decades, now values ethnography even more than when he began.[1]

Engaging Ethnography

The book's first part, *Engaging Ethnography*, contains three chapters about fieldwork in New York City's Elmhurst-Corona district. Chapter 1, "Color Full before Color Blind: The Emergence of Multiracial Neighborhood Politics in Queens, New York City," summarizes the major findings and arguments about this fieldwork arena in my book *The Future of Us All*. It was first presented as a talk to a multidisciplinary scholarly audience at the Russell Sage Foundation (which included sociologist Robert Merton, who, gratifyingly, told me that he enjoyed it). It was later published in the *American Anthropologist*, and here all demographic figures and projections are updated with more recent information.

This essay illustrates the "doing" of ethnography as this process is defined and historicized in Chapter 4 ("Ethnography"). Chapter 1 also exemplifies what "an ethnography of the present" with "a concern about the outcome," as advocated in Chapter 6 ("The Ethnographic Present"), might be, in this case in "perhaps the most ethnically mixed community in the world." The background sections about Elmhurst-Corona in the 1970s, before my fieldwork began in 1983, illustrate the importance of historical contextualization (more of this occurs in *The Future of Us All*). The significance of women leaders in these neighborhoods is what I found there "on the ground," although a feminist perspective no doubt ensured that I deliberately paid attention to both men and women (as I had in earlier fieldwork in Ghana and did from the 1970s onward as a Gray Panther participant). The lesson I draw about the importance of inclusive "color full before color blind" political action is also a fieldwork-derived conclusion. Indeed, had I done my fieldwork in this neighborhood ten years earlier, my findings on both scores would have been quite different.

Chapter 2, "The Organization of Festivals and Ceremonies among Americans and Immigrants in Queens, New York," was also written for a multidisciplinary academic audience, this time in Sweden, and halfway through my 1983–1996 Elmhurst-Corona fieldwork. The framework of four contrasting categories of local ritual events emerged while I was sitting in a Houston airport in 1988—a fieldwork-derived "theory of significance" that then led me to attend as many of these events as I could. I had not anticipated the range and degree of public ritual activity I encountered, and my Queens College students who later read this essay, most from similar or even these same neighborhoods, were surprised as well.

This chapter also illustrates the comparative and theoretical side of Chapter 4's "anthropological triangle" of ethnography, comparison, and contextualization. I enjoyed reflecting on Meyer Fortes's classic approach to the interlocking cycle of Talis and Namoos rituals and on Stanley Tambiah's similar portrayal of rituals in a Thai village. I also found helpful more recent thinking about ritual by Tambiah and Fredrik Barth. Bits of this analysis reappeared in *The Future of Us All*, but Chapter 2 here examines the public ritual efflorescence following racial change, immigration, and fiscal crisis in Queens with greater focus and coherence.

Chapter 3, "What Ethnographies Leave Out," answered a request from the editor of *Xcp: Cross-Cultural Poetics*, Mark Nowak. He asked for a contribution to a special issue on "Fieldnotes and Notebooks," and what he wanted, I realized, was something less conventionally academic. The two fieldnote episodes I proposed, of a "revival" at a Protestant church I was studying and "international day" at an elementary school, had struck me with their short-story–like ironies when they occurred. I knew I was not the person to attempt to recast them in that genre, but Mark agreed that on their own they were suitable for his journal issue.

In this book's context, these events show what raw notes from the field look like. Many of my Queens College students who read this piece—of diverse religious and cultural backgrounds, many from immigrant families—found the revival unfamiliar and remote, but not the international day events: most had participated in similar "rituals of inclusion" themselves.

Ethnography, Past and Present

The second section, *Ethnography, Past and Present*, moves away from fieldwork in Queens to the distinctive features and history of ethnography. Chapter 4, "Ethnography," introduces the "anthropological triangle" formula of ethnography, comparison (where theory comes in), and contextualization. It then briefly surveys the development of ethnography by such germinal figures as Lewis Henry Morgan, Frank Cushing, Franz Boas, Bronislaw Malinowski, Margaret Mead, William Foote Whyte, and Max Gluckman, who reappear in other chapters. Finally, it examines the "funnel"-like, wide-to-narrow course of ethnographic fieldwork: through situated listening, observation, and interviewing to utilizing fieldnotes in writing ethnographic accounts. This chapter embodies the didactic tone and tight word budget of two encyclopedia entries (on "ethnography" and "field observational research") that are combined here.[2]

Like most of this volume's essays, Chapter 5, "Anthropology's Hidden Colonialism: Assistants and Their Ethnographers," was first presented in oral form, in this instance at an American Anthropological Association (AAA) panel on "Scholarly Canons and the Replication of Hierarchies" organized by George Bond. It reemphasizes the "color full before color blind" theme by showing how ethnography in its formative years was frequently produced not by "lone strangers"[3] but by hierarchical multiracial partnerships and teams of white professionals directing assistants of color, who were often silenced and displaced, thus mirroring U.S. and European colonialism. (Barbara Tedlock further complicates "lone stranger" narratives by detailing the role of "incorporated wives" in many male anthropologists' "two-person single careers."[4])

The standard "color-blind" history of ethnography needs rewriting, and since Chapter 5 was first published more contributions to themes raised in it have been made (or learned about by me) by Garrick Bailey, Andrew Bank, Judith Berman, Lane Hirabayashi, Ira Jacknis, Gordon Jensen and Luh Ketet Suryani, Joan Mark, Z. K. Matthews and Monica Wilson, Lyn Schumaker, Gerald Sullivan, Wayne Suttles, and Michael Young (as noted in "See also" references in Chapter 5's endnotes). In addition, Hugh Baker has brought the fascinating career of Hong Kong fieldwork assistant C. T. Leung into view.[5]

Chapter 6, "The Ethnographic Present," first appeared in a leading British anthropology journal (*Man: The Journal of the Royal Anthropological Institute*), and as Queens College students often reminded me, it is written in the most academic in-group style and format of the essays in this volume. Responding to the impact of 1980s postmodernism, it affirms the centrality of ethnography for an "anthropology of the present." The essays in the first, third, and fourth sections of this book are intended to illustrate this.

As Chapter 6 establishes, I found some aspects of postmodernist textual critiques unexpectedly congenial. My anthropological perspective was formed in the context of 1960s demands for "relevance" and for recognition and delineation of larger structures of power.[6] I was not much impressed with Levi-Strauss's structuralism, and the structural Marxism of the 1970s seemed overly abstract and tinker toy-ish. Political economy as it emerged in that decade was a welcomed carryover from the 1960s "critique from power," mainly for its contextual and comparative importance.[7] From the 1970s onward, feminism—politically, personally, professionally—was more important to me, with a much deeper impact on the way I saw the world and thought about power. It affected what I studied and wrote about, including two books, *The Future of Us All* and *Gray Panthers*, that turned out to be largely about women political activists.[8]

During the 1980s, as my Gray Panther involvement reemerged in New York and I began a team research project on racial change and immigration in that city, I also became editor of a Cornell University Press book series that I named *The Anthropology of Contemporary Issues*, which over the next two decades numbered fifty-two titles. Most were ethnographies, two-thirds were based on fieldwork in the United States, and they included a broad range of theoretical orientations: political economy, feminism, symbolic and psychological anthropology, migration studies, ethnoaesthetics, social history, the anthropology of Judaism, legal and medical anthropology, lesbian and gay studies, social gerontology, postmodernism. My editing experience made me receptive to anthropological concerns with "writing about writing," and I was an early reader of George Marcus and James Clifford.[9] Indeed, it was a suggestion by Clifford in 1984 that we needed to think about "the writing that precedes ethnographic writing—fieldnotes" that led to the 1985 AAA panel that eventually became *Fieldnotes*, with Clifford among its contributors.[10]

Postmodern anthropology, and Clifford and Marcus's *Writing Culture* (1986) in particular, provoked, inspired, and rankled. *Fieldnotes*, as well as *Localizing Strategies* (1990), edited by Richard Fardon and discussed in Chapter 6, reaffirmed a fieldwork-rooted, if more critically self-conscious, ethnography as still central to anthropology. They were followed by other such edited volumes—Ruth Behar and Deborah Gordon's *Women Writing Culture* (1995); Ellen Lewin and William Leap's *Out in the Field* (1996); Akhil Gupta and James Ferguson's *Anthropological Locations* (1997); Allison James, Jenny Hockey, and Andrew Dawson's *After Writing Culture* (1997); Karen Fog Olwig and Kirsten Hastrup's *Siting Culture* (1997); Irma McClaurin's *Black Feminist Anthropology* (2001)—as well as by Clifford's *Routes* (1997) and *On The Edges of Anthropology* (2003) and a continuing stream of overview essays by Marcus (such as those of 1995, 2006, 2009, 2010).

At the same time, hefty multiauthored and theoretically ecumenical volumes reemphasizing the broad range of post-1960s approaches also appeared: *Assessing Cultural Anthropology,* edited by Robert Borofsky (1994); the *Encyclopedia of Social and Cultural Anthropology,* edited by Alan Barnard and Jonathan Spencer (1996); *Handbook of Methods in Cultural Anthropology* ("meaningful," "person-centered," "discourse-centered," "direct systematic observation," "structured interviewing," "feminist," "transnational"), edited by H. Russell Bernard (1998); and *American*

Anthropology, 1971–1995: Papers from the American Anthropologist, edited by Regna Darnell (2002). Moreover, Darnell's insightful *Invisible Genealogies: A History of Americanist Anthropology* (2001) added greater time depth to assertions that much in pre-postmodern anthropology was of enduring, and even prescient, relevance to anthropology's present and future.

In the twenty-first century so far there has been no single "next big thing" in anthropology to follow postmodernism. The "convergence of applied, practicing, and public anthropology" that Louise Lamphere pointed to in 2004 has become more visible in professional meetings and journals, as well as in career trajectories,[11] but it has not displaced other interests and pursuits. The rise of digital media and communication in human social life is affecting how and what anthropologists study, and its impact will loom even larger in years to come.[12] Overall, the field (in multiple senses) of social and cultural anthropology is both broadening and consolidating. As Ulf Hannerz put it in 2010:

> Most of us simply want to get on with our work, which by now does not appear to be inevitably shaped by any of the more dramatic theoretical divides or confrontations of the later decades of the past century. . . . Recent thought within the discipline has tended to move away from grand theory, into a fertile middle ground where new connections cross-cut such divides as those between global, regional and local scales, between structures and events, between ethnography and history, between objectivism and experimental genres of writing, and between theory and practical concerns. . . . No real state of crisis here.[13]

Within this terrain, several recent volumes affirm that ethnography remains an indispensable resource.[14]

Comparison and Contextualization

The third section, *Comparison and Contextualization*, begins with Chapter 7, "Worth Holding Onto: The Participatory Discrepancies of Political Activism." This essay derives from an AAA panel I organized honoring ethnomusicologist Charles Keil.[15] Exemplifying the comparison side of the anthropological triangle, it applies Keil's theory of "participatory discrepancies" to the dynamics of political meetings in three fieldwork locations: Accra, Ghana; Gray Panthers in New York City; and Elmhurst-Corona. The question it addresses—why people keep coming to meetings—is one I had long pondered, and reading Keil's work suggested an intriguing answer.

Chapter 8, "Intermarriage and the Future of Races in America," began with wanting to understand the wider context of interracial marriages in the genealogies of white Elmhurst-Corona residents I interviewed. As I probed the history and current trends of intermarriage in the United States I found much that resonated with the differing Elmhurst-Corona residential experiences of African Americans and of Asian and Latin American newcomers: less neighboring interaction and intermarriage among whites and blacks, more among whites and Asians and Latin Americans.

Propinquity, of course, does not explain everything about marriage or politics; ideologies, histories, concepts of identity, group and personal experiences, and inconstant sources and flows of migration and arrivals are also important. In contrast to sociologists and some anthropologists who analyze immigration almost solely in terms of "assimilation" (and assimilation to what? you might ask[16]), I see the present and future as more complicated and open than that. Chapter 8 concludes with six future scenarios relating intermarriage and political trends, all of which are likely to occur in combination. A "Postscript" at the end of the chapter reports the most recent New York City housing segregation and U.S. interracial marriage figures.

My team research project in Elmhurst-Corona was designed to bring the study of race and immigration under one tent—as against the separate development of research on race, racism, and race relations on one hand and immigration, the immigrant experience, and immigration policy on the other. It was for this reason that I chose to work in the area of Queens, the most diverse New York City borough, with the greatest proportional representation of whites, blacks, Latin Americans, and Asians. Race was examined most directly by Steven Gregory writing about African Americans—who did not arrive in North America as immigrants—in his book *Black Corona: Race and the Politics of Place in an Urban Community* (1998), and by me, focusing on white Americans. Gregory and I also co-organized an AAA panel on race and coedited the resulting volume, *Race* (1994), in which an earlier version of Chapter 8 first appeared.[17]

Immigration was a major topic of our other team members studying post-1965 immigrants who arrived in the United States as adults: Chen

Hsiang-shui in *Chinatown No More: Taiwan Immigrants in Contemporary New York* (1992); Kyeyoung Park in *The Korean American Dream: Immigrants and Small Business in New York City* (1997); Madhulika Khandelwal in *Becoming American, Being Indian: An Immigrant Community in New York City* (2002); and Milagros Ricourt and Ruby Danta in *Hispanas de Queens: Latino Panethnicity in a New York City Neighborhood* (2003).

However, the whites of Elmhurst-Corona needed to be understood through the frame of immigration too, as most were children or, like me, grandchildren of European immigrants. Chapter 9, "Rethinking Migration, Ancient to Future," first published in a special journal issue honoring Ulf Hannerz, addresses my frustration with the "assimilation" approach and places current immigration within a larger historical context. It offers a comparative canvas of seven successive processes, all still continuing today: expansion, refuge seeking, colonization, enforced transportation, trade and labor diaspora, and emigration.

This view of "the past of us all" begins with "deep history": the expansion of "anatomically modern humans" throughout Africa and to other continents. Starting the analysis of human migration here also returns me to my deep history. In the 1950s, I read and reread Anne Terry White's children's books *Prehistoric America* (1951) and *The First Men in the World* (1953) and then later, anthropologist William Howells's *Mankind in the Making* (1959).[18] My high school biology teacher Anne Schwerner, whom I idolized, encouraged this interest in human origins and dispersals, and during 1960 I read still other physical anthropologists for a forty-page biology term paper on the fossil record. Decades later, when in 2002 I began teaching a four-field senior seminar, I assigned a current overview of modern human dispersals over the past hundred and fifty thousand years, and I began reading contemporary physical and biological anthropologists and archaeologists on prehistoric expansions more widely.[19]

Schwerner's son Michael was one of three civil rights workers killed by Ku Klux Klansmen in Mississippi in 1964. I was then an anthropology major moving from human evolution to ethnography and also closely following Civil Rights Movement activities and legislation. This disturbing news helped solidify my leanings toward an anthropology "relevant" to race and current issues. Anne Schwerner died in 1996, and sometime after, I met her son Stephen when he spoke in New York about the 1960s racial justice movement. I told him how great an influence his mother had been on me, and he responded that she had studied anthropology at Hunter College and wanted to pursue it but became a high school teacher.

Ethnography and Society

Anthropology in the 1960s and its aftermath is the topic of Chapter 10, "Politics, Theory, and the Nature of Cultural Things," which begins the book's final section, *Ethnography and Society*. I was an undergraduate and graduate anthropology student at Columbia University from 1963 to 1969 when I departed for fieldwork in Ghana. As Darnell observes, "every practicing anthropologist has a unique genealogy . . . tracing her or his relationships to the ideas, institutions, and social networks of the profession."[20]

More on that in a moment. But first, I want to add that we also have other prior and "coeval" social relationships, as persons and as "citizens."[21] These include

1. The families, communities, life circumstances, and political climates that bring us to anthropology, that continue and change as we practice it, and that, in conjunction with the "ideas, institutions, and social networks" of the profession, shape (if they do not overdetermine) what and where we "choose" to study. The theories we embrace are products of who we are in total.[22] Theory is autobiographical, I contend in Chapter 10, as much as fieldwork is autobiographical, a postmodern insight perhaps fuzzily understood all along.
2. The people whom we study and study among, and with whom we share one globe. Their lives preexist our arrivals, continue during and after fieldwork, and may be affected by what we write about them. They include those persons who assist us in various ways (Chapter 5). If these "informants" do not also have major impacts on how we see and write about the world, then what are we there for?[23]
3. The audiences we inform in various ways about what we learn as anthropologists. These include other professional colleagues and students, of course, but also "society at large."

Returning to the 1960s, Chapter 10 revisits this disruptive era in the profession and at Columbia. Many anthropologists then publically professed the belief that the discipline could no longer "remain aloof from the great issues of our times." They included Marvin Harris, who had learned this in the 1950s, and whose work and example I consider here. This chapter was first written for an AAA panel honoring Harris, who was present and thanked me for these reminiscences and reflections.

Although Harris registered the strongest impact on me, other Columbia teachers shaped me too. In my first anthropology course, archaeologist Robert Stigler's well-organized and content-rich classes set a standard I tried to meet when I became a teacher. Lambros Comitas (like Harris and Stigler, a Columbia PhD), Jaap van Velsen (a visiting professor and student of Max Gluckman), and George Bond (trained at the London School of Economics) nurtured and guided my social anthropology inclinations; Allen Johnson (a product of Berkeley and Stanford) expanded my understanding of theory and fieldwork methods.[24] All four had deep appreciations of ethnography. Among guest speakers, M. N. Srinivas (then at the Delhi School of Economics in India) and Fredrik Barth (from the University of Bergen, Norway, who spoke about Darfur[25]) were fieldworkers and thinkers whose work I already admired and continued to follow.

Chapter 11, "Keeping Ethnography Alive in an Urbanizing World," asks how we may preserve wide-ranging ethnography and not retreat to interviews alone, in the dense, increasingly enormous cities of our urbanizing world. After first steps in a Brazilian village, all my fieldwork has been in urban settings: Accra, the Gray Panther movement in Berkeley and New York, and Queens. It is the latter experience I return to in this essay, highlighting sites for participant observation that team member Chen Hsiang-shui and I found especially productive. I conclude Chapter 11 by considering the interplay among the contextual, comparative, and ethnographic sides of the anthropological triangle that I experienced in thinking and writing about Queens.

A Queens College student once asked why I discussed Chen's fieldwork here and not that of our other team colleagues. The answer is that this chapter was originally presented to students at the Institute of Anthropology, National Tsing Hua University in Taiwan, where Chen, a faculty member, invited me to speak. In addressing the topic of ethnography's continuing importance for anthropology, I wanted to acquaint the students with his New York work, which some might not have read or fully appreciated. Our other team members certainly found productive locations for ethnography in Queens as well, and their ethnographies richly demonstrate this.[26]

The final chapter, "Going Public: Responsibilities and Strategies in the Aftermath of Ethnography," considers ethnography in "the public sphere" via a revisionist look at Boas, an alternative genealogy for anthropological advocacy, and my own community-based and media experiences after publication of *The Future of Us All.* This essay first appeared in an issue of *Human Organization* honoring Donald Stull, who has written informatively about his extensive "third stage" activities following fieldwork among Americans, immigrants, and the meatpacking industry in Garden City, Kansas.[27]

PART I

Engaging Ethnography

Chapter 1

Color Full Before Color Blind: The Emergence of Multiracial Neighborhood Politics in Queens, New York City

The United States is in the midst of a great transition. Within a few decades, Americans of African, Asian, and Latin American ancestry will outnumber those of European origin. According to a recent U.S. Census Bureau projection, by 2042, the proportion of whites will fall from its present 65 percent to 50 percent, and by 2050, the country's population will be 46 percent white, 30 percent Latin American (or "Hispanic"), 15 percent black, and 9 percent Asian. The great transition among America's children will arrive even sooner. By the year 2020, fewer than half of children under age 18 will be white.[1]

The pace of multiracial change is faster on the nation's coasts and in its cities than in its heartland and suburbs.[2] New York City crossed the "majority minority" threshold in the early 1980s,[3] and by 1990, the city's white population stood at 43 percent, down from 52 percent in 1980. Two decades later in 2010, New York City was 33 percent white, 29 percent Latin American, 23 percent black, 13 percent Asian, and 2 percent biracial or multiracial (a category first enumerated in 2000).

It is in New York's diverse, changing neighborhoods, such as Elmhurst-Corona in northwest Queens, that clues about the future of us all may first be glimpsed. Elmhurst-Corona underwent *its* "majority minority" transition in the 1970s. Between 1960 and 1970, the neighborhood's white population fell from 98 percent to 67 percent, then to 34 percent in 1980, and

18 percent in 1990. Over these same decades, immigrant and African American newcomers arrived in substantial numbers, and by 1990, Elmhurst-Corona was 45 percent Latin American, 26 percent Asian, and 10 percent black. Established residents of German, Irish, Polish, Italian, Jewish, and other European ancestries now lived among Africans, African Americans, Chinese, Colombians, Cubans, Dominicans, Ecuadorians, Filipinos, Haitians, Indians, Koreans, Mexicans, Puerto Ricans, and other new neighbors. In 1992, New York's Department of City Planning called Elmhurst-Corona "perhaps the most ethnically mixed community in the world."[4]

My fieldwork in this neighborhood began in 1983, and I followed its changing political life over more than a dozen years. I worked with a team of researchers who mirrored the cultural and linguistic complexity of the Elmhurst-Corona population. Their work focused on Chinese, Korean, African American, Indian, and the diverse Latin American residents. My assignment was the white folks.[5]

Our team's overall charge was to assess how far Elmhurst-Corona's diverse population had come in forming what Lani Guinier terms "an integrated body politic in which all perspectives are represented, and in which all people work together to find common ground."[6] I took primary responsibility for this by focusing on what Jane Jacobs defines as the "district-level" political field. Anthropologists envision any political "field" they study as a set of linked "arenas" in which ongoing political events may be observed; the field also extends beyond these "enclaves of action" to include "encapsulating" structures of power at larger-scale levels.[7]

In her classic *Death and Life of Great American Cities,* Jacobs distinguished three levels of urban existence: "the city as a whole," in which people find jobs, visit museums, support baseball teams, and vote for mayor; "the street neighborhood" of immediate daily interaction; and "the district," which "mediates between the politically powerless street neighborhoods, and the inherently powerful city as a whole." In contemporary New York City, she noted, districts range from eighty thousand to two hundred thousand residents in size.

Jacobs envisaged district-level political power emerging from "churches, PTAs, business associations, political clubs, civic groups, and block associations." For a district "to be big and powerful enough to fight City Hall," political "interweaving" of its groups and associations was required. In a "successful" district, "working relationships [exist] among people, usually leaders, who enlarge their local public life beyond the neighborhoods of streets and specific organizations or institutions, and [who] form relationships with people whose roots and backgrounds are in entirely different constituencies. It takes surprisingly few people to weld a district into a real Thing. A hundred or so do it in a population a thousand times their size."[8]

The composition and scale of Elmhurst-Corona's district-level political field matched Jacobs's description. Within it, I could readily do what an ethnographer does: observe ongoing events and listen to speech in action.[9] Its participants included black and immigrant newcomers, but the majority continued to be long-established white residents. Some local whites were antagonistic or indifferent to their new neighbors. Others sought accommodation and even formed new friendships. All were intensely aware of change going on around them. It was impossible to do otherwise.

A Neighborhood Remade

Already by 1970, salsa stars Tito Puente and Orquesta Broadway were appearing on Roosevelt Avenue, and Dominicans and Colombians referred to sections of Corona and Elmhurst as "Sabana Iglesias" and "Chapinerito," named after locales in their homelands. Korean Christian churches sprouted up everywhere, joined by Spanish-language Protestant congregations, a Pakistani mosque, a Hindu temple, and a Chinese Zen Buddhist church. Enormous crowds came for Colombian, Ecuadorian, and Korean festivals in Flushing Meadows–Corona Park, where Latin American leagues also played soccer every weekend. New Asian and Latin American stores appeared on the district's commercial strips, and languages other than English could be heard on subway platforms, in Elmhurst Hospital, at local libraries, in coin laundries, and on every block and apartment building floor.

Latin American and Asian immigrants settled gradually throughout the area, in all of its thirty-five census tracts. The white population had already begun leaving in the 1950s, and their moves to suburbs and other parts of the United States continued, resulting in vacant apartments and homes. The number of white households shrank less than the overall white population, however, with one or two older persons remaining by the 1990s from what had been larger, growing households in earlier decades.

African Americans arrived under very different circumstances from those of the diverse immigrants. Following a federal housing discrimination suit at the forty-six-hundred–unit Lefrak City apartment complex in 1970, white flight occurred there, and by 1980, Lefrak City was 65 percent black. Most black newcomers settled here or nearby so that even in 1990, only 3 of the 35 census tracts contained 86 percent of Elmhurst-Corona's black population. The historically white local real estate sector, now including large numbers of immigrant-owned firms, had opened up to Latin American, Asian, and even Haitian renters and home buyers, but not to African Americans.[10]

I traced the emerging relations among Elmhurst-Corona's whites, blacks, and immigrants from 1983 to 1996 through participant observation and also back to a 1960 baseline with archival sources. My fieldwork centered on Community Board 4 (CB4). The most immediate layer of government in New York City, the fifty-nine local community boards of up to fifty appointed members each, were created in the late 1960s as part of "the nation's most ambitious attempt at urban decentralization."[11] Their purview includes land-use review, city budget recommendations, and the monitoring of municipal service delivery. Their maturation as arenas for local politics coincided with Elmhurst-Corona's growing ethnic and racial diversity.

I attended a hundred and twenty-three meetings and public hearings of CB4 and its district services cabinet. From there I worked outward, to fifty meetings of civic associations, small business groups, redistricting bodies, and mayoral commissions and "town hall" events. I also observed eighty-three public rituals, which ranged from Christmas tree lightings, ethnic festivals, protest rallies, and block cleanups to award ceremonies, park openings, anti-drug marches, and International Day programs in schools. I attended seventy-five services and social events at three historically white Protestant churches and visited several other white, African American, Asian, and Latin American houses of worship. Moreover, I spent numerous hours in walks throughout the area and in parks, an indoor shopping mall, Elmhurst Hospital, the local police precinct house, libraries, senior centers, and restaurants. I used formal interviewing strategically and sparingly, and in my 1,230 pages of fieldnotes, participant observation outnumbers interviews by 10 to 1.

African Americans Misperceived

In 1970, just 9 percent of Lefrak City's tenant population was black, and this included many Africans working for the United Nations and other international organizations. Following landlord Samuel Lefrak's agreement to end discriminatory rental practices, African American lower-middle-class city employees, teachers, and white-collar workers who could afford the prevailing rents found they were now treated on a first-come, first-served basis and sought out Lefrak's roomy apartments. By 1975, the complex was two-thirds black, and Elmhurst-Corona's surrounding white residents had noted the change. When some whites saw black faces, however, they made uninformed assumptions.

In January 1975, a rumor that Lefrak City "is being loaded with welfare cases" was reported at Community Board 4, where no Lefrak City tenant, white or black, had yet been appointed.[12] One CB4 leader averred, "People have moved out [of Lefrak City] because of the bad conditions there, due to welfare tenants. As soon as landlords begin to rent to them, the buildings deteriorate and we will have another South Bronx." Representatives from the still mainly white Lefrak City Tenants Association (LCTA) were invited to CB4, where they insisted the problem was not "welfare cases" (it turned out that the tiny percentage of these was smaller than the figure for Queens overall) but rather cuts in maintenance and security by Lefrak Management. The complex had been overbuilt in relation to the rental market, and Lefrak had hundreds of vacant apartments, a situation that had persisted ever since the complex opened in 1962.

Slowly, as Elmhurst-Corona whites began to meet black Lefrak leaders, they also began to understand that their own neighborhood's fate was inextricably linked to that of Lefrak City. By 1979, white Corona civic groups were supporting the now black-led Lefrak City Tenant Association in a rent strike, and Community Board 4 and the LCTA joined forces against Queens politicians maneuvering to move twenty-six hundred Social Security Administration jobs from Lefrak City to another Queens neighborhood. In economic terms, Lefrak City's black population in 1979 had a higher mean family income than its white Corona neighbors. This would continue. In 1990, Elmhurst-Corona's average household incomes by race were closer to each other than anywhere else in Queens. Blacks stood at slightly over $35,000 and whites slightly under that figure; Asian incomes were $36,000 and Latin American ones $33,000.

An "Illegal Aliens" Panic

Much as white Elmhurst-Corona leaders had misperceived Lefrak City's growing black population as "welfare cases," they also misdefined Elmhurst-Corona's immigrant newcomers as "illegal aliens." Both designations masked real issues—Lefrak's overbuilding and maintenance reductions in the first instance and rapid population growth and overcrowded schools and housing in the second. In both cases, progress in facing these issues was made only after perceptions were revised, hysteria over newcomers subsided, and leaders began to redefine problems as ones affecting the "quality of life" of all Elmhurst-Corona residents, white and black, American and immigrant, alike.

The phrase "illegal aliens" first appeared in Community Board 4's minutes in 1971 in connection with the emerging problem of school crowding. Young immigrant families with children were replacing aging whites in Elmhurst-Corona, and School Board 24, which was controlled by members elected from still overwhelmingly white neighborhoods in southwest Queens, was responding with makeshift measures, mainly prefabricated "mini-schools" that filled former school playgrounds.

In addition, white and immigrant realtors, landlords, and home owners were satisfying the growing demand for housing in Elmhurst-Corona by adding illegal room rentals and basement and garage units to the local housing supply. And worse, overzoning under the city's 1961 ordinance permitted developers to buy and demolish existing one- and two-family homes and replace them with brick-box "infills" that housed six or more units. Nonetheless, one white Elmhurst civic leader insisted, "this is a job for the INS." As far as he was concerned, if "illegal aliens" were dealt with properly by the Immigration and Naturalization Service, "the housing and neighborhood deterioration problem would solve itself."

In 1974, Community Board 4 held its first public hearing on the "illegal aliens" issue, and panic then set in. An August 25 *New York Daily News* story headlined "Illegal Aliens, a Flood Tide in Elmhurst" quoted Community Board 4's white chairman referring to immigrant newcomers as "people pollution." "My parents were immigrants," he continued, "and this country was built by immigrants. But our community is being overrun. Our schools, housing, and many jobs are being taken by people who have no legal right to be here." More public forums were held in 1974 and 1975, and INS and elected officials inflamed the situation with inflated estimates of New York's undocumented population.[13]

Cooler heads eventually prevailed. The white male Community Board 4 district manager pressed for city housing code enforcement, and a black female Democratic district leader who represented Corona reminded the district cabinet of "the legal residents of Hispanic origin who are good hardworking people." A careful numerical analysis after the 1980 census would have shown that the vast majority of Elmhurst-Corona's immigrant population consisted of visa and green-card holders, naturalized citizens, and their children. But by the end of the 1970s, the "illegal aliens" question had in effect been redefined locally as a housing and school crowding issue.

Fiscal Crisis and Quality of Life

The prospect for solutions to housing and school problems, however, worsened after the city's 1975 fiscal crisis, which eclipsed the Elmhurst-Corona flare-ups over new black and immigrant neighbors. In 1975, Manhattan's major banks cut off credit to the city, and ultimate budgetary and policy control passed from public to private hands. Massive cuts in municipal services quickly followed.

Overall, the city budget shrank 22 percent between 1975 and 1983, and service cuts affected every aspect of life in neighborhood New York. The transit fare was raised; 129 years of free college education ended with the imposition of tuition; public school layoffs resulted in fewer teachers and paraprofessionals and a 25 percent increase in class size. Library hours were curtailed. Summer youth jobs and senior citizen, recreation, and cultural programs were scaled back. Five city hospitals closed. Fire Department response time increased. Building inspectors fell from 625 in 1975 to 382 by 1980 (and to only 7 for all of Queens by 1994). Sanitation department staff declined 48 percent by 1984. Park and playground workers were cut 25 percent during 1975, 29 percent more by 1984, and shifted from fixed assignments to mobile teams servicing several locations.

In Elmhurst-Corona, the *Newtown Crier,* a local civic association publication, reported in March 1976: "Home burglaries and muggings have been on the rise. Our police are trying to do their job, but do not have enough manpower. The sanitation pickups have dwindled to one a week in some sections and overall our streets are filthy. We are informed some of the classes in our schools are so large that teachers are having problems maintaining control."

The aftereffects of the 1975 fiscal crisis defined the content of neighborhood politics for the next two decades. These assaults on what Elmhurst-Corona residents call "quality of life" have troubled whites, blacks, and immigrants alike.

The phrase "quality of life" resounded in the community board, civic association, and mayoral town hall meetings I attended during the 1980s and 1990s. The most succinct definition I heard was offered at a 1993 CB4 meeting, where a member explained: "Quality of life—the problems that are important to us." These problems included crowding on Elmhurst-Corona's subway lines, competition for street parking as population grew and commercial vehicles were parked illegally, abandonment of stolen cars on neighborhood streets, increasing numbers of illegal garment factories, streetside dumping of commercial and household garbage, a noticeable rise in prostitution, and placement of homeless families in local motels. But the five quality-of-life issues that mattered most and provoked sustained civic action among Elmhurst-Corona residents were school crowding, lack of youth recreation facilities, housing code violations, drug sales, and dissatisfaction with police response.

Parapolitics and Wardens

A sense of estrangement from "the city" and mayoral power existed among white Elmhurst-Corona civic activists by the 1980s. "We are stepchildren; Manhattan is the favored son." "Mayor Koch and his goddam hoodlums are against Corona." These comments at Community Board 4 meetings reflected not only continuing assaults on quality of life but a weakened power of numbers. Elmhurst's Democratic Club folded in the 1970s. Corona's Democratic Club survived but with less political muscle. And with fewer whites and more immigrants, the total number of votes cast by CD4 residents fell off, and the responsiveness of elected officials and city agencies diminished. "We don't have no political push," one white civic activist lamented. "We're just being plopped on," said another.

As electoral politics proved less effective, Elmhurst-Corona's parapolitical civic activism became more important. F. G. Bailey locates "parapolitical" activity in the "lesser arenas, those which are partly regulated by, and partly independent of, large encapsulating political structures; and which fight battles with these larger structures in a way [that] seldom ends in victory, rarely in dramatic defeat, but usually in a long drawn stalemate and defeat by attrition."[14]

It began with individuals I call "wardens," persons who on their own attempted to do something about "problems that are important to us."

Often it was garbage—misplaced, mispackaged, sitting out too long—that provoked the first step. Two white elderly sisters spoke to their new neighbors about garbage and dog litter. A retired hotel worker visited each new household in his co-op building to explain rules for placing garbage in the incinerator room. With more serious problems, or where personal requests proved insufficient, wardens notified the sanitation department, the local police precinct, or the Community Board 4 office. Lefrak City wardens surveyed the avenue in front of their complex and recorded drug-seller descriptions and buyer license-plate numbers to report to the police. Residents throughout Elmhurst-Corona phoned in illegally parked vehicle and prostitution locations.

Wardens formed the leadership of the thirty-five block, tenant, co-op, and civic associations that existed in Elmhurst-Corona by 1985. Tenant and co-op groups had the most diverse memberships, because they sought to mobilize all building residents, but their efforts were directed primarily at internal matters and landlords and management. And the neighborhood's pattern of housing segregation was also evident in these organizations: most Elmhurst groups were white, Latin American, and Asian; the Lefrak City Tenants Association was predominantly black. Four larger-scale, and politically active, Elmhurst and Corona homeowner civic associations were predominantly white, with only a handful of Latin American or Asian members. It was in the smaller block associations, on streets of one- and two-family homes, that the most significant multiracial organizing took place.

A Block Association Mobilizes

The leading civic warden in Elmhurst-Corona by the 1990s, Lucy Schilero, attended the first meeting of her block association, formed to deal with parking congestion, in 1984. A freelance beautician whose Italian immigrant parents lived on the same street, she sat in the back row. Meeting attendance fell off until 1986, when a rumor circulated that the police precinct house located on this block might be moved elsewhere.

"We bought our homes with a police station here," Schilero explained as she began circulating a petition to keep the precinct headquarters where it was. She first went door-to-door on her block and then to churches, stores, subway stations, and streets and apartment buildings in the surrounding area. "All the people on our block helped, 50 people. We had everything in Spanish, Greek, Italian, Chinese, Korean, [and] French. I met Iranians [and] Turkish [people], to help translate." Schilero also met tenant leaders from several Elmhurst apartment buildings who were fighting illegal rent increases and evictions and battling with absentee investors who had purchased occupied units in buildings converted to co-ops.

As a result of her petition work, Schilero's personal network began to change.

> Now, I have new ethnic friends: Hindu, Spanish—a lot—Chinese. My Ecuadorian neighbor is a good friend, and in touch with Spanish residents. [White] friends in Maspeth and Middle Village [in southwest Queens] say to me, 'How can you live here? It's like Manhattan.' I tell them we have to live with one another or we won't survive. The Hindus and Shiites are the hardest to relate with; the man at the Geeta Temple, he's been great, but he won't come to meetings. I want to get Haitians, I want to bring one with me on my rounds. The newcomers are people we want to keep here. They are hardworking people, like the old immigrants.

In 1986, Schilero formed the Coalition of United Residents for a Safer Community, comprising her block association and the tenant groups she met through petitioning. She shared information with leaders of these groups on quality-of-life issues such as drug selling, sanitation, police response, and illegal occupancy. Through her coalition network she was able to circulate petitions rapidly, including one to keep open the Elmhurst Hospital clinics facing proposed budget cuts in 1991. At coalition meetings, Schilero also reported on what she learned at Community Board 4, which she joined in 1990, and on her contacts with other civic groups and elected officials. Two weeks before each meeting, Schilero called leaders of the coalition groups; other members expanded her telephone tree along Chinese, Spanish, and Greek branches. During meetings, people at the back of the room translated for non-English speakers, and by 1990, Korean, Bengali, Urdu, and Vietnamese were also in use within the coalition network. In 1996, Lucy Schilero's coalition numbered two thousand members of forty block, tenant, co-op, and business associations in the northern half of Elmhurst-Corona. Her meetings drew up to four hundred people and now included Mexican and Russian immigrants, African Americans from Lefrak City, and whites from neighboring Jackson Heights.

New Immigrant Leadership

Latin Americans and Asians together constituted a majority of Elmhurst-Corona's population by 1980, but their involvement in civic politics did not reflect their numbers. Enormous organizational energy, however, went into a vast world of immigrant associations and houses of worship.

There were scores of Colombian, Dominican, Ecuadorian, and other Latin American nationality-based associations in Queens, focused largely on home country politics, sports, and cultural activities. Queenswide Chinese organizations drew Elmhurst-Corona members, but most of their activities occurred elsewhere. Associational lines divided South Asian immigrants by country, region, language, and religion, mirroring the complexities of their homelands; some of these groups met in Elmhurst-Corona, but they drew upon a Queens or New York metropolitan area membership base. Immigrant churches, temples, and mosques were plentiful, but only the Korean Central Presbyterian Church made an impact on Elmhurst-Corona civic life when in 1991 it began a Sunday afternoon street cleanup. Echoing views of many white residents, one warden said of the new houses of worship, "They are *in* Elmhurst, but not *of it*."

A few Latin Americans and Asians did join civic associations headed by whites, but only in the mid-1980s did two new organizations that addressed issues that mattered to immigrant residents begin to stake out places in the district-level political field.

In 1978, Puerto Rico–born Haydee Zambrana moved to Elmhurst and soon met other Latin Americans who shared her concerns about the lack of social services for Spanish speakers and the need for a Latin American presence in Queens politics. In 1980, she formed *Ciudadanos Conscientes de Queens*/Concerned Citizens of Queens, or CCQ. From a small Elmhurst office, she referred people to appropriate government agencies, sometimes providing advocacy and English translation herself. She also processed citizenship applications, which by 1984 totaled one thousand a year. By 1986, CCQ's volunteer and paid staff provided counseling on entitlement eligibility and vocational training programs, held English classes and seminars for business proprietors, and ran a New York State–funded hotline to inform undocumented immigrants of their rights. The following year, CCQ received a federal grant to process legalization applications, and in 1989, it was funded to run citizenship and English classes for newly legalized immigrants now eligible for naturalization.

Zambrana was impatient with the many nationality-based Latin American organizations in Queens and felt little of their energies went to local issues. In 1986, she told the Mayor's Commission on Hispanic Concerns, "My priority is to help the Hispanic community become part of the American political process." She went about this by registering voters, backing Latin American candidates for Elmhurst-Corona's district school board, and lobbying the borough president to appoint more Latin Americans to Queens community boards. In 1985, she joined CB4, and its Latin American membership that year doubled from three to six.

That same year, Sung Jin Chun and Seung Ha Hong founded the Korean American Association of Mid-Queens. Chun, a chemist and teacher in Korea, had arrived in Elmhurst in 1970 and established a real estate business. Hong immigrated in 1971, worked for an American baker, and in 1984 bought a bakery in Elmhurst. On the day his bakery opened, he received a fifty-dollar sanitation fine. Although the law only required merchants to sweep their sidewalk within one hour of opening, which he did, when he complained about the fine to a sanitation department supervisor he was told, "You want another?" Hong decided he had to create personal relationships with local officials.

The two men began by visiting Korean business owners throughout Elmhurst and listening to their problems. Many were already members of citywide associations of Korean greengrocers, dry cleaners, or other types of business, but they understood the need for a new local Korean organization as well. Chun also met with Elmhurst-Corona's police precinct commander after an incident of alleged police brutality involving a Korean taxi driver. This opened a dialogue that continued; when the police needed Korean translation, or problems involving Koreans arose, the commanding officer would call Seung Ha Hong.

Chun and Hong also established personal ties with whites active in Elmhurst civic politics, became Elmhurst Lions, and participated in Christmas tree lighting and Memorial Day rituals. One of their Mid-Queens association members, a Korean woman whose long-practiced English was better than that of most Korean immigrants, was appointed to Community Board 4. Linkages were also created with African American wardens at Lefrak

City. Chun and Hong continued to provide leadership to the Mid-Queens Association, which during 1996 registered two thousand Korean American voters.

White-Black Alliances

The arrival of new Latin American and Asian members on Community Board 4 in the mid-1980s coincided with a shift from male to female leadership. In 1985, Rose Renda Rothschild, an Italian American woman long active in PTA work and a CB4 member since 1977, was elected chairperson. The following year, she became district manager. Previously, she had headed the health committee on which nearly all the board's female members served. This position had also introduced her to city agency staff and programs throughout Elmhurst-Corona, as well as to many blacks, Latin Americans, and Asians who lived or worked in the neighborhood.

Under the male chairperson who preceded Rothschild, relations between CB4 and the community's African American residents were minimal. The several thousand black voters in the Lefrak area, however, were approaching Elmhurst-Corona's declining white electorate in size and already formed an important constituency for Corona's African American State Assembly member Helen Marshall. In 1987, Marshall put Rothschild on the agenda of her own Lefrak City town hall meeting, providing Rothschild with her first large black audience. The two women continued to work closely, and when Rothschild received a Democratic Club award in 1995, it was Marshall, now a City Council member, who introduced her to the several hundred Queens party faithful attending the event.

In 1985, Edna Baskin, an African American Lefrak City resident and a tenant association member, began attending CB4 meetings. She was frustrated that no LCTA channel to the community board existed, and she reported what she learned at CB4 to residents of her building, including parents of children she babysat in her home-based day care business.

Then, in fall 1986, a crisis began mounting at the Lefrak City branch library. Many children came there after school, and as the weather grew colder, their numbers increased. The librarians were unable to provide supervision, and a library security guard was dispatched to assist them. Early in 1987, the library announced that the guard would be discontinued. Helma Goldmark, a white Lefrak area resident and CB4 member, was concerned about both young and elderly users of the library and requested that the guard remain.

In February 1987, a library official came to a CB4 meeting attended by Goldmark, Rothschild, Baskin, the branch librarians, and a dozen Lefrak area residents, half white and half black. Rothschild began the meeting. "It's quieted down with a guard. Kids today are 10 going on 40, but if they see a security guard there will be less playing around." The library official defended the withdrawal of the guard and blamed "these latchkey kids" and "the parents" for difficulties.

Rothschild objected. "You are taking a negative approach. So far [you are saying] the kids are from Murder Incorporated. I'm here doing *my* job, which is to get *you* to do *your* job." Baskin followed: "I speak as a parent [of two grown-up sons]. I pass every day. I've seen the librarian physically and verbally assaulted by a 175-pound, six-foot, 14-year-old." Rothschild backed Baskin up. "Kids are tired after being closed in all day. My son is 6'3", 17 years old. As Edna said, you should try a security guard." Rovenia McGowan, a black Lefrak area resident and a schoolteacher, and Ken Daniels, a white Lefrak resident and CB4 member, added that schools, department stores, and their own buildings had security guards. "If we don't get a guard, we may lose the library," McGowan pleaded.

The library official had attempted to split the white and black residents, blaming black children and parents for the problem. Instead, he encountered local solidarity, with black and white adults requesting help to deal with troublemakers and to allow black neighborhood children and white senior citizens to use the library in peace. The guard remained.

White Americans Regroup

Throughout Elmhurst-Corona, whites were forming personal relationships with their new neighbors. In most of the area, these neighbors were Latin American or Asian. A not untypical example of these new ties was one retired white woman who tutored two Korean and two Argentinean–Puerto Rican children who lived on her apartment building floor, taking them to the library, bowling, and movies. In exchange, her female Puerto Rican neighbor often cooked for her, and her Korean female neighbor did her nails.

Whites also encountered neighborhood newcomers at senior centers and in their churches. Two historically white Protestant churches disbanded as their congregations shrank, but a dozen others survived by welcoming Latin Americans, Asians, and blacks. A Presbyterian church pastored by a conservative German American minister was the most racially diverse setting I encountered in Elmhurst-Corona, with active white American, Indonesian, Filipino, Cuban, Mexican, African, black American, and Indo- and Afro-Caribbean members. Roman Catholic churches had a large infusion of Latin American parishioners, but the creation of Spanish-language masses and other activities frequently provoked conflict. To overcome this at St. Leo's Church in Corona, a pre-Easter Stations of the Cross procession through the neighborhood, long dormant, was revived in 1986, with readings and choral response alternatively in English, Italian, and Spanish.

Black-white interaction, or black-immigrant interaction for that matter, was constrained by the pattern of residential segregation. Many whites, however, did have cordial workplace relationships with African Americans. Moreover, both the Corona Democratic Party and the growing number of black community board members reinforced ties among white and black Elmhurst-Corona wardens. By 1993, eight black members comprised nearly a fifth of CB4's membership, and several of them served on the board's executive committee.

Elmhurst-Corona whites also found that many of those thwarting their quality of life were white. These included Manhattan "permanent government" real estate and corporate interests[15] who received tax abatements and exemptions, white police who lived outside the city and expressed contempt for Elmhurst-Corona, white businessmen who ceaselessly encroached on residentially zoned property, and white southwest Queens school board members more interested in controlling district office jobs and opposing curriculum reform than in school crowding in Elmhurst-Corona. The three local schools finally built in the 1990s came not with help from the school board but as a result of parapolitical lobbying by Elmhurst-Corona wardens.

Listen to Women

At no one's request and by no one's design, Elmhurst-Corona was transformed from a solidly white neighborhood in 1960 to "perhaps the most ethnically mixed community in the world" by the 1990s. The United States is now undergoing a similar "majority minority" transition. Its arrival on a national scale later in this century will not repeat the story I have recounted, nor will the many local transitions from now to then follow any single script. Still, if our goal as citizens and neighbors is "an integrated body politic in which all perspectives are represented, and in which all people work together to find common ground," we may ask what lessons can be drawn from the Elmhurst-Corona experience. Here I wish to stress three:

1. Listen to women (they listen to each other)
2. Government matters
3. Be color full before color blind

Early in my fieldwork, a white warden, Bill Donnelly, compared Elmhurst during the 1930s with his contemporary neighborhood.

> In those days only the rich had telephones. We had no telephone, and yet I couldn't do anything and get home before my mother knew about it, and met me on the way in the door with a smack. So my father called it the "mothers' union"—all the mothers were plugged into the clothesline, he said. Well, the world hasn't changed. The school bus for the primary school stops in front of my house. One morning a year ago, the kids were all lined up, and a mother was coming down the block, a new American from Korea, with a kid late for the bus. And a little [Indian] boy on the end of the line—you could see this little lawyer's mind at work—he peels off and heads for home because he's got a good idea. His mother wasn't there, she didn't come with him; he's going home. So the Korean mother packs her kid on the bus, and then she steps over and says to this little boy who's going up the road, "Where you go?" He says, "Home, I'm sick, I've got a cold." She opens his mouth, looks in, and says, "No sick. On bus." He goes on the bus, and I said to myself the mothers' union is alive and working. The fathers can bitch and belly all they want, but the mothers are going to make sure that it all works out.

In the 1980s, women began moving into Elmhurst-Corona's district-level political field and unblocking the channels between whites, immigrants, and blacks. As Herbert Gans observes, "In communities where similarity of backgrounds is scarce, collective action requires a sizeable amount of interpersonal negotiation and compromise and [also] leaders who can apply personal skills that persuade people to ignore their differences."[16] It was women more than men who supplied this leadership, and we should be prepared for more female leadership everywhere as America's majority-minority transition unfolds.

Why was it women more than men who formed a network of cross-racial ties in Elmhurst-Corona? Nancy Chodorow would trace these patterns to socialization that incorporates daughters into a world of women characterized by "relational" identification and "connection to other people," while sons exit this world to adopt male roles emphasizing "positional" identification and individual achievement. Consequently, as Deborah Tannen observes, women's ways of talking are more likely to stress "a community of connection"; men's talk operates "to preserve their independence in a hierarchical world." Further, as Temma Kaplan posits, "the gender system of their society assigns women the responsibility of guarding their neighbors, children, and mates against danger"; under conditions of change, "a sense of community that emerges from shared routines binds women to one another" and "politicizes the networks of daily life." Carol Hardy-Fanta concludes that women more than men "focus on connecting people to other people to achieve change" but that such "participatory qualities are [not] the unique realm of women [and] these skills and values are within the abilities of men."[17]

In Elmhurst-Corona, women certainly acted to "guard their children." When one district cabinet meeting turned to park projects, Rose Rothschild remarked, "I always suggest preschool buildings [in park plans] because I'm a mother. Men never look at that." Nonetheless, some men did champion library, after-school, and recreation programs for youth. In terms of race, women moved sooner from categorical to personal ties,[18] relating more readily to individual women of another race as women than did men with other men. The "positional" and "hierarchical" values that continue to mark race relations in the United States are not only more characteristic of male socialization and gender roles, they are reinforced by the structural relationships of workplaces. Many of Elmhurst-Corona's women leaders were housewives or worked from their homes, while men were more likely to be employed in formal organizations. Women who entered civic politics, moreover, frequently had experience in school, religious, or block association groups, in which improvisation and abilities to involve others were more important than tables of organization and titled positions.[19]

Government Matters

In the contemporary United States, government is involved at every step in the movement toward common ground. The reasons why people of so many diverse origins live together in Elmhurst-Corona are not simply the result of individual choices disconnected from government policies. Individual whites, blacks, and immigrants indeed chose to stay in, move to, or leave Elmhurst-Corona, but they did so in response to shifting job opportunities, federal highway and housing programs, suburban zoning restrictions, inconsistent fair-housing law enforcement, and changing immigration policies—all the result of government actions.

As neighborhood New Yorkers, they endured assaults on quality of life resulting from the 1975 fiscal crisis and continuing mayoral budget cuts. In Elmhurst-Corona, zoning regulations and diminished housing-code enforcement defined neighborhood realities for all residents and set the stage for struggles to change them. Individuals innovated new alliances and forms of organization, but this took place within "city trenches"[20] shaped by community boards, district cabinets, and school boards.

Contemporary antigovernment conservatives maintain that declining quality of life in neighborhood New York is inevitable. They expect those who can to practice "choice" and move away and those who cannot to "trust the market" and "display a healthy respect for the natural economic development of the city."[21] Elmhurst-Corona civic activists had their own ideas about what was "natural." They did not accept this faith in "market" solutions to inappropriate zoning, unsafe housing, overcrowded schools, and unresponsive police. Their local efforts resulted in new schools, downzoning, a return of "cops on the beat" in the mid-1980s, and restoration of police numbers to 1975 levels after 1990.

Without a community board, there would have been no public forum at which white, black, Latin American, and Asian leaders had a place to interact. Each racial and ethnic group in Elmhurst-Corona would have confronted mayoral and permanent government power directly, without the power of numbers and lubricatory expertise[22] that CB4 made possible. The board was pivotal to the still-ongoing creation in this diverse neighborhood of what F. G. Bailey calls a political "community." He explains that members of a political community create "a common culture [and] conceive of themselves as an entity ranged against a world outside." Those beyond the community "are likely to be judged in an instrumental fashion, not 'in the round.' They are not [interacted with as] human beings to the same extent as those of us who belong within the community."[23]

Elmhurst-Corona in the 1980s and 1990s was not a political community in any complete sense, but probably no urban district ever is. For many of its wardens, however, lines of race and ethnicity had become crossable. CB4 members knew each other by name, embraced at meetings, and were in a position to see beyond stereotypes of "blacks," "immigrants," and "outer-borough white ethnics."

In Elmhurst-Corona, the intolerant tendencies of the 1970s were reversed as civic politics acquired new leaders and more diverse participants. This occurred within what Cornel West calls "a public sphere in which critical exchange and engagement takes place. Principled alliances—tension ridden, yes, but principled alliances and coalitions. That's the new kind of public sphere that we are talking about. There will be no fundamental social change in America unless we come together [within it]."[24] Indeed, government matters.

Color Full before Color blind

Finally, suppose the worst. In the year 2050, the predominantly white upper fifth of Americans lives in gated suburbs and edge cities. Its schools, police, health care, recreation facilities, transportation, and communication links are all private. Taxes everywhere are a pittance. For the rest of the population—now white, Latin American, black, Asian, and multiracial with no majority group—public schools, hospitals, parks, sanitation services, and mass transit function poorly. Most wages permit only minimal subsistence. Crime and the underground economy sustain enormous numbers, and the few police officers and government inspectors do not interfere. Government statistics on income, poverty, and race are neither published nor collected. The era of big government is over. "Individual choice" and "the market" reign. People live in a "color-blind" society.

The more divided the power of numbers, the more likely the worst will prevail. No racial or ethnic group will be able to counter this on its own, and only the upper fifth can afford to be "color blind." To the extent that the rest of us find ourselves in settings filled only with people who look like us, we will be doomed to political ineffectiveness. People will need to ensure deliberately that block and civic associations, local government bodies, civic ritual audiences, workplaces, and leadership slates are *color full*—diverse and inclusive. In Elmhurst-Corona, people have been moving in this direction, some more consciously than others, and learning from both successes and failures. An exchange at Community Board 4 following a zoning defeat in 1988 highlighted the need to strengthen the power of numbers.

Judy D'Andrea: The high-power developers in this city are trying to eliminate the community review process because we stand in their way and they make political contributions to high-power politicians.

Ron Laney: We have no power. The Mayor opposed us.

Judy D' Andrea: It goes back to the community. [In Bayside] they get buses and go. We are not like that. We had seven people at the public hearing. If we had 7,000 it would be different.

The point is not to be, or pretend to be, "color blind." Racial categories, after all, are something we learn to see from childhood, and they are in constant use around us.[25] Our goals, rather, should be to see racial identity as one among the many aspects of every person and to acknowledge and value the full range of human physical and cultural diversity in what always has been and is now an increasingly interconnected, color-full world. Thinking consciously, not "blindly," about race in order to work toward representative and proportional inclusiveness is not racist. And it can be politically empowering when it results in color-*full* ranks of local leadership and supporters.

Early in my fieldwork, Elmhurst warden Bill Donnelly told me, "All of life, every place, is the same thing—trying to get people to see that we're all in the same damn thing together. I've been standing on the street corners and hollering for fifty years, and it doesn't amount to nothing. [But] let one [other] person [say], 'Yeah, we're in the same boat together,' then everyone says, 'Hot damn, we're in this same boat together. Let's get together and paddle this boat.' "

Chapter 2

The Organization of Festivals and Ceremonies Among Americans and Immigrants in Queens

On a Friday night in March 1990, I attended an awards ceremony and buffet dinner sponsored by the Coalition of United Residents for a Safer Community at the Knights of Columbus hall in Elmhurst, Queens. I was invited by the coalition's organizer, Lucy Schilero, an Italian American woman in her thirties who had lived most of her life in a house in Elmhurst, just one block from its border with Corona. During the past twenty years, Elmhurst and Corona had been transformed from outer-city neighborhoods[1] of white homeowners and apartment renters—mainly immigrant and second- and third-generation Italians, Germans, Irish, Greeks, Jews, and other European ethnic groups—into neighborhoods in which Chinese, Colombian, Indian, Dominican, Puerto Rican, African American, Cuban, Korean, and diverse other newcomers now constituted a numerical majority.

Schilero was introduced by Joe Bellacicco, a successful businessman who had remained in the old neighborhood. She in turn introduced the public officials at the two head tables facing the seated audience of a hundred and fifty persons. They included the captain of the local police precinct (coterminous with Community District 4), the Queens borough commander of the New York Police Department, the Community District 4 Manager, representatives of the New York City mayor and the Queens borough president (all white), and a U.S. Department of Commerce representative (African American), who urged that everyone cooperate to prevent an undercount in the upcoming decennial U.S. census.

Schilero recalled the accomplishments of the five-year-old coalition. She mentioned support for rezoning the district to prevent overdevelopment;

pressure on government agencies to close illegal rooming houses, such as the one in which two children recently died in a fire; protests over street drug selling; working to keep the police precinct house from being relocated elsewhere in Community District 4 (CD4); and winning approval for construction of two new schools to serve the overcrowded Elmhurst-Corona area.

Next, wooden plaques with brass plates engraved with each person's name and the coalition's appreciation were presented in three groups. First, to ten local police officers and the CD4 liaison staff member from the Queens borough president's office, a Nicaraguan woman; next, to leaders of each of the coalition member block and tenant associations; and finally, to several children and two adult Spanish and Chinese translators who worked directly with Schilero on coalition activities.

Following testimonials to Schilero by dignitaries at the head tables, a representative of Mayor David Dinkins read a proclamation congratulating her and the coalition for their efforts. Several of the speakers had commented on the impressive numerical turnout, especially for a Friday night, and how this demonstrated the civic interest of those in the audience. Schilero then invited everyone to eat the food prepared and contributed by coalition members, including two twelve-foot Italian hero sandwiches supplied by Bellacicco. The event lasted from eight p.m. to ten p.m.

The audience was two-thirds Latin American and Asian, including Puerto Ricans, Cubans, Chinese, and Bangladeshis. Except for the whites, who were mainly elderly, the audience was also diverse in age. Demographically, it reflected the section of Elmhurst-Corona the coalition served. No one at the head table could fail to have noticed the ethnic diversity of the audience, nor could those in the audience (where I was) have missed hearing several languages being spoken or seeing the rainbow of faces around themselves. Yet aside from the awards to the two translators, ethnicity went unnoted and unmarked in the evening's program. The focus was strictly on the neighborhood problems that constituted an agenda of what were referred to locally as "quality of life" issues. These concerns formed a basis here and elsewhere in Elmhurst-Corona for interethnic and interracial agreement and action.

Public Rituals and Anthropological Analysis

It is possible to take a single ritual in Community District 4 (or any community) and use it, as Max Gluckman did with a bridge-opening ceremony in Zululand,[2] to introduce an analysis of political dynamics in an ethnically and racially diverse society. But the force of such an analysis would depend, as does Gluckman's, upon the scope of fieldwork concerning other rituals and political activities. Such a presentation represents a rhetorical choice in ethnographic writing and not a methodological prescription.[3]

This single-event approach exemplifies the work of anthropologists who have analyzed what I call *metropolitan* ethnic and communal festivals in American and British cities and towns.[4] These studies focus on individual events that either are organized on a community-wide basis or attract participants of a particular ethnic group from a wide, metropolitan region. Queens had its own metropolitan equivalent in the annual Queens Festival, a large "county fair" held from 1978 to 1998 that attracted up to one million persons to its many stages, booths, tents, and simultaneous performances. I studied this two-day festival between 1985 and 1994 but will reserve analysis of it for another occasion.

Still, I wonder whether events like the more mundane, less spectacular Elmhurst-Corona rituals I will consider here also occur less prominently in the locales of these metropolitan festivals and whether a more complex and textured analysis of evolving ethnic and racial relations might be possible by studying their equivalents elsewhere. In this regard, I find still compelling the point made by Meyer Fortes in his classic 1936 paper "Ritual Festivals and Social Cohesion in the Hinterland of the Gold Coast."[5] Fortes demonstrated that the meaning of Tallensi public ceremonies and festivals is not to be found in any single event but in the local ensemble of linked events. The approaches to rituals of E. E. Evans-Pritchard, Victor Turner, Stanley Tambiah, and Fredrik Barth in pastoral, horticultural, and rural agricultural settings also follow this course.[6] So will my approach to public ceremonies and festivals in Elmhurst-Corona.

Beginning in 1984, I observed scores of public ceremonies and festivals in Community District 4 and nearby areas of Queens. Not all of these events ignored or underplayed ethnic and racial symbolism, as did the coalition awards ceremony. One group of events, which I call *rituals of inclusion*, in fact celebrated Elmhurst-Corona's ethnic diversity. These events at schools, hospital, and churches pointedly featured ethnic foods, music, and costume; they openly appealed for ethnic harmony; and they deliberately used languages in addition to English during their program.

A second group of events also celebrated or focused on ethnicity, but these *rituals of ethnic celebration* were organized by participants of a single ethnic group, such as Koreans, Ecuadorians, Colombians, African Americans, or Italian Americans. A mood of pride or assertion characterized such activities, in which I include ethnic festivals and fairs; events that stressed pan–Latin American solidarity among Spanish-speaking immigrants of diverse nationalities; and a revitalized, Italian-symboled Fourth of July celebration in a section of Corona once, but no longer, predominantly Italian.[7]

A third category, *rituals of continuity*, ignored or underplayed ethnicity. Yet, unlike the coalition awards ceremony, they focused not on the community's current quality-of-life concerns but on the way things used to be. These Memorial Day celebrations, holiday school programs, and Christmas tree lightings recalled a neighborhood past that newcomers did not share, a time when ethnic diversity meant European nationalities, and, although it is never stated, when everyone was white.

The coalition awards ceremony typified a fourth category, *quality-of-life rituals*. These events underplayed ethnicity and stressed inclusive communal values, rather than ethnically parochial ones. Quality-of-life events in CD4 included park openings, an annual art show, street clean-up efforts, and demonstrations against drugs and for improved law enforcement. Audiences at quality-of-life events were most often ethnically and racially diverse. But even when their audiences were predominantly of one group, these events nonetheless stressed commitment to the quality-of-life values that participants shared with other residents of Elmhurst-Corona and Queens and not to values of common ethnicity.

Rituals of Inclusion

In ceremonies of inclusion, symbols of ethnic diversity and expressions of panethnic communal harmony were used overtly to structure events. An example was the Three Kings Day program at Elmhurst Hospital, which I attended in 1986, 1987, and 1988. The ceremony marked the feast of Epiphany celebrated widely in Latin American countries and elsewhere but observed only as a church calendar holiday by most Christians in the United States. The 1986 event featured Dominican, Puerto Rican, and Colombian dances performed by a troupe of Latin American children who attended a weekly dance school at a Roman Catholic church in Corona. The dances preceded Christmas and Chanukah songs sung by a class of Latin American, Asian, white, and black children from a nearby public school. In between the performances, the hospital's Roman Catholic chaplain, a nun, delivered a message stressing racial and ethnic harmony. The racially and ethnically mixed audience was composed of hospital staff and patients, the children's parents, community organization leaders, and the Community District 4 manager, an Italian American woman. The children's engaging dance and song produced many smiles, side comments between adults in the audience, and frequent applause during the one-hour midday event.

Similar programs were held in Elmhurst and Corona public schools. Corona's Public School 16's "Cultural Sharing Day" in 1988 presented a guest Chinese dance company and Spanish and Latin American dances performed by students. The audience consisted of the student body and a group of community leaders. These included the Queens borough president, who addressed the assembly, representatives of the mayor and governor, the Community District 4 manager, Board of Education officials, and Chinese community leaders. At another school, "International Day" in 1986, 1987, and 1988 began with a parade through the surrounding neighborhood by the entire school, all wearing ethnic costumes. This was followed by "African," Filipino, Swiss, and other ethnic dances performed outdoors by each class (all of which were ethnically diverse) for an audience of parents and, finally, with the "tasting" by teachers, parents, and adult guests of ethnic foods prepared by parents and served in each classroom.

A Roman Catholic church annually undertook a "Stations of the Cross" procession, which I observed in 1986 and 1988, of up to 200 parishioners through the streets of Corona on a Saturday preceding Easter. Readings at each station alternated among English, Italian, and Spanish. The church, St. Leo's, was founded in 1904 to serve an Italian immigrant parish, but by the 1980s, Latin American neighborhood residents were the majority among weekly attendants.

Hospital, school, and church are institutions open to serve any who live in their surrounding community. Their ceremonies of inclusion began (or in the case of the Stations of the Cross procession, was revived) following the arrival of immigrant and African American newcomers in the 1970s and 1980s. The organizers, mainly white Americans, used the events to unify and build support among multiethnic and multiracial staffs, patients, parents, and parishioners, as well as with local government officials.

The themes of ethnic harmony and of honoring cultural differences and traditions were invoked in these rituals. The symbols of ethnicity were song, dance, food, costume, and greetings or a few formulaic words in languages other than English. The authenticity of the "cultures" so presented was limited (except perhaps for the foods prepared by Latin American and Asian school parents) and was repackaged in domesticated, American formats. The bearers of the richest arrays of ethnic and cultural symbols were children, not adults. For white and black Americans, the symbolization of European and African and West Indian cultures was even more attenuated—limited to foreign-language popular or religious songs, Negro spirituals, or costume and dance of the sort presented to tourists. The more complicated and challenging values and popular cultures of adult immigrants and African Americans living in Elmhurst-Corona found their expression elsewhere.

Rituals of Ethnic Celebration

This next set of events celebrated or asserted particular ethnic identities. In what was probably the largest gathering of Koreans outside Korea, the Korean Harvest and Folklore Festival attracted upwards of twenty thousand Koreans each September to Flushing Meadows–Corona Park, a large public park bordering Community District 4. Presented annually since 1982 by the New York City association of Korean greengrocers, the festival included food booths, popular entertainers from Korea, and folk arts performances. New York Mayor Edward Koch addressed throngs seated on rows of folding chairs or picnic blankets in 1986, as did Mayor Dinkins in 1990, and other elected officials also appeared or sent telegrams and proclamations. In 1987, a measure of pan-Asian/Pacific symbolism appeared when performances by Chinese, Indian, and Hawai'ian dancers were included on the stage.

A more assertive Korean presence in Community District 4 occurred at a 1985 demonstration in front of the local police precinct house. This event protested two incidents of verbal ethnic insult and physical beating of Koreans by local police officers. More than two hundred Koreans were present at the demonstration, including ethnic community leaders from outside Elmhurst-Corona. The protest featured as guest speaker Reverend Herbert Daughtry of the Black United Front, a militant African American group based in New York's borough of Brooklyn. The event received press coverage in American and Korean media.

In July 1984, a Colombian Independence Day festival brought thousands of Colombians from within and beyond Elmhurst-Corona to a small triangular park on a shopping street in CD4. Behavior by a few—beer and alcohol drinking, pot smoking, public urination—that would be less obvious in a large public park here intruded on surrounding Elmhurst residential streets. A mixed delegation of local homeowners—Latin American, white, Indian, Filipino—protested to Community Board 4 members, and in 1985 a permit for the event was denied.

In 1986, the Colombian festival moved to the same large park where the Korean event was held. It was organized by Centro Civico Colombiano, an umbrella group of many Colombian organizations. In 1987, the festival attracted hundreds of thousands of Colombians and other Latin Americans. They enjoyed music, food booths, picnicking, and dancing. Surrounding the stage and sound system were advertising slogans and logos of Colombian and American businesses sponsoring the event. A similar Ecuadorian festival was held each summer in the same park, attracting crowds smaller than the Colombian event but larger than the Korean festival.

Two events within CD4 were organized to celebrate pan–Latin American identity, still a politically weak ideal in Queens, where the Latin American population is extremely diverse. In 1985, Spanish-language radio station WJIT sponsored a fund-raising event for a boy who was gravely ill in Colombia and broadcast for twenty-four hours from a nightclub in Elmhurst. Although the location made it convenient for the many Colombians who live in this area to bring cash and check contributions to the nightclub, the appeal was made on a pan–Latin American basis. Each year, WJIT chose one charitable cause—the previous year it had been Crippled Children of Puerto Rico, and the event was held elsewhere in the city.

The second pan–Latin American event was a Christmas tree lighting ceremony sponsored by *Ciudadanos Conscientes de Queens*/Concerned Citizens of Queens, the only multiservice social agency designed to serve the borough's hundreds of thousands of Latin American residents. Held for the first time in 1986, the 1987 event was attended by forty persons of diverse Latin American nationalities, including CCQ staffers, local Corona merchants, and Latin American community activists. Several Latin American Christmas songs were followed by a few American ones, after which those gathered walked to the nearby CCQ office for a buffet dinner.

A "Multi-Cultural Book Fair Specializing in Black Heritage Children's Books" was held first in 1988, and several times later, in front of a large shopping mall on a major Elmhurst commercial thoroughfare. It was sponsored by Concerned Community Adults (CCA), an organization focused on education, recreation, and public safety issues confronting the mainly black youth in the Lefrak City apartment complex in Corona. The titles for sale were celebratory of African American and African culture and history: biographies of Marcus Garvey, Jesse Jackson, and Oprah Winfrey; *Traditional African Musical Instruments*; *What Color Was Jesus?*; and others. The day-long book fair had no air of ethnic assertion and attracted a mix of black, white, Asian, and Latin American passersby who stopped to make purchases or chat at several folding tables on which books were displayed.

CCA's leader, an African American woman who had resided in Lefrak City for nine years, organized the event. Five African American adults, an immigrant Nigerian woman, an Indian librarian from the Lefrak branch, the white CD4 youth coordinator, and a Colombian college student studying youth services in Elmhurst-Corona assisted her. The mixed nature of this group resulted more from the organizer's "center woman"[8] mode of opportunistic organizing than a calculated attempt at multiethnic symbolism.

Most rituals of ethnic celebration in Community District 4 were staged either in the large public park, where a metropolitanwide rather than local assemblage of coethnics could gather, or, like the book fair, at the district's perimeter, in commercial zones at a remove from quiet residential streets. The Korean anti–police brutality demonstration, however, occurred on a residential street in front of the precinct house; it was disruptive of local routine, which was its point. The 1984 Colombian celebration that similarly disrupted residential tranquility—which was not its point—later relocated to the park where its metropolitan audience could be more appropriately accommodated.

The last ritual of ethnic celebration I will discuss was the annual public assertion of Italian identity during a Fourth of July picnic and fireworks display sponsored by a local businessman popularly known as "Tough Tony." The event took place at a small triangular park (commonly called "Spaghetti Park") festooned with paper Italian flags and opposite Tough Tony's pricey Italian restaurant in the heart of once-Italian Corona.

In 1987, by four p.m., some two to three dozen Italian American men in their twenties and thirties arrived to mingle with and jostle each other and to listen to the loud sound system playing Frank Sinatra and disco (locally seen as white music, in opposition to rap, symbolically the music of local African American and Latin American youth). By six p.m., a crowd of two hundred had gathered, mixed in age and gender and 80 percent Italian. One Italian teenage girl wore a "Sicilian is Sensational" t-shirt. Free hot dogs and soda were available. Many older Italians were served at umbrella-covered tables inside and next to the park or went directly to the head of the short food and drink line. The few Latin Americans, Asians, or blacks waited patiently in line (as I did) and ate standing or sat on the park benches.

About nine p.m., the fireworks display, which I attended in 1988, commenced. The young Italian men put up wooden sawhorse barriers along the two ends and both curbs of a block-long street adjacent to one of the park's three sides. Standing within the barriers, and surrounded by hundreds of onlookers, the men strutted back and forth in their cleared street space. As they joked with each other, they slowly set up firework launchers. The audience was racially mixed, predominantly non-Italian, and included both Corona residents and people from outside the neighborhood who had arrived to watch the fireworks. For a few hours, the street belonged to the men, who included employees and friends of Tough Tony, and Corona was theirs again. The men, however, did not represent the majority of Corona's Italian population, many of whom had better jobs and more education or had moved to suburban or more expensive Queens and Manhattan neighborhoods. Significantly, no public officials or Italian American leaders of Corona's many organizations appeared at this event, and no speeches were made.

Rituals of Continuity

Rituals of continuity in Elmhurst-Corona were organized by leaders of its established white population. They celebrated the community's past but inescapably involved the neighborhood's present diverse population as well, as audience or, in some cases, as program participants.

Elmhurst's Memorial Day ceremony commemorated the sacrifice of local residents killed and wounded during the First and Second World Wars and the Vietnam War. Amid the symbolism of flag lowering, military uniforms, and patriotic music in 1986, three Spanish surnames were read along with Irish, Jewish, and German surnames in the list of "Elmhurst boys" who died in Vietnam. In 1987, the two new Korean members of the Elmhurst Lions Club stood at attention alongside their white American fellow Lion businessmen members. In addition to white Americans who came to the park expressly for the ceremony, a racially mixed group of park users enjoying a day off watched the event.

The same park, named for nineteenth-century local resident Clement Clark Moore, author of "'Twas the Night Before Christmas," was in 1983 the site of a revival of Elmhurst's annual Christmas tree lighting and reading of Moore's poem. The audience of neighborhood children, which dwindled each year until a final tree lighting in 1987, was predominantly Asian and Latin American. Christmas carols sung by a Korean Methodist church choir framed greetings from the white American city councilman and community organization leaders. (This Korean congregation occupied the church building of the Elmhurst Methodist congregation founded by white Americans in 1839 and that had disbanded in the late 1970s.)

In Corona, just before Thanksgiving each year, Public School 14 presented a program of popular songs of the 1920s, 1930s, and 1940s to which senior citizens, mainly Italian and Jewish, from a nearby senior citizen center and a nursing home were invited. Many of the Italian women who attended were themselves graduates of this neighborhood school. Themes of remembrance, patriotism, and neighborhood continuity were stressed in song, an elaborate pledge-of-allegiance-to-the-flag musicale, and remarks from the school principal, whose own Jewish immigrant father, age 91, was introduced at the 1987 program. The school district superintendent also spoke, stressing the theme of generational reciprocity and recalling memories of his Italian immigrant grandfather. Ironically, none of the children performing, the majority of whom were Latin American, Asian, and black, were themselves the grandchildren of the senior citizens in the audience. The grandchildren of these onlookers did not live in Corona. Neither did many of the schoolchildren's own grandparents, who resided in the Dominican Republic, Pakistan, China, Ecuador, and elsewhere.

Corona's Christmas tree lighting ceremony was revived in 1981, but unlike Elmhurst's grew larger in attendance each year. Several thousand people and a television news camera crew were on hand in 1988 to witness the lights being turned on and the arrival of Santa Claus on a hook-and-ladder fire truck. The event was held in the same "Spaghetti Park" as the Fourth of July picnic but featured sponsorship by several Corona civic and business associations and speeches from the local city councilman, an

Italian American and Corona resident, and the area's New York State assemblywoman, an African American. Children from Public School 14 (which presented the pre-Thanksgiving musicale), a Corona Boy Scout troop, and St. Leo's Roman Catholic Church participated in caroling, and Corona residents of all ages and ethnic groups attended. At the evening's conclusion, the participants were invited into the Democratic Party club hall across the street, where the mainly elderly Italian American members provided refreshments to the neighborhood children.

Corona's hundredth birthday celebration in 1985, also a "Spaghetti Park" event, overlay the Fourth of July celebration it accompanied and turned that year's activities from an Italian ethnic celebration into a broader ceremony of continuity. Italian flags were present, but so were an equal number of American flags. An Italian singer and four-piece combo provided music, but the much larger crowd of several thousand—nearly half white and half Latin American, with small numbers of Asians and blacks—were *all* served hot dogs, sodas, and beer in long, orderly lines. The celebration was sponsored by the Corona Community Development Corporation and the Corona Heights Businessmen's Association; local merchants provided refreshments, including a ten-foot "Happy Birthday Corona" cake, decorated with an American flag, from a local bakery. Democratic Party club leaders were active participants, and two voter registration tables were set up at the park's edge. Short formal remarks at the bandstand by the city councilman and the president of the businessmen's association stressed civic pride and the need for voting in order to ensure park and street maintenance for Corona. Italian ethnicity this day was entwined with neighborhood continuity, not with symbolic occupation of the street by a group of Italian men.

Quality-of-Life Rituals

The quality-of-life values Lucy Schilero enunciated at the 1990 coalition awards ceremony fueled many of the demonstrations, dedications, cleanup days, and awards dinners I observed in Elmhurst-Corona. These quality-of-life events consistently avoided mention of the neighborhood's ethnic and racial diversity, stressing family-based community life, concern for children and the elderly, opposition to overdevelopment, public and private compliance with sanitation standards, and police action against drug dealers. In short, quality-of-life events expressed communal commitments to the locality and its conventional standards.

Drug sales in Elmhurst-Corona and perceived police unresponsiveness in reducing local crime were hotly debated at Community Board 4 monthly meetings. The board consisted of about forty CD4 residents, each of whom was active in various civic organizations; they were appointed by local city council members and the Queens borough president to make recommendations on land-use and municipal budget issues. In 1986, the board held a Saturday morning demonstration at the local police precinct house to protest inaction on the crime situation. Although the event was small, the dozen who participated included white, Puerto Rican, Korean, and Chinese board members and community residents, each of whom presented their complaints personally to the precinct captain. A "March against Crack," also in 1986, proceeded down a street frequented by drug dealers in front of Lefrak City. The appreciative comments from the mainly white Community Board 4 members at their next monthly meeting centered on the drug issue: "People are fed up"; "We've got to get those drug dealers off 57th Avenue." No comment was voiced about the racial identity of the mainly African American marchers (or about the immigrant Jamaican drug dealers, for that matter).

Ceremonies to open new community facilities typically brought together audiences of diverse ethnic and racial composition. In 1987, many groups and leaders joined to dedicate a new public park located between a residential Corona street and a senior citizen residence. They included Italian homeowners; black, Latin American, and Korean residents of the senior residence; the African American international secretary of the Transit Workers Union, the residence's sponsor; the Latin American Chinese architect who designed the park; a predominantly Latin American public school class who entertained with folk dances (including the Virginia reel); and a large delegation of public officials. A few months later, a similarly racially and ethnically diverse group of Roman Catholic Church officials, St. Leo's parishioners and parochial school children, and public leaders celebrated the opening of a new residence for a dozen developmentally disabled adults—themselves white, Latin American, and black—in a renovated convent building belonging to the Corona church.

Since the late 1970s, block association leader Carmela George had organized an annual neighborhood cleanup day in a four-block area around her

Corona home. On a Saturday morning in May, a Sanitation Department truck would arrive and the residents throw out old furniture, appliances, and other trash; they used brooms to sweep driveways and sidewalks into the gutters, which were washed down by a Sanitation Department street-sweeper truck. When I had first met Carmela, an Italian American then in her sixties and a life-long Corona resident, I learned that she still personally greeted each new Latin American, Chinese, Korean, and Guyanese Indian family that moved into her immediate neighborhood. She also explained on which days of the week to place garbage bags outdoors for curbside pickup, and she invited them to participate in the May cleanup.

Edna Baskin, the African American leader of Concerned Community Adults, a youth advocacy group in Lefrak City, and organizer of the Black Heritage book fair, also used the symbolism of street cleaning. Beginning in 1987, Baskin led a group of a dozen African American, black immigrant, and Latin American youth in a summer campaign for clean sidewalks on the commercial blocks surrounding her apartment complex (one of which was the site of the 1986 antidrug march). The youth swept the sidewalks three mornings each week and distributed flyers to merchants urging them to cooperate.

Many of these merchants were Korean and belonged to the Mid-Queens Korean American Association, active throughout CD4. The association donated funds for cleanup implements and garbage bags and also gifts for the youth. In 1987 and 1988, they hosted Mrs. Baskin, the youth, other CCA members, the District 4 manager, and civic organization leaders at a Korean restaurant to celebrate the cleanup campaign. Mrs. Baskin, in turn, at her CCA awards dinner at the end of each summer, presented certificates of appreciation to Korean association leaders, among others who assisted her efforts. Although all were aware of African American–Korean conflict in other parts of New York City and of the significance of cooperation between these two ethnic groups in CD4, the rhetoric of the dinner events focused on local quality-of-life values, not racial harmony or conflict prevention.

Public Rituals and Local Politics

Most of the rituals I attended in Elmhurst-Corona were held outdoors. The public was invited to attend by the organizers, and the events were advertised with flyers, posters, and newspaper announcements. These events required official permission and cooperation from public agencies—the Community District 4 office, the local police precinct, and New York City's Parks and Sanitation departments. Organizers of public ceremonies, festivals, and protests therefore came into contact with the local political structure even before an event transpired.

These rituals were not tangential to local politics. They *were* local politics. Public rituals had their own particular roles and impacts within an unfolding field of political relations among established residents and newcomers in CD4. They constituted a set of local political arenas that intersected with Community Board 4 public hearings and votes; civic and ethnic organization meetings; municipal agency policy determinations about locations and level of effort in public services; meetings with and requests tendered to elected officials by local residents; election campaigns for public office; and informal contacts among officials, leaders, and residents, including those occurring during ritual events.

Elmhurst and Corona housed large numbers of immigrants who were not citizens and could not vote. White American civic leaders were aware that the total number of votes the area now delivered was small compared to that of many other Queens community districts and also to that of other portions of the electoral districts of officials representing segments of CD4. (Community districts and electoral districts are not coterminous in New York City; typically, parts of several community districts are included in each electoral district and vice versa.) Public rituals in this context were a parapolitical means to voice community needs to elected officials and municipal bureaucrats who gravitated toward high-voter-turnout neighborhoods rather than low-voter-turnout (high immigrant) areas. Rituals could validate local leadership claims by producing numbers of supporters; impressing invited public officials, who might be given both awards and opportunities to address assembled audiences; and solidifying local leaders' positions among their followers. Elmhurst-Corona's continuously evolving political field thus included these public rituals. It also encompassed claims for support and resources made later to public officials—informally, in funding requests, in public meetings—by the leaders who staged CD4's public events and ceremonies.

CD4's panoply of public rituals was linked by leading actors in community politics who appeared and reappeared at different events. Rose Rothschild, the Community District 4 manager, for example, was present at many of the events I report here. Several elected officials and civic and ethnic association leaders were frequent participants as well. Political careers were built in part through rituals, as well as in other settings. Public rituals were particularly important in navigating the entry of CD4's newcomer groups into local political life. Seung Ha Hong and Sung Jin Chun, two founders of the Mid-Queens Korean American Association, for example, absented themselves from the 1985 police-brutality protest. But they joined the CB4 demonstration against police unresponsiveness in 1986; attended Elmhurst Christmas tree lightings in 1985, 1986, and 1987; welcomed white American community leaders as their guests at the Korean Harvest and Folklore festival in 1986 and 1987; were introduced with local dignitaries and fellow Lions at the 1987 Elmhurst Memorial Day ceremony; and participated in both their own organization's and Edna Baskin's summer cleanup campaign dinners in 1987 and 1988.

Unlike Mrs. Baskin, most African American leaders in Lefrak City were relatively uninvolved in CD4 civic politics before the 1990s. The tenant association avoided such activity, as it had felt rebuffed in earlier contacts. Mrs. Baskin used her group's participation in quality-of-life events to develop personal ties with community organization leaders and elected officials and to obtain public resources for youth activities in the underserved Lefrak City area.

Compared to these Korean immigrant and African American involvements in Elmhurst-Corona rituals during the 1980s, the Latin American, Chinese, and Indian presence was more circumscribed. Colombian, Ecuadorian, and other Latin American leaders were active in organizing rituals of ethnic celebration for their own nationalities on a metropolitan basis; they were in contact thereby with citywide and Queens borough–wide elected officials but not with Elmhurst-Corona leaders. The pan–Latin American events *within* CD4 did not attract non–Latin American local officials or leaders. Latin American Elmhurst-Corona residents did participate in local public rituals as audience members, but not yet as organizers, official guests, or honorees. Chinese in Elmhurst-Corona equaled Koreans in number but were as organizationally invisible in local rituals as Latin Americans. This was not the case in Community District 7 (Flushing) to the east of CD4. There, several Chinese organizations were politically active and participated in many local rituals.[9] Elmhurst-Corona's Indians, who slightly trailed Chinese and Koreans in numbers, were by 1990 only beginning to become active in civic politics and local rituals elsewhere in Queens but not yet in CD4.

The Precession of Public Rituals in Elmhurst-Corona, Queens

Some Elmhurst-Corona festivals and ceremonies were staged annually (the Three Kings Day celebration, the Stations of the Cross procession, Corona's Fourth of July, the Christmas tree lightings) and enjoyed the repeated quality that is one hallmark of "ritual."[10] Other events, such as demonstrations, facility openings, and award presentations, were repetitive in form yet staged on each occasion by a different organization or group. All were new rituals, begun (or recently revived) in the context of massive demographic change in the 1970s and 1980s. They had an experimental, contingent, constitutive quality that reflected, I believe, a search for order and purpose in the lives of those who resided in this multilingual, multiethnic, multiracial community.

However, the ceremonies and festivals of Community District 4 clearly did not possess the organic, integrated, communal qualities of rituals in the small, culturally homogeneous settings of classic ethnographic accounts.[11] In Elmhurst-Corona, no one (except the ethnographer) attended or even knew of the existence of all of them. They are conducted in different languages and for different audiences. The values that charged different rituals—continuity and priority, ethnic celebration and assertion, panethnic harmony, or quality-of-life inclusiveness—signaled different visions of what the neighborhood was or should be. Where did order lie within such diversity?

The search for order would turn up empty, I contend, if one treated these events as self-contained texts and read in, into, or across them the symbolic constellations they might reveal. Certainly more thorough ethnographic exposition is possible of symbolic conventions in the discourses of white old-time reminiscers, or immigrant popular culture celebrants, or asserters of Korean civil rights or Italian neighborhood priority, or service-provider panethnic harmonists, or neighborhood quality-of-life activists. But that would leave us with a ragged "postcultural situation," with an ethnography of people as "morally disconnected" from each other as were the separate "cultures" (and those of their ethnographers) in anthropology's historically neutral days of the "ethnographic present."[12] It would also undermine the fact that the same person may on different occasions engage in two or more of these discourses and be moved by their organizing symbols.

The order lies not in texts but in context. Stressing both the semantics and pragmatics of rituals, Tambiah writes that "multivalent meanings and multiple uses must be dialectally and recursively related to one another and to the larger sociocultural whole."[13] Barth directs attention to the analysis of rituals "as a product of history" that "turns our attention away from constructing models of order and pattern in cultural manifestations, and towards the search for events that cause and shape these manifestations."[14]

National immigration policies, economic and political conditions overseas, and the U.S. civil rights revolution brought immigrants and African Americans to new homes in Elmhurst-Corona. Established residents and newcomers alike made the most of their personal situations within a context of laws and government agencies that regulated work opportunities, housing, education, and the reproduction of neighborhood "quality of life." At the same time, their current circumstances rub against visions of the past, of a return to one's homeland, and of a more just future. These material/ideological contradictions, as my colleagues and I discovered, led to debate and differing motives for political action within each of CD4's ethnic components.

As Koreans pondered the diminishing returns of small business success, some pursued confrontation with those who harassed them; others sought accommodation in local civic alliances; still others found salvation in Korean Christian churches.[15]

Chinese followed a more direct political route, with a half-dozen Flushing and Queenswide organizations each separately pursuing contacts with elected officials, mobilizing voters, and backing candidates for elective office.[16]

Indian professionals sought suburban escape but found their complaisance challenged by anti-Indian violence and by social problems plaguing less educated or less-well-off Indian immigrants who would not suburbanize and remained in Queens outer-city neighborhoods.[17]

Latin Americans might organize their lives for eventual return to their homelands, pursue individual assimilation in the United States, or lack the certitude and resources for choosing either course. Latin American female leaders more frequently sought to organize across nationality lines and to bring social services to "los Hispanos de Queens"; male leaders focused on events in their home countries and on political careers in organizations of their co-nationals in the United States.[18]

African Americans, with long historical memories, debated the wisdom both of militant "empowerment" political strategies—remembering past accomplishments and defeats when no "rainbow" of non-black allies could be counted on—and of quality-of-life politics in a Queens that was increasingly multiracial.[19]

White Americans might resist multiethnic alliances, remembering or reviving a white neighborhood past, or embrace them pragmatically. They used such new alliances to preserve a lower-middle-class/working-class "quality of life" threatened from above by elite Manhattan social planners or gentrifier shock troops and from below by persons surviving on meager "safety net" social programs who might be "dumped" on any neighborhood that let down its guard.

In these political circumstances, rituals of inclusion and quality-of-life rituals arose and waxed. Rituals of ethnic celebration might empower ethnic leaders who entered American civic arenas and might assert the messages of those not being heard. Rituals of continuity expressed prior claims of the remaining local white Americans, but in practice they also required the presence of newcomers as audience, if not for their very enactment.

Order did emerge, I concluded, in the diversity of public rituals I observed. Here, individual residents might find the different forms of coherence and purpose in their personal lives expressed in different rituals (and also in worship, leisure pursuit, and interpersonal relations). But the nature of the political community also shaped the local ritual process. Established residents and newcomers who entered it had no choice but to deal with each other. Their mutual engagement in turn produced a precession of values.

Parochial rituals of continuity were being transformed. They either were becoming expressions of a "new" white ethnic minority or were appropriating communal symbols of inclusion (Christmas carols sung in Korean and Spanish) and of quality-of-life commitment (generational continuity).

Rituals of ethnic celebration were becoming spatially marginal to the locality (moving from residential community to peripheral commercial strip or metropolitan park) or were temporally marginal (occurring one day or night a year). They were also attracting participants of other ethnic groups (thereby becoming more political in American terms—more color full) and thus conveying to their audiences emergent inclusive sentiments.

Rituals of inclusion were domesticating the authentic, living ethnic cultures of adult newcomers and limiting expression to the few symbolic forms by which white ancestral European ethnicity is enacted in the contemporary United States—music, dance, food, costume, greetings. At the same time, they brought together in common audiences those who defined the current and future local political community.

Communal, ethnically unmarked, quality-of-life rituals were presenting, at best, a political platform around which local residents might unite and, at least, an agenda around which those of each ethnic camp who defined their place locally, not elsewhere, might find temporary allies. As the community changed over time, quality-of-life values become thematic features of all categories of public ritual. We see in formation, perhaps, a community's new ceremonies of continuity.

Chapter 3

What Ethnographies Leave Out

In 1927 Margaret Mead prepared to write her second book on Samoa, *Social Organization of Manu'a* (published in 1930). Having completed *Coming of Age in Samoa* (scheduled to appear in 1928), which aimed at a popular audience, she now wanted to write a "monograph" to establish her place among "scholars." Before beginning, she read a handful of what we now call "classic" ethnographies. "I gathered together a pile of the famous monographs of the period—Rivers' *The Todas* (1906), Malinowski's *Argonauts of the Western Pacific* (1922), [John] Roscoe's *The Baganda* (1911), and [George] Grinnell's *The Cheyenne* (1923)—and studied their arrangements."[1]

What Mead discovered, of course, was that the "arrangements" of each work were unique; there was no all-purpose model to which her Samoan data could be affixed and a monograph result. Each author presented a mass of material, and each had designed an internal architecture upon which this mass was hung. These two properties—rich ethnographic detail and cohesive supporting framework—continue to animate the anthropological aesthetic. We applaud works that contain both, and we remain unsatisfied by those with too little ethnography (they are "thin") or too much architecture ("too theoretical") or those in which the architecture is inadequate to support the ethnography ("too much detail," "not well-organized").

Mead's teacher Franz Boas understood how an ethnography could fail in its architectural mission and had told her, "The trouble with a monograph is that you need the end at the beginning, and this is true of every chapter—you need each chapter in all the others."[2] (Good advice for all ethnographic writers upon completing their first draft!) Boas, however, misunderstood from where the desired cohesiveness arose. He imagined it lay within "the culture" an ethnographer studied. As his student Marian Smith explained, "Masses of data may therefore be worked over with no clear knowledge of what is to be gained at the end. A new hypothesis or a new slant [the architecture] will 'emerge' or be 'revealed' or 'suggested.' The data will 'speak for themselves.' This is the procedure by which the exponent of the natural history approach prefers to arrive at a hypothesis: they do not come from systematic thought but from systematically ordered data."[3]

Anthropologists long ago freed themselves from such illusions: even in 1927, Mead was looking for architectural inspiration outside her Samoan fieldnotes. We know that a range of conscious and unconscious biases molds what we see, hear, and record in field notebooks. We attempt to reveal and control these biases, not deny them.[4] We no longer pretend that there is nothing on our desk between the fieldnotes and the ethnography we produce. We acknowledge that along with fieldnote indexes and a progression of writing outlines, we turn to the substantive and theoretical writings of others for comparison and contextualization.[5] When I wrote my ethnography of Elmhurst-Corona, my desk was covered with (1) two boxes of fieldnotes in the center, with my index to them sitting on top; (2) a succession of constantly evolving chapter and section outlines on the left, each keyed to fieldnotes, newspaper clipping files, and cited works; (3) file drawers, maps, and piles of books and photocopied materials on the right; (4) the computer screen where the ethnography was typed off to one side; and (5) the printer where it all came out on the other.

As index categories are formulated, writing outlines refined and expanded, and sources to cite reviewed and selected, we respond to the architectural pole of our aesthetic and move away from the fieldnotes. Yet the other pole, the desire to present as much "well-hung" ethnographic detail as the architecture will bear, constantly sends us back to the notes themselves. Anthropologist Sol Tax once told a despondent M. N. Srinivas, whose Rampura fieldnotes had just been consumed in a fire, "that no social anthropologist, not even the most industrious, has ever published more than a small portion of his data."[6] Tax had spent six years doing fieldwork in Guatemala, and his classic ethnography, *Penny Capitalism* (1951), chock-full of ethnographic detail, plus a set of articles, came nowhere near utilizing all his fieldnotes.[7]

Still, most anthropologists, who, like Srinivas, have less extensive fieldwork experience than Tax, remain driven to "use" the fieldnotes they produce in a comprehensive ethnography. There are different ways to do so. Some ethnographies are more through-composed and analytic, others more raw and immediate, with many fieldnote examples.[8] All, however, will leave out most of the direct experience captured in an ethnographer's fieldnotes. Indeed, they must do so if anthropology's two-poled aesthetic is to work its power.

Yet this direct experience is not omitted without regrets. There remain certain events that do not find a place within the architecture the ethnographer creates but which nonetheless remain etched in one's headnotes. What follows are two such fieldnote accounts from my Queens research that "got lost" or severely compressed as my book's architecture took shape and prevailed. The notes bring these episodes into my consciousness with a vividness no one else can share, but they also tell stories that may be appreciated by others. The first account finds established white residents claiming their place within the new multiethnic, multiracial reality of Queens. The second describes newcomer children who were growing up amid it.

Elmhurst Baptist Church Revival

Background

Elmhurst Baptist was one of three historically white Protestant churches I studied, and I had been there six times before attending the two evening revival services described in these fieldnotes. The church was pastored by Reverend Kelly Grimsley, a white American. His wife, Susie Grimsley, was Filipina. In addition to its English language service, Elmhurst Baptist also rented space to independent Spanish, Korean, and Haitian congregations.

I took no notes during church services but jotted down brief handwritten scratch notes in the subway on my way home, then typed out a full fieldnote account the following day. Aside from correcting typographical errors, printing out abbreviations in full, and adding a few words in brackets, these and the following set of fieldnotes appear as I typed them. The section on Elmhurst Baptist Church in *The Future of Us All* (pages 338–340) draws on my fieldnotes of twenty services and events, church programs and documents, newspaper clippings, and an interview with two members.

18 May 1988

I arrived at the church at 7:30 on a rainy night, and the large banner announcing the revival looked wet but still bright and white against the dark stone church walls. The revival services program, to be used for all three nights, was distributed by Earl and the other older white American usher.

[Reverend] Kelly [Grimsley] said that this was an experiment for the Elmhurst Baptist Church. There has never been a revival in the 15 years he has been here. We have a full house tonight: the Boy Scouts, the Koreans and the AA [Alcoholics Anonymous] are all meeting in the church.

The congregation and choir, about 45, included two dozen Filipinos of all ages; about ten white Americans, mainly older people, women and a few men, but one young white man and woman; three Hispanics, a woman and a couple, who are [all] regulars; Claudia, the West Indian woman, and her daughter later at the coffee hour; one man who may have been Korean; and two [other] black people, a woman who came for [a] short time and left, and a man who came late, perhaps a Haitian. Susie [Grimsley], Kelly's wife, was in the choir, which was mainly Filipino tonight, with Claudia.

The older Filipino man who is [the church's] financial secretary led off the service with four or five hymns. The hymns sung in this church are mainly American hymns, of the 19th and 20th century. Some are published by the Rodeheaver Company, and Fanny Crosby is a composer of one or two we sang. "Love Lifted Me" was sung tonight.[9]

Kelly asked another older Filipino man, "a friend of our church," whom I have not seen at the service before, to give the invocation prayer. When we came to the [individual] testimonies, a Filipino man sitting with the invocation leader in the front row came up to the pulpit and introduced himself as Mr. Acosta, a minister from Iloilo in the Philippines. He is visiting New York, and was told about this revival by a woman [medical] doctor, whom he pointed out in the congregation. She is a regular member, about age 50. He gave a very well presented sermon on the need to accept Christ out of love, not out of fear. It was a well-paced, measured, rehearsed presentation, with several stories interspersed in his exhortations. It was a hotter emotional tone than anything I have heard here before from Kelly, who later told me he did not know that this was going to happen.

The [volunteered] congregational prayer, which followed, opened things up. Bert [Pueblos, a Filipino member] gave a prayer, addressing "Lord" throughout, and [he] was followed by the invocation giver; [by] a young white man with a beard, who speaks with the fervor of an ex-druggie Jesus person, about how God helps him, a sinner, in his life; and by the woman doctor, who was very fervent and tight in her presentation. Three of [these] four were Filipino, and all expressed firm religious commitments on a personal level of [a] believer's expression that is different from Kelly's more social, haven in a heartless world, liberal sermons.

Kelly said again [that] this was an experiment. "We don't know what will happen. Perhaps I am too low-key for a revival, but tonight I will start things off, tomorrow Reverend Michael Easterling of the Madison Baptist Church in Manhattan, will put us on a roll, and by Friday night we will be out of control." His sermon, as he often does, criticized the TV evangelists for their hypocrisy, and also the glitter and glitz of modern life and pursuits. His examples of the lack of witness to Christ were the Chambers murder of Jennifer Levin, the case of the East Harlem white minister accused of sexual abuse of two teenage girls, and current cases of sexual excess or accusation. He also spoke, in his liberal tone, against the oppression in South Africa, of Palestinians in Israel, and the homeless and the contrast between the rich and poor in the US. He said [that] we are divided by race, age, sex, and turf, but we are all united under God. Christ's forgiveness of our sins was a gift of God's that we don't deserve; it was given purely out of love.

The service lasted about two hours.

Afterwards, [at] the coffee hour in the church hall, I asked Kelly if he felt it unusual that the control of the service was distributed among several others (a multivocality), sort of like the early church with gifts of the spirit appearing spontaneously. He said yes to my question, and added quickly that he didn't know Reverend Acosta would speak, and that made another sermon, his [own], almost unnecessary. He also said he hoped that the Antioch [Baptist Church] choir [coming on Friday] would not tone down for a "white" audience, which black churches sometimes do. (An ironic way to see it, in that this church is not white, but half Filipino, and only a third or less white, if historically it is a white church.)

The whites here included Vic, the [church] treasurer; the woman who has lived in Elmhurst for 68 years, and a woman who looks like his sister[10] and [who] sang a duet with the Filipino financial secretary from the choir; the woman from the South who lives in Rego Park, and told me she doesn't like the TV evangelists, but is from the South, "So I know revivals."

Bert Pueblos sings in the choir, as do his wife, who served coffee, his two sons, and his daughter, who sat next to Susie [Grimsley]; he introduced them all to me. Bert—Kelly thanked [him for it] in the service—made the [revival] banner in front, and the flyers [advertising the revival].

Annefiora, the organist and choir director, talked with me. She has been at the church for 17 years, and has seen big changes in the congregation. She is Italian, and taught in Latin America for three-and-a-half years, so she speaks fluent Spanish. She lives in Jamaica Estates, where many "Asians" are moving in: "Filipinos, Chinese, Koreans." She teaches music at Newtown High School, and said they are getting a new principal; the current one is there just a few years, [and] is moving to Long Island. She said she finds the Asian students more disciplined, and harder working than the Latin Americans. I told her about the [New Immigrants and Older Americans] Project, and she asked about the music that is used at the Presbyterian and Lutheran churches [I am attending], as well as about the [ethnic] composition of the congregations.

20 May 1988

It was a warm night, unlike the last two rainy evenings. Ruby [Danta, a member of my research team][11] and I arrived at 7:30, and met Kelly and Bert standing in front waiting for the Antioch [Baptist] minister and choir to arrive. I asked how things were last night—about the same number of people [they said]. Reverend Easterling had a different approach: he gave a questionnaire, which Bert showed me, about being born again and again as a concept, rather than being born again just once as some other churches practice.

Inside people were sitting and waiting, talking with each other quietly. Claudia [the West Indian Elmhurst Baptist member] had another daughter, Pat [with] her husband and little girl, who sat with Claudia. Next to her was the regular Hispanic woman. The other regular couple, [a] Puerto Rican woman and Nicaraguan man Ruby found out, came in and sat in the same pew with a younger couple, perhaps their son and his wife (this woman was introduced to Ruby as Puerto Rican). There were about 26 Filipinos tonight, including the choir members now sitting in the congregation, and dressed casually except for the older men and the woman doctor. There were about ten elderly whites, the men in ties and jackets. The younger bearded white man came with a young black woman whom I haven't seen before.

The Hispanic woman went forward after a while, and began leading people in hymns, asking for requests. She seemed to take the initiative in getting things started, asking [Claudia's daughter] Pat to play piano, which she did, serviceably, but not very well.

Kelly then came to the altar and began, saying that the [Antioch Baptist] choir is here, having had trouble finding the church. He was relaxed, and talked about the first two nights a bit. "It's the same crowd" here, an older white man told me in the coffee hour, and it was.

Reverend Laura Sinclair, in her mid 30s, came to the altar to join Kelly in one of the heavy wood chairs. She wore an afro, a black robe (Kelly always wears a jacket and tie), and a *kente*-styled long scarf falling on both sides of her robe. She spoke very forcefully and dramatically, with a[n American] black English accent, and very clear enunciation. Eight women in blue robes, her choir, came in and sat in the front row. One had a young child with her. Another woman, the church's youth director, also came, sitting in the congregation with her young daughter. They both came with the choir from their place, as did a young black man who came much later in the service. The pianist and choir director, a man in his mid 20s, came in with them, and asked for help in moving the piano sideways so he could face the choir standing in front, and also see the congregation.

Their first selection was a wonderful moving gospel piece, with one of the members leading the women. They all began to sway together with the gospel piano before beginning to sing. This was a rocking performance, not the watered down "white church" presentation that Kelly feared might happen. Reverend Sinclair then welcomed everyone, and said that while people meditated on the next selection she wanted them to think about the two words " 'I Can.' After the choir is through, I'll be back with 'I Can.' "

[Individual] testimonies followed. An Antioch member began with a short thanks to God because her sister had hip surgery recently, and everything was all right. Another said she wanted to just thank the Lord for this day. The young white man spoke, as did a Filipino man. The testimonies, except the white man's, were fairly short tonight. An elderly white woman finished the testimonies.

The congregational prayer was at first silent, Kelly not leading off, and then Bert spoke, but that was all. The choir followed with another hymn, much slower, featuring a solo from one of the women. They all swayed in time as she sang, as did one of the young Filipino women who seemed quite enthusiastic about the music. I looked around a couple of times while they sang. The elderly whites were less expressive than the Filipinos, but no one seemed dismayed or uninvolved in the music. Only on a few occasions did people clap with the choir, and here more Filipinos and Hispanics and Claudia clapped than did the elderly whites.

Reverend Sinclair gave "I Can," contrasting the "I Can't" attitude as an expression of sin. "I can't go to church because I'm too tired [or because] I don't have the right dress." Later, in the coffee hour, Bert's children were joking with his wife about how they had heard and said these things. She also mentioned South Africa, Martin Luther King, John F. Kennedy, oppression in the South, the homeless and hungry, showing the "I Can" attitude to overcome sin.

The pianist then sang "Amazing Grace" to the tune of "Danny Boy." This is an Andrae Crouch arrangement,[12] as I asked him [about it] later in the coffee hour. He seemed surprised that I knew this, and was caught, and said that he listened a lot to Andrae Crouch, and his arrangement was similar. Several Elmhurst Baptist members told him how much they liked his solo, including several elderly white women.

The offering was collected by the white usher, the Nicaraguan man, the (Filipino) financial secretary, and Bert.

The [Antioch] choir then began singing, in a gently but firmly bouncing manner, "Come, Come to Jesus." Reverend Sinclair said if there is anyone who has never accepted Jesus, now they could come forward, and stand with Kelly, and pledge their faith in Jesus before everyone. No one did, as the choir sang on and people began singing with them, and clapping at Reverend Sinclair's urging. Things were [now] heating up, and exciting.

Next she said, if anyone would like to renew their faith in Jesus they could come forward, but if they wanted to make that renewal in their heart, silently, and stay where they were, that was all right too. People sang another verse or so, and then an older Filipino woman in front came forward, and Kelly put his arm around her.

She was soon followed by the Hispanic woman, and then by the Rego Park white woman from the South. A few moments later, another eight older whites all came forward, including all but three men or so of the elderly whites present. The two sisters, in Elmhurst 68 years, were among them. They all stood as we sang "Come, Come to Jesus."

It was remarkable. A symbolic embrace of "their" church by the older whites, nearly all of them, in a changed congregation where they are the minority, and in a service led by a black Baptist minister and choir. They were symbolically demonstrating both their claim to the church, and their right to be here, to be included, if they are no longer "the owners" they once might have been.

The coffee hour was very open and friendly. The Filipinos, though tending to sit together, and joking and talking together, also socialized with the others. Many, especially the elderly whites I thought, made an effort to speak with the [Antioch] choir members, and make them feel welcome, though they also tended to stick together, knowing each other and not the [Elmhurst Baptist] congregation members. It was a friendly atmosphere, with about 60 people. Again the service lasted two hours, and I left a bit before 10 pm.

Public School 89 International Festival

Background

In addition to this account, I observed the PS 89 International Festival in 1986 and 1988, and my description in *The Future of Us All* (pages 333–334) draws on all three sets of fieldnotes, programs, newspaper clippings, and an interview with school principal Cleonice LoSecco. The book also provides extensive coverage of Community Board 4's district cabinet and its district manager Rose Rothschild. Hsiang-shui Chen, Steven Gregory, and Milagros Ricourt were all members of my "New Americans and Old Immigrants" research team.[13] For this event, I took scratch notes during the outdoor activities, added to them following classroom visits, and typed this fieldnote account shortly afterward.

27 May 1987

I arrived at PS 89 at 8:45 am and met Chen and Steve, who both took pictures. Milagros arrived later, after the parade. The crowd was very much as last year, the same mix of faces among the children, and [also among] the parents, mainly women, many Hispanic and Asian—including Koreans, Chinese, and South Asians, with some Indian women in various styles of South Asian dress. There were, as last year, a few men, [and] grandparents, and this year one or two newspaper photographers, [including] one from *Newsday*.

The day was not nice, in the 50s or 60s, jacket weather, and raining very lightly through the march and dancing. The kids were lined up [to one side of the school] on Gleane Street on the sidewalk, with police barricades at the end opening on to Britton Avenue, and in the midblock. An art show was posted on the fence in front of the school facing Britton Avenue. Many of the mothers were carrying food, in bags or in dishes wrapped in foil. A police "No Parking Wednesday" printed notice was fixed to the telephone poles on Britton Avenue; hand lettered on it was "miercoles" ["Wednesday" in Spanish]. A printed program was passed out to the crowd by a student.

Traffic was still moving on Britton as the parade was about to begin. Yesterday at the district cabinet [meeting] Rose [Rothschild] had made a fuss about the marching through the street, calling it unsafe, but, I think, really being bothered about something else—perhaps conflict between her and [PS 89's principal] "think-headed Mrs. LoSecco," as she termed her, dating to when Rose was PTA president at PS 89. The public address system, as last year, was terrible—a large, long table piled with about six components, yet inaudible sound when announcements were made, and loud, but undistinct music for marching and dancing. Mr. Steven Klein, the parade coordinator, who last year was dressed in a tuxedo, today had on a cream colored double-breasted suit, ruffled shirt, large bow tie, and Borsolino hat. Steve, who thought he looked a lot like [his teacher, anthropologist] Stanley Diamond (he does), later talked with him. Klein said when he came to the school about seven years ago the kids just paraded through the street. He introduced the dances, which is one of the things he teaches in PS 89.

At 9 am the school color guard came to the middle of the cleared space on Gleane Street next to the school. A Hispanic girl carried the American flag; she was dressed in blue and purple, the western dress from the OKLAHOMA production group who later did the Virginia Reel. Behind her were three school flags carried by: a Hispanic boy with white shirt and pants, vest, and straw cowboy hat, also in the OKLAHOMA group; a black boy in the outfit of the [French] minuet dancers; and a black girl in a long dress. After a recorded "Star Spangled Banner" was played, without any singing, the color guard returned to the street and the school building, and the parade began.

The first group was boys in black pants, white shirts, white lace ties, and paper cocked hats, something like pirate hats. The girls wore long dresses. A teacher of Class 4–15 told me this group would dance the minuet; the costumes were "like the court of Louis XIV or XV." The first minuet dance class carried crayoned paper flags, of their own countries presumably. The next class had yellow paper sashes with their home countries written, crossing their chests. These included: Dominican Republic, Puerto Rico, El Salvador, Colombia, Venezuela, Bolivia, Mexico, Nicaragua, Peru, Guyana, India, China, Philippines, Ecuador, Korea, America, Laos, New Orleans, Guatemala, Honduras, Viet Nam, Italy, Cuba, Nepal, Costa Rica. One of these classes had banners: "The International Festival PS 89"; "PS 89 Bilingual Class 5-401," a Spanish language class.

As they marched out, they went right into the street, with help from the [110th Precinct] Police. Britton Avenue had been cleared of traffic; a police van blocked the Gleane Street intersection; and a police scooter, followed by a school car with p.a. system playing march music, led off the parade down Britton. It followed the same route, pretty much, as last year: turning north on Layton, coming back down Petitt, and returning on Ithaca to Britton, where the kids went back into the school on the Hampton Street side.

Following the minuet classes, 5-411 [and] 5-401, came class 403 with several paper signs: "Computers"; "Bits and Bytes"; "We Are the World"; "Languages." Another class had a paper collage of pictures, including a large one of astronaut Sally Ride, with the message: "We Are the Future."

Class 5-409 were wearing the western outfits. One of the kids said they were for a school production of OKLAHOMA, and they would do a dance from that. This class had [a] banner with a score of paper flags on it. They also had a sign with a world globe and the message lettered: "Friendship."

Class 4-405 were dressed in white, with couples of boys and girls carrying flower arches about three feet across. The kids told me this was for a Filipino dance they would do. They had been rehearsing since April, a boy said. The teacher looked Filipina; I remember that her class did a Filipino stick dance last year. Actually, none of the dances or costumes from last year were repeated this year; overall the costumes were more imaginative, with more classes dressed uniformly in costumes oriented to the dance they performed. Classes with students all in their own [various] national dress were fewer this year; perhaps half or more last year, but less than half this year.

The kids in a class dressed in blue with orange polka dot costumes—long dresses of this material for the girls—told me they would do "a Spanish dance." Another class was led by a hand-colored map of the 48 US states, with the legend: "This land is made for you and me." These kids were going to do a Swiss dance; the boys had shorts and colored suspenders.

A class in [various] home country dress, carrying handmade flags, had a banner reading: "Visit the World—Come to PS89." Another, dressed similarly, had a "Peace—Goodwill" banner. Class 2-103 banner: "Bienvenidos—Welcome." Class 2-102: "Different People from Different Countries." More paper flags were carried by the first and second grades that finished off the parade.

I saw the Korean bilingual class again, with the same teacher as last year, with most of the kids in Korean dress. I also saw a dozen or so Chinese kids, the girls in Chinese [satin] tops and pants. I talked to the teacher who said this was a bilingual first grade, just started at PS 89 in September 1986. Her children were from Hong Kong, Taiwan, and mainland China, she said, and speak Cantonese, Taiwanese, and Mandarin.

Class 1-17 banner: "We've Got the Spirit." Class 1-16: "We Are the Children of the Rainbow," wearing [various] home country dress.

A class in Greek costume, with boys wearing white skirts and white stockings (many of them; some wearing pants under the skirts) were in the middle of the march, as I had walked up to Petitt to join up there. One girl said: "We're doing a Greece dance" (sic) when [I] asked her what the costume was. Another class had a banner reading: "Celebrate our Nations," with many flags on it.

A few people along the way watched the parade. The cool and rainy-damp weather accounted for fewer watching than last year no doubt. The Little Friends preschool [children] at Ithaca and Britton were out on their front steps watching. As the parade came back into the school, the police directed traffic at the Hampton-Britton intersection, stopping cars for kids to pass, then halting the parade for the cars to continue up Hampton toward Roosevelt.

As I returned to the Gleane Street side of the school for the dances, I met Rose Rothschild. She was in a bad mood about the children having marched in the street, not on the sidewalk as she had stated they would yesterday [at the district cabinet meeting]. She said she would write "the commissioner" to complain that the 110th Precinct had allowed this to happen. She said they did not have a parade permit; she wouldn't give them one. "I'll give [outspoken Elmhurst civic activist] Ron Laney a permit, for spite, and see what they do."

As I arrived the dances had begun. (See program for numbers and classes.)

1. Minuet (France), had the same amazing mix of faces—Asian, Hispanic, fewer white, a few black—as last year. As they finished, a mother said, "Que lindo!" ["How cute!" in Spanish]. They then left around the corner to enter PS 89 through the Britton Street front entrance. The p.a. system was lousy.
2. Virginia Reel (U.S.A.). The girls wore long dresses with bonnets or kerchiefs, and the boys white shirts and pants, colored vests, and straw cowboy hats. At Mr. Klein's urging, people began clapping . . . 1, 2, 1, 2. The crowd was a couple of hundred, mainly mothers, with Asian and Hispanic women predominating by far.
3. Flower Dance (Philippines).
4. Flamenco (Spain). The girls wore long, ankle length skirts, of a blue material with orange polka dots. The boys wore black pants, white shirts, and polka dot cloth sashes around their waists. The kids seemed quite well rehearsed, and one could hear the spirited foot-tapping on the streets of the flamenco rhythms.
5. Swedish Schottische (Sweden). Boys in white short pants, with dark print colored suspenders; girls in white blouses, blue skirts, and white aprons. European peasanty looking costumes.
6. Jiffy Mixer (U.S.A.). Boys and girls were all dressed in white, with colored elbow bands, waist sashes, and (for some) bow ties for the boys. Girls in two classes wore headbands with three small feathers over their foreheads; the others had spangly red headbands. One class had blue pants and skirts instead of white like the other two.
7. Jingo Lo Ba (African). This was the biggest hit of the day, with wildly enthusiastic applause and shouts from the audience. This was Mrs. Montgomery's second grade class; she is black, and last year did a Jamaican dance. The girls were dressed in black leotards, with tiger skin cloth miniskirt and bra-top cloth wrapper; the boys in Hausa-style over shirts and black pants. The kids danced enthusiastically, shaking their hair around, and moving their arms up and down. Mrs. Montgomery looked like a West African woman, with a blouse top and waist tie of the same cloth as the kids, black skirt, and nicely tied head cloth. The kids looked mainly Indian and East

Asian, with a few Hispanics. I noticed no white or black kids, but Chen saw one black kid.

8. Children's Polka (Germany). Several kids were wearing their coats, in the cold, overcast weather. The rain had stopped but the feeling was still damp. The crowd was the same size as last year. There were many cameras, including Ellen Young, the unsuccessful [Chinese] School Board [24] candidate in 1986, who had a second grade child in PS 89; also several videocams, including one for the school, set up next to Mr. Klein's p.a. table.
9. Tamborine and Spring Dance (China). This was the Chinese bilingual first grade class. Nine girls, each with two ring-hoops with bells, were dressed in Chinese-style shirt and pants. Ten boys with wrist bells, dressed in short pants and running shoes, waited on the side as the girls danced. When they finished, four of the girls took off their costumes, shook out their pony tails, had red paper carnations put in their hair, and joined the ten boys. While they danced, the other girls stood on the sideline with the teacher who was directing the boys and girls, and they mouthed the words to the recorded song.
10. Dei Leider Strompf (Switzerland). The girls wore white blouses, blue skirts, and white aprons; the boys white short pants, blue suspenders, and bow ties. Like their costumes, their dance was very similar to 5, the Swedish dance.
11. Miserlou (Greece). Boys and girls wore white skirts, though some boys had pants on underneath, while others wore the white stockings of the Greek outfit. The girls wore several paper flowers in headbands. The music was "Never on Sunday." Two of the teachers directing the classes in this dance were black.
12. Two long chorus lines of three classes stretched up and down the entire dance area, with six lead dancers in front; they danced quite well, while many in the two lines barely made it. They all wore black pants, white tops and gloves, white socks, cardboard bow tie and three shirt-button bibs, gold or silver spangled top hats, and carried black white-tipped canes. Very Broadway looking. They danced to [the song] "New York, New York."

To end, Mr. Klein introduced Dr. Thomas Piro, the assistant principal. He explained that [PS 89 Principal] Mrs. LoSecco could not be here today, but International Day was an important tradition for the parents, the teachers, staff, and children. "It seems that every year it gets bigger and better. It's a day when we recognize the backgrounds of many of the children who come to our school." Most of the parents had deserted Gleane Street and the cold by now, so by the time Dr. Piro ended the audience was just about gone. Dr. Piro thanked Mr. Klein, the staff, and the 110th Precinct. Ms. McCarthy, the other assistant principal, wound up: "Thank you for coming and giving us your children."

At that point it was 10:45. Everyone was invited into the school for food and to visit the classrooms. A man dressed in Indian shirt and pants with white vest and turban, who had been taking pictures, invited us in when we told him who we were; he turned out to be a white American teacher, caught in the spirit of International Day, I guess.

Steve, Chen, and I went to buy more film, and then returned to visit several classes. We went into the mini-school [building] to find the Chinese bilingual class where Chen talked with the teacher, a parent, some of the kids, and Ellen Young. We also ate there, and [again] next door in the Spanish bilingual first grade, 1-13A & B. The place was full of mothers, the kids having gone to the lunchroom for the school lunch. We talked with the teacher who showed [us] a chart the class had made listing the birthplaces of students and their parents. She pointed out that most of the kids were born in the US. The parents were from Argentina, 2; Chile, 1; Colombia, 32; Costa Rica, 2; Dominican Republic, 15; Ecuador, 16; El Salvador, 5; France, 1; Mexico, 6; Peru, 5; US, 5; Uruguay, 2.

Another teacher told us this may be the last year of such a large International Day. Next year several classes and 24 teachers will be moved to other schools in the district to relieve the overcrowding. In addition, Mr. Klein told Steve, Rose Rothschild at the Community Board [office] is giving them difficulty.

We talked with another group of first grade girls in a regular class, and Steve took their picture before we left. They were Indian, Puerto Rican, Vietnamese, and Chinese. The Chinese girl was told by another Puerto Rican girl that "Carlos" said she was his girlfriend. She said to tell Carlos to come out in the hall; she wanted to punch him in the nose.

Rakhee, the Indian girl, told me they had their "home country" food in the class today. She had brought "samosa—the triangle, you know?"

PART II

Ethnography, Past and Present

Chapter 4

Ethnography

The word "ethnography" has a double meaning in anthropology: ethnography as *product* (ethnographic writings—the books and articles written by anthropologists) and ethnography as *process* (participant observation or fieldwork). The product depends upon the process but not in any simple A→B relationship. In constructing ethnographies, anthropologists do more than merely "write up" the fieldnotes they record as part of the process of doing fieldwork. If ethnographies can be seen as the building blocks and testing grounds of anthropological theory, then it must also be accepted that ethnographies and the ethnographic process from which they derive are shaped and molded by theory.

Ethnography (in both senses) may profitably be envisioned as one side of an anthropological triangle. The other two sides are *comparison* and *contextualization*. Together, the three sides of this triangle define the operational system by which anthropologists acquire and use ethnographic data in writing ethnographies. Fieldnotes are filtered through and interpreted against comparative theory and contextual documentary materials. As they are read, ethnographies stimulate comparative theoretical thinking, which in turn suggests new problems and interpretations to be resolved through further ethnographic fieldwork. Ethnographies, and the comparative theoretical reflection they spur, also regularly lead to new demands and rising standards for documentary contextualization (more history; more ecological or demographic backgrounding; more attention to state policy, economic trends, and the world system). This anthropological triangle of ethnography, comparison, and contextualization is, in essence, the way in which sociocultural anthropology works as a discipline to explain and interpret human cultures and social life.[1]

Ethnographies as they have evolved over the past hundred and sixty years constitute a genre, a form of writing conditioned by the process of knowledge construction epitomized in this anthropological triangle. Ethnographies consequently differ from travel writing, gazetteers, interview-based surveys, or even the personal fieldwork accounts of anthropologists (which form a separate genre). Ethnography, both product and process, has a history and pattern of development of its own.

A Brief History of Ethnography

As a written account, ethnography focuses on a particular population, place, and time, with the deliberate goal of describing it to others. So, often, did the writings of nineteenth-century explorers, missionaries, military agents, journalists, travelers, and reformers, and these contain much information useful to anthropologists. What distinguishes the first ethnography, Louis Henry Morgan's *The League of the Ho-de-no-sau-nee, or Iroquois* (1851), from these other writings are two qualities: its attempt to depict the structure and operation of Iroquois society from the Iroquois viewpoint (the ethnographic side of the anthropological triangle) and its grounding in the monogenist anthropological theorizing of its time (the comparative side of the triangle), ideas to which Morgan would make major additions and reformulations. Morgan's book detailed Iroquois matrilineal kinship, political and ceremonial life, material culture, and religion, the ethnographic basis for this information being Morgan's partnership with the Western-educated Iroquois Ely S. Parker, his translator and cultural interpreter. The book's attention to history, geography, the impact of white settlers, and contemporary land-rights issues also established standards for pre- and postfieldwork contextualization (the third side of the triangle) that anthropologists continue to heed.

Morgan's ethnography, still authoritative and readable, was not joined by comparable works until the 1880s. What ensued instead were increased efforts to provide standardized guides for gathering ethnographic data to local "men on the spot" (few were women) in accord with the comparative goals of armchair theorists. Although Morgan did collect kinship data himself from American Indian groups on field trips during the 1860s, much of the material he used in later writings arrived from missionary and other amateurs in India, Australia, and elsewhere who filled in and returned his kinship schedules. In England, E. B. Tylor played a key role in drafting *Notes and Queries on Anthropology*, first published in 1874 for use around the globe; he and other comparativists, such as James Frazer, helped shape up the resulting local work for publication, often first as articles in the *Journal of the Anthropological Institute*, which dates to 1872. Through these efforts, ethnographic standards slowly improved, and theoretical perspectives became more overt, but contextualization retreated, a victim of antihistorical and ethnocentric evolutionism or diffusionism.

The fieldwork of Frank Cushing among the Zuni Indians in the early 1880s made a great leap forward in ethnographic method. Cushing learned to speak Zuni, resided at the pueblo over a four-year period, and combined observation of ongoing events with the seated-informant questioning more typical of anthropological guide-users. Cushing's sensitive *Zuñi Fetiches* (1883) revealed the inner world of these people's cosmology, mythology, and symbolism and its connection to practical activities. So did his major work *Zuñi Breadstuff* (1920), but its initial publication during 1884–1885 in an obscure journal insulated its impact at the time. Cushing's lack of influence on students and his death in 1899 combined to make his ethnographic advances a false start for anthropology.[2]

Franz Boas's ethnographic research among the Inuit in 1883–1884 moved less thoroughly in the participant observation direction than Cushing, and his subsequent fieldwork through the 1890s among the native Americans of the Northwest Coast consisted mainly of the transcription of texts recited by seated informants.[3] It was this approach that he taught his cohorts of students during the first three decades of the twentieth century at Columbia University, and they took it with them as anthropology departments sprouted in the United States. Their goal was the "salvage ethnography" of "memory cultures" and not the direct participant observation of human life as it is lived. In view of the devastated circumstances of Native American reservations, the Boasians recognized no alternative until acculturation and community studies became acceptable choices in the 1930s. Until then, American ethnographies increased in number and improved in contextualization as historical interests supplanted evolutionary theory. But they stultified in method as participant observation regressed, and in theory as well, with little invigoration from the ethnographic side of the anthropological triangle.

In British anthropology, the division of labor between the armchair theorist and the person on the spot, already dead in the United States, entered obsolescence in the 1890s when Tylor and Frazer's Oxford-trained protégé Baldwin Spencer collaborated in participant observation with a seasoned local expert on Aboriginal life, Frank Gillen. Their *Central Tribes of Native Australia* (1899) provided a vivid and detailed view of cosmology, ritual, and social organization that not only revealed unheralded cultural complexity amid technological simplicity but sparked new theoretical currents in the work of Émile Durkheim and Sigmund Freud.

Even before Spencer and Gillen's work was published, in 1898 a team of Cambridge scientists arrived on the spot themselves in the Torres Strait islands just north of Australia. Though less theoretically or ethnographically provocative, their results moved fieldwork practice beyond even the Australian ethnographers via crystallization of the genealogical method of anthropological inquiry by team member W. H. R. Rivers. Rivers demonstrated that systematic collection of genealogies could produce far more than kinship terminologies. Community history, migration trajectories, marriage patterns, demography, inheritance and succession, and the relation of rules to actual occurrences could all be studied. With his application of this method in *The Todas* (1906), an ethnography of a South Indian group, Rivers also found that prior knowledge of kinship connections enriched his understanding of Toda participation in ongoing ritual events.[4]

These British ethnographic innovations were incorporated into a 1912 revision of *Notes and Queries.* Novice ethnographer Bronislaw Malinowski carried this with him to New Guinea in 1914 but soon became discouraged with the limits of even this more sophisticated use of the seated informant. In his groundbreaking Trobriand Islands fieldwork of 1915–1918, Malinowski bettered Cushing. Not only did he learn the language, he more actively entered the scenes of daily life and made the speech in action he heard and recorded there the basis of his ethnography. Moreover, he maintained detailed fieldnotes that he analyzed topically while still in the field and constantly reread to plan further research activities.[5] He found that topics such as economics, law, land use, and magic intruded on each other—the events recorded in his fieldnotes could be analyzed from several of these institutional perspectives. Thus was his functionalism born, "the mass of gears all turning and grinding on each other," as his American contemporary Ralph Linton put it.[6]

Malinowski's students, a robust and gifted group, produced dozens of classic ethnographies during the 1930s, 1940s and 1950s. Perhaps the most influential is E. E. Evans-Pritchard's *The Nuer* (1940). Rich in ethnographic details, it is nonetheless highly selective in their presentation, subordinating them to a powerful theory of how descent ideology organizes group life and cattle management against the vagaries of annual ecological transformation and population movement. In this work, influenced by the thinking of A. R. Radcliffe-Brown, a strong relationship was evident between the comparative and ethnographic sides of the anthropological triangle, and its impact was marked over the next quarter century. As critiques of *The Nuer* later mounted, it was the historical-contextual side of the triangle that was seen as most in need of bolstering.

In the United States, Malinowskian-style ethnography took hold and Boasian fieldwork methods were largely superseded. Margaret Mead, one of Boas's later students, independently invented an ethnographic approach equivalent to Malinowski's, against her mentor's advice.[7] From the 1940s, on both sides of the Atlantic and beyond, a combination of strong ethnography but weak contextualization was widely visible in both anthropological theory and in ethnographies themselves. New demands for improved contextualization arose with the impact of ecology, regional analysis, history, and world systems in the 1960s and thereafter. Today, there are hundreds of classic ethnographies, although perhaps none since *The Nuer* would be as readily so designated by a majority of anthropologists or has been as widely read.

In sociology, there is less agreement about the disciplinary origin of ethnographic research methods. Conventionally, the monographs of the University of Chicago sociology department during the 1920s and 1930s are cited: studies of itinerant "hobo" workers, youth gangs, dancehall employees and patrons; Italians, Poles, Jews, French Canadians, Mexicans, and Chinese; and central city "gold coast" apartment, artist colony, and rooming-house dwellers.[8] Two decades before this research, however, W. E. B. Du Bois used similar methods (both he and the Chicago school were inspired by British and American survey and settlement house movements) to produce *The Philadelphia Negro* (1899), which depicted life in an inner-city neighborhood of southern migrant and northern-born African Americans. Even earlier, Frederick Engels in 1844 studied new classes, Irish labor migration, urban spatial arrangements, symbolic attachments, and modes of observable behavior in Manchester and other rapidly industrializing British cities, although his *Condition of the Working Class in England* was not published in English until 1892.

Since the 1920s, there has been much cross-fertilization between anthropological and sociological ethnography. A few of the "Chicago school" studies were conducted by researchers identifiable as anthropologists. Moreover, both the Lynds, authors of *Middletown* (1929), a study of Muncie, Indiana, which credits anthropologists Rivers and Clark Wissler, a Boasian, for methodological inspiration, and William Foote Whyte, author of *Street Corner Society* (1943, 1955), a study of Boston's Italian North End influenced by Harvard anthropologists, are considered major figures in the development of American sociology.[9] In England, Max Gluckman, a Manchester social anthropologist who did fieldwork in Africa, was influential in the development of ethnographic fieldwork by British sociologists in schools, gangs, and workplaces during the 1950s and later.[10]

In recent decades, both anthropologists and sociologists have undertaken ethnographic research in a wide range of traditional and innovative settings, at home and abroad. So, increasingly, do scholars from folklore, education, environmental psychology, political science, and other disciplines. Ethnography, however, remains central to credentialing, teaching, publishing, and theory construction in social and cultural anthropology, and it occupies a more marginal position in other fields.

Selection, Access, Rapport

The selection of a particular population or site for ethnographic research is ordinarily related to some unanswered question or outstanding problem in the body of comparative anthropological theory. Personal connections or predilections of researchers also shape this selection, but the fieldworker still must justify his or her choice in terms of some significant theory to which the project is addressed. Usually this is made explicit in a written proposal for funds to underwrite the fieldwork.

Although ethnography is thus lodged from conception in comparative anthropological theory, the comparative side of the anthropological triangle molds the ethnographic process in two further ways. First, anthropologists are imbued with a cross-cultural perspective by training and career-long reading. When addressing any aspect of social life—marriage, leadership, ethnicity, television viewing—they recall and refer to examples of similarities and differences in the global range of societies with which they are familiar. Unlike other social sciences that see Western experience as the center and as the norm, anthropology fixes each case within the widest coordinates—social formations globally, throughout human history.

Second, the comparative perspective focuses ethnographic attention on trends and transitions, not just on similarities and differences at random (which are infinite). Rather than treating each ethnographic instance as unique (which in terms of extreme cultural relativism, it is), ethnographers place the social phenomena they observe within comparative frames (foraging, horticultural, agricultural, pastoral, industrial, colonial, neocolonial economies; cooperative, competitive, individualistic societies; gender subordination, complementarity, or equality; etc.). Ethnographic results in turn provoke debate, revision, and innovation in such theorizing. And behind this, and behind the ethnographic process itself, lies the problem of identifying what is most deserving of close attention within the flux of daily life—the patterns of behavior and change that effect shifts in the social order at large.

Significant theories bring ethnographers to particular locations, actors, and activities, and once they arrive, they begin to observe and listen. Often they must learn to listen—learn the language, the local vocabulary, and current verbal conventions. Ethnographic fieldwork now turns away from theoretical discourse to the viewpoints and concepts of the people (informants, subjects, actors, consultants) themselves. Ethnographers aim to document how the people see and talk about their everyday social activities and groupings and about the wider worlds they live in. Their normal scenes of activity, topics of conversation, and standards of evaluation are the objects of ethnographic fieldwork.

This does not begin by announcing "I'm your ethnographer; when can I interview you?" Ethnographers must be honest about their role and sponsorship (covert fieldwork remains controversial and rare), but their paramount aim is to listen and to move as quickly as possible into the natural settings of social life, the places people would be, doing what they would be doing if the ethnographer were not there. This involves a continuing process of requesting and obtaining access to the many locations, activities, and groups that comprise the overall fieldwork arena. As ethnographers observe and listen in a wide-ranging manner, within parameters set by the significant theories that bring them there, they begin to understand culturally meaningful behavioral conventions and to formulate culturally appropriate utterances. This indexes a second continuing process: building interpersonal rapport with informants, a topic that preoccupies many autobiographical accounts of ethnographic fieldwork, one of the most instructive being Whyte's 1955 Appendix to *Street Corner Society*.

As the ethnographic process unfolds, the fieldworker must constantly make decisions about where to be, who to listen to, what events to follow, and what to safely ignore and leave out. These decisions are guided both by the significant theories prefiguring fieldwork and by new theories of significance that arise in the field. These latter theories—hunches, hypotheses, ideas about connections and relationships—emerge as listening and observation proceed. They suggest which persons and activities to focus upon, what places and events to attend to, and which objects and their circulation to follow.

As this occurs, the fieldwork "funnel" narrows, to use Michael Agar's apt metaphor.[11] The early phase of securing access and building rapport is wide, open, and nearly all encompassing. As theories of significance emerge, pan out, or are discarded, the funnel of informants, events, and activities narrows. Goals crystallize. Research design sharpens.[12]

Discovery Procedures: Listening

Ethnography's greatest strength is situated listening. Interviews become useful at later stages of fieldwork, but ethnographic research begins by listening to what British anthropologist Audrey Richards called "speech in action."[13] Here the actors control topicality—talking to each other about what they usually do—and the researcher secures access to their turf—the locations they usually occupy. Early on, as rapport begins to be established, fieldworkers deliberately place themselves in a wide range of such situations so that they can sample widely. Then, as the research funnel narrows and other methods are deployed, the ethnographer becomes more selective about where to listen.

The importance of situated listening was emphasized memorably by Whyte. After he asked an intrusive question during illicit gambling activities, stopping the ongoing flow of behavior, Whyte's key informant Doc told him, "Go easy on that 'who,' 'what,' 'why,' 'when,' 'where' stuff, Bill. You ask those questions and people will clam up on you. If people accept you, you can just hang around, and you'll learn the answers in the long run without even having to ask the questions." Whyte said, "I found that this was true. As I sat and listened, I learned the answers to questions that I would not even have had the sense to ask if I had been getting my information solely on an interview basis."[14]

Situated listening becomes the basis for understanding both what can be talked about in later conversations and interviews and what categories and evaluations the actors use to observe and interpret ongoing behavior.

Discovery Procedures: Observing

Many veteran ethnographers bristle when they are told that their methods are not quantitative. Using both emic categories articulated by the actors and etic categories formulated by the community of social science observers, ethnographers count, sample, and calculate ratios, proportions, and probabilities as part of their fieldwork activities.[15] These countable quantities include numbers of people in events, their positions, their comings and goings; objects and inventories; and exchanges, movements, orderings, sequences, associations, assemblages, and arrangements of many sorts.

Malinowski's classic *Argonauts of the Western Pacific* (1922) incorporated his numerous observations of the inter-island *kula* exchange of seashell valuables—necklaces traded for armlets—as canoes from one community arrived at another, exchanges were conducted, and then additional exchanges of foodstuffs, timber, greenstone, pottery, and other items followed. Who exchanged what, the order, etiquette, volume, frequency, and other variables were all counted and analyzed. In Whyte's *Street Corner Society* (1943), the size, composition, duration of activity, and initiation of interaction were recorded and analyzed for numerous group events. Whyte even demonstrated quantitatively a relationship between hierarchical group leadership structure and bowling scores.

Discovery Procedures: Interviewing

Interviewing is problematic.[16] Human beings are apt to reinterpret or reformulate the past to make it conform to their ongoing sense of the present. Moreover, the ever-present danger of an observer effect in fieldwork—that the presence of the ethnographer affects and reshapes an actor's behavior and response—is especially difficult to control in an artificial one-to-one interview situation, where normal social activity is suspended.

Still, interviews are essential in ethnography. They are best left for later stages of the ethnographic encounter, when, to use Agar's funnel metaphor, the speech events of fieldwork move from wide and open to narrow and more focused. After the investigator has become at ease with the language and local codes and references and has successfully gained access to natural conversations and amassed a stock of cultural knowledge via situated listening, deliberate intervention into speech events may begin. These steps may be graded from least to most intrusive and controlled.

1. Still on the informants' turf and still in the accustomed activities of daily life, the ethnographer begins to enter natural conversations as a speaker and begins to shift topicality to her or his own interests. This process starts gently, with the ethnographer moving appropriately into rounds of chatting, gossiping, and ordinary comment. As cultural competence increases and as theories of significance emerge, the ethnographer attempts to direct conversations by introducing questions and suggesting topics for responses from informants.
2. After an initial period of fieldwork—a few months, perhaps—arranged interviews may begin. This class of speech events is disruptive: the informant is removed from her or his turf to the ethnographer's household or office, or an everyday location is transformed into a scene of ethnographer-informant dialogue, an activity that would otherwise not be occurring there. Typically, the earliest of these deliberate breaks in time-place behavioral flow reserve topicality for the actor. In such open-ended or discovery interviews, the informant is encouraged to move the conversation according to his or her own interests.
3. In later and more productive interviews, the ethnographer begins to assert control. General topics are introduced, allowing informants to expand freely upon their own points of view and knowledge. In more structured ethnographic interviews, topicality is more firmly shaped and directed by the fieldworker. Informant responses now move away from orations and free commentaries and to more specific responses to questions.
4. In the most focused forms of interviewing, the ethnographer controls both turf and topicality as fully as possible. Questionnaires and interview schedules may be used, and the objective is to obtain particular types and pieces of data. These may include household interviews,

psychological tests, and reports of disputes or may encompass repeated interview sessions to secure lengthy life histories, with the ethnographer guiding the subject according to preset standards of scope and comprehensiveness.

5. Though not a major part of ethnographic practice, in some instances, and when still on the informants' turf, the ethnographer may ask direct and pointed questions and attempt to secure precise pieces of data for his or her records. Interventions of this sort are especially dangerous—the inappropriateness of such seizures of topicality in everyday settings may be jarring to the actors. Typically, speech events of this sort occur in the final phase of fieldwork, when local rapport is at its peak, research goals are most pressing, and the fieldwork funnel approaches its vanishing point.

Notes and Records

The production of notes and records begins to move ethnographic research toward its ultimate written products. Focused interview sessions with seated informants often permit direct transcription of verbal statements. In open-ended and ethnographic interviews, brief written notes—what Simon Ottenberg terms "scratch notes"—are taken during the session, and these form the basis for the construction later of fuller written fieldnotes.[17] Field-workers often go through this two-step process even when interviews are tape recorded, both as a backup to and index of the taped session and because of the analytic gains many ethnographers note in transforming their scratch notes into fuller descriptive fieldnotes.

During ethnographic research in natural behavior stream settings, similar brief jottings may be inscribed, but major attention is directed to observing the event in progress. Often it is not even possible to record scratch notes, and both they and fuller fieldnote description follow later. Margaret Mead wrote about the nagging pressure to type up fieldnotes from scratch notes and about the danger of scratch notes growing "cold" when this was delayed, even by one day. She also wrote of the satisfaction of being caught up in this work and of the importance for later ethnographic writing of the insights gained in expanding scratch notes into descriptive fieldnotes.[18]

Ottenberg sees this process as the interaction of scratch notes and "headnotes"—the stored memories and interpretations that arise from direct participant observation as filtered by the ethnographer's overall theoretical stance. Headnotes form an essential complement to fieldnotes (and to more formal fieldwork data sets or records). Headnotes are employed to make sense of one's fieldnotes when they are re-read later for ethnographic writing projects. The importance of headnotes is particularly evident when one ethnographer attempts to use another's fieldnotes and quickly realizes how difficult it is to understand them without headnotes of one's own.

Fieldnotes typically are kept in running chronological order and may be (minimally) indexed separately by actor and topic. Additionally, ethnographers usually generate various records—well-defined sets of data organized by topic, person, or other category. These may include records of household composition, land holdings, ritual performances, life histories, folktales, and so on. Sometimes, decisions to collect sets of records are part of the initial research design, and pre-set forms to enter such data may be brought with the investigator to the field setting. In other cases, a decision to collect a systematic body of records develops during fieldwork, often emerging within general running fieldnotes and then being separated out in new record files.

Fieldnotes and records present ethnographers with great masses of information—hundreds, even thousands of pages—that while accumulating may be arranged only by chronological order or by topic. Malinowski urged that ethnographers constantly re-read and begin to organize and analyze their notes while still conducting fieldwork, but commonly the more focused work of indexing them occurs when fieldwork is over. As ethnographers then turn to ethnographic writing, they readdress the theoretical discourse they turned away from in fieldwork.[19] Fieldnotes and records must now be related directly to the comparative and contextual sides of the anthropological knowledge-construction triangle.

The Ethnographic Writing Process

On paper, two types of documents (each with many iterations and subdivisions) link fieldnotes and ethnographic writings. Book or article *outlines* key the writing process to comparative theoretical ideas and contextual data sources against which fieldnote evidence will be weighed and interpreted. *Indexes* of fieldnotes and records are developed and refined to locate relevant data for the topics of concerns in the writing outlines.

The ethnographer then works back and forth along the fieldnote-index-outline-ethnography continuum.

At the same time, considerations are made as to format, style, readership, manner of presentation, and direct use of fieldnotes and informant statements. These issues are considered both through emulation of admired models of ethnographic writing and through attention to a critical literature on ethnographic writing that arose in the 1980s.[20] This postmodernist concern with "the crisis of representation" adds to earlier forms of ethnographic criticism that focus mainly on faults of contextualization and that have produced ever-higher standards in historical, political economic, ecological, demographic, statistical, and legal backgrounding.

Conclusion

Ethnographic research produces results that can be obtained in no other way. The ethnographic tradition entails "the description of people's activities, their interactions with each other, [and] their verbal behavior[, which should be] copious and detailed. Cumulative development consists above all in the fact that such data, provided they are adequate, never become obsolete and can be used by analysts in researching questions not visualized by the researchers who collected them."[21]

Chapter 5

Anthropology's Hidden Colonialism: Assistants and Their Ethnographers

This chapter concerns hidden issues of scholarly history, the interpersonal context of fieldwork, and intellectual colonialism in the study of "other cultures." For more than a hundred years, members of the communities and cultures studied by anthropologists have been major providers of information, translation, fieldnotes, and fieldwork. Although professional ethnographers—usually white, mostly male—have normally assumed full authorship for their ethnographic products, the remarkable contribution of these assistants—mainly persons of color—is not widely appreciated or understood. In no major treatment of the discipline is it portrayed as a fundamental part of the history of anthropology.

Anthropologists remain as uncertain about what to call these locally recruited fieldworkers (research assistants, key informants?) as they do the people they study (natives, locals, informants, collaborators, respondents, subjects, "the other"?).[1] This is due in part to our failure to appreciate that anthropologist-assistant relationships have a history, a changing set of relationships that this chapter attempts to outline. It is organized in six sections, each dealing with a stage in the unfolding assistant-anthropologist relationship and each section also focused upon ethnographic research in a major world area. This circular-staircase analysis is not intended to suggest that fieldwork in each region developed along a unique course, still less to provide an exhaustive review of relations with local assistants, but rather to highlight particular cases and sequences in anthropology's collective history.

The Informant: Melanesia

In Bronislaw Malinowski's now famous diary, he recorded his first session with an informant in 1914.[2] This man was Ahuia Ova, resident of a Motu village near the colonial British New Guinea capital Port Moresby. Ova was already familiar with the role of the seated informant who would answer the ethnographer's pre-set questions, questions most frequently posed from printed guides such as the Royal Anthropological Institute's *Notes and Queries* (first edition 1874). Ova had served in 1904 as informant to C. G. Seligman, an alumnus of the pioneering 1898 Cambridge University Torres Strait Expedition, and was his principal source for the chapters on Koita culture, some hundred and fifty pages of Seligman's massive survey volume *The Melanesians of British New Guinea*, published in 1910.

With another expedition veteran, W. H. R. Rivers, Seligman had put on-the-spot fieldwork with informants at the center of an emerging British anthropology, and he served as mentor to Malinowski in his first extensive New Guinea fieldwork in Mailu in 1914–1915. Malinowski later broke decisively from *Notes and Queries* inquisition in his historic Trobriand Islands fieldwork in 1915–1918 and redefined the informant as someone to listen to and speak with in natural, everyday settings, as well as in arranged interviews.[3] Malinowski would influence the development of anthropological fieldwork immensely, but he did not work again with Ova. Others did, however, and Ahuia Ova's autobiography, as edited by F. E. Williams, was followed by an update by Cyril Belshaw in 1951, the year of Ova's death, and research by Reg Shelley.[4] These writings allow us to envision the career of a man caught up in the throes of colonial society, one who played an important role in working with a series of New Guinea coastal ethnographers.

Ahuia Ova is an example of the local cultural expert. There would be many more such men and women informing anthropologists in Melanesia and other world areas over the succeeding years. The dilemma for ethnographers who found it difficult not to acknowledge their dependence upon persons such as Ova has been addressed in various ways in Melanesian studies. Ralph Bulmer enlisted and credited a local collaborator, Saem Majnep, in a coauthored study, *Birds of My Kalam Country* (1977). Other anthropologists have made their Ahuia Ovas the subject of book-length life histories: Roger Keesing in *'Elota's Story: The Life and Times of a Solomon Islands Big Man* (1978) and Andrew Strathern in *Ongka: A Self Account by a New Guinea Big-Man* (1979).[5]

The Native's Point of View: North America

In his Northwest Coast fieldwork, beginning in the 1880s, Franz Boas envisioned his goal as capturing the native's point of view through texts that recorded myths and folktales or that described ritual and technological activities. His informants included the literate *metis* George Hunt, raised in a Kwakwaka'wakw (Kwakiutl) village, whom Boas taught to transcribe Kwakwala texts on his own. A stream of Hunt's materials arrived by mail in New York to be edited by Boas in several volumes, some of which listed Hunt as coauthor.[6]

Partnerships like this characterized the work of many of Boas's students. In his preface to *Havasupai Ethnography* (1928), the resolute Boasian Leslie Spier wrote, "My principal informant, Sinyella, was an energetic and well-informed old man, aged 71. So much material is directly autobiographical, that it would have been possible to present this sketch as an account of his life."[7] This option was not taken, however, and the volume consists of topical chapters ranging from "Economic Life" to "Social Relations" to "Historical Tales," with Spier as sole author.

The Boas-Hunt and Spier-Sinyella collaborations were later surpassed in a monumental ethnographic trilogy on the Ingalik Indians of Alaska, a far better organized achievement than Boas's Kwakiutl corpus. These volumes list anthropologist Cornelius Osgood as author, yet he details carefully the role of Billy Williams, his Ingalik informant in 1934 and 1937. Williams came to understand fully the Yale anthropologist's objectives, and he was responsible, in Osgood's words, for "the great majority of my data," including "more than ninety-five percent" of the descriptions of ritual.[8]

The Boasian single-informant model clearly influenced many of those who became prominent figures as the discipline of anthropology achieved academic standing in the early decades of the twentieth century. Meanwhile, another ethnographic role for American Indians developed at the Bureau of American Ethnology (BAE) and other museum-oriented research centers. Here Native Americans became staff members, writing the ethnography of their own and closely related peoples. The Plains Indians Francis La Flesche, who was published in seven BAE volumes, and James Murie were two of the most industrious,[9] but their careers were not without affronts of a racist and intellectually colonialist sort.

La Flesche normally wore tie and suit to his Smithsonian Institution office. Yet, as his biographer Margot Liberty has revealed, when he died in 1932, his *American Anthropologist* obituary photograph was retouched to remove his usual attire, leaving only the buffalo robe he had once been persuaded to don over his shirt and tie for this single shot. We can compare the original with the altered version in the plates accompanying Liberty's two biographical essays.[10] In death, La Flesche's Indian identity was seen as superseding his professional accomplishments.

Attached to the Chicago Field Museum, the BAE, and the American Museum of Natural History, Murie worked early in the century with white anthropologists Alice Fletcher, George Dorsey, and Clark Wissler, each of whom (to varying degrees) acknowledged his contributions. But few of Murie's own manuscripts were published in his lifetime: his two-volume *Ceremonies of the Pawnee*, completed in 1921, finally appeared in 1981. Ralph Linton, however, used Murie's fieldnotes (deposited at the Chicago museum) in writing five papers on the Pawnee, a group he had never worked among, and without any mention of Murie.

Murie died in 1921, and Linton's papers appeared between 1922 and 1926. In their biography of Linton, Adelin Linton and Charles Wagley imply that Linton acknowledged both Murie and Dorsey in his Pawnee publications. Douglas Parks, however, states that Linton drew upon and quoted Murie's unpublished materials but did not acknowledge him in any of his five Pawnee papers, although he did cite unpublished work by Dorsey. This is certainly the case in the two of Linton's five papers that I have examined; in each, "unpublished" material is attributed to Dorsey, and Murie's name appears nowhere at all.[11]

More creditably to the discipline, the intimate informant-anthropologist partnerships that Boas had set in motion led one of his students, Paul Radin, as well as later generations, to find ways to acknowledge more fully the assistants upon whom their work depended. These assistants continued to be included in prefaces and introductions but also in fieldwork memoirs and, most tellingly in my opinion, book-length life histories. Beginning with Radin's *Autobiography of a Winnebago Indian* (1920), this genre had taken on a life of its own by the 1930s. It is ironic, perhaps, that the most detailed of these publications—Walter Dyk's *Son of Old Man Hat* (1938), Clellan Ford's *Smoke from Their Fires* (1941), and Leo Simmons's *Sun Chief* (1942)—like Radin's, vividly depict the clash and blend between Indian and U.S. or Canadian cultures that Boas studiously neglected.[12] In these volumes, the native's point of view overturned the cultural reconstruction and salvage goals that Boas had set for Americanist studies and that remained evident in many conventional ethnographic monographs.

The Assistant: Indonesia

With the blossoming of more fieldwork in the active Malinowskian style, and among living cultures as opposed to memory cultures, the seated query responder, text reciter, or life-history narrator began to recede in significance.[13] For the new 1930s ethnographers in the Pacific, Asia, Africa, and Latin America, it was numbers of persons in daily and ceremonial activities who were now objects of observation and interlocutors in conversation. At the same time, it became common to enlist, and pay, one local cultural guide as a member of the ethnographic team. This person might translate, introduce, negotiate, gather facts, and even conduct interviews and write fieldnotes to facilitate the work of the professional ethnographer.

I Made Kaler, a Balinese who joined Margaret Mead and Gregory Bateson's field team in 1936–1939, filled this role par excellence, as Mead recounts vividly in her autobiography *Blackberry Winter* (1972) and her Balinese *Letters from the Field* (1977). A loose thread here, however, appears in the letter I Made Kaler wrote Mead in 1938 asking her if he could publish his own study of one aspect of Balinese culture: "Anyhow with this letter I do you a request. But when you think it will be bad for your Bali book, I won't do it. Do you think I can write a short article about the cockfight. But I tell you if you think this action will be a bit bad for your book, I won't do it, I don't want to make profit of any of the stuff we have collected. It belongs all to you."[14]

I do not know what happened to this Balinese analysis of the Balinese cockfight. "The stuff we have collected belongs all to you." We, anthropologists and assistants, lost something irreplaceable here. A much later analysis of this Balinese cultural focus by Clifford Geertz has become famous and has stimulated much commentary by other anthropologists.[15] Geertz's fieldwork methods in Indonesia involved a broad range of informants and much less reliance on a key assistant than had Mead and Bateson's approach.[16] Still, it is unfortunate that I Made Kaler's Balinese perspective has never been published in its own right as part of a more inclusive ethnographic record.

Collaboration: Mesoamerica

A more complex set of relationships between locals and ethnographers evolved during the 1930s research of American anthropologists in Mesoamerica. Robert Redfield worked first solely with his wife Margaret

Park Redfield in their aborted 1926–1927 study of the Nahuatl-speaking Mexican town Tepotzlan. They used informants in then-standard interview fashion but also drew upon historical and linguistic writings of Tepotztecanos literate in Spanish.[17] In Redfield's 1930–1933 study of Chan Kom, he collaborated with local schoolteacher Alfonso Villa Rojas, who spoke both Spanish and Mayan, and the resulting monograph appeared as a coauthored volume. Villa went on to study another Yucatan community on his own as part of Redfield's four-community research project, and his *Maya of East Central Quintana Roo* (1945) became one of many publications from this eminent Mexican anthropologist.[18]

Following the Yucatan project, Redfield and his American student Sol Tax worked in Guatemala from 1934 to 1941. Redfield continually prodded Tax to conduct more intensive fieldwork and to pay greater attention to natural conversations, an approach Redfield had not used in Tepotzlan and that he credited to Villa and not to Malinowski, with whose work he was certainly familiar. Tax had difficulty embracing this advice, preferring to develop close working relationships with Indian collaborators such as Santiago Yach, whose life history he recorded, and Juan Rosales, whom he employed to conduct research and record fieldnotes.[19]

Rosales also shared his fieldnotes with Charles Wagley, who did fieldwork in Guatemala in 1937, and some of these notes were appended to Wagley's *Social and Religious Life of a Guatemalan Village* (1949). But Wagley's principal fieldwork assistant was Carmelo San Jose, a Spanish- and Mayan-speaking Ladino. Earlier in the 1930s, Boas student Ruth Bunzel also worked in Guatemala, in Chichicastenango, a town Tax later studied. Bunzel used the single-informant text-transcription approach of her teacher. This variety of collaborative relationships offers an intriguing interpretive key to the body of Guatemalan ethnography from this coterie of researchers.[20]

Post–World War II ethnography in Mesoamerica witnessed further evolution along the lines established in the 1930s. Oscar Lewis, with a large team that included Mexican researchers, restudied Tepotzlan in 1943–1947 and produced a major body of publications, some of which challenged Redfield's earlier conclusions. Relationships established by Redfield and Tax brought several Mexican and Guatemalan anthropologists to the University of Chicago. The extensive Chiapas research project launched from Harvard in 1957 employed old and new methods of using informants, including teaching them to use tape recorders and then to transcribe typewritten bilingual Mayan-Spanish texts, which they supplied for analysis to the U.S.

professional and student ethnographers. Later, James Sexton used written diaries and tape-recorded accounts to dramatic effect in portraying the turbulent change witnessed by one Guatemalan Indian informant: the results of Protestant evangelization, military rule, and endemic violence.[21]

Decolonization: Africa

In the early twentieth century, a body of works by African colonial subjects addressed issues that anthropologists would return to decades later—land tenure, politics, customary law, race relations, and "social change." Books by Gold Coast (later Ghana) authors, such as *Fanti Customary Law* (1897) and *Fanti National Constitution* (1906) by John Mensah Sarbah and *Gold Coast Native Institutions* (1903) by J. E. Casely Hayford, and also by South African authors, such as *Native Life in South Africa* (1916) by Sol Plaatje and *The Black Problem* (1920) by D. D. T. Jabavu, watered the seedlings of African nationalism but not of anthropology. By the 1920s, as Robert Thornton has shown, a combination of missionary, academic professional, and political interests among European ruling groups had resulted in an anthropology of Africa that portrayed a primitive, timeless, and tribal present.[22] This contrasted greatly with the themes that preoccupied contemporary African writers.[23]

The opposed orientations of these two traditions of writing about Africa are evident in the ethnographic essays on the Gã published between 1910 and 1920 by A. B. Quartey-Papafio in the British *Journal of the Africa Society*[24] and the monographs two decades later by the English government ethnographer and Malinowski student M. J. Field—*Religion and Medicine of the Gã People* (1937) and *Social Organization of the Gã People* (1940). Both authors wrote about the indigenous inhabitants of Accra, the capital city of Ghana. While Quartey-Papafio, himself a Gã, dealt with kinship, political structure, and ritual, as did Field, he also described modern occupations, labor migration of educated Gã to other African colonies, and political maneuvers against the British occupiers by Gã leaders in collusion with Hausa and Yoruba immigrants. Field, who did not cite Quartey-Papafio, presented an altogether more primitive and tradition-bound portrait of Gã culture and society.

A major attempt to correct anthropology's false start in Africa was evident in the work in Northern Rhodesia under the Rhodes-Livingstone Institute banner by British social anthropologists, many of leftward political attachments, before and after World War II. Their urban research led to a stream of publications, notably from A. L. Epstein and J. Clyde Mitchell. For both political and practical reasons, the anthropologists depended upon African research assistants. These men went where whites could not and recorded extensive fieldnotes, which were used in the resulting analyses. Textual acknowledgments traced the assistants' accomplishments, but the most revealing and grateful of these was from American anthropologist Hortense Powdermaker, regarding Frederick Phiri, a Rhodes-Livingstone Institute assistant who worked with her in Luanshya in 1953–1954. Her books *Copper Town: Changing Africa* (1962) and *Stranger and Friend* (1967) describe her and Phiri's fieldwork in detail. Phiri later pursued higher education in Britain in community relations but not in anthropology.[25]

Few Africans became anthropologists until the Decade of Independence in the 1960s. Jomo Kenyatta, who studied with Malinowski in the 1930s, was an exception; his *Facing Mount Kenya* (1938) returned to land tenure issues raised decades earlier by Plaatje, Casely Hayford, and others. The transition from assistants to professionals was not accomplished gradually, although a few publications by assistants at African research institutes staffed mainly by whites did begin to appear in the 1950s and 1960s. PhD-level careers were few, but the work of professional anthropologists Archie Mafeje, a South African, and Maxwell Owusu, a Ghanaian, exemplified the persisting concern with politics and decolonization begun by their countrymen early in the century.[26]

The continuing reluctance of some white anthropologists to accord professional equality to their African counterparts has been described by Ugandan anthropologist Christine Obbo. Her own work from the 1970s onward has added to the rich heritage of African interests in Africa and matches the best urban ethnography by expatriates. Still, in a 1990 essay, she depicts the ungracious and uncollegial attempts of some white researchers throughout her career to surreptitiously appropriate and use her fieldnotes and analyses.[27]

Application: United States

The desire to use anthropological research to address social problems in the United States led to the formation of the Society for Applied Anthropology in 1941 and to continuing work since by action, advocacy, and practicing anthropologists. Many of the first applied anthropologists were strongly influenced by the studies of human interaction pioneered in the 1930s by a group of Harvard anthropologists, several of whom became leaders in the use of anthropology in industry and other fields.[28]

In this group was William Foote Whyte, whose *Street Corner Society* (1943) justly became an ethnographic classic. Whyte's close relationship to Doc, an Italian American working-class Bostonian who collaborated in his fieldwork, is described in this book and in later writing that traces Doc's career.[29] Such an insider-outsider pairing is widely taken as an ideal by many ethnographers, even if the payoffs for each partner have not received much attention in anthropology's recurrent "rethinkings," "critiques," and "crises" since the 1960s.

Several of the founding applied group were among the twenty-one anthropologists who worked as researchers in U.S. government concentration camps for Japanese Americans between 1942 and 1946. Their job was to conduct studies of the culture and social organization of the internees. It was impossible for white anthropologists to move freely in the camps, and Japanese American research assistants, among them university graduates with social science training, provided the bulk of the data.

Despite a large body of resulting publications during the 1940s,[30] this formative period in the application of anthropology and in outsider-insider collaboration received little scrutiny through the 1950s or during the "radical anthropology" reorientations of the 1960s and 1970s. The first critical assessments of this period appeared in anthropology journals only in the 1980s.[31] Few anthropologists even today understand how a large group of their colleagues, with several prominent names among them, applied their craft in the government camps. Nor, I venture, do courses in the history of anthropology devote much attention to their efforts.

None of the camp anthropologists continued research on Japanese Americans after World War II. Only one Japanese American was to be awarded a PhD in anthropology for work on the topic that had engaged so many of his senior colleagues during the war years—Toshio Yatsushiro, for *Political and Socio-cultural Issues at Poston and Manzanar Relocation Centers* (1953), a Cornell University dissertation.[32] (A handful of Japanese Americans did produce sociology dissertations on the wartime experience.[33]) The few other Japanese Americans who became professional anthropologists in the immediate postwar years studied such cultures as the Navajo and the Nias Islanders of Indonesia. Only in the 1970s did a second Japanese American anthropologist pursue PhD research concerning her own group.[34] A rich literature of memoirs and novels about the concentration camp experience by Japanese Americans themselves, however, has emerged.[35] Qualities that mark these writings by "natives" about their own culture are ones that many anthropologists today view as enriching ethnography.

Conclusion

By the 1930s, anthropologists of diverse non-Western nationality and ancestry were making important contributions as professionals to the emerging discipline. They included Sir Peter Buck (Te Rangi Hiroa), Kenyatta, Fei Xiaotong, A. Aiyappan, D. N. Majumdar, Manuel Gamio, Julio de la Fuente, Villa Rojas, William Jones, Ella Deloria, Allison Davis, St. Clair Drake, and Arthur Huff Fauset.[36] In the United States, since the 1930s, their ranks have grown proportionately scarcely at all, and several notable such scholars have faced limited career choices.[37] The record of the discipline remains meager in terms of training and of according professional standing to ethnographers of color who study their own peoples. As of 1989, some 93 percent of anthropologists in full-time U.S. faculty positions were white, a figure even higher than the 89 percent white for all full-time faculty in U.S. institutions of higher education.[38] In the academy, one might conclude, the "native's point of view" is still largely unwelcomed from the natives themselves.

Anthropology's future must do better in this regard than anthropology's past. If the discipline is to move into a phase of political maturity and responsibility in a color-full world, we need to face up to our historical antecedents. And as we do, we need to recognize that we have a richer history than some of our ancestors have acknowledged or wished to be recorded. It seems to me no longer possible that the history of anthropology should be taught without including in it Ahuia Ova, George Hunt, Billy Williams, Francis La Flesche, James Murie, I Made Kaler, Alfonso Villa Rojas, Juan Rosales, A. B. Quartey-Papafio, the Rhodes-Livingstone Institute African staff members (who, beyond Frederick Phiri, need to be named), Doc, the Japanese American internee fieldworkers (who, in addition to Toshio Yatsushiro, also need to be named), and other assistants and native scholars who were producers of our ethnographic heritage and history.

Globally representative voices are there—inadequately recognized, or disciplinarily silenced in various ways (like Murie, Kaler, and Quartey-Papafio), but still there. Ethnographers and assistants together made anthropology. We need to revise our textbooks and write new ones.[39]

Chapter 6

The Ethnographic Present

I intend this chapter's title, "The Ethnographic Present," to be ambiguous, to apply to more than may be obvious. I wish to approach its topic from four connecting angles, considering (1) the ethnographic present as the present state of ethnography; (2) the ethnographic present as a mode of presenting ethnography; (3) the ethnographic present as the ethnographer's presence during fieldwork; and (4) the ethnographic method as a gift, or present, from our founders. If this hints of reflexive or autocritical concerns, let me advise that I am not about to rehearse or refine postmodern (or more pointedly, post–Marcus-and-Clifford[1]) anthropology. I am more in danger of being branded old-fashioned for a strongly proethnographic stance or mired in 1960s politics in calling for an ethnography of the present.

The 1980s was a decade of debate and questioning about the nature of ethnography. The dominating figures were James Clifford and George Marcus.[2] Their work, with a large ancillary literature, has been much discussed by proponents and skeptics.[3] Yet, from the "fieldnotes up" perspective proposed in *Fieldnotes: The Makings of Anthropology* (1990) and advocated in this chapter, as much about the nature and purpose of ethnography was left out of these programs and polemics as was included in them.[4]

If one effect of *Fieldnotes* (although not the intent) was to orient ethnographic debate to issues beyond those in Clifford and Marcus's *Writing Culture* (1986) and Marcus and Michael Fischer's *Anthropology as Cultural Critique* (1986), it joined two British publications that moved us in a similar direction—*Localizing Strategies: Regional Traditions in Ethnographic Writing* (1990) and the first proceedings from the meetings of the Group for Debates in Anthropological Theory, held in Manchester in 1988.[5] Here I will consider points raised in these three efforts, as well as other work from the 1980s on the nature of ethnography, particularly Johannes Fabian's *Time and the Other* (1983).

The Present State of Ethnography

Our first barometer of the present state of ethnography, *Localizing Strategies*, brought together papers from a 1987 conference at the University of St. Andrews, Scotland. Its purpose was to assess how individual regional ethnographic writing traditions—as much as "metropolitan" theory—affect the production of ethnography. The topic was also given consideration in 1986 by Arjun Appadurai in a discussion of regional "gate keeping" concepts, such as caste in India and "honor" in the Mediterranean.[6] Although the conference theme had been set in 1985, the appearance of *Writing Culture* and *Anthropology as Cultural Critique* in 1986 influenced discussion to a considerable extent. Positioning in relation to Clifford, Marcus, and Stephen Tyler pervaded editor Richard Fardon's introduction and figured in varying proportions in essays by the contributors.

Fardon contrasted the inattention to regional issues and foundational ethnographies by Clifford and the essentially formal considerations of Marcus and Fischer with a need to assess what contribution the texts they did spotlight "make towards understanding specific others in other places, as part of a history of such attempts." He viewed with reservation the textualist "concern for ethnography [that] is ethnographically unspecific. It invites us to sacrifice the specificity of research in particular places at certain times in order to treat all research as so many refractions of an ethnographic master process."[7]

More affirmatively, Fardon turned to the issue of how "the authorship of ethnographic accounts and of fieldwork experience is also enabled, inter alia, by the example of precedent writings," also a topic of Nancy Lutkehaus and Robert Smith's essays in *Fieldnotes*.[8] Fardon emphasized that in anthropology, there are "several traditions of regional scholarship, each with its specific history."[9] A dozen such traditions were examined by his contributors. David McKnight, for example, showed how earlier debates and concerns for pristineness led ethnographers of Australian Aborigines to block out much of the "living actuality" in front of them and perennially thus arrive "after it is too late." Wendy James contrasted the center-outward, romantic ethnology of Ethiopia with the grassroots, fieldwork-oriented ethnography of the Sudan, leaving no doubt about which attracted her sympathies.[10]

Localizing Strategies cautioned us to be aware of and to work through the accretions of regional ethnographic traditions, but it also warned against forgoing them altogether. Even if regions were artificial creations, a point made by David Parkin in contrasting Max Gluckman's "Central Africa" with Audrey Richards's "East Africa," enough "living actuality" has emerged within regional scholarships to provide a critical proving ground for ethnographic output.[11] This makes it necessary for nonregionalists to have at least a modest grasp of the exemplary regional ethnography when dealing with the "burning issues of anthropological theory" that so frequently arise in particular regions.[12] The essays in Fardon's collection show a persisting respect, even awe, for the foundational (if imperfect) regional ethnographies. Ethnographic self-awareness of all sorts is called for in *Localizing Strategies*, but, as Parkin puts it, "If there are indeed problems in ethnographic description, they will not be solved by less detailed fieldwork and writing."[13]

But what is "ethnographic description" or "detailed fieldwork"? Can we do more than point to favorite ethnographies in which these properties may be found? The Fardon volume leaves hazy what is being defended. Bruce Kapferer disdains the postmodernist celebration of "experience and subjectivist anthropology as a thing in itself" but counters this only by advising that "the subjective and the objective [be] in balance. The validity of the description is in their interdependence." Michael Gilsenan is downright pessimistic: "We sense that at this period anthropology is all margins anyhow and that there is no specifically and uniquely anthropological object, method, or theory."[14]

Assertions of things that ethnography is not—this time, science—but again, not of what it is arose during the 1988 Manchester debate, "Social Anthropology Is a Generalizing Science or It Is Nothing," our second barometer of the state of ethnography. The proponents were Keith Hart and Anthony Good, the opponents Anthony Cohen and Judith Okely. The outcome that the proposition lost is less interesting than the arguments and floor comments.

Hart began with an all-out defense of the proposition.

> We have lost our way; and this may be because we can no longer see the connection between the social purposes of knowledge and

> the pursuit of knowledge for its own sake. Science has two great objects—nature (everything out there that we did not consciously make up) and society itself (which is both a part of nature and the result of human intentions, however misguided). A democratic society has to break down intrinsic barriers to its own development—poverty, ignorance, injustice. To do so it needs science. Whatever we plan to do is more likely to succeed if we employ reason to find out how essential things work.[15]

Cohen followed, not attacking Hart's position as much as arguing for the ethnographic portrayal of individuals as active and creative, a task that can combat prejudiced images of simplicity and sameness in other cultures and need imply no "retreat into the reflexive." Good responded, citing Ladislav Holy and Milan Stuchlik's *Actions, Norms and Representations* (1983), that scientific ethnography should include cultural interpretation and be aimed "to help those we study—concern for whose welfare we parade like stigmata in front of students, readers, and the general public."[16]

Okely's statement exposed the discomfort caused by the label "science" and probably swung the vote. "The current meaning of 'science' as proffered to social scientists is little more than scientism. It is still contaminated by positivism. We have been bewitched, bothered and bewildered by a limited definition of science."[17]

The ensuing debate revealed a common fear that government support for British anthropological research would continue to dwindle, because it shared the same funding pot with other social sciences and must meet "positivist" canons, presumably reliability, statistical sampling, and quantification. The debaters proposed counterstrategies—redefining "science" in terms of its historical Enlightenment heritage; "pretending" to be scientists for "strategic reasons" (getting grants), even while fearing to be found out; or adopting some unspecified "critical perspective" toward positivist dominance.[18] Like the contributors to *Localizing Strategies,* the Manchester debaters and audience offered no defense of ethnography as a method different from either "scientism" or a "retreat into the reflexive." In this, British anthropologists, as I argued in *Fieldnotes*, were not alone.[19]

The only step in a proethnography direction was the tentative proposal by Wim van Binsbergen that models of historical method are closer to anthropology than those of natural science.[20] No one responded to this point, although, earlier, Hart had mentioned that "scientific anthropologists are likely to insist that their subject matter is largely historical."[21] We will consider presently the ethnographic method as a gift to be valued in its own terms, "the ethnographic present" bequeathed by our predecessors. But first we need to examine this reconstitution of anthropology as history and how this is related to still other facets of the ethnographic present.

The Ethnographic Present as Mode of Presentation

The phrase "the ethnographic present" has been a familiar term to me since my student days in the 1960s.[22] In recent definitions, it is for Fabian "the practice of giving accounts of other cultures and societies in the present tense" and for McKnight "the present which existed in the traditional past and not the period when the ethnographer was in the field."[23] Both Fabian and McKnight see something wrong with the ethnographic present, but they are identifying two different—if related—problems.

Fabian is concerned with the artificiality and freezing of time that descriptions in the present tense impart. Ethnography written in the present tense implies a view of human behavior as conventional, predictable, and rule determined—a culturology. Such writing conveys none of the independence of rule and action or structure and agency experienced in the ethnographer's own world, nor does it present behavior as contingent, situational, or deliberate.[24] The ethnographic present, for Fabian, functions to take the society so described out of the time stream of history in which ethnographers and their own societies exist. There is more to it than this, but let us consider McKnight's concerns before we come back to Fabian's.

McKnight is not opposed to doing history—to reconstructing society as it existed in the past—but rather to the pretense that certain aspects of the present may be ignored, while other aspects are taken to represent "traditional" life—the way things were before white influence, in the case of Australian Aborigines—and then written about in the present tense.[25] One side of this problem, as McKnight showed, is that what was thus ignored in earlier decades later became the new research agenda and was then studied at the expense of still other aspects of the present, again "after it is too late." The nature of what was and is ignored also has a political dimension connected to the concern with "poverty, ignorance, injustice" pointed to by Hart and to an anthropological "critique from power" Parkin contrasts with the postmodernist "literary critique."[26]

The example of A. R. Radcliffe-Brown, to which McKnight drew attention, is instructive. In his field research in Australia, Radcliffe-Brown apparently stayed longer on Dorre and Bernier Islands than in any other location. Yet his accounts of social organization never dealt with the "living actuality" of what were detention centers there, where diseased Aborigines from many parts of Western Australia were sent forcibly in chains, segregated by sex, and suffered high casualty rates.[27]

Bronislaw Malinowski's use of the ethnographic present conflated the problems identified by both Fabian and McKnight. In his voluminous ethnographic corpus on the Trobriands, he wrote resolutely in the present tense, and only in item 43, section 4, appendix 2 in his last Trobriand volume did he deal with "Decay of Custom under European Influence." After acknowledging imposed constraints on chiefly power, economic changes, and limitations on polygamy and warfare, he wrote:

> The empirical facts which the ethnographer has before him in the Trobriands nowadays are not natives unaffected by European influences but natives to a considerable extent transformed by these influences. The Trobriander as he was, even two or three generations ago, has become by now a thing of the past, to be reconstructed, not to be observed. The subject matter of field-work is the changing Melanesian or African. He has become already a citizen of the world, is affected by contacts with the world-wide civilization. I was not yet under [this point of view] in doing my field-work. This perhaps is the most serious shortcoming of my whole anthropological research in Melanesia.[28]

In *Fieldnotes*, I called attention to the reconstructed and recollected nature of the texts on myths, tales, and techniques that Franz Boas collected on the Northwest Coast and to the radically different present revealed in his letters. In these, he noted denominational and ecstatic Christian churches, missionary influence, Indian mixed farming, migrant farmwork, sawmills, work camps, salmon canneries, racial mixing, a European-style wedding ceremony, celebration of Dominion Day, and an 1890 reunion with the Bella Coola, now cannery workers and migrant laborers, whom he had met first in Berlin.[29]

All this is more than a matter of Radcliffe-Brown, Malinowski, or Boas arriving "after it is too late." Imagine what anthropology would look like today if Boas's texts concerned conversions to Christianity, work histories, and the mundane folklore of a multiracial, polyethnic society; if Malinowski had charted the expeditions of pearl buyers and provided case materials involving the resident magistrate, chiefs, and their subjects; if Radcliffe-Brown had written "Three Tribes in Western Australia's Concentration Camps"; and if these were the authoritative, foundational ethnographies on which anthropology had developed.

That none of this happened took considerable effort. Boas, Malinowski, Radcliffe-Brown, and others deliberately screened out what was going on around them to create an ethnographic present rather than an ethnography of the present. For anthropology, "the native's point of view," which Boas and Malinowski professed to render, has been from the start the ethnographer's normative view of what the native is about.[30] In Africa, where Robert Thornton has traced the ideological, professional, and intellectual stakes in these creations, a double distortion arose. Tribal cultures described in the ethnographic present did not include Western-induced aspects of the present, including war and imperial repression. Neither did they deal with "ease of mobility, multi-lingualism, and the presence of numerous religious cults in the same communities," aspects of the African past and present that an image of separate cultures obscured and dismissed.[31] I think we must conclude that the post-1960s crises of anthropology all have their roots in the very origins of professional ethnography.

Perhaps a third set of distortions arose as well, within the supposedly pure, uncontaminated domains of cosmology, myth, and genealogy. The historian David Henige takes subversive delight in showing how quickly Christian missionary influences and other oral and written transmissions "fed back" into non-Western "traditions" on the edges of European exploration and imperial expansion.[32] This happened earlier and more pervasively than many past or present anthropologists acknowledge: "The first Indian the Pilgrims met in Massachusetts spoke to them in English, much to their surprise. It appears that he and others had learned English from earlier English visitors and fishermen. Even these, though, had already met Indians who spoke English, dressed in English style clothing, and paddled canoes of Basque design, all presumably adopted from yet earlier, but otherwise unrecorded visitations."[33]

It gives one pause to realize that those world regions in which genealogical supports for authority were "spontaneously" presented to anthropologists—Polynesia, Africa, the Middle East—were the same terrains in which nineteenth-century Hebraist Christian missionaries preceded them, or which had long histories of Biblical and Koranic influence.[34]

We may now return to Fabian's appraisal of the ethnographic present. He argues that anthropological writings award place and time differently to the industrial West: Here and Now—and to the Rest: There and Then. He identifies a radical contradiction between the "coevalness," or contemporaneity, of the personal interaction between ethnographer and informants (the "Other," in his vocabulary) during fieldwork (and indeed during the courses of their lives) and the assignment into time frames created by anthropology that remove the informants from a shared human time stream. These frames have included Victorian and neoevolutionary stages and types, the ethnographic present, and categories such as "preliterate" (waiting for something to arrive) and "Third World" (out of *this* world). Writing results in relegation rather than interrelation. At best, non-Western peoples might have ethnohistories, to be determined by trait distributions or decoded from indigenous conceptions of time, but this does not put them into the swim of the anthropologists' own historical currents.

Fabian's critique, which I find compelling, is sustained on the high ground of theoretical "discourses" and eschews analysis of specific ethnographic works.[35] (I note here the provocative analysis he makes of pronoun use in ethnographic writing,[36] even if this remains at a general rather than textual level.) He comes closest to an ethnographic example in proposing that the national character projects directed by Margaret Mead and Clyde Kluckhohn in the early 1950s put Soviet culture "at a distance" by essentializing it out of coeval time, thus adding ice to the Cold War,[37] but even here he does not dig very deep into specific writings.

In consequence, Fabian offers no remedies for ethnographic writing and points to no examples of an anthropology that embraces "coevalness," what I am calling an ethnography of the present. He acknowledges some anthropological victories in disputing assumptions about the moral, aesthetic, intellectual, or political superiority of the West but again provides no ethnographic references that would point us to effective prescriptions. Certainly, in view of Fabian's compelling ethnographic and historical work on Congo,[38] his vision of coeval sensitivity amounts to more than an aim of "recognizing cotemporality as the condition for truly dialectical confrontation between persons as well as societies." Fabian concludes with a call for "processual and materialist theory" that will "incorporate the idea of totality."[39] I take this to mean ethnography placed within the context of the global expansion and post-Columbian reticulation of humanity.

If we seek to restore ethnographic accounts to coevalness, to the single time stream all humanity shares, we need to reconsider anthropological attitudes to the past. The discipline has always had some such attitude, alternating from active to passive—from nineteenth-century evolutionist stages and Boasian trait distribution–based reconstructions (active) to functionalist and configurationist avoidance (passive) to neoevolutionist generalizations and specificities (active) to structuralist disinterest (passive) to a neo-Marxist focus on colonialism and modes of production (active).[40]

In the current anthropological climate, an active attitude toward the past prevails, with three tendencies: an interest in the past on its own terms; an interest in the past to illuminate the present; and an interest in the present as "current history,"[41] situated between the past and the future. All three tendencies are supportable endeavors, but they have different implications for "the ethnographic present" in the two remaining senses: time in the field and methodological legacy.

The long-standing anthropological interest in the past on its own terms is exemplified in Eric Wolf's *Europe and the People without History* (1982), which he compares with earlier culture histories of Alfred Kroeber and Ralph Linton but which is inspired by contemporary humanistic and political perspectives acknowledging a world of racism, Eurocentricity, and persisting North/South inequalities. Wolf writes a theoretically honed history of interrelations and interconnections within and between Europe, the Americas, Africa, and Asia over five centuries from 1400 AD. The story trails off in the early twentieth century, and in this book, Wolf does not draw precise connections between the history he tells and specific ethnographic locations or issues in the present. The tools Wolf might use to do so would no doubt begin with the capitalist mode of production's opposition between capital and labor. Wolf anticipated that the scholarship his book might provoke would similarly explore the past on its own terms.[42] The family resemblances of *Europe and the People without History* are thus to such historical works as William McNeill's *Plagues and Peoples* (1976), Philip Curtin's *Cross-cultural Trade in World History* (1984), and Alfred Crosby's *Ecological Imperialism* (1986), as well as to such anthropological histories as Clifford Geertz's *Negara* (1980), Jack Goody's *Development of Family and Marriage in Europe* (1983) and *Logic of Writing* (1986), Marvin Harris's *Cannibals and Kings* (1977), and Sidney Mintz's *Sweetness and Power* (1985).

The second current anthropological interest in the past—as a means to illuminate the present—*is* attuned to specific current ethnographic settings. For example, Nicholas Dirks has pored over nineteenth-century land records of the Tamil kingdom of Pudukkottai to examine political, economic, and ritual processes that he relates directly to similar processes in contemporary India.[43] He concludes, "colonialism seems to have created much of what is now accepted as Indian 'tradition,' including an autonomous caste structure with the Brahman clearly at the head, village-based systems of exchange, isolated ceremonial residues of the old regime state, and fetishistic competition for ritual goods that no longer [play] a vital role in the political system."[44]

Dirks uses his study of the past to criticize reigning theoretical positions in Indian ethnography, particularly those of Louis Dumont and the ethnosociology of McKim Marriott and Ronald Inden in which Dirks was trained at the University of Chicago.[45]

The weight of Dirks's presentation is historical, and insights from ethnographic fieldwork play a secondary part. In this regard, it is similar to the political economy approach, in which debates about modes of production, ethnic and national consciousness, and colonialism and resistance concern the past first and the present second.[46] Perhaps it was in part to this work that Hart referred in remarking that "scientific anthropologists [in his Enlightenment-heritage sense] are likely to insist that their subject matter is largely historical."[47] Certainly Hart's *Political Economy of West African Agriculture* (1982) is a prime example of an interest in the past to illuminate a specific present.

In the third tendency of the current active attitude to the past, fieldwork and the ethnographic method are foregrounded. Sally Falk Moore characterizes this as "fieldwork treated as current history. . . . Past history immediately becomes germane. How was the present produced? But the fieldworker must also ask, 'What is the present producing? What part of the activity being observed will be durable, and what will disappear?' The identification of change-in-the-making [and] conjectures about the future thus become an implicit part of the understanding of the present."[48]

Moore speaks of this orientation as focused on "process," which is directional, and urges consideration of potential outcome as a guiding concern in fieldwork. She contrasts this with "practice" (referring to Sherry Ortner), which subsumes iterative "instantiation" within "structure" and does not predicate a future-oriented fieldwork strategy.[49]

From a political viewpoint, such a strategy matters above all. As Dell Hymes wrote decades ago in a key document of the anthropological "critique from power": "Recognizing ourselves as members of an emerging world community, we cannot avoid hope (or despair) for it. When we study local communities, we cannot escape assumptions, open or hidden, as to that for which they hope and as to what can be hoped for them. The *general* problem, then, is not simply empirical—what has occurred; nor only methodological and theoretical—how to study what has occurred, how best to explain it. It is also a moral problem, a problem of one's commitments in, and to, the world [and] a concern with the outcome."[50]

Whatever the words used, "process" or "practice" (and Ortner might agree with Moore's and Hymes's sentiments[51]), it is the vigor and growth of this third tendency, of an ethnography of the present situated between past and future, that is crucial. It opens space for the ethnographic method that the first two tendencies do not, useful as they may be for understanding "the larger-scale, the supra-local domain as generalized background."[52]

I believe further that the first and second tendencies entail principally an ideological, not an operational, relevance to advocacy and political action. A social and cultural anthropology buried, or up to its neck, in the past offers little of the findings and interpretations that an ethnography of the present can provide to those who struggle in the present. Ironically, the most radical and critical of past-oriented intellectuals may be seen as conservative, or irrelevant, by those too occupied in ongoing work to indulge in window-shopping for late-model ideologies. We are in part responsible for any such barriers to dialogue and engagement that we encounter. Anthropologists armed with both ideology and ethnography need to step forward rather than waiting to be called.

The Ethnographic Present as Time in the Field

One casualty of the heady debates about ethnography during the 1980s was the ethnographic method itself. It was a major argument of *Fieldnotes* that since the method's emergence with Frank Hamilton Cushing, Boas, and W. H. R. Rivers and its consolidation by Malinowski and Mead, anthropologists have done a better job of using than of articulating it.[53] We have transmitted the ethnographic method informally and anecdotally or by pointing to exemplary works. The ethnographic method, as I describe it in *Fieldnotes* and represent it here, fell under a shadow from the 1950s on as research funding moved from the pre-war research schemes and teams of foundation and government largesse[54] to the individual research proposal. In competitive funding, successful individual proposals quickly came to require the accoutrements of the experimental model as practiced in sociology, economics, and psychology—hypothesis testing, sampling, and a focus on reliability.[55]

By the 1960s, a new anthropological "methods" literature emerged in response to this fiscal environment. "Science" became a watchword in the "behavioral science" sense, with the retort of "positivism!" moving from mutters to curses and, eventually, to print. The increasingly hard-shelled scientific thrust inevitably came to include a "quantitative extreme" in the United States, as well as the "scientistic" streak that the Manchester debaters in 1988 voted against, now with similar funding pressures prevalent in Britain.

Opposing this has been a multistranded humanist, interpretationist, and postmodernist thrust.[56] It became as popular during the 1980s[57] as "science" was in the 1960s and early 1970s. What began with personal accounts of fieldwork by Claude Levi-Strauss and Laura Bohannan in the 1950s led to a spate of books that moved from collections of how-I-did-it articles in the early 1970s to full-length, I-did-it-my-way confessional accounts. Because ethnographers in the field continued all along to do more than gather records to test hypotheses and because everyone admitted that "rapport" was somehow involved, it was inevitable that this reaction to the behavioral science research model would surface. By the 1980s, a soft-skinned variant, ethnographic sojourn as personal memoir, was evoking its own "anti-antiscience" retort. We had a fierce match going on in which little communication was traveling back and forth.

Let an umpire step in. I take as my foil Fabian's presentation of the coeval encounter of ethnographer and actor/informant/"Other." Fabian offers a forceful and sustained portrayal of fieldwork as intersubjective dialogue and communication between actor and ethnographer. The ethnographer, he asserts, "must be involved in interpersonal and, *a fortiori,* in intercultural production and communication of knowledge."[58] With that, I agree. Those who would argue against this position would imperil the ethnographic method. But is that it? From the "fieldnotes up" viewpoint, Fabian's position is, first, too general, and, second, too narrow.

It is too general because communicative events in fieldwork are not all alike. They vary from those that occur naturally on the actor's turf to those arranged by the ethnographer and from communicative events the actors produce to those the ethnographer seeks to direct in interviews and record elicitation (see Chapter 4). One of the defining characteristics of the ethnographic method is the recording of "speech in action," as Audrey Richards labeled Malinowski's great breakthrough from *Notes and Queries*–style inquisition.[59] As Barrie Sharpe poses it: "In ordinary talk and action [cultural conceptions] only appear piecemeal. The fragments which appear in the everyday flow of action are puzzling to a stranger (not just to an ethnographer), yet if these 'data' are extracted from their context the practical sense is destroyed, whilst the formal rules and systems are elaborated. The aim of local fieldwork is not just to get data, but to understand the sociology of information in particular communities."[60]

Such situated listening to what informants say to each other in real-time practice (or processes) and discoveries of how to enter appropriately into such speech events are the foundation for our recovery of cultural knowledge, interpretation, and meaning. Three key contributors to ethnographic debates can back me up. Moore advocates as the first "preferred form of raw data events that are in no sense staged for the sake of the anthropologist, together with local commentaries on them." Parkin argues that "when the vernacular is seen *at work* in detailed case studies, then we are surely that much closer to speaking through our informants." Fredrik Barth sounds a warning: "Recent reflexive anthropological writing has focused too egocentrically on the native's dialogue with ourselves and too little on their dialogue with one another."[61]

The interpersonal, dialogic encounters between informant and ethnographer, which occur outside the historical time flow of the actors' social lives, are supplementary to listening to speech in action.[62] Like various forms of interviews and oral record collection, they constitute only part of the ethnographic method. For these reasons, I suggest that the identification made by Fabian and others of ethnographic practice with dialogic communication, or the co-invention of culture, is too general.[63]

Fabian's position is also too narrow. I regret that he compromises his valuable insight with antagonism to countable, quantifiable fieldwork evidence derived from the observation of ongoing behavior.[64] Such descriptive record collection, both that designed prior to fieldwork and, perhaps more important, that which results from decisions about systematicity based on fieldwork-derived theories of significance, historically has been part of the ethnographic method—not all of it—and I find no convincing reason to give it up.[65] Fabian resorts to parody to make his case and rejects as "visualism" even the use of "maps, charts, and tables," which he himself uses impressively in his Congo ethnography.[66]

We may join Fabian in denouncing "the dehumanizing effects of overly scientistic methods" (again, no specific example is cited) and agree that "the urge to visualize a great multitude of pieces of information as orderly arrangements, systems, and *tableaux*" should be resisted when it is based on thin evidence and does not accord with what we can learn through communicative events.[67] But Fabian's "privileging" of the oral-aural over the observational, despite any disclaimer, channels ethnographic activities too narrowly. We need in fieldwork to call on all these senses, and even others, as he avers at least once.[68]

If we constitute the object of ethnography not as a contest between communication and visualization, emic and etic, culture and behavior, ideology and practice, or symbol and process but as the interpenetration of webs of significance and sequences of human action—in events[69]—then the narrowness of Fabian's position emerges. To continue to brand this "dualism" and thus attach a history of philosophical sins is going overboard.[70] As Anthony Leeds has insisted, we live in a universe where monads, dualities, multiplicities, and continua are all realities, and we need to recognize and use each of them appropriately.[71]

After all, to hammer your thumb and to say "ouch!" rather than "adzei!" or something else are different but interpenetrating aspects of a single event. So equally were Hawai'ian and European cultural construals and flesh-and-blood human interactions and their disastrous consequences in disease, depopulation, and ecological collapse upon the arrival of the *Discovery* and the *Resolution* at Kealakekua Bay in 1778.[72] There *is* an "out there" out there—Hart's "nature," Wolf's "structural power," Moore's "supra-local domain"[73]—whether it is subjected to varying cultural intuitions or to none.

The Ethnographic Present as Gift

Time in the field, the ethnographic presence, is a complex set of activities—listening to speech in action, learning how to ask, arranging dialogic exchanges, conducting interviews, requesting specific pieces of information, observing behavior in predetermined times and places and among combinations of actors, and, especially in the early stages of fieldwork, seeing and hearing in a wide-ranging and open manner.[74] These activities and the field-based writings they result in have a cumulative history that I traced in *Fieldnotes*.[75] They constitute the ethnographic method that, until recently, most anthropologists have adopted in practice, despite theoretical emphases on particular types of data and fieldwork activities. Broadly, the ethnographic method results in wide-ranging fieldnotes and more specific records of sequences of data collected according to plan. In interplay with the ethnographer's headnotes (her or his memories and interpretations), these written materials are indexed and organized according to theoretical schemes and interpretive frames and used to write papers and monographs that are new improvisations on ethnographic modes of presentation and that display convention or innovation in their rhetorical strategies.[76]

In the postmodern camp (and elsewhere[77]), some anthropologists today reject the ethnographic method; they are writing memoirs, novels, and autobiographies related to fieldwork experiences.[78] I have no desire to put such writing out of business; in fact, it has a history in anthropology, parallel to that of ethnography, which dates back more than a century to Cushing's "Adventures in Zuni."[79] But neither do I think it correct to call everything that begins in the field "ethnography," as some do.[80] To do so is to lose sight of what the ethnographic present, as a gift, is.

I wish to focus on what we may be losing and why it is important, politically as well as for other reasons, that it not be lost. I agree with Parkin that, contra anthropological postmodernism, there is much to salvage from previous generations of fieldworkers.[81] I also take James's point that the critique of ethnography made by African anthropologists such as Asmaron Legesse is so telling because it exposes methodological weaknesses and ethnographic prejudices "in order to save and justify the enquiry itself."[82] Yet why, precisely, is the ethnographic method more valuable than the humanistic impressions of fieldwork memoirists or the positivist excesses of scientistic extremists?

In my judgment, the issue comes down to distinguishing among reliability, validity, and what may be called "I-was-there" Truth. I leave such Truth to truth seekers and truth finders, as there is no disputing the urge to tell us "what is really going on because I was really there."

Much more can be said about reliability, which is "the repeatability, including intersubjective replicability, of scientific observations."[83] Reliability preoccupies those who hold anthropology to be a behavioral science and who thus place severe limits on what the ethnographic method should include. It is a valuable quality in laboratory, medical, and product safety research, as well as in some social research operations. As an anthropological advocate, I have both been on the receiving end of reliability strictures against the validity of my research on community health clinics and used reliability to defend quantitative analyses of the employment of women anthropologists against sophistry.[84] In each case, entrenched power holders were threatened by the research results.

In a general sense, reliability as the crowning feature of fieldwork-based ethnography limits us in precisely the ways to which Okely and Fabian object, and they are right.[85] Realistically, we do not require our fieldwork to be replicated before we advance our findings, nor do we wish to limit our ethnography only to what is replicable. Yet this is not to say that we should have no standards of criticism of fieldwork and ethnography, for then we would be back to assertions of "I-was-there" Truth.[86]

My argument is that ethnography aims at enhancing validity, not reliability—at maximizing "the degree to which scientific [I adopt Hart's definition here] observations actually measure or record what they purport to measure."[87] What the ethnographic method aims to achieve is accounts that support the claims the ethnographer makes. In terms of validity, there *are* better and worse ethnographic accounts. Fardon writes that textualist criticism does not "help us decide which are better and why. Writing about writing fails to engage the subject of the writing, or the history of writing about that subject."[88] I do not think, however, that the many cauldrons of regional ethnographic tradition are a sufficient alternative. As readers of book reviews in anthropology know all too well, criticism often returns to unchallengeable "I-was-there" Truth—the crusty, field-wise reviewer who knows "what is really going on because I was really there" (or nearby).

Without valid ethnography, we cannot have an ethnography of the present with any political uses—to advocates, activists, feminists, and those concerned with "change-in-the-making" and with "one's commitments in and to the world." There has been some concern with ethnographic validity for purposes of "data quality-control" in quantitative cross-cultural studies,[89] but it is excessively formal and buries points of value to ethnographers (of whom probably few have read these studies) in a welter of other considerations. We need to do better.

In *Fieldnotes*, I proposed a start.[90] I offered three canons of ethnographic validity. To summarize, the first is theoretical candor. This means that an ethnography is more valid when it is explicit about the theoretical decisions that structure fieldwork, both those based on the significant theories with which one comes to the research locale and the terrain-specific theories of significance that emerge in ethnographic practice.

The second canon is the portrayal of the ethnographer's path in conducting fieldwork. An ethnographer achieves greater validity when he or she identifies the range of informants encountered, the kinds of information they provided, and their social and cultural characteristics in relation to the totality of persons inhabiting the locale that the ethnography describes.

The third canon is fieldnote evidence. Here, the criterion is not the more the better or that fieldnote evidence be available archivally if not presented in ethnography. However much such commitments enhance validity, and they do,[91] my point is that the relationship between fieldnote evidence and ethnographic conclusions should be made explicit.[92] Fieldnote evidence need not be overbearing; considerations of rhetorical effectiveness and readability are also important in ethnographic writing, from both an editor's and an activist's point of view.

An ethnography that is silent on these three canons places its validity in question and rests on trust[93] without explaining why it is deserved. If we persist without any canons of validity and rely on each other's "I-was-there" Truth or submit to the constraints of reliability, then I see no way to enjoy and transmit our ethnographic gift, no reason to maintain faith in fieldwork, and a diminished future for anthropology.

Toward Ethnographies of the Present

By the 1990s, many anthropologists had revitalized their discipline's conceptualization of culture.[94] We began in the nineteenth century with an evolutionary view of culture—the ladder steps and trajectory stages (hand-axe to machine gun, promiscuity to nuclear family) envisioned in Victorian museums and theories and criticized by Boas.[95] We replaced this with pluralized cultures but isolated them from each other in functional and configurational, then typological and structural, descriptions. We also separated them from each other and ourselves by misusing the ethnographic present. We created "a moral disunity"[96] against the worldview of a unitary species that physical anthropology and attacks on racism were constructing. Now we are back to culture but with a vastly different conception of it.[97] Today we see culture everywhere, under continuous creation—fluid, interconnected, diffusing, interpenetrating, homogenizing, diverging, hegemonizing, resisting, reformulating, creolizing, open rather than closed, partial rather than total, crossing its own boundaries, persisting where we do not expect it to, changing where we do.[98]

This view of culture is not entirely new. It popped up over and over again during the era of cultures. In West Africa, Goody questioned the spatial movement of new religious "cults" as a postcolonial phenomenon and urged that we see such ritual traffic as continuous with Africa's deep historical roots. Aidan Southall pointed to multilingualism and the crossing of language and even language-family boundaries by cultural concepts throughout a wide East African region. Wolf revived Alexander Lesser's early call that we envision "human societies as inextricably involved with other aggregates, near and far, in weblike, netlike connections."[99]

In the 1980s, such conceptualizations of culture appeared everywhere, from Appadurai, Barth, Bernard Cohn, John Comaroff, Geertz, Ulf Hannerz, Moore, John Peel, Robert J. Smith, and more.[100] Clifford advanced a view of cultures and culture similar to that of these anthropologists. Yet his was a more uncertain and more ironic vision, calling the present world situation "post-cultural."[101] If the new view of culture is really postmodern, as some might argue, then I am happy to join Goody, Southall, Wolf, Lesser, and the other aforementioned anthropologists as a postmodernist. But that would apply this label more broadly than it warrants. For all these, unlike historian Clifford, have been practitioners of the ethnographic method, and if they turn to history, it is with that experience fixed within them. Coherences, processes, political regimes, even world systems remain central to anthropology.[102] All is not margins and edges.

As we craft our ethnographies of the present, we do so with our new version of culture's insistence on interconnection, partial rather than total description, and ubiquity of human creativity. As Geertz puts it, it is now the ethnographer's task "to enlarge the possibility of intelligible discourse between people quite different from one another in interest, outlook, wealth, and power, and yet contained in a world where, tumbled as they are in endless connection, it is increasingly difficult to get out of each other's way."[103]

There is no reason to desert anthropological interests in the past, but I hope the center of gravity in social and cultural anthropology will be an ethnography of the present as "current history," situated between past and future.[104] We offer a powerful vision of a single, interlocked, culture-full humanity. And in the ethnographic method, we are bequeathed a powerful means to display that vision—from the roots and meaning of famine in contemporary Darfur to the persistence of racism dividing black and white in Australia; from the creation of use values by homeless persons in Manhattan's public spaces to the survival of African American Carolina culture amid gentrification in Washington, D.C.[105]

Let us remember the lessons of the political and feminist critiques of anthropology issued in the 1960s and 1970s. Let us heed Parkin's call to end "the last waltz" of postmodern romanticism, scholasticism, and self-concentration, as much as some have enjoyed it.[106] Let us be grateful for the ethnographic method we have been bestowed and extend that "we" universally.[107] Others are addressing the continuing reticulation of global humanity with methods other than ethnography and with assumptions and ideologies we are quick to criticize. Let us remember that some of these others—if Thornton, Henige, Fabian, Wolf, and Sanjek[108] are correct—are Others whom anthropology has colluded in creating. I hope that anthropology will eventually cease arriving "after it is too late." The ethnographic present, in all its senses, is ours to use or to lose.

PART III

Comparison and Contextualization

Chapter 7

Worth Holding Onto: The Participatory Discrepancies of Political Activism

Over the course of four decades I have attended hundreds of political meetings. Among them have been meetings of the Dzodze Social and Cultural Union (DSCU), an Ewe hometown association in Accra, Ghana; meetings of Gray Panther networks in Berkeley, California and New York City; and meetings of Community Board 4, its district cabinet, and block, civic, tenant, ethnic, and merchant associations in Elmhurst-Corona, Queens. To nonmembers, many of these meetings might seem boring. "Not much was happening" would have been the response, as it was from some of the undergraduates whom I have assigned to attend and write fieldnotes about Queens community board meetings. I, of course, disagree, proud of the compliment from a reviewer of *The Future of Us All* about my "apparently inexhaustible capacity for absorbing the minutiae of local politics."[1] (Anyway, I took it to be a compliment.)

In making sense of these meetings, I focused on the political economic conditions that brought the various groups into being and sustained their endeavors. I learned about their internal organization, goals, ideologies, histories, successes, and failures. And I have been intrigued by leadership, both its personal roots and the qualities that make a leader effective.[2] These are certainly critical issues for anthropologists studying urban political activism. Yet I have had a back-burner feeling that there was something more I could not explain. Simply put, what was it that drew members of these various political groups to keep coming to meetings?

Political economic factors and explanations do not suffice here. They may help illuminate which categories of persons become members, but many individuals within these categories never do. The forty-five or so members who attended meetings of the DSCU during 1969–1971 were a minority of the more than three hundred adults from Dzodze then living in Ghana's capital. Only a tiny portion of persons who first became active in political causes during the 1920s and 1930s ever joined the Gray Panthers after their retirements. Dozens of Elmhurst-Corona residents appointed to Community Board 4 between 1983 and 1996 flagged in attendance, resigned, or by mutual consent were not reappointed, and thousands more never attended a meeting or even knew of CB4's existence.

Overall, only 5 percent of Americans are involved in any political activity or organization.[3] Most of these are ordinary members who come to meetings and may occasionally participate in "actions" planned by organization leaders, such as demonstrating and marching, attending government hearings, leafleting, monitoring public services, or lobbying and writing letters to public officials. Meeting attenders, nonetheless, are the integument supporting activist leaders. They constitute potential troops for various actions, as well as supplying leaders with the authority to speak on their organization's behalf. (A leader with no following gets nowhere.) But why do rank and file organization members who are not leaders continue to attend political meetings?

Charles Keil's conceptualization of "participatory discrepancies" (PDs), applied to musical performances, can help move this question about political participation off the back burner. To anticipate my argument: members *like* seemingly "boring" meetings, and focusing on PDs may help us understand why they do.

PDs and Politics

Beginning with *Urban Blues* (1966), Keil has shifted the interpretive terrain in ethnomusicology from a focus on text (notes and bars) and background context[4] to one on performance, which includes musicians, audiences, and their mutual ongoing aesthetic responses and judgments.[5] As his colleague Steven Feld has emphasized, this shift was a product of Keil's ethnographic observations but also of his experience as a musician and music listener.[6] Three innovative perspectives (that are as applicable to "live" politics as to live music) follow: first, Keil's foregrounding of participation; second, his emphasis on how "participatory discrepancies" produce compelling, groove-making experiences; and third, his use of these discoveries to critique class domination and state power.

In music, Keil stresses, we need to focus on "moving, playing, grooving, jamming," on forms of participation by everyone present. Those participating are not all doing the same thing, but they are engaged with each other in coproducing and coexperiencing a performance. When participation (in many diverse musical styles) reaches a peak, then "a groove," or those copresent "getting into the groove" with each other, may occur. Feld paraphrases this as "crystallizations of collaborative expectancies in time."[7]

Keil next points to how it is "*slight* variations," or participatory discrepancies, which both constitute the groove and make it satisfying. "As humans on this planet we groove on the repetition and redundancy of information with minor but frequent variations. Slight variations become magical, hypnotizing, mesmerizing. They give you deep identification or participatory consciousness." Feld amplifies this: "patterned expectancies in time established by regularities of sonic, syntactic, or semantic elements set the ground for the 'groove.'"[8]

Finally, Keil insists that participation is an endangered heritage, one traceable to our pre–class society origins and one that needs active encouragement and preservation: "All humans were full participants once upon a time, and I believe we still experience much music and perhaps some other portions of reality this way. At the very least, it is important to recognize this capacity in human beings. Participation is the opposite of alienation from nature, from society, from the body, from labor, and is therefore worth holding onto wherever we can still find some of it."

Working against participation in music is the force of commercialized mediation, and working against participatory consciousness in general is the dominance of the hierarchical, class-stratified state. Feld adds that participatory "working together works out and works through the tension between egalitarianism and individualism."[9] This "working together" is needed more than ever in modern societies, in which the weak and disorganized power of numbers of the masses (the 99 percent) confronts both the centralized, polarizing power of resources (the 1 percent) and its usual ally, bureaucratic or "lubricatory" power.[10]

Let me summarize the implications of Keil's insights for studying political activism. We need to move beyond political economic context and explanation and beyond explication of issues and ideologies to participatory political events as they happen: meetings, actions, activities of leaders. Here, following Keil's example, ethnography, as well as reflections on personal experience, need to be deployed. Sites of participation and occasions during which grooves may be achieved (as observed by the ethnographer and evidenced by the actors), as well as their underlying participatory discrepancies, need to be identified. All this must be placed within a political field of grassroots opposition by the power of numbers to the reigning unequal distribution of resources and to the powers of the state—circumstances that characterized the Ewe hometown association, Gray Panther, and Elmhurst-Corona meetings to which we now turn.

The Dzodze Social and Cultural Union

DSCU meetings occurred once a month on Sunday afternoons in a school building, with meetings of the dozen "organizers," later renamed the "executive committee," taking place in between. Members all had at least one parent from Dzodze in Ghana's Volta Region or, in a few cases, were married to someone from that town. The main reason for the formation of the association in 1969 was the desire of a group of young, educated men to advocate and lobby government officials for development projects in Dzodze, in particular, roads, a dam, improved school facilities, and a septic tank latrine. Quickly the group was criticized for not including any less-educated or illiterate members, and it expanded to be inclusive of all Dzodze people living in Accra, even switching the official meeting language from English to Ewe.[11]

Most members were male, but during the course of the first two years, women were encouraged to join, and three female seats were added to the executive committee. A program of social events was organized, including an Easter dance in Dzodze, a Christmas party in Accra, and parties or gift presentations for members leaving for overseas, marrying, or sponsoring memorial services for deceased kin. Members lived scattered throughout Greater Accra, and DSCU meetings and activities presented them with an embodied sense of their power of numbers—of comembership in a group concerned with the hometown where most had spent at least part of their childhood, to which all paid annual or more frequent visits, and to which they expected to retire.

Participatory discrepancies occurred not in the course of a single meeting but from one meeting to the next. The drama of each meeting lay not in the occurrence of something new—although this might happen—but in "slight variations" in the agenda, in those "regularities of syntactic and semantic elements" which made for a "crystallization of collaborative expectancies." The same was true of Gray Panther and Queens CB4 meetings. The form and content of DSCU meetings were set: opening and closing prayer; reading of the minutes from the previous meeting; financial update (most members were perennially in arrears with their annual dues); reports from executive committee leaders on their meetings and correspondence with government officials and with Dzodze chiefs and *atsyofos* (funeral association heads); and finally, "other matters," when personal activities might be announced or questions asked. Interest focused on how each expected agenda segment played out *this time.* In addition, from time to time a guest speaker was featured, officers elected, or the DSCU constitution amended and ratified.

Participation was intense. The principal executive committee leaders were expected to report at length on their actions related to development efforts, including meetings in Accra and Dzodze, and were freely questioned by members. The minutes, constitution, financial situation, and announcements of arrears or individual contributions all provoked considerable discussion. When during my first meeting I mentioned to one of my hosts that so far fifteen of the thirty people attending had spoken—a high level of participation, I was thinking—she assumed I thought otherwise and reassured me that the rest would speak when it came to "other matters."

Planning the 1971 round of Easter events in Dzodze—an *atopa* drumming contest by the funeral society groups; libations; a *durbar* (court) of chiefs; remarks by notables; meetings with local leaders; a soccer match; and an evening dance, featuring highlife, soul, rumba, reggae, smoochy, and Santana numbers, with music by the Dynamites band from Accra—all involved numerous members "working together" and "in groove" with each other. Indeed, this successful weekend resembled a "polka event" as described by Keil and his colleagues:

> Every polka event is built by polka people. The wedding is perhaps the prototype: find and rent a hall; buy booze; pick the band or bands; send out invitations (or, for a dance, put up posters, pass out slingers, sell tickets); and make sure that all the tasks of preparation are spread evenly yet done so well that everyone can be equally happy on that happy day. Similarly, the time, energy, and volunteer

> labor required to produce a parish dance or a lawn fete or a booster club monthly "meeting" are considerable, and the return on this investment is carefully measured by everyone in terms of the number of people who come and how good a time they have.[12]

The Gray Panthers of New York City

Between 1982 and 1987, I was the convener of the Gray Panthers of New York City.[13] This was an alliance of the existing Gray Panther networks in the city, which numbered between five and nine during these years. Each of the constituent Manhattan, Queens, and Brooklyn local networks met on its own, usually monthly, with its own agenda and a guest speaker. Their combined dues-paying membership numbered five hundred and fifty, but only some two dozen actually participated in Gray Panther actions focused on health, housing, peace, or Social Security. Often held in coalition with other activist organizations, these events included forums, demonstrations, radio and television appearances, letter writing, testifying at public hearings, lobbying elected officials and government agency personnel, and producing flyers and background documents on issues. Most members were elderly, mainly in their seventies. Then in my late thirties and early forties, I was one of only four younger active members.

Following my 1981 election to the national Gray Panthers steering committee, I decided to organize this citywide alliance to pool the energies of each network's more active members. As convener, I chaired monthly citywide leadership meetings attended by the five to nine local network conveners, one or two of their active members, and the chairs of the citywide peace, health, housing, environment, and Social Security "task forces." The meeting agenda included updates from each network convener, task force reports on meetings and actions, and announcements of forums and demonstrations, which were also published in *The City Panther*, a monthly newsletter mailed to all five hundred and fifty New York City Gray Panther members.

I had my own notion of what made "a good meeting." It was not merely participation but a balance between participation during the meeting and reports of actions accomplished or planned in between meetings. Each task force remained independently "active"—doing things beyond holding its own meetings—but an enjoyable groove was reachable at the citywide meetings, and this occurred most consistently during 1983 and 1984. Although certainly different from the Kaluli *dulugu ganalan* performative groove, a good Gray Panther meeting approached "maximized participation [with] each voice . . . socially ratified as cooperative agent, linked and immersed in a myriad of human relations that continually activate the pleasures of [Gray Panther] identity."[14] Like an Ewe or Dagomba master drummer,[15] my task as convener was to steer participation toward the groove—to make sure there was something new and worth hearing during each point in the predictable agenda—and to move on when there was not.

Two things worked against the groove: a few individual members who wished to seize the agenda and go off *clave* and the failing energy or health of active members. One of the discordants was a man obsessed with military waste and foreign policy. He had been asked to leave the Central Queens Gray Panthers for his frequent monopolization of meeting time by reading long *New York Times* stories or his own lengthy unpublished letters to the editor of that newspaper. He moved his membership to the Forest Hills Gray Panthers, where as convener he continued his activities before a shrinking but loyal audience. When he came to the citywide meetings and took the floor, eyes wandered to the ceiling and to me as chairperson. The "tension between egalitarianism"—letting everyone participate—and "individualism"—his tilting of the agenda to his own speech making—was palpable. As the elected leader, I was sanctioned to respond with my own "individualism" by cutting him off.

The other discordant was a woman in her early sixties who was a victim of a Social Security provision reducing benefits for persons born between 1917 and 1921, the so-called "notch babies." Everyone agreed the provision was unfair, but as a member of the Social Security Task Force, she used its agenda time to speak about this and only this issue, meeting after meeting. Again eyes wandered, and I had to cut her off and then try to reestablish a meeting groove.

The longer-term problem was that Gray Panthers who had joined the movement in the 1970s were aging or becoming infirm and were not being replaced by new, younger cohorts. This was a national problem. The number of networks had grown from thirty in 1975 to ninety in 1981 to more than one hundred by the mid-1980s, but most were also by then shrinking in size and mounting fewer actions. In 1990, Gray Panther founder Maggie Kuhn, then eighty-five, reported of that year's national convention: "The crowd was noticeably older than in years past. The organization has aged with me, and many of the members are in their later seventies and eighties."[16] By the mid-1990s, there were only forty networks nationwide.

In New York City, the trend was already apparent in the mid-1980s. Several active task force leaders and the founding convener of the Greenwich Village Gray Panthers died or curtailed their activities due to health problems. In fact, the disruptive military budget monologist had "taken over" the Forest Hills network, as one Queens Gray Panther put it, following the incapacity of that group's founder. More and more network and task force meetings were becoming talk sessions, and troops for Gray Panther actions or coalition activities were becoming fewer. As the volume of outside activities to report diminished, the agenda PDs were less compelling, and the groove of the citywide meetings waned. Due to work demands at Queens College, I resigned as convener of the Gray Panthers of New York City in 1987. In subsequent years, the number of networks fell to just one, and in 2001, the four remaining Manhattan West Side Gray Panthers suspended meeting.[17]

Community Board 4

Between 1983 and 1996, I attended 89 meetings and public hearings of Community Board 4 in Elmhurst-Corona, Queens, a multiracial, multiethnic, multilingual neighborhood of more than 137,000. CB4 was one of New York's fifty-nine community boards, which together constitute the local-level tier of decentralized municipal government. Its appointed members had advisory power over zoning changes, municipal budget allocation, and city agency performance. Most members were active in neighborhood civic, tenant, block, PTA, merchant, or immigrant associations, as well as houses of worship. A majority were established "white ethnics" of Italian, Irish, German, Jewish, and other European roots, but as the neighborhood's African American and Latino and Asian immigrant populations increased, members of these backgrounds were appointed to CB4 in growing numbers.

Much of the monthly meeting agenda time was devoted to land-use matters and to guest speakers, primarily city agency supervisors or elected officials. In addition, CB4 standing committees on zoning, housing, public safety, parks, youth, health and social services, arts and culture, transportation, and consumer affairs made reports, and the full-time district manager updated board members on citizen complaints and on meetings with city agency staff. Beyond this predictable agenda, members felt free to introduce anything they defined as a "quality of life" issue that fell within the board's purview—such as unresponsive policing, housing code violations, street drug sales—and some that technically did not—such as school crowding.

Consensus was by no means assured, and divided votes, arguments, tirades, and tension-ridden accusations occasionally arose (as they did at DSCU and Gray Panther meetings). On the other hand, a "good meeting," or in-groove portions of a meeting, might also occur. These episodes met Feld's characterization: "Instantly perceived, and often attended by pleasurable sensations ranging from arousal to relaxation," with CB4 members "appreciating subtleties vis-à-vis overt regularities."[18] These subtleties were contributed by individual participants, who used embellishment, humor, or deliberate orchestration from the chair to do so.

An example of embellishment that occurred early on at most CB4 meetings and quickly got people "into the grove" was provided by long-standing CB4 member Don Mallozzi, a gruff, bluff, cigar-chomping, retired post office worker active in the Corona Democratic Club and civic activities. Following the pledge of allegiance to the flag, Mallozzi could be counted on to raise his hand and, with mock solemnity, declare: "I move that we dispense with the reading of the minutes of the previous meeting." This set-piece ritual brought smiles as people looked his way, and if he hesitated, the chairperson might ask, "Mr. Mallozzi, do you have a motion?" When he was absent, people would take note of it at this point, and someone else, less elegantly or affirmatively, would make the motion. Don Mallozzi also embellished airings of quality-of-life issues with pithy comments, for example, remarking, "Connelly's a lot of hot air" during a report by public safety committee members of their meeting with the local police precinct captain. And to conclude a discussion of city tax favors for real estate developers, he announced, "I'm damned if I'm going to pay more taxes and give the mayor's curly-haired boys tax abatements. Let them pay taxes like everyone else," a comment that crystallized the meeting's sentiment and brought smiles.

Ken Daniels had headed the Lefrak City Tenants Association in the 1970s when that apartment complex was mainly white, and unlike most whites, he did not move out after it became predominantly black. He was a member of CB4's neighborhood stabilization committee, formed to press Lefrak management to provide adequate security and maintenance. He also collected neighborhood reports of local drug selling and numbers betting and was in frequent touch with the police precinct—on one occasion after drug dealers set his car on fire in retaliation. Always addressing the board in a serious and earnest manner, he adopted the same demeanor when he reported his discovery that boxes of Malomars sold at the Lefrak City Waldbaum's supermarket inevitably contained one stale cookie. He brought this up at several board meetings; wrote as chair of the CB4 consumer affairs committee to the manufacturer of the chocolate-covered, marshmallow-filled Malomars; and doggedly continued to gather evidence on the "one stale Malomar per box" problem. (He also pursued problems of underweight turkeys, moldy cheese, and insufficient sale items at Waldbaum's.) For board members, Daniels's consumer affairs committee reports became an anticipated moment of humor—of enjoyable participatory discrepancies—and remarks like "and now from the Malomar kid" introduced his updates on this quality-of-life saga.

Rose Rothschild, a former PTA president, joined CB4 in 1977, was elected chairperson in 1985, and became district manager in 1986. A skillful, one-to-one marshaler of support from CB4 members and other Elmhurst-Corona community activists, she also mastered city budget, zoning code, and agency ins and outs, thus augmenting both her own and the board's lubricatory power. Her ability to orchestrate a satisfying meeting for participants and still produce workable results—goals sometimes in conflict—was evident the night of a board vote on a new parking garage proposed by St. John's Hospital in Elmhurst.

More than a hundred local residents had come to a prior public hearing to oppose the garage. At the subsequent CB4 meeting, several board members voiced a raft of arguments against the garage, most of which were irrelevant to the technical land-use provision on which a CB4 vote was required. A few members attempted to sharpen the focus to this provision, but Rothschild allowed all objections to the garage to be aired, whether on point or not, and a wordy, overstated list of six objections was moved and passed. She then summarized the applicable arguments in concise form for the minutes, and by letter informed the relevant city agency of the board's opposition. She later told me that the wording of the motion was "ridiculous" and if conveyed as voted "could make the thing look silly." Nonetheless, she had let everybody speak.

Within the Flow of Humanity

Members of the Dzodze Social and Cultural Union, the Gray Panthers of New York City, and Community Board 4 enjoyed their meetings. As John Storm Roberts writes of African and African-derived musics, "Those who use the word 'monotonous' in criticism are on the wrong cultural wave length. 'The more you hear it the more harmony it has.'"[19] Members of these three urban political groups appreciated meeting grooves that "require and focus different kinds of participation. . . . People express their opinions by participating [and thus] make a contribution to the success of the occasion." Like Ghanaian master drummers, successful leaders valued and made use of participatory discrepancies "to enhance possibilities for personal happiness and community realization [and] because they believe that involvement will lead to caring and that a participant will find a way to complement a situation."[20]

Still, if PDs help us understand why members keep returning, why do they come in the first place? I share Keil's affirmation of the far more participatory nature of human cultures past and his desire to hold onto and promote participation where we find it in the present. When it finds its groove, participation provides its own rewards. As an eighty-three-year-old African American retired steel worker put it in Keil and his colleagues' *My Music*: "We all come here, we all sing together, talk together, eat together, be together while we're here. So when we depart, upon having to die or something, well, we could look on and say that was my friend, we could say we done such and such together."[21]

Dzodze people in Accra had a wide range of participatory alternatives—funeral association dance groups; daily opportunities to converse with others in residential buildings, bars, or visits to each other's homes; Presbyterian and Roman Catholic Ewe-language congregations; and DSCU meetings. In the United States, it is not only commercialized mediated entertainment, in ever more isolating forms, that blocks participation but also American cultural values that "alienate ourselves from others through a tenacious insistence upon individual rights rather than social relatedness."[22] Some Americans nevertheless resist, for reasons we need to understand better. In Elmhurst-Corona, they may find participatory grooves in houses of worship, bowling leagues, socializing after work and in homes, or in civic activism.

Moreover, many CB4 members, like most Gray Panthers, were retired and thus may have embraced organizational participation "because membership affords them excursions into a structured social milieu [and] the opportunity to interact with others in a convivial, reliable setting." What brought these older members to meetings, then, was "the implicit desire to remain within the flow of humanity, perhaps no longer playing as important a role there as before, but there nevertheless, to be of use again if called upon, still a functioning social unit, still interested, talking, alive."[23]

There is a danger in romanticizing participation, but as an anthropologist introduced while a student to its significance via the teaching and writings of Stanley Diamond,[24] I am convinced that anthropology cannot stress this perspective too strongly. Our critique of alienation, individualism, and state power is firmly warranted, more now than ever. And we need to sustain it by ethnographies of participation, both in classless societies like the Tiv or Kaluli or Anaguta and in those pockets of participation we describe and even celebrate[25] in our own.

Chapter 8

Intermarriage and the Future of Races in America

Through four centuries, white and black Americans have lived together and apart—in closer propinquity through the first twenty-five decades, during which slavery existed, than in the fifteen decades since. Across these years, the power of race has been expressed and mediated through sex. Forced disruption of black conjugal ties and kinship networks, white-on-black rape, sexual mythology and fear, legal bars to interracial marriage, and the overriding of kinship by race are historic features of the United States' continuing "American Dilemma."[1]

The post-Emancipation decades have been marked by still-entrenched patterns of black-white residential segregation.[2] In the early 1940s, St. Clair Drake and Horace Cayton characterized racial division in Chicago as "a pattern of relations which reduces to a minimum any neighborly contacts, school contacts, or chance meetings in stores, taverns, and movie houses between Negroes and whites." In 1990, some 30 percent of black Americans still lived in neighborhoods at least 90 percent black, and 68 percent of whites lived in neighborhoods nearly all white. (The slightly more segregated 1980 figures were 34 percent of blacks and 76 percent of whites).[3] In view of this history, it is unsurprising that the prevalence of white-black intermarriage remained low, at 3 percent for married black Americans in 1990 (up from 2 percent in 1980) and far less than 1 percent for whites.[4]

Despite the low prevalence of white-black intermarriage throughout U.S. history, numbers of white males have been ready to "bed but not wed" black women.[5] The long history of sexual abuse and exploitation inspired no enthusiasm by African Americans for marriage with whites, whose negative attitude to interracial marriage was epitomized by the rhetorical question "Would you want your daughter to marry a Negro?" which required no answer. Still, black and white opinion divided around state laws forbidding interracial marriage. Many such laws were proposed by whites during the Jim Crow decades of the late nineteenth and early twentieth centuries. In 1921, the black scholar and activist W. E. B. Du Bois reiterated the widely held African American position opposing such laws:

> We have not asked amalgamation; we have resisted it. It has been forced upon us by brute strength, ignorance, poverty, degradation and fraud. It is the white race that has left its trail of bastards and outraged women and then raised holy hands to heaven and deplored "race mixture." No, we are not demanding and do not want amalgamation, but the reasons are ours and not yours. It is not because we are unworthy of intermarriage—either physically or mentally or morally. It is because no real men accept any alliance except on terms of absolute equal regard and because we are abundantly satisfied with our own race and blood. And at the same time we as free men must say that whenever two human beings of any nation or race desire each other in marriage, the denial of their legal right to marry is simply wrong.[6]

Led by Du Bois and the NAACP, African American opposition to laws barring interracial marriage was aimed at the overtly racist presumption of black inferiority the laws contained.[7] At the same time, black opinion also resisted the more subtle racist viewpoint of white liberals who favored interracial marriage as a "solution" to America's race problem. This position, holding that through intermarriage African Americans eventually would melt into the white population and disappear, was advocated by anthropologists Franz Boas and Ralph Linton.[8] Boas wrote in a 1921 *Yale Review Quarterly* article, "The Negro in America" (later reprinted in his posthumous 1945 volume *Race and Democratic Society*):

> The greatest hope for the immediate future lies in a lessening of the contrast between Negroes and whites. Intermixture will decrease the contrast between the extreme racial forms, and in the course of time, this will lead to a lessening of the consciousness of race distinction.

> If conditions were ever such that it could be doubtful whether a person were of Negro descent or not, the consciousness of race would necessarily be much weakened. In a race of octoroons, living among Whites, the color question would probably disappear. It would seem, therefore, to be in the interest of society to permit rather than to restrict marriages between white men and Negro women. It would be futile to expect our people would tolerate intermarriages in the opposite direction. . . . Thus it seems that man being what he is, the Negro problem will not disappear in America until Negro blood has been so much diluted that it will no longer be recognized, just as anti-Semitism will not disappear until the last vestige of the Jew as a Jew has disappeared.[9]

Boas had calculated in a 1909 paper that with unrestricted mating in a population where 90 percent was of one type and 10 percent of another, the minority type would effectively disappear in one hundred years.[10] Although Boas and Linton opposed the more grossly racist position that "miscegenation" was biologically objectionable, their recommended "paling out of blacks as the ultimate solution," as Joseph Washington has remarked, denied "equality for the black male" and ruled out cultural "acceptance of blackness as a firm and rich experience"; their recommendation remained "unconsciously bent on genocide."[11]

Sexual contact between interacting populations is a universal feature of human history, but its behavioral specifics—whether coerced or chosen, in or out of marriage, at high or low rates—are historical, political, and cultural issues requiring analysis and explanation. In recent decades, white-black intermarriage rates have been slowly increasing. There were 51,000 such couples in the United States in 1960; 65,000 in 1970; 167,000 in 1980; and 211,000 in 1990.[12] Black-white intermarriage rates are higher in the North than in the South, in the West than in the East, and in locales where there is a small percentage of blacks than in places where the percentage is large.[13] Still, the 3 percent rate of intermarriage for African Americans in 1990 was much smaller than that for other non-European groups. "Data from the 1990 Current Population Survey indicate that 17 percent of married Asian Americans have a non-Asian spouse. About the same level of intermarriage is seen among Latinos."[14] American Indian intermarriage rates were even higher.

Race and Ethnicity

In the 1980 U.S. census, 1.4 million persons identified themselves as American Indian by race, yet 5.3 million whites claimed some American Indian ancestry on the separate ethnic origin question.[15] For many of these persons, the Indian ancestry was remote, but for others it was not. More than half of American Indians in 1980 were married to non-Indian spouses, most of whom were white.[16] The high rate of intermarriage helps to destabilize an ethnicity-versus-race distinction in this case. By race, some 1.4 million Native Americans see themselves as Indian, in contrast to white,[17] yet millions more whites view their Indian ancestry as ethnicity. Cultural and political identification are also involved, as some former "whites" changed their race to Indian in the 1990 census.[18]

It is intermarriage, primarily, I believe, that has transformed American Indian racial difference[19] into ethnicity for some whites. Such transformation historically also accorded ambiguously defined European "others" an unambiguous white racial status in the United States. The boundaries of "white" in the nation's history expanded continuously with this "naturalization" of non-British Europeans. In 1751, Benjamin Franklin railed against German "*aliens*" whose presence interfered with the dominance of "purely White People."[20] Later, nativist and white supremacist groups targeted Italians, Greeks, Slavs, and Jews, all today considered white and marriageable by the majority of white Americans.[21]

In eighteenth-century New York, intermarriage solidified English, Dutch, and French residents[22] and accorded each an ethnicity. Over time, as differences of language, diet, worship, and popular culture were attenuated, these white ethnicities stood for little more than ancestral origin claims.[23] Nineteenth-century intermarriage similarly accorded Irish, Germans, and other Europeans ethnicity within the white racial fold. A third wave of intermarriage, beginning near the turn of the twentieth century, extended ethnicity to southern and eastern European "new immigrants."[24] Among intermarrying whites, ethnicity supplied contrast at symbolic cultural points (surnames, cuisines, festivities, language) even as these became progressively vitiated in substance with each U.S.-born generation. Children inherited the ethnic identities of *both* their parents.

Historically, intermarriage between Europeans had begun immediately after immigration, even across language boundaries. In the late 1600s, English settler Richard Alsop of Newtown (later Elmhurst), New York, married his Dutch wife, Hannah, "whom he courted through an interpreter" according to local tradition.[25] Their match initiated more extensive eighteenth-century Dutch-English intermarriage in this Queens County township, settled in 1652. Later, during a period of heavy European immigration to New York City in the 1840s and 1850s, although statistics are lacking, there were certainly cases of "Irish-German, Irish-Chinese, Irish-French, German-French, [and] English-French [intermarriage], and numerous instances of immigrants marrying native [white] Americans."[26]

A comprehensive study of intermarriage in New York City during 1908–1912, the peak "new immigration" years, found first-generation intermarriage rates of 6 percent for southern Italian immigrants, 8 percent for Hungarians, 15 percent for Irish, 22 percent for Greeks, 27 percent for Swedes, 38 percent for Norwegians, 40 percent for French, 50 percent for Scots, 52 percent for north Germans, and 55 percent for south Germans. (Immigrant Jewish groups had intermarriage rates of 5 percent or less.) Marriages occurred in virtually every ethnic combination; among Norwegian female immigrants, for example, foreign-born husbands included 36 Swedes, 16 Danes, 9 English, 9 Germans, 9 Irish, 6 Italians, 3 Scots, 3 Swiss, 2 Austrians, 2 Russians (1 of these being Jewish), and 1 each from Canada, Finland, Greece, Portugal, and Turkey. In addition, Norwegian immigrant women married 4 nonwhite or non–North American husbands—British West Indian, Chinese, Japanese, and Peruvian.[27]

The historical realities of intermarriage in relation to ethnicity do not support the influential interpretation of sociologist Milton Gordon, who sees intermarriage as the final step in cultural and structural assimilation.[28] With intermarriage beginning immediately upon each new wave of European immigration, I suggest that it became the social vehicle through which cultural contrasts among "people we marry" were construed as ethnic by the white population. Over time, as intermarriage increased with each generation, there was less and less cultural stuff requiring assimilation. Gordon's intermarriage caboose was in fact an engine of cultural change for white Americans.

Race, the point at which intermarriage was shunned, was construed as biologically defined *difference*, and race obviated recognition or discussion of cultural contrasts within white kinship networks. Offspring of any white-black pairings or marriages were considered black; they did not inherit the ethnicity of their white parent in a socially recognized manner, and they were not incorporated into their white parent's kinship network.

Today's substantial white-Asian and white-Hispanic intermarriage rates raise the question of whether a contemporary round of race-to-ethnicity conversion may be occurring. Will white Americans accord ethnicity through intermarriage across what have been racial lines and recognize, say, Polish-Mexican, or Jewish-Chinese, or French-German-Puerto Rican, or WASP-Korean kinspersons?

The grounds barely exist for a parallel conversion of race to ethnicity across the white-black line, where intermarriage remains low. There are undoubtedly more than 5.3 million whites (the number who acknowledged some American Indian ancestry in 1980) who are unaware of or do not admit African ancestry. By 1960, Robert Stuckert estimated, 23 million white Americans had some degree of post-1492 African genetic ancestry.[29] The cultural calculus of race in the United States, however, still does not permit black ethnicity among the multiple ethnic strands a white American may claim.[30] A white person may be Croatian-Irish, but not Croatian-Irish-African American. In the eyes of whites, at least up to now, such a person is black, and race overrides ethnicity.[31]

But today there are other eyes, other ways of seeing. Increasingly, these others appear in central institutional locations—city neighborhoods, universities, public and corporate bureaucracies—alongside white and black Americans. Predictions of a U.S. "majority minority" future with Americans of non-European ancestry amounting to more than half of the population are widely acknowledged (see Chapter 1).

A white-black-Hispanic-Asian-American Indian formula constitutes the current U.S. racial framework. Anthropologist Jack Forbes traced the bureaucratic origin of this racial grid to the Nixon administration, beginning in 1973.[32] As policy discussion moved through federal interagency committees and received input from Republican officials who promoted a new "Hispanic" label, five "mutually exclusive categories" were promulgated for official government use in a 1977 Office of Management and Budget (OMB) circular titled "Race and Ethnic Standards for Federal Statistics and Administrative Reporting." The five were

1. "American Indian and Alaskan Native," which applied to North America only.
2. "Asian and Pacific Islander," with its western border inclusive of Pakistan.

3. "Black," which included persons of African origin from south of "North Africa" but did not specify where "white" North Africa began.
4. "Hispanic," which included all inhabitants of Western Hemisphere Spanish-speaking nations and their descendants, plus Spaniards from Europe.
5. "White," including persons who trace their origins to the "original peoples" of Europe (except Spain), North Africa, and the Middle East eastward to the Pakistan border.[33]

This state-defined view of five races has been increasingly evident in political and street-level discourse.[34] If we grant that race has always been a concept of state-level social ordering, one that frequently disregards linguistic, cultural, and immigrant or creole ethnic difference, then white, black, Hispanic, Asian, and American Indian are races as the U.S. social order defines race. When people in the contemporary United States talk about "racial" politics, discrimination, or violence, it is this white-black-Hispanic-Asian-American Indian framework they use.

Some sociologists prefer to subordinate or avoid "race" as a concept, preferring to use only "ethnicity."[35] Putting ethnicity at the center, however, results in seeing African Americans as a problematic exception to general processes applying to everyone else and underplaying the historic legal and popular denial of equality to Native, Asian, and Hispanic Americans.[36] The ahistoric construction of African Americans as a late-arriving urban ethnic group, downplaying the significance of race, was articulated by neoconservatives in the 1950s and 1960s.[37] The alternative position—that we need both race and ethnicity as concepts—continued to be maintained through the ethnicity-focused 1970s and 1980s. From this viewpoint, both repressive processes of exclusion (race) and expressive processes of inclusion (ethnicity) must be taken into account.[38]

Historical Perspectives on Interracial Marriage

From my New York standpoint, the emergence of Hispanic and Asian populations in substantial numbers and the addition of these terms to the biracial black-white framework are recent. Although the first person other than native Munsee to live in what became New York City was Juan Rodriguez, described in 1612 as "a mulatto from San Domingo,"[39] only with growing numbers of Puerto Ricans in the 1930s did a new racial category of persons not white and not black take popular hold. Moreover, even into the 1950s, individual Puerto Ricans experienced societal pressure to identify as white or black.[40]

With a large post-1965 Latin American immigration to the city, its Hispanic or Latino (in Spanish, *Hispano* or *Latinoamericano*, and in street English, "Spanish"[41]) population became a fixed part of the city's "humanscape." Chinese resided in New York by the 1830s in small numbers and by the 1870s were widely seen by whites as an exotic marginal group, not white and not black.[42] The political significance of Asians dates from the large influx of diverse Asian immigrants after 1965, and political calculation now includes them.

This New York racial history differs from the Southwest and Pacific regions, where the implanted mid-nineteenth-century U.S. social order included Hispanics and Asians from the start or soon thereafter. Mexicans in the Southwest and California and Chinese and then Japanese in the Pacific and mountain states were subjected to second-class citizenship, racial mythology, targeted violence, labor exploitation, and legal and social bars to marriage with whites, similar to what blacks continued to experience after Emancipation in the East and South.[43] Blacks arrived in substantial numbers in the Southwest and Pacific states later than whites, mainly after 1940. Their position was then consistent with that in the East and South—residential segregation, job restriction, and low black-white intermarriage rates. By the 1970s, a white-black-Hispanic-Asian racial formula existed nationwide, reinforced by continuing Latin American and Asian immigration.

In the 1960s, the intermarriage rates—both prevalence (existing marriages) and incidence (new marriages)—rose sharply for Asians and Latinos, reflecting mainly marriages to whites. For Japanese Americans, the well-studied Seattle case is typical of the picture elsewhere: intermarriage climbed from rates of less than 10 percent before 1950 to 17 percent in the early 1960s, 30 percent later in the decade, and over 50 percent by 1975.[44] Among Chinese Americans nationally during the 1960s, some 11.5 percent of males and 12.8 percent of females married white spouses.[45] Los Angeles County marriage licenses in 1979 showed a 50 percent interracial incidence for Japanese, 30 percent for Chinese, and 19 percent for Koreans.[46] In New York City, Chinese intermarried, again mainly with whites, at a 27 percent incidence in both 1972 and 1982.[47] In the 1980 U.S. census, the prevalence of intermarriage with whites was 27 percent among Japanese Americans, 25 percent among Koreans, 22 percent among Filipinos, 17 percent among Vietnamese, 13 percent among Indians, and 10 percent among Chinese.[48]

Mexican American intermarriage, also mainly with whites, occurred before 1960 at prevalences of 10 percent or less in Los Angeles, Albuquerque, and San Antonio. By 1963, incidence in Los Angeles climbed to 25 percent; intermarriage rates for Spanish-surnamed California residents were even higher: 38 percent in 1962 and 34 percent in 1974.[49] In eight Arizona counties, the incidence of "Chicano-Anglo" marriage was 16 percent in 1960, 24 percent in 1970, and 28 percent in 1980.[50] The incidence of intermarriage in Albuquerque was similar, 24 percent in 1971; in San Antonio, a predominantly Mexican American city, 16 percent in 1973; and in heavily Mexican American rural South Texas it remained at less than 10 percent through the 1970s.[51] Nationally, the prevalence of Mexican American intermarriage was 17 percent in both 1980 and 1990.[52]

Puerto Rican intermarriage in 1980 was 26 percent nationally (a figure that included marriages to blacks and other Hispanics as well as to whites).[53] An analysis of 1975 marriage licenses issued in New York City, where the largest concentration of mainland Puerto Ricans lived, found that 12 percent of males and 15 percent of females married non-Hispanic spouses that year.[54] In 1990, the national intermarriage rate for all Puerto Ricans was 19 percent and 40 percent among those born on the mainland.[55] The New York 1975 marriage license study also tallied the incidence of intermarriage to non-Hispanic spouses for male and female Cubans (23 and 32 percent), Central Americans (24 and 23 percent), South Americans (16 and 22 percent), and Dominicans (6 and 8 percent); unknown but substantial proportions of these were marriages to white spouses.[56] In 1980, 13 percent of all Hispanic Americans intermarried, most of them to whites.[57]

It is noteworthy that Asian and Hispanic intermarriage with whites increased only after blacks became part of the West Coast social order in substantial numbers. African Americans' low intermarriage rate demonstrates their persisting identification by race rather than ethnicity on the part of whites. Asians and Mexicans, who undeniably formed the reserve labor pool in the western states before blacks arrived, became marriageable—and ethnic—to whites only after the U.S. black-white racial regime was established.

In New York City, where blacks long occupied this labor market position, Asian and Hispanic intermarriage with whites achieved high rates (although in tiny numbers) decades earlier. Marriage registry data for 1908–1912 shows rates of intermarriage to white spouses (both U.S. born and immigrant) of 53 percent for 34 Chinese who married during those years, 60 percent for 42 Japanese, 44 percent for 155 Cubans, 37 percent for 79 Puerto Ricans, 63 percent for 35 Mexicans, and 78 percent for 40 Central and South Americans. In the same years, the rate of intermarriage with white spouses of 4,748 blacks was 1 percent. Overall, during 1908–1912, some 63 blacks (51 African Americans and 12 black immigrants) married whites, compared to 82 Asians and 309 Latin Americans.[58]

To recap, by 1980, nationwide, 13 percent of Hispanics and 25 percent of Asians were married outside their group, mainly to white spouses. Black-white rates in 1980 stood at 2 percent. By 1990, after a decade of heavy Latin American and Asian immigration—which masked rising intermarriage rates for earlier arrivals and the U.S. born—1 in 6 of married Asians and Hispanics in the United States were married interracially. This compared with 1 in 33 blacks.[59]

Since the 1960s, Hispanics and Asians have become more likely to marry whites with each generation of residence in the United States and as income and education levels increase. The same factors apply historically to white interethnic marriage, and today the majority of white Americans are of multiple European ancestries.[60] At the same time, a small but growing number of "unhyphenated whites" answer only "American" or give no response when queried about their ethnicity. Two-thirds of this ethnic-less segment of the white population consists of southern whites and is more rural and less well-educated than white Americans overall. The other third is well off, northern, and likely to be Roman Catholic.[61]

Intermarriage, Kinship, and Community

By the late 1980s, just 1 percent of white Americans were married interracially, with three in four of these marriages to Hispanic and Asian (or other) husbands and wives and one in four to black spouses.[62] If we assume each intermarried white spouse had sixteen white relatives and assume these kin did not reject the intermarried couple, then potentially one sixth of white Americans had a nonwhite affinal relative and perhaps also a racially mixed kinsperson, the offspring of the interracial marriage. Looking from the other side of these interracial marriages, many more Hispanic and Asian Americans had white and perhaps half-white relatives. Such existing and growing interracial kinship links were far fewer between black and white Americans or between blacks and Hispanics or Asians, for that matter.[63]

My data on white American kinship networks in Elmhurst-Corona, Queens, are limited but are consistent with the national picture. In sixteen intensive interviews with white residents, I found widespread white ethnic intermarriage—WASP-Italian, Italian-Irish, Polish-Russian, German-Scotch-English, and so on. Five of the sixteen networks of those I interviewed also included an interracial marriage. Two were with Hispanic (Mexican, Puerto Rican) and two with Asian (Chinese, Korean) spouses. Three of these four had been well accepted by white relatives, and the fourth had just occurred. The fifth marriage was to a black spouse and received little approval within the white kinship network.[64]

Political Scenarios

Political readings of projected future U.S. racial composition do not as yet take into account the trends in intermarriage, the racial self-identification of mixed persons, or the significance of intermarriage within kinship networks. Nonetheless, these themes seem critical for ethnographic exploration of the unfolding race-sex-power configuration of the United States. To encourage this, I will discuss six alternative scenarios identifiable in public and academic discourse. These scenarios are not mutually exclusive, in my opinion, and each may offer a glimpse of one facet of our future. There are also, and will continue to be, advocates and supporters for each of these alternatives.

Scenario 1: A Social Order in Which Racial Groups Compete and Contend for Relative Political Advantage

Activists and analysts who consider U.S. politics to be fundamentally racially based range considerably in political orientation.[65] Interpreting politics in New York City, economist Robert Fitch argues that an apartheid-like, divide-and-rule, elite strategy underpinned the move to create a large number (fifty-one) of small racially and ethnically defined districts in the

1991 City Council redistricting (which was still in effect two decades later). Struggles over boundaries were phrased in racial terms, with demands for more black and Hispanic seats (including specific Caribbean and Dominican districts) and for creation of an Asian district. As the reality set in that blacks were more residentially concentrated than Hispanics and Asians (so also are whites) and that black electoral districts were far easier to draw than Latino ones, black-Hispanic conflict between political activists surfaced. Fitch saw this division as serving the entrenched white political interests of the city's "permanent government."[66]

Intermarriage patterns might mitigate racial separateness and promote alliance along the lines where they are strongest. In this regard, it is significant to note that the *New York Times* during the 1980s increasingly published notices of interracial marriages in the city's higher circles, often with photographs. I counted eighteen such announcements in 1991, twelve of them white-Asian intermarriages, four white-Hispanic, one white-black, and one black-Asian.

Factors other than redistricting or marriage patterns, of course, affect racial categorization and mobilization. The most important of these is continuing immigration bringing new Latin American, Asian, Caribbean, and African arrivals, who will be counted and appealed to in racial and ethnic terms. Another such factor is continuing exhortation by political leaders who advocate racial or ethnic voting or forms of racial or ethnic chauvinism and separatism, sometimes provoking greater impact among persons outside their assumed constituencies than within them.

Scenario 2: People-of-Color Unity Among Black, Hispanic, and Asian Groups

Political analyst Manning Marable spotlighted issues that confront all U.S. residents of color in a widely read essay calling for a rethinking of African American political strategy.[67] People-of-color ideology has many spokespersons among political activists, but in New York City, where action on common issues of housing, education, and health-care services would benefit from it, this ideology, Angelo Falcon contends, has little force in either community or city politics.[68] My prediction is that it will encounter greatest support first in glass-ceiling workplace situations, where qualified professionals of color find opportunities and promotions blocked by discrimination from whites.

Current intermarriage patterns are in line with a relative underdevelopment of people-of-color unity. Most intermarriages involving Asians, Latin Americans, and blacks are with whites, not other persons of color—in 1987, 93 percent of Asian, Hispanic, and American Indian interracial unions nationally were with whites and 7 percent with blacks, whereas 83 percent of black interracial marriages were with whites and 17 percent with other persons of color.[69] Nonetheless, incidents of racial harassment in public settings, housing discrimination in mainly white neighborhoods, and incidents of racial violence continue to provide a potential common platform for people-of-color alliance.

Scenario 3: Transition from a White-Black Racial Order to a Light-Dark Order in Which Asians and Some Hispanics Align with Whites

In this scenario, advanced by several sociologists, Asians, whose intermarriage rates with whites are already high, will blend into the white population, as will lighter Hispanics. Hispanics of visible African ancestry and family background will be pushed off the Anglo-conformist immigrant track and join black Americans and black Caribbean and African immigrants in continuing racial subordination.[70]

The intermarriage numbers might be evidence for supporters of this scenario, but the racial identification of half-white and half-Asian or half-Hispanic persons is not predictable merely from numbers. Although some children of such interracial marriages do identify as "white" or as racially neutral "Americans," others choose to identify with their Asian or Hispanic parent. For some, this is determined in part by their physical appearance and place of residence, but for others it is a deliberate political or ethnic affirmation.[71]

No one knows what proportion will assimilate to white or identify as Asian or Hispanic or claim, for example, Chinese or Mexican ethnic strands along with European ones, as do the 5.3 million whites that claim an American Indian strand. It appears that mixed persons have some degree of choice in self-identification, depending upon class, closeness to each parent, region of residence, or physical appearance. But there is little reason to state firmly that a widening of the "white" grouping will occur in contrast with a persisting "African American" or widening "black" one. This may happen for some persons and in some places, but others, of all colors, may contest it.

Scenario 4: Increasing Use of Racially Mixed Identification

College campuses, where racial identify is frequently of heightened concern, are cauldrons in which formation of organizations of racially mixed persons occurs. Many such groups have emerged, with some consisting of "hapa," or half-Asian and half-white persons; some of "biracial" persons, usually of black and white parentage; and others of more complex racially mixed backgrounds.[72] Persons in these groups may both affirm their dual or multiple origins and reject or accept membership in organizations addressing Asian or black racial interests. Self-identification of persons of interracial parentage also needs more study in workplace and community settings. Ideological attachments to college identity politics may shift when the white-black-Hispanic-Asian formula is imposed by employers or by politics. On the other hand, emergent biracial and multiracial identities may begin to change this hegemonic racial formula.

Since the 1980s, racially mixed spokespersons have called for revision of the U.S. Census race question to offer a more affirmative choice than "other race."[73] This occurred in the 2000 census, when individuals were able to select two (or more) races to identify themselves. Before 2000, the introduction of a proposed new "biracial" or "mixed" census category was successfully resisted by African American leaders, in particular, who feared that growing numbers of offspring of black-white marriages, or their parents, might select it and thus reduce "black" numbers.

Some African Americans may also find objectionable an ideological message that seeks to expand biracial or multiple race identification by calling attention to white racial ancestry in their own, as well as Hispanic and Native American, histories. For black Americans, racial mixing in past generations, we have noted, usually was imposed and unwelcome or, when freely chosen, was denied acceptance by whites. It differed substantially from the current situation in which some black-white marriages now do enjoy the "equal regard" long ago demanded by Du Bois.[74]

The issue is not going away. Today there are children of interracial marriages proclaiming their "sense of wholeness that is more than the sum of the parts of a person's heritages . . . of being 'both' and 'neither' throughout life" and also that "we are everywhere, and the United States will have to adjust to our presence in many ways."[75]

Scenario 5: Latin American–Style Views of Race as Appearance, Not Ancestry, May Gain Ascendance

Great masses of Latin Americans who are U.S. residents or may become so in the future acknowledge their racially mixed backgrounds—although not usually in an immediate parental generation but rather in the formative periods of their ancestral home-country histories. In Latin America, some elites and regional subpopulations maintain they are of unmixed European descent, but millions of Mexicans (and post-1848 Mexican Americans), Puerto Ricans, Dominicans, Colombians, and others acknowledge varying combinations of European, American Indian, and African ancestry.

Centuries of white racial dominance are reflected in continuing notions that light skin, straight hair, and European facial features are prestigious, but families and kinship networks frequently include persons who vary widely in racial physiognomy. Racial terms translatable as "white," "black," or "Indian" refer to appearance, not beliefs about the absence or presence of African or American Indian ancestry. In addition, other terms exist to identify persons of intermediate combinations of skin color, hair form, and facial features, much as white Americans distinguish blonds, brunets, and redheads and pale to olive-skinned complexions.[76]

As sociologist Clara Rodriguez has pointed out, in recent decades, increasing numbers of Hispanics have selected "other" on the U.S. census race question, rejecting "white" and "black" as choices. Some, she notes, may read this as a cultural question, viewing themselves culturally as other than white American or black American.[77] When I mentioned this choice of "other" in one of my Queens College classes, two Egyptian sisters raised in New York joined a Colombian friend in saying, "That's what we do."

Increasing numbers of Americans like these may choose "other" when the choice is white or black, but they are likely to use more specific and affirmative self-identifications in everyday life. How do persons from world regions or of mixed ancestries not conforming to stereotypic white, black, or East Asian racial images describe themselves and others like them? Will new concepts of race as appearance, not ancestry, and new vocabularies ("brown people"?) gain greater currency?

Nomenclature for shades and hues in cosmetics marketing might be an interesting place to probe this issue. With a quarter of the U.S. population of non-European ancestry by the 1990s, cosmetics firms were marketing new lines to a broader spectrum of customers, with such names as Color Deeps, Shades of You, and All Skins.[78]

Scenario 6: A People-of-All-Colors Ideology Promoting Unity Among Working- and Middle-Class Persons and Identifying Their Class Enemies

Marable argued for this strategy, as well as for people-of-color unity, although he left unspecified the linkage between these two political scenarios.[79] In the Queens community district I studied a quality-of-life politics had established itself amid the racial changes of the 1970s and 1980s: it underplayed race and stressed common needs for improved city services and local programs. Its chief obstacles to success remained the control of information, organization, and procedure by nonlocal, upper-middle-class bureaucrats and city elites, as well as the continuing force of racially defined political competition.

Perhaps a more deliberate "color-full" consciousness and practice, rather than silence about race, will be required to strengthen the power of numbers against the power of resources, which benefits most from "color-blind" ideology and proscription.

Conclusion

I repeat that all six scenarios are likely to occur simultaneously, find supporters and advocates, and affect thinking about race in the future. In the year 2050 or 2100, it may be less easy than today to assign persons a place within the white-black-Hispanic-Asian-American Indian framework. Growing numbers of racially mixed persons and complex kinship networks that cross these racial lines will be more prevalent. Another factor moving kinship ties in this direction is the adoption of children across racial and international lines by white Americans as their birthrate declines. In 1986, some ten thousand foreign-born children were adopted, the largest number from South Korea. And in 1988, Congress approved funds to bring up to thirty thousand Amerasian children and their family members from Vietnam to the United States. By 2002, foreign adoptions had doubled to twenty thousand; China and Russia each accounted for one quarter of these children, with Guatemala and South Korea the third- and fourth-place source countries.[80]

The white population may increasingly divide into two groups. The first will consist of those who object to interracial marriage, continue to practice racial exclusion, and define fewer and fewer U.S. residents as white. In a

1991 poll, 66 percent of white Americans opposed interracial marriage with blacks—one in five believed it should be barred by law—and 45 percent opposed intermarriage with Hispanics or Asians.[81] The second group will consist of those who, along with persons of other and mixed racial identities, maintain social ties and practice politics that increasingly discount racial division and accord ethnicity across today's racial boundaries.

In the end, the critical racial issue will continue to be the place that persons of African descent occupy within the U.S. social order. As Michael Banton put it, "Good race relations would be ethnic relations," but white and black Americans are not there yet.[82] If even partial transformation into ethnicity of Asian and Hispanic racial identity is effected through intermarriage, will denial of ethnicity to African Americans continue, reinforced and symbolized by continuing low rates of intermarriage? Will today's patterns of housing, education, and employment discrimination for large numbers of black Americans be dismantled or persist?[83]

We have unfinished business. However it is drawn, the color line remains a problem of the twenty-first-century United States.

Postscript

Black-white residential segregation in America's cities declined slightly during the 1990s, by 3 percent, and in the 2001–2010 decade by 5 percent. In the New York metropolitan area, the declines were smaller, only 1 percent and 2 percent. More broadly, according to sociologists John Logan and Brian Stults, "Systematic discrimination in the housing market has not ended, and for the most part it is not prosecuted. Fair housing laws by and large are enforced only when minority home seekers can document discrimination and pursue a civil court case without assistance from public officials. Americans do not want to believe that discrimination still exists. Yet studies that track the experience of minority persons in the rental or homeowner market continue to find that they are treated differently than comparable whites."[84]

At the same time, interracial marriage has become more common. In 2000, some 7 percent of all married couples were interracial (including Hispanic/non-Hispanic unions), and by 2008, the figure was 8 percent. The prevalence of black intermarriage rose to 7 percent of couples in 2000 and 9 percent in 2008. Among whites, 5 percent of all marriages were interracial by 2008, as were 17 percent of Hispanic marriages and 16 percent of Asian marriages. Of 3.8 million new marriages in 2008, one in seven, or 15 percent, were interracial, including 9 percent of marrying whites, 16 percent of blacks, 26 percent of Hispanics, and 31 percent of Asians.[85]

Attitudes toward interracial marriage have shifted sharply. Among persons of all races under age 30, by 2009 some 80 percent or more approved the idea of a relative marrying a spouse of a different race. Even among whites of all ages, nearly two-thirds (64 percent) said they would not object if a family member married an African American.[86]

Increases in interracial marriage are projected to continue. "More than half of whites . . . may well belong to multiracial kin groups within the lifetimes of people born today." Moreover, although only 2 percent of Americans identified themselves by two or more races in 2000, when multiple responses to the U.S. Census race question were first permitted, "projections suggest the number of multiple-origin Americans (both multiracial and part Hispanic) will increase to 189 million by 2100, making up one-third of the total U.S. population."[87]

Chapter 9

Rethinking Migration, Ancient to Future

Rising tides in the movement of information, commodities, and people characterize the contemporary world, and anthropologists of the present have been vigorous in charting these proliferating forms of transnational circulation.[1] Taking a global view, Arjun Appadurai discerns "a general rupture in the tenor of intersocietal relations" marking "the extended present" and attributes this to first, the impact of electronic media and second, the pace and ubiquity of contemporary migration. Of the latter, he writes, "Few persons in the world today do not have a friend, relative, or coworker who is not on the road to somewhere else or coming back home."[2]

In the year 2000, some 130 million human beings lived outside their nation of birth.[3] In social anthropology, the dominant concept for investigating this massive intercourse of people has been immigration—the self-directed movement of individuals from one nation-state to another.[4] We have learned much from the harvest of immigration studies and have by no means exhausted the productivity of this approach. Yet in making sense of the contemporary world, we find that there is a conceptual narrowness to immigration as a master framework, a narrowness that may be summarized under four headings:

1. Treating human migration primarily in terms of contemporary legal categories
2. Paying insufficient attention to national citizen-making processes as experienced both by immigrants and by others
3. Failing to treat immigration as ideology as well as experience
4. Subscribing to a presentist orientation that foregrounds movers versus other groups

Immigration as Legal Category

Contemporary global immigration cannot be studied apart from the enormous legal apparatuses that define and channel it. In the United States, since 1965, these have included an evolving and increasingly intricate complex of ceilings and quotas; visa categories; and immigrant, refugee, and asylum statuses, including that of illegal or undocumented alien.[5] Intersecting with this and with the legal structures and processing procedures of other nations is a complex array of paragovernmental nongovernmental organizations (NGOs), human rights monitoring groups, pro- and anti-immigration lobbies, dual citizenship arrangements, and government programs for extraterritorial diasporees.[6] Research that exemplifies careful attention to this legal domain includes Michel Laguerre on the strategies by which Haitians obtain U.S. immigrant visas; Johanna Lessinger on the ties of expatriate non-resident Indian (NRI) investors to their homeland; Jacqueline Hagan on the utilization of Immigration Reform and Control Act (IRCA) legalization provisions by undocumented Guatemalan Mayan migrants; Alex Stepick on U.S. refugee and immigrant statuses in relation to Haitian and Cuban "boat people"; and Jon Holtzman on Nuer refugees in Africa and North America.[7]

Researchers who do not master the legal technicalities that apply to the immigrant and refugee populations they study are not doing their job. But the rub arises when legal categories are used to narrowly define the parameters of study, and the wider social fields within which immigrants and others operate are rendered hazy or invisible (which does not mar the careful work of Laguerre, Lessinger, Hagan, Stepick, and Holtzman). In addition, the legally framed immigration standpoint tends to obscure historical continuities between past migrations within nation-states or colonial dominions and contemporary migrations that cross national borders.[8]

Immigrant and Other Citizens

Several scholars have considered how cultural concepts relating to race, language, and culture influence official and popular ideas of what a nation is and how its citizenry should behave, speak, worship, dress, or even "look."[9] From this perspective, citizenship in contemporary nation-states has an ethnocultural aspect, making it something more than merely a legal status. In past decades, U.S. society awarded what Renato Rosaldo terms "first-class" citizenship[10] to the offspring of "white" European immigrants—persons who spoke "American" English (and, in public, no other language); were Christian or, latterly, "Judaeo-Christian"; were educated in U.S. schools in which the triumphalist mythos of American continental settlement and frontier expansion was inculcated; and who had largely forgotten or never learned the languages of their European background and their cultural "roots."[11]

Whether in terms of "Anglo-conformity"[12] or "assimilation," assessing the attainment of such cultural citizenship has dominated U.S. immigration studies. Even as there is debate over whether today's non-European immigrants will or will not similarly "assimilate"[13] and speculation about how cultural conceptions of U.S. citizenship are being stretched—for example, by adding Islam, Hinduism, and Buddhism to the Judaeo-Christian formula and by expanding the definition of "white" (see Chapter 8)—the assimilation framework continues to dominate immigration studies.[14]

An alternative and more complicated picture emerges, however, when diverse nonimmigrant groups become part of the analytic terrain.[15] African Americans were forcibly transported to the New World. Their circumstances of arrival and life since are not understandable in terms of immigration and assimilation; nor do their concepts of "home"[16] resonate with those of past European or contemporary transnational immigrants; nor do reflections on the African American experience by black intellectuals[17] bear any resemblance to immigrant narratives. Similarly, American Indians, Mexicans in areas conquered by the United States, Native Hawaiians, and Puerto Ricans were not immigrants, nor is their descendants' popular or political consciousness intelligible in terms of the immigration paradigm.[18] These peoples crossed no border to enter the United States. Of Chicanos, Patricia Zavella writes, "After the U.S.-Mexican war the border literally migrated to them."[19] And Hawaiians, Haunani-Kay Trask emphasizes, "are not transplants from somewhere else, but indigenous to our archipelago. [Following] Western foreigners in 1778 [came] disease, mass death, and land dispossession; cultural destruction including language banning; American military invasion in 1893 and forced annexation in 1898."[20]

Immigration as Ideology

Immigration has several ideological dimensions. Immigrant populations form their own notions of what immigration is all about, as with the

"American fever" that grips some Koreans[21] or the cultural expectation of overseas immigration as part of adulthood in many Caribbean societies.[22] At times, immigration may become a highly charged political issue, and ideological battles over it may be waged via media representations[23] or in local political struggles.[24] But the ideological (and hegemonic) dimension I wish to bring into focus here is immigration's place in "the official version of the national community promulgated by the nation-state."[25]

The U.S. case is particularly telling. As Trask notes, "It is characteristic of American ideology to reiterate that 'we are all immigrants.'"[26] This frankly counterfactual representation of U.S. history—this "master narrative of migration and melting pot"[27]—is echoed occasionally even by immigration researchers themselves. Nancy Foner, Ruben Rumbaut, and Steven Gold, for instance, write unproblematically of the United States as "a nation of immigrants," and Marcelo Suarez-Orozco, in homage to Oscar Handlin, remarks, "The history of the United States is in fundamental aspects the history of immigration."[28]

This narrative has operated over time to impart the European colonizers' mythos of productive entitlement in a "wilderness" and Manifest Destiny on a "frontier" to later-arriving European labor diasporees and their descendants, groups who played no original part in conquering or exploiting the land and non-European peoples. By defining themselves as new entries into a "nation of immigrants," these later arrivals learned to misread history, to "Anglo-conform," and to become eligible for the rewards of first-class citizenship. The unstated message of this U.S. "master narrative" has been marginalization and erasure of the lived experiences of Native, African, Chicano, Hawaiian, and Puerto Rican Americans, as well as of Asian immigrants, who were not permitted to become citizens until 1952.

Beyond a Presentist Perspective

Immigration as analytic concept inescapably foregrounds recent or current movers over other groups that also must be foregrounded to fully understand "the national experience." It was not as immigrant border-crossers that ancestral Native Americans arrived in North and South America, Polynesians in Hawai'i, Africans in the thirteen colonies, or Spaniards in pre-1848 Mexico and in Puerto Rico, where they mixed with Indians and Africans. Modern nations, in fact, all encompass a diverse set of origins and arrivals, facts at odds with nationalist mythos of peoplehood and cultural citizenship and also with the presentist perspective of immigration studies. Taking a global view, Robert Foster cautions that "all definitions of the national essence selectively ignore competing definitions" and thus provoke "struggles over the constitution of an authorized, collectively held past."[29]

Concerned with understanding both the present and an emergent, planetary future, Ulf Hannerz has "retrieved" Alfred Kroeber's vision of the "ancient ecumene" stretching from Gibraltar to China and invited us to envision a contemporary "global ecumene" of even more extensive "interactions, relationships, and networks."[30] As Kroeber put it, "While any national culture may and must for certain purposes be viewed and analyzed by itself, any such culture is necessarily in some degree an artificial unit segregated off for expediency."[31] Although Kroeber's interest was in the ecumene-wide movement of ideas and techniques, anthropologists have also long been interested in the physical movement of people.[32] If we adopt this larger Kroeber-Hannerz space-time canvas, we need to think beyond the current immigration studies perspective of population movements within an embordered world of nation-states and refocus to include "the culture of all humanity at all periods and all places."[33] Several of the forms of population movement that even today continue in the modern world epoch in fact preceded the emergence of nation-states and a globe fully carved up by political borders.

Upon this wider canvas, human migration may be disassembled into a set of seven processes: expansion, refuge seeking, colonization, enforced transportation, trade diaspora, labor diaspora, and emigration.[34] These processes are sequential in historical appearance and cumulative in impact, each earlier process continuing to occur after each later one emerged. We live and do fieldwork in a world formed (and still being formed) by all of these processes and their compounded results. Thus, American Indians arrived in the New World via expansion, as did Polynesians in Hawai'i; Africans in the thirteen colonies by enforced transportation; Spaniards in Mexico and Puerto Rico by colonization. In contrast to the present-day legal categories of state-regulated immigration, a broader anthropological view of human migration may help to improve upon current weakly formulated distinctions of "immigrant and involuntary 'minorities'" or "immigrants and established residents,"[35] as well as to illuminate deeply rooted political sentiments and movements existing in contemporary multiethnic, multiracial, multilingual political fields.

Expansion

"Expansion," a term given resonance in anthropology by Marshall Sahlins,[36] is the process of outward movement at a population's geographical margins, frequently as a consequence of numerical growth, and either maintaining the existing mode of production or adapting it to differing ecological conditions. Expansion is how "anatomically modern human" foragers between about 150,000 and 10,000 BP spread throughout six continents following their appearance and dispersal in Africa and arrival in Palestine (by 90,000 BP), South Asia (70,000 BP), Australia–New Guinea (60,000–40,000 BP), Europe (40,000 BP), Japan (32,000 BP), Central Asia (20,000 BP), North China–Siberia (15,000 BP), and the New World (at least 12,000 BP).[37] For the last major phase of hunter-gatherer expansion—into the Alaskan-Canadian Arctic beginning around 4500 BP—the archaeological, biological, and linguistic evidence is well synthesized by Don Dumond.[38]

One group of paleoanthropologists and geneticists, whom we may term "ramifiers," models this long process of expansion as adaptive radiation, with a continuous spawning outward of new populations.[39] Other anthropologists have stressed intensive, persisting intercultural exchange between expanding and neighboring populations, arguing from ethnographic and linguistic research among recent hunter-gatherers.[40] The viewpoint of this group, which we may call "reticulators," is embraced by contemporary paleoanthropologists, who see local mixing (including with Neanderthals and Denisovans) and exchange as intrinsic to "anatomically modern human" global expansion.[41] A similar division occurs among historical linguists: ramifiers propose diverging, adaptive radiation models[42]; reticulators point to linguistic evidence of intercultural processes traceable in individual languages.[43]

Neolithic food-producing expansions began around ten thousand years ago. For Europe, Luigi Cavalli-Sforza posits a "demic expansion" model,[44] one both criticized and modified but also applied elsewhere.[45] Intercultural cultivator-forager interactions accompanied these food-producer or food production expansions and ranged from hunter-gatherer retreat to asymmetric ties (Pygmy-Bantu villager relations being a well-known case[46]) to amalgamation and absorption. Population expansion along econiche margins also marked the movement of Polynesians into the eastern Pacific islands, as it did the preceding western Pacific movements in which coastal

Lapita settlers encountered inland horticulturalists descended from still earlier population expansions.[47] The Nilotic neolithic and the Bantu iron age expansions in middle and southern Africa involved considerable techno-economic adaptation as populations moved at their margins into varied ecological settings[48]; here Igor Kopytoff and Jan Vansina stress reticulating intercultural relations among the new food-producing settlements, as well as with preexisting foragers.[49]

"Predatory" expansions by stateless agricultural and pastoral populations into lands of others on their margins was the topic of Sahlins's 1961 paper on Nuer and Tiv lineage organization. (This raises the topic of refuge seeking by the vanquished, to which we turn momentarily.) Peaceful, or largely peaceful, expansions as a form of migration, however, also continued after the emergence of states. (I exclude annual transhumance or nomad-sedentary population exchanges as processes of migration, although such groups may also expand these ecological adaptations at their geographical margins.[50]) Ethnographic cases include pastoral Fulani "migratory drift" across the sub-Saharan savannah from the Atlantic to the Nile, both within and beyond state-organized areas; expansion of Ewe fishermen westward from Ghana along the African coast to Gambia and southward to Angola; interpenetration by Hakka cultivators of poorer, hilly areas among southern Chinese villages occupying more productive paddy lands; and "peaceable encroachments" by farmers into Ecuador's eastern Andean slope and Pacific coast plain.[51]

Refuge Seeking

The Fulani concept *perol* refers "to flight from intolerable conditions of a political or ideological nature."[52] Such refuge seeking to preserve life and livelihood emerged as a process of human migration when neolithic horticulturalists began to displace foragers and to fight over land. It no doubt occurred behind the expanding margin of cultivation in European and other "demic expansions" and perhaps took forms comparable to those described by Mervyn Meggitt for Mae Enga intersettlement warfare in highland New Guinea. In areas of Africa where larger-scale political units, which Aidan Southall termed "segmentary states," existed, bigger numbers of people traveled greater distances, seeking refuge in the wake of interpolity conflict, a situation meticulously documented for the Tswana by Isaac Schapera and treated more broadly by Kopytoff.[53]

With military conquests by ancient and pre-modern states, colonization of newly subjected lands by the victors involved either keeping the losers in place to tax and exploit or enforced transportation of them elsewhere. Some refuge seekers, however, escaped both of these outcomes by fleeing beyond the new regimes' reaches. Refuge seeking became prevalent in locales of state-directed slave raiding, with many so-called "acephalous" peoples in West Africa, for example, owing their settlement location and pattern, or even their ethnogenesis, to refuge seeking migrations to safer ground.[54] At the other end of the trans-Atlantic system, refuge seeking by enslaved individuals and groups resulted in maroon settlements in the United States, Brazil, Surinam, and elsewhere.[55]

Refuge-seeking migrations occurred during several episodes in Jewish history, as well as among other persecuted religious populations within premodern and contemporary states—the Sudanese Copts under Islamist military rule are a contemporary instance.[56] In the eleventh and twelfth centuries, Jews were expelled from France and England and moved eastward in Europe, many eventually to Poland. Later, fleeing the Inquisition in 1492, more than a hundred thousand left Spain and became the Ladino-speaking Sephardim of Holland, Italy, the Balkans, North Africa, and the Middle East. Still later, Russian pogroms (beginning in 1881) and the threat of twenty-five-year military conscription caused millions of Jews again to seek refuge, this time mainly in the United States.[57]

Flights from "intolerable conditions of a political or ideological nature" have accelerated since World War II.[58] Ethnographic studies include those by Sarah Mahler, of Salvadorans on Long Island, New York; Stepick and Nina Glick Schiller, of Haitians in New York and Miami; and Holtzman and Rogaia Abusharaf, of southern and northern Sudanese in neighboring African countries and North America.[59] Anthropologist Shahram Khosravi, himself an "illegal" border crosser from Iran, describes the day-to-day lives of contemporary refuge seekers.[60] In 2011, the world contained some 42.4 million "forcibly displaced" persons, according to the United Nations High Commissioner for Refugees, including 26 million seeking refuge within their own country and 12 million who were "stateless"; the largest refugee populations were from Afghanistan, Iraq, Somalia, Sudan, and Congo.[61]

Colonization

Expanding states that occupy and rule the territory of conquered peoples—Babylon, Rome, Imperial China, Tahuantinsuyu, Spain, Asante, Hawai'i, the United States—also impose upon their acquired lands new uses and administrative policies that involve the migration of numbers of their core population, movements we can term "colonization." Although the word "diaspora" was first used by the ancient Greeks to refer to their overseas military conquests and migrations,[62] its major association more recently has been with peaceful or coerced movements that follow historically in the wake of colonizations. For these reasons, I would subtract the European "imperial diaspora" cases from Robin Cohen's diaspora roster and refer to the administrators of "an empire comprising a quarter of the planet" not as a British "diaspora" but rather as a migration of colonizers.[63]

Colonizer migrations in their initial phase often involve small numbers of state-directed traders and other advance personnel, as in the gradual incorporations of northeast Asia by Russia, Canada's First Nations by France and England, and Ainu-occupied Hokkaido by Japan.[64] (Earlier Japanese-Emishi and -Ainu encounters to the south are perhaps better understood as agricultural expansion with absorption of farmers and hunter-gatherers on the margin.) Mature colonizations deploy combinations of military, officials, and settlers, as in Roman Britain, provincial Asante, Kamehameha's Hawai'i, English-occupied Ireland, Dutch South Africa, and Ch'ing-era Taiwan.[65] Colonization may also beget more remote colonization, as with the expansion of West African slave-dealing states in the context of European coastal trading operations or the nineteenth-century *Mfecane* conquest states formed by Nguni colonizers who migrated northward throughout south central Africa.[66]

The westward colonizing migration by United States settlers involved displacement of Native Americans, payments for land and its unconsulted inhabitants by one colonizer power to another (to France for the "Louisiana Purchase" and to Spain for Florida), annexations of Texas and Hawai'i at the request of numerical minorities of white settlers, and warfare against Mexicans. Coercive colonization does not end with formal conquest; Martin Leggasick shows how over decades, whites using both legal and extra-legal means have relentlessly appropriated new parcels of land from descendants of indigenous South Africans.[67]

Enforced Transportation

For reasons either political or economic, states and their agents may move people, almost always against their will, from one location to another. An early example is the sixth-century-BC removal of Jews from Judah to Babylon by Nebuchadnezzar. The Inca elites of Tahuantinsuyu moved populations and consolidated people in towns as part of their imperial design; "recalcitrant elements" in newly conquered areas were removed to core or longer-settled provinces, and *mitimaes* from these areas were resettled in the new domains, with all subjects wearing distinctive headdress to mark their origin. A similar policy of enforced population movement was practiced by the Asante state.[68]

Ireland's seventeenth-century population and economy were completely reorganized within five decades by colonizing power England. In 1605, James I declared dominion over Ulster, soon divided into its present six counties. The native population was scattered to reserves amounting to one-fifth of the land area and ruled over by newly arrived English nobles. British and lowland Scot farmers were imported to work the land, with the native Irish becoming a reserve labor supply. In 1651, Cromwell's Protestants seized power in England and then invaded the rest of Catholic Ireland. One quarter of the Irish population died, and eighty thousand were transported as slaves to join West Africans and New England Indians on Caribbean plantations. In 1653, the remaining Irish population was ordered to move from the eastern and southern plains to the hilly west or face death. Ireland's new large plains estates then became suppliers of wheat and cattle to England, with Irish labor permitted to reside only where needed.[69]

The human migration largest in number and longest in duration in world history was the enforced transportation of more than 10 million landed Africans to the "New World" created by European colonizations.[70] A few firsthand accounts by Africans who had themselves been enslaved and transported bring alive the violent, disruptive reality experienced by millions more.[71] For those who survived and became coerced and uncompensated laborers in colonizer regimes, further episodes of enforced transportation of one's self, kin, and friends were an ever-present threat. The enslaved black population of New York City in the 1740s, for example, included persons who had arrived directly from Africa, as well as others transshipped from Curaçao, Jamaica, Antigua, and St. John and "Spanish Negroes" or "Cuba men" who had been free sailors captured by privateers and then sold. Following their dubious conviction of conspiracy to revolt in 1741, seventy enslaved black New Yorkers were in turn transported to the "Spanish W. Indies, Madeira, Hispaniola, Cape Francois, St. Thomas, Surinam, Portugal, Curacoa, Statia, [and] Newfoundland."[72]

Enforced transportation of Native Americans began with the first reservations: Mashpee on Cape Cod in 1660, Poosepatuck on Long Island in 1666, Pequot in Connecticut in 1683. In 1830, an Indian Removal Act passed by Congress gave the U.S. president power to transfer eastern groups to trans-Mississippi western lands; this followed discovery of gold on Cherokee land in Georgia two years earlier and resulted first in concentrating seventeen thousand Cherokee in stockades and then, in 1838, forcing them west to Oklahoma along a "Trail of Tears" on which half of them died. Concentration of the Dakota Sioux on a reserve by whites in 1868 proved too generous after gold was discovered in the Black Hills; in 1876, a new treaty creating a smaller reservation—minus the Black Hills—was imposed. Even more land was lost by 1889, one year before the massacre at Wounded Knee.[73]

Migrations by enforced transportation during World War II included the removal to concentration camps of 120,000 Japanese Americans, two-thirds of them citizens; personal accounts convey the disempowering uncertainty of not knowing what the outcome might be.[74] In Europe, six million Jews, Roma, and others were transported to Nazi death camps from Germany, Holland, France, Italy, Croatia, Hungary, Greece, Bulgaria, Romania, Poland, and the German-occupied USSR.[75] More enforced transportations (and no doubt some willing movements) accompanied the partition of India and Pakistan in 1947 and the "ethnic cleansings" in the former Yugoslavia during the 1990s.

Diaspora

Recently the term "diaspora" has "grown in popularity and come into expanding use."[76] Chaliand and Rageau's *Penguin Atlas of Diasporas* (1995) discusses Jewish, Armenian, Gypsy, black, Chinese, Indian, Irish, Greek, Lebanese, Palestinian, Vietnamese, Korean, Assyro-Chaldean, Cape Verdean, and Japanese diasporas. Cohen's *Global Diasporas: An Introduction* (1997) adds African, Italian, Phoenician, Sikh, Caribbean, and post-USSR Russian cases; Spanish, Portuguese, Dutch, German, French, and British "imperial diasporas"; and cites another scholar's Cuban, Mexican, Pakistani, Maghrebi, Turk, and Polish instances. Hausa, Sierra Leone Creole, Dominican, and Puerto Rican "diasporas" have also been identified.[77] Self-designated Haitian diasporees give the term their own particular twist.[78]

The Cavalli-Sforzas even titled their overview of prehistoric hunter-gatherer and neolithic expansions *The Great Human Diasporas* (1995). So who is not a diasporee now?

Some uses of "diaspora," as Hannerz notes, are simply "metaphorical."[79] Others perhaps are merely euphonious. But Chaliand and Rageau and Cohen attempt to identify common elements and define types in formulating their diaspora rosters. A problem, however, is that they begin with three distinct ethno-diasporas—sets of population movements consciously understood and referred to as "diasporas" by their subjects: the Jewish Diaspora, the African Diaspora, and the Armenian Diaspora. Then, as social-science–minded diasporologists, they compare them with numerous other cases in order to isolate key variables. At the opposite extreme, James Clifford restricts his considerations of the diaspora concept to representations of the African and Jewish cases.[80] I take a different approach, consistent with a more wide-ranging view of human migration. I propose that the Jewish, African, and Armenian (emic) ethno-diasporas might also be understood analytically—as historical amalgams of (etic) enforced transportation, refuge seeking, trade and labor diasporas as I am about to define them, and emigration.

The process of diaspora, as I will use the term, thus occurs when people voluntarily leave their home area for distant regions within or beyond the state in which they reside and continue to remain in contact in various ways with their place of origin. ("Almost always [such] migration is followed by a counter stream moving back to the migrants' place of origin."[81])

Unlike expansions, diasporas are spatially discontinuous, with distances and other peoples separating their component population clusters. And unlike refuge seeking, diaspora involves continuing and relatively unimpeded ties to points of origin. Unlike colonization, moreover, diaspora involves no dominion over or dispossession and enforced transportation of others, although diasporas often do follow in the wake of other peoples' colonizations. And unlike don't-look-back emigration, diaspora includes occasional, frequent, or long-postponed returns home.

Bear in mind that diaspora henceforth in this chapter is considered as one of several processes of human migration, not a self-characterization by ethnocultural groups that constitute their complex migration histories as "diasporas" and that more such groups are likely to do in the future. Trade or labor diasporas as defined here may mark a phase in a particular group's history, with other migration processes preceding or following them.

Trade Diasporas

The earliest diasporas were trade diasporas, and their nature and history is superbly synthesized by Philip Curtin.[82] In his view, they first appeared following the earliest cities some five thousand years ago and comprised networks of trading specialists who physically left their home communities and learned the language and commercial culture of their foreign hosts. They included "movers" (such as caravan leaders), who traveled, as well as "stayers" (such as brokers and lodging providers), who lived abroad, often in their own "stranger" quarters.[83]

Historic trade diasporas considered by Curtin include the Phoenicians operating in the Greek Mediterranean by 800 BC and, later, farther out; Greek-speaking Romans who ranged beyond the empire to Aden, Oman, and India; Chinese trading by land to Afghanistan and Iran and by sea as far as Indonesia and East Africa; south Indians reaching peak influence in mainland and island Southeast Asia by 400–500 AD[84]; Muslim Arabs traveling beyond *dar al Islam* in Europe, West Africa, Malaysia, and China; Gujarati Indians throughout the Indian Ocean after 1400 AD; medieval Italians; Aztec *pochteca*; seventeenth-century Armenians; and others.

Periods of "voluntaristic"[85] diaspora in Jewish history occurred in between episodes of enforced transportation and refuge seeking.[86] After Cyrus of Persia conquered Babylon, Jews were permitted to return to Judah, but some also dispersed to Egypt, Syria, and Turkey; still others stayed in Babylon, and all these communities remained linked through Hellenic and Roman times. In Christian Europe before the Jewish massacres of the First Crusade in 1096, "Jews were free individuals on the whole"[87] and lived in religiously intermixed locations. Unlike Christians, however, these medieval Jews were permitted to trade, an activity their diasporic connections facilitated. And though as second-class subjects, but still People of the Book rather than pagans, Jews through Ottoman times dispersed relatively peacefully and widely throughout the Arabic-speaking Muslim Mediterranean world.

A number of West African trade diasporas have been well studied. These include the Mande-speaking Wangara (or Dyula, or Juula) diaspora, beginning in the western Sudan, and the Hausa-Kanuri-Tuareg diaspora of the central Sudan, both of which extended into forest and coastal zones.[88] In southeastern Nigeria, the Aro diaspora of oracle agents and armed trading settlements extended beyond the Arochukwu homeland among both fellow

Igbo and other language speakers, a case in which the analytic categories of diaspora and colonization are both relevant.[89] A Sierra Leone Krio (or Creole) trade diaspora, including the development of a Krio-dominated multiethnic settlement on Fernando Po, flourished along the West African coast in the nineteenth century before European traders economically squeezed it out.[90]

Subject to Asante until its defeat by the British in 1874, residents from the Kwawu (or Kwahu) "traditional area" then commenced their diaspora within the Gold Coast colony and elsewhere in West Africa. Individual Kwawus entered the rubber and cocoa trades and sold imported goods inland. By World War I, they had established credit accounts with European firms and were using both railroad lines and trucks to transport goods. Clusters of Kwawus appeared in many towns, including Ghana's capital, Accra, where by 1960 they numbered eleven thousand.[91]

Kwawus accounted for one quarter of the 423 residents of the multiethnic street in Accra I studied in the early 1970s. Nearly half of them were members of a single kin group headed by a successful businessman-landlord. Born in 1912, at age seventeen he went to work in an Akim town for an uncle who owned a shop selling alcoholic beverages and other items. At age twenty-seven, he moved to an Ewe town, dealing in automotive spare parts on his own, and when he was thirty-three to Accra, first trading in cloth and three years later beginning to import a variety of goods from overseas. By age fifty-eight, he owned two stores and two residential buildings in Accra, a cinema in a large Kwawu town, and a spacious home in Obomeng, his hometown. Four years earlier, he had been elected "headman" by fellow Obomeng businessmen in Accra and was confirmed by the Obomenghene, the hometown chief. He traveled frequently to Obomeng (a trip of many hours), sometimes two or more weekends a month and always for the large Easter gathering, when most Kwawus returned to their hometowns.

Labor Diasporas

With the rise of industrial capitalism and its demand for proletarianized wage labor, longstanding intrasociety rural-to-urban movements—usually as household economy expansions[92]—intensified, and large-scale interregional and international labor diasporas and emigrations began.[93] "Pushes" were real, via enclosures and reserves, the negative consequences of absent labor power,[94] landlord exploitation, and the impact of commercial agricultural and land markets undermining rural viability. "Pulls" to the locations where wage work was available were also real. Who went where involved economic considerations (travel costs, wage levels), the availability of kin or friendship ties to assist in finding housing and employment, and the specific immigration policies of nation-states and colonial governments.

The first well-described labor diaspora was that of the Roman Catholic Irish. Frederick Engels found them in Manchester in 1844 and estimated that one million were already at work in the new English industrial towns, with fifty thousand more arriving each year, their numbers bidding down the wages of English workers.[95] The Irish went also to the United States, some 4.5 million between 1840 and 1920,[96] and to Australia. Relatives of my maternal grandmother, who arrived in New York from County Wexford in 1904, resided in all three countries; moreover, she and my maternal grandfather from County Mayo traveled back to Ireland several times and sent money for younger family members to immigrate. In County Clare in the early 1930s, Conrad Arensberg noted "a marked tendency for emigration from a local region to perpetuate itself. One little settlement called Cross is said locally to be supported by the Shanghai police force. The first man to go is now Chief of Police in the International Settlement there, and many places in the Force have gone to men of Cross."[97]

A slightly later labor diaspora (along with many individual instances of refuge seeking) brought millions of mainly rural and poor African Americans from south to north between 1890 and 1960.[98] In 1897, W. E. B. Du Bois studied an early phase of this movement, documenting relations between southern migrant and northern-born black Philadelphians, as well as their interaction with whites.[99] Labor diasporas from several countries in Europe during the nineteenth and early twentieth centuries included as destinations the United States,[100] Brazil, and Argentina; fieldwork in the 1910s and 1920s among Poles, Sicilians, and other immigrant groups was conducted by several University of Chicago sociologists in their home city.[101] Another labor diaspora to the United States, following Mexico's revolution and peaking in the 1920s, was studied by Manuel Gamio.[102]

At about the same time and for similar reasons, labor diasporas in south and central Africa brought rural migrants to wage employment in white colonizer cities, farms, and mines. In the early 1930s, Monica Hunter studied one such group, the South African Mpondo, on their "reserve," on white farms where half the male population worked, and in the towns of East London and Grahamstown. (This was no obscure precursor of "multi-sited ethnography."[103] Hunter, later Monica Wilson, was a student of Malinowski, and her book, *Reaction to Conquest*, was published in the canonical International African Institute series. I read it while a graduate student in the late 1960s and absorbed her conception of problem and method as part of my ethnographic training.)

In the 1950s, a cohort of anthropologists began to document the global Indian labor diaspora, which between the 1830s and 1920s brought 1.3 million indentured and additional self-financed migrants to British, French, and Dutch colonial territories in the Indian and Caribbean oceans, Africa, and Fiji and to colonizer nations Canada and the United States.[104] In the 1950s in England and 1960s in the United States, a second Indian labor diaspora of prospective factory workers, professionals, and eventually a wide range of arrivals began.[105] In both places, the newer immigrants encountered descendants of the first diaspora, including East African Indian "twice migrants."[106] Today, the constantly reticulating global Indian labor and trade diaspora involves complex cultural and economic interaction between numerous overseas clusters and their homeland.[107]

A second cohort of anthropologists in the 1950s (preceded in the 1930s by University of Chicago sociologist Paul Siu) turned to the southern Chinese labor/trading diaspora first historically discernible in Manila in the early 1500s. At its peak between 1842 and 1900, some four hundred thousand Chinese traveled to the United States and British white colonizer dominions, mainly as contract laborers; four hundred thousand more went to the Caribbean and Latin America; and 1.5 million went to Southeast Asia.[108] Anthropologists have also studied the Chinese of Calcutta, who date to the 1770s and some of whom have now "twice migrated" to Toronto. Recent working- and middle-class migrants and investors from Hong Kong, Taiwan, and mainland China now residing in Great Britain, Europe, and the United States have been studied as well.[109]

In 1965, anthropologist Robert Manners presciently called attention to the economic importance of labor diasporee remittances for Caribbean islands, Southern Europe, and Mexico. He anticipated that fieldworkers would soon be moving beyond localized "community studies" to research in wider regional and overseas "social fields."[110] A dozen years later, a volume that exemplified Manners's prediction offered essays by anthropologists with "field experience at *both* ends of the migration chain."[111] In it,

Stuart Philpott analyzed the social mechanisms that tied together Montserratians in Britain and in their Caribbean home island. Robin Palmer described a labor "diaspora," beginning in the nineteenth century, from one north Italian town to Britain.[112] Many of these migrants worked in the London food industry while they maintained communication with their stay-at-home *paesani*, supported residential investment and community construction projects in their home village, and were a political force in their wider Italian region of origin. Other pioneer fieldwork in this vein included Raymond Wiest's analysis of labor diasporees' remittances in a Mexican village and Robert Rhoades's cautions about pressures on home community investment in relation to changing employment opportunities in destination countries. More recently, Linda Basch and Nina Glick Schiller have documented transnationally coordinated Grenadian, Vincentian, and Haitian familial, organizational, and political strategies.[113]

In my 1970s Ghana fieldwork, I studied a hometown association of Ewe migrants from the Volta Region town of Dzodze living in Accra (see Chapter 7). Unlike the Kwawu traders, most Ewes had migrated from their relatively poor region to other parts of Ghana as cocoa laborers and then small-scale farmers or as wage-labor workers in government or private firms. Dzodze people also returned to their hometown for visits and Easter reunions (the distance from Accra to both Dodze and Kwawu was similar) and built or added to homes there as they could afford. Association members desired to improve the physical and educational amenities of their hometown, because they expected to retire to Dzodze, wanted the option of sending children to schools there, and wished to impress friends who accompanied them on visits. Accordingly, they attempted to mobilize Dzodze's traditional chiefs and influential funeral association heads and lobbied government and political party figures in their efforts to secure development projects.

Some recent research on "transnationalism"[114] describes activities and fieldwork approaches that resonate with Philpott, Palmer, and my Accra research—diasporees sending and bringing gifts home, providing lodging and job leads for newly arrived kin and friends, attending festivals and influencing politics in their home community, and researchers interviewing people about links between diaspora and home community households, as well as observing diasporee association meetings. Although from the actors' points of view, all these cases equally concern "reconceived deterritorialized units,"[115] the legal nexus of "transnationalism" does make a difference.

When the Ghana Business Protection Order was issued in 1970, it was Lebanese diasporee businessmen who were expelled and Kwawus and other Ghanaians who moved into the commercial niches they occupied.

Emigration

The last process, emigration, or the don't-look-back exit for a new existence elsewhere,[116] perhaps has a distant origin in moves by persons who committed real or suspected interpersonal, kinship, or ritual offences and departed to begin life as strangers in a new setting.[117] But as a form of human migration characterizing sizable groups of people, emigration is the historical converse and complement of diaspora. The difference sometimes is one of intention, and intentions may be unclear or change and are difficult to study definitively. Within any diaspora, certainly, there are both some persons determined from the start to emigrate and others who wind up doing so after severing or losing personal connection to their home community.

There are, nonetheless, some unambiguous historical emigrations. From the start, the late nineteenth-century migrations of Andalusian agricultural laborers from Spain to Hawaii and then from Hawaii to California were don't-look-back movements to what were anticipated to be better circumstances.[118] Other emigrations have been undertaken by liberated enforced transportees to areas they considered true, near, or substitute homelands. Thus, neither the black British, Afro–Nova Scotians, and African Americans who traveled in the late eighteenth and early nineteenth centuries to Sierra Leone and Liberia nor Brazilian exslaves who returned to various points in West Africa remained tied to the colonial "New World" they were exiting.[119] Emigration also describes the movement of 67,000 Jews who left Western Europe for Israel between 1945 and 1970.[120] The more numerous contemporaneous departures of Jews from Arab countries for Israel may perhaps more appropriately be seen as refuge seeking.[121]

Conclusion

In his essay "The Withering Away of the Nation?" Hannerz quotes Salman Rushdie's celebration of "intermingling"—"the transformation that comes out of new and unexpected combinations of human beings, cultures, ideas, politics, movies, songs. It is the great possibility that mass migration gives the world."[122] This echos Appadurai's point, with which this chapter opened—that the present is marked by "a general rupture in the tenor of intersocietal relations" attributable to the impact of mass media and global immigration.

My argument is that a third moving element is also present: the ground, or sometimes underground (due to oppressive and ideological concepts of cultural citizenship) over which current immigrations flow. The "ethnoscapes"[123] into which immigrants arrive in contemporary nation-states are not homogeneous and rock solid. They are fully interpretable only in terms of the complex political juxtapositions and inequalities that past expansions, refuge seekings, colonizations, enforced transportations, diasporas, and emigrations have produced.

The reticulationst perspective that Hannerz has done much to advance in interpreting current global flows,[124] and that Rushdie celebrates, needs also to be directed deep down into national and ethnocultural histories if mutual perceptions and dynamics in the present are to be fully understood. Immigration studies, in contrast, foreground a ramifying viewpoint of divergence, cultural singularities, and recent, on-the-surface arrivals. We do need to study today's immigrant movers, but we also must pay heed to where and among whom they are arriving.

PART IV

Ethnography and Society

Chapter 10

Politics, Theory, and the Nature of Cultural Things

Since anthropology's "postmodern turn" in the 1980s, we have understood that ethnography is autobiographical.[1] In the sense that writing ethnography depends upon recalling and recounting one's presence in fieldwork events, with the help of fieldnotes and records, this is certainly true. Yet this is a relatively trivial point, I believe, compared to the substantive and theoretical purposes of doing ethnography. This autobiographical truism becomes objectionable when used to justify making the author the major personage in memoirs that are presented as ethnography.[2]

A more far-reaching argument I wish to advance is that anthropological theory is also autobiographical—even more significantly so than ethnography—and for both its producers and consumers.[3] I was a student in the Department of Anthropology at Columbia University in the 1960s, and my first fieldwork in Brazil in 1965[4] was supervised by Marvin Harris, later my graduate advisor. The times we lived in molded the body of work Harris produced in the 1950s and 1960s, including *The Nature of Cultural Things* (1964), the text I consider here. The times also molded my reading and my application of what I read. If I offer some "glimpses of the unmentionable" from the Morningside Heights of the 1960s,[5] it is to historicize in part a major transition in anthropology, to sketch in some of its political context, and to affirm the lived (autobiographical) component of anthropology's theoretical developments. In so doing, I ask readers to accept Judith Okely's point: "Any autobiography by the anthropologist, while emerging from a unique and personal experience, evokes resonances of recognition from others. There are solidarities as well as contrasts to be examined, and systematized for the enrichment of the discipline. The autobiography is not a linear progress of the lone individual outside history, let alone outside cultures and the practice of anthropology."[6]

Anthropology through the 1960s

Anthropology's 1960s transition[7] was marked by the passing of the tribe, the eclipse of the community study, and the move beyond the village.[8] During that decade, anthropology lost much of its political immaturity and faced anew the Third World[9] and also life at home.[10] It is not my argument that similar lights had never flashed in the discipline before the 1960s. They indeed had.[11] Anthropology at Columbia, moreover, had long had leftward connections beyond the classroom. Discussion and activism during the 1930s, particularly concerning anti-Nazism and antiracism,[12] had left an intellectual legacy to which Harris and I were heirs, and to which I had direct exposure in a class with Alexander Lesser, a Franz Boas student and faculty member during the 1920s and 1930s. The socialist and Marxist interests of Columbia students in the late 1940s to the early 1950s,[13] particularly in the nature of the state, were also an influence on Harris's work and my reading of it. They included Sidney Mintz, Eric Wolf, Robert Manners, Marshall Sahlins, Eleanor Leacock, Sally Falk Moore, and Anthony Leeds, all of whom I read in the 1960s, and Morton Fried, Robert Murphy, and Stanley Diamond, whom I both read and heard in classes.

If the icy blast of the 1939 Hitler-Stalin pact and the chill wind of the 1950s McCarthy era cooled open expression of these tendencies in academic anthropology during intervening years, things had changed by the mid-1960s. The Civil Rights Movement and opposition to the war in Indochina and, more broadly, to U.S. intervention and imperialism in the Third World were the backdrop to what was happening then on the Columbia campus. While an anthropology student, I met SDSers, NCLCers, ISers, RCPers, Maoists, Weathermen, PLs, and MLs, as well as PhDs. Learning not only the initials but also the political positions, leading members, and roles in campus politics of this variety of leftist groups was part of student life in the 1960s. (SDS = Students for a Democratic Society; NCLC = National Caucus of Labor Committees, the Lyndon LaRouche, then known as Lyn Marcus, group; IS = International Socialists, a Trotskyite group; RCP = Revolutionary Communist Party, the renamed RU, or Revolutionary Union, followers of Bob Avakian; Maoists included RCPers, some

NCLCers, members of still other groups, and individual activists; Weathermen were an adventurist successor group of former SDSers; PL = Progressive Labor; ML = Marxist-Leninist, an epithet used for Communist Party, or CP, members by Maoist antagonists.)

I admired the SDS platform (and also the Black Panther Party's ten-point program), and I marched and demonstrated but never became a member of SDS or any other political group. This was partly a cultural choice. I was captivated by the music and style of rhythm and blues and jazz musicians Sam Cooke, Jackie Wilson, King Curtis, Eric Dolphy, Miles Davis, and Jackie McLean. Not a "red-diaper baby" (a child of left-wing parents) myself, I was not attracted to the movement culture of folk music, flannel shirts, and work shoes. I was also increasingly committed, intellectually and emotionally, to the anthropology I was learning at Columbia in undergraduate and graduate classes from 1963 to 1969. I found in Harris's writings of the 1950s and early 1960s a means of understanding race at home and in the world and colonialism and inequality in Latin America, Asia, and Africa.

During the 1960s, individual student discoveries of current and earlier anthropological political engagements occurred within a shifting disciplinary context. The profession as a whole changed, and ideas of former mavericks or seers became common stock. Poverty, colonialism and neocolonialism, inequality, and rural dislocation became standard anthropological topics, ones that could no longer be avoided by the 1970s. By the 1980s, many anthropologists embraced world-system perspectives as articulated by Andre Gunder Frank, Immanuel Wallerstein, and Wolf.[14]

This 1960s transition did not occur smoothly. We can glimpse one autobiographical experience of it in P. H. Gulliver's thoughtful 1985 reconsideration of his role as Tanganyika (Tanzania) government anthropologist during the 1950s. "Social anthropology developed in the era of metropolitan colonialism [and] anthropologists failed in their local-level research to take account of the dependency of local societies and cultures on the wider, embracing political economy." He did not assert that a logical unfolding brought the profession to this realization. Rather, he pointed to critics of anthropological practice, namely Talal Asad, Gerald Berreman, and Kathleen Gough. The latter two wrote openly about the Vietnam War, American counterinsurgency research, and the desirability of bringing into academic discourse the thinking of socialist and activist writers Paul Baran, Paul Sweezy, Frank, Franz Fanon, Kwame Nkrumah, and others. "I agree in general with those kinds of critical accusations," Gulliver wrote. (The Asad volume was more historical in focus and forecast the anthropological romance with French Marxism that blossomed during the 1970s.)[15]

Gulliver's arrival at this position, like that of others, occurred in the midst of serious disruptions in anthropology. Gough and her husband David Aberle left the United States for Canada because neither wished to be arbiters of their male students' draftability, a role in which teaching at an American university inescapably cast them. Fierce debates about ethics and the conduct of overseas research were divisive as well.[16] As Wolf recalled in an interview in 1987, "I think that what the Vietnam experience—and subsequently other kinds of events—demonstrated to everyone was that there was a connection between culture and power. I came into anthropology [in the 1940s] when it was still innocent and pristine, and by the late 70s we were aware that difficulties, complexities, and guilt had accumulated. For myself, lots of old friends no longer talk to me, and it has happened not only to me, but to others."[17]

During the 1960s and 1970s, a wide range of Marxist and progressive writings was openly discussed in anthropology. For some, like me, these concepts were filtered via anthropologists and the socialist thinkers mentioned by Berreman and Gough. Others joined Marxist study groups. Beyond the still impressive *Communist Manifesto* and Engels's *Origin of the Family* and *Condition of the Working Class in England*, I cannot claim systematic exposure to the Marxist canon. Continuing activism in the 1970s and later regarding health care, housing, peace, and equity for women in anthropology,[18] as much as continuing reading in and beyond anthropology (but mainly in), occupied me, and I am more a "visceral" or "gut" progressive than a "cerebral" Marxist, as Raymond Firth once put it.[19] Yet this has always seemed to me a skewed choice of adjectives. For "gut" versus "cerebral," why not "engaged" versus "contemplative" or "involved" versus "aloof" or "activist" versus "textualist" or "participant" versus "observer"?

Whatever the adjectives, anthropological struggle and disruption in the 1960s amounted to more than a chronicle of good ideas chasing out bad ones, and I find William Roseberry's history of the rise of anthropological political economy during the 1970s and 1980s incomplete in this regard (as well as deficient in omitting Leacock's 1969 study of institutionalized racism in New York City schools from his appraisal of her work).[20] Entering anthropology when I did, I experienced more a 1960s paradigm rift than

Roseberry's paradigm shift of the 1970s. That experience also predisposes me to view historical transitions more as the result of disruptive human action than intellectual unfolding or logical arrival.

Which brings me to *The Nature of Cultural Things*, a book about human action written in the early 1960s. This is Marvin Harris's most dissonant book, quite unlike his later widely read popular volumes.[21] It cannot be understood apart from his 1950s fieldwork in Brazil and Mozambique, and it underpins what followed in his influential *Rise of Anthropological Theory* in 1968 and later work through the 1990s.

Who Wrote the Book?

Marvin Harris's first fieldwork was in a community in Bahia, Brazil, in 1950–1951. His first publication, "Race Relations in Minhas Velhas," appeared one year later in *Race and Class in Rural Brazil*, a volume edited by his Columbia mentor Charles Wagley.[22] Here, in the context of a rich ethnographic report, he announced themes that would occupy him for years to come: contradiction between cultural expression and actual behavior, the different ways Brazilian and U.S. cultures label individuals of mixed African and European ancestry, the organization and consequences of social inequality.[23] Harris rooted current race relations in history, tracing the arrival of whites and blacks in Minhas Velhas. And he predicted racial tension in Brazil would increase as the darker middle strata grew in number and urban concentration. His later studies in Brazil demonstrated the absence of "a descent rule" for racial identity (as existed in the United States) and probed the cognitive organization of the large vocabulary of racial terms.[24]

A 1958 comparative study cowritten with Wagley, *Minorities in the New World*, included a historical overview of African Americans in the United States.[25] It traced the persisting "American dilemma" between democratic ideals and racial discrimination through the 1954 Supreme Court school desegregation decision and slow pace of implementation. In Harris's *Patterns of Race in the Americas* (1964), he tied contrasting regimes of North American, Brazilian, and highland Latin American race relations to the labor requirements of differing historical forms of agricultural and industrial production.[26] This succinct 99-page volume originated in a network television lecture and indicated Harris's emerging commitment to bringing his ideas to publics beyond professional anthropology.

His 1956–1957 field research in Mozambique had also pushed him in this direction. In 1958, against academic advice that it might close Portuguese Africa to him and other American researchers, he published *Portugal's African "Wards,"* a 36-page report issued by the American Committee on Africa, a nongovernmental organization dedicated to African self-determination. In clear, direct prose, Harris described the lack of Portuguese citizenship rights for Mozambique's majority, the "unmitigated exploitation" of the illegal *shibalo* forced-labor system, the decisive role Mozambique migrant labor played in the profitability of South African gold mines, and the history of South Africa–Portugal labor and shipping agreements that structured the regional economy. As in Brazil and the United States, the "contradiction between value-system and behavior" was for Harris "the crux of the matter. Little in the way of real understanding of these matters is to be derived from the invocation of a nation's 'traditions,' 'soul,' or 'national character.' Racism is a phenomenon which is produced in relation to fairly well-defined circumstances of a socio-economic nature."[27]

Portugal's African "Wards" was written "to discharge what I conceive to be a moral obligation. Under these circumstances, I cannot confine my writing to such 'neutral' or purely technical subjects as would lead to no involvement in politically controversial issues."[28] Still, Harris also published a paper on his Mozambique research in the scholarly journal *Africa*, there detailing the relationship between labor migration to South Africa and the internal structure of Thonga patrilineages at home.[29] A 1966 paper updated the political chronicle, including the emergence of FRELIMO, the Mozambique liberation movement headed by Eduardo Mondlane, who, I learned, was a friend of Harris and was later assassinated in 1969.[30]

In the early 1960s, Harris added the ecology of rural poverty to his focus on race and colonialism. His study of India's agrarian regime attacked analyses of the Hindu taboo on cow slaughter that identified "irrational" rather than "economic, and mundane" causes for its persistence.[31] Harris argued that milk production, admittedly below European and U.S. levels, was only one aspect of cattle utilization in India. Others included fuel provision (use of cow dung for cooking) and traction, for both of which there were fewer cattle than the vast population required. In addition, non-Hindu and Harijan (or "untouchable") groups consumed what beef became available, and India's large leather industry was an important component of its national economy. Harris also described the political economy of cow ownership and access to plough teams in a country where 10 percent of the population owned 50 percent of the land and 22 percent owned no land at all. He challenged American press reports that the cattle population competed with the human population for food, and cautioned that Western market rationality applied to Indian realities would result in greater, not less, mass immiseration.

In 1967, Harris published a version of the cow paper in *Natural History*, the American Museum of Natural History magazine for a popular audience.[32] This now became a venue for many Harris articles, as well as for an American Anthropological Association symposium on "War: The Anthropology of Armed Conflict and Aggression," organized by Columbia professors Morton Fried, Harris, and Robert Murphy. The symposium resulted from the 1966 AAA national meeting, during which a large group of AAA Fellows opposed to the Vietnam war sponsored a resolution protesting inhumane U.S. actions and urging rapid peaceful settlement.[33] They also called for more attention at future meetings to "critical issues of contemporary society."

The resolution reflected many of the organizers' experiences in the campus antiwar teach-in movement.[34] Hoping to involve the widest range of anthropologists, Fried, Harris, and Murphy organized not another teach-in but a 1967 AAA plenary session that ranged from "primitive" warfare and the evolution of human aggression to the effects of U.S. bombing in Vietnam and the impact of a massive U.S. defense establishment on the national economy and quality of life. In their introduction to the 1968 book version, they wrote, "the present period of intense and growing unrest brought on by our Vietnam involvement has produced a crisis of conscience which has called into question the right of anthropologists to remain aloof from the great issues of our times."[35]

Just four months after the 1967 AAA symposium, students protesting Columbia's war-related research and expansion plans occupied five university buildings. The occupation ended eight days later, when police forcibly removed them in the early morning of April 30, 1968, arresting 720 people. Harris had stood in a Columbia faculty human chain around one of the buildings with anthropologists Alexander Alland, Ralph Holloway, and visiting professor Jaap van Velsen, and he was physically displaced as the police moved in.

Harris wrote a trenchant analysis of the events for *The Nation* a month later.[36] He assigned blame to a conservative, intransigent university administration that misled its own faculty about Defense Department research contracts related to the Vietnam War and that promoted a callous plan to use public park land for a university gym, which was opposed by leaders of the neighboring Harlem community. As a Columbia undergraduate, I had received a glossy fundraising packet in 1965 about the planned gym. What caught my eye was the basement entrance and facility for Harlem youth separated by a locked door from the several upper floors Columbia students would enjoy.

Harris did not condone the occupation but did support the university strike that followed the police bust. In addition to his campus and department involvement, he arranged with his "History of Anthropological Theory" students to teach the remainder of the course in two marathon sessions off campus. There we listened to him lecture from the galleys of *The Rise of Anthropological Theory*, published later that year. It was affectionately acronymed "RAT," which was also the name of a New York underground newspaper that covered the 1968 Columbia events.

The Nature of Cultural Things

During a 1965 seminar preceding my summer undergraduate fieldwork in Brazil, Harris assigned me the two chapters on verbal behavior from his new book, *The Nature of Cultural Things.* I did not make much sense of this, however, until I read the entire book in January 1967, just before beginning graduate classes and in the same momentous week when I read Edmund Leach's not dissimilar *Pul Eliya* (1961). Now I got it. By then I understood more fully the scope of Harris's work on Brazil, the United States, Mozambique, and India. As I now related the book's arguments to his other writings, its implicit political vision sank in. Later, when I planned my 1969–1971 Ghana fieldwork and wrote my 1972 dissertation, I returned to it frequently.

The book begins with the point that anthropological concepts are abstractions and thus should be judged useful to the degree they are related to the ongoing "behavior stream" events in which an ethnographer is situated while conducting fieldwork. (This subsumes the point that ethnography is autobiographical.) An ethnographer has three options: (1) come-what-may fieldwork according to no systematic plan, (2) framing research to uncover the concepts and categories of significance to the actors, or (3) anthropological description based on events of observed human behavior. To accord significance to human action and to test theories of human history, the first option was deemed unproductive and wasteful.

Harris viewed the second option, which he discussed in two chapters (the ones I read in 1965), as problematic but clearly part of what ethnography is about. His fieldwork in Brazil and Mozambique and his studies of race in the Americas and the ecology of Indian society convinced him, however, that the concepts and categories of the actors often provide a skewed guide to material, behavioral, unequal, and countable realities. This prior research context is not explicit in *The Nature of Cultural Things*, perhaps flawing the book for many readers, but in light of Harris's work it was impossible for me to read it in any other way.

Harris dissected this second, or "emic," option as advocated in "the new ethnography," the ethnoscience movement in anthropology that was of rising prominence in the early 1960s. Ethnoscientists had evinced no substantive interest in issues of inequality or Third World struggle. The thrust of Harris's argument was that the new ethnosemantics of categories and concepts stressed cultural uniformity when, for Brazilian racial terms at least, cognitive variability, ambiguity, and diversity were demonstrable properties that needed to be explained.

The Nature of Cultural Things crystallized this point for me and not only at an abstract intellectual level. As a Sunday school student and altar boy at Holy Trinity Lutheran Church in New Rochelle, New York, I had been fascinated and puzzled by the variety of what those in this congregation actually believed. After hearing all shades of opinion from Sunday school teachers and other church members about whether or not hell existed, what were the wages of sin in the afterlife for both Lutherans and non-Lutherans, and what exactly one consumed at the communion table, I was amazed to learn official Lutheran doctrine when I attended confirmation classes with the church's new minister. It clearly was not what everyone in that church believed. I was not even sure that it fell at the center of a congregation that ranged from a Sunday school teacher who tolerated my enthusiastic report on Hinduism when we studied non-Christian religions to a fellow confirmation class student who threatened me physically after my brother and I brought to church a Jewish friend staying with us over the weekend.

I had concluded that this was not a body of believers, but a body of behavers. Each week, people showed up, sat where they should, performed their roles, and the church went on, despite the disparity in belief. Behavior was observable and predictable. Meaning, at least in the sense of Christian belief, was multiple and somehow beyond the point of what held things together. So I had already learned about the emic/etic mystery I would later find at the heart of Harris's anthropology.

From today's viewpoint it is worth remembering that the now bland "new ethnography" of the early 1960s was then widely touted as anthropology's yellow brick road to "science." Today's body of sociolinguistic work that contextualizes cognition and cultural expression in ongoing behavior was not then in existence. Refusing to trade the substantive issues of inequality, to which he had devoted his professional life, for the ethnoscientific quest of abstract elegance and parsimony, Harris elaborated his third fieldwork option.

Purposefully using dissonant language, his "etic" approach provided a framework for constructing ethnographic behavioral accounts rooted in directly observable physical activity and reaching upward to complex social entities such as "General Motors, the Pentagon, the Catholic Church, [and] Columbia University."[37] Resolutely, be began at the lowest level, with human action and its environmental effects. He proceeded to "episodes" of such activity over time, connected by specific actors, locations, or commodities and artifacts and then to critical behavioral "nodes": recurring activities that result from and summarize sequences of human action. These lower-level yardsticks for ethnographic description were offered not as fieldwork prescription but rather to demonstrate their logical ordering and to urge attention to the behavioral underpinnings of ethnographic generalization and, for that matter, the actors' generalizations.

The higher levels of Harris's framework were similar to familiar anthropological approaches to social and political organization. They began with observable "scenes," including multiactor scenes; moved to linked sequences of scenes, or "serials"; and then proceeded to groups and interconnected complexes of groups. Groups ranged from work crews and husband-wife pairs to corporations and public bureaucracies, and they varied in size, frequency of assemblage, behavioral repertoire, and temporal permanence.

Four points about this ethnographic framework seemed noteworthy then, and still do:

1. The terrain to which it applied—"the great stream of uninterrupted behavior" that extended back in time to human origins—embraced all human history and the entire contemporary world, using the same conceptual approach to link them together.
2. The focus on "environmental effect" at the smallest level of human action tied in ecology, technology, the labor theory of value (I had read enough Marx to understand that), economic inequality, and biological consequences of human activity. Culture and nature, people and planet, were mutually implicated.
3. The approach grounded "interaction" in a wider field of human activity. This included for research more that was palpable and consequential than competing sociologically inclined role analyses and Parsonian-influenced theoretical schemes, which began with "interaction."
4. The vertical connecting of levels—from individual action to entities such as multinational corporations—meant that theories that explained higher-level phenomena had implications at the lowest levels, where the higher levels were rooted and continuously reproduced. Ethnographic description and analysis could move up and down, but they had to account for the most immediate levels of human activity if what they claimed about higher levels was valid.[38]

Immediate Applications

The theoretical vision of *The Nature of Cultural Things*, amplified in later publications,[39] influenced many anthropologists. Among them was a group of Columbia students and colleagues who participated in research in the 1960s and early 1970s directly inspired by this book.

The earliest were two graduate students who studied the etics and emics of garbage collection on Morningside Heights. Muriel Schein and Sydney Diamond's formal attempt to "apply the program of actonic ethnographic descriptions as rigorously as possible" included comparison of their etic data with sanitation worker statements. They found that verbal descriptions of garbage collection culture varied from one worker to another and also over time. Using their behavioral observations, the ethnographers were able to distinguish official rules (lids are always replaced on cans), interpretive statements (the bosses don't really expect us to replace lids), experiential statements (workers usually don't replace lids), and personal statements (I don't replace lids). Their performative and contextual view of work culture moved beyond the strict "white room" ethnosemantic method then advocated by the "new ethnography."[40]

A largely unpublished project that involved several dozen Columbia researchers commenced in 1967 when Harris began experiments with videotaping behavioral episodes.[41] The focus quickly narrowed to household behavior, with fixed cameras recording daily sequences in living rooms and kitchens. The contractual guarantees of privacy and control provided to the participating families, who were already involved in hospital-based research projects, exceeded the norm in anthropology at the time. White, black, and Puerto Rican husband-wife and female-headed families were studied, with ethnographic interviewing supplementing videotape analyses. For one family, I analyzed three types of nonverbal behavior in a one-hour taped sequence: initiation of activity, where a second actor repeated action begun by the first; results of contested control of objects; and interpersonal physical displacement. Other students focused on commands and requests and their outcomes, a measure of authority encompassing verbal performance and behavioral response. Although three dissertations resulted, only a brief report by Harris was published.[42] Perhaps the major conclusion was that concepts such as "authority," "household head," "matrifocal," and "organized" or "disorganized" at best summarize extremely complex patterns of intrahousehold activity and should be used cautiously in the absence of careful research.

My fieldwork in Accra was organized to assess contending propositions about urban Ghanaians: that they associated primarily with coethnics or that they interacted mainly within class lines that crossed "tribal" boundaries. Lani Sanjek and I collected data from forty adults regarding with whom they interacted over four-day sequences of behavior. This revealed that these urban Ghanaians associated most often with others of different ethnicity but the same class position.[43] This social network approach was inspired both by *The Nature of Cultural Things* and by Manchester anthropologist A. L. Epstein's network method deployed in urban Northern Rhodesia (later Zambia).[44] The ethnographic sensibility inculcated by Harris's book and by hours of close watching and coding of videotaped behavior also resulted in detailed records of household residence over time, gender roles, interhousehold linkages, male and female domestic careers, and children's work.[45]

Another veteran of Harris's videotape research cohort, Orna Johnson, used video equipment in fieldwork in Shimaa, a Matsigenka (Machiguenga) community in the Peruvian Amazon. Video records of four households were utilized to identify command/compliance authority structures. In addition, careful analysis of interpersonal food exchange during videotaped meals revealed situational factors underlying patterns of gender segregation and interaction. Johnson noted, "The importance of these factors is not apparent from talking to people. It is only after specific behavioral acts are observed that the structural principles ordering social action begin to emerge."[46] Allen Johnson, also a participant in Harris's Columbia videotape project, developed a fieldwork method in Shimaa to sample behavior stream events rather than trace them in temporal sequences. By randomizing visits to Matsigenka households and noting ongoing activities upon arrival, Johnson amassed a body of behavioral observations that led to his rethinking the concepts "production" and "work."[47]

Wider Theoretical Terrains and Trajectories

At the same time I was assimilating *The Nature of Cultural Things*, I and other Columbia students were reading work that pointed in a similar direction by British-trained anthropologists Fredrik Barth, Epstein, Raymond Firth, Edmund Leach, and Jaap van Velsen.[48] However, they did not connect fieldwork-rooted sequences of human activity all the way up to multinational corporations and imperialist states, as Harris's book did. In addition, writings by Malcolm X, Frantz Fanon, and Kwame Nkrumah made significant impressions about wider political perspectives. And I give important place to the "independent socialist" journal *Monthly Review*, which in the 1960s demonstrated interest in anthropology more than once. Here I read Gough's "Anthropology and Imperialism" essay before its more mildly titled version, "New Proposals for Anthropologists," in *Current Anthropology*.[49] Through *Monthly Review*, we found radical economists Paul Baran, Paul Sweezy, and Harry Magdoff.[50] I first read Andre Gunder Frank there, but I also read him and others in the Radical Education Project's broadsheets and pamphlets.[51] Of special importance to me was Bob Fitch and Mary Oppenheimer's *Ghana: End of an Illusion*, a Monthly Review Press publication that set me on my fieldwork path to Accra.[52] I also remember several books by later neoconservative David Horowitz, then a cool demystifier of Cold War ideology.[53]

When submitting an "economic anthropology" bibliography for my graduate exams in 1969, I was too timid to include such nonanthropological writing, even Frank's 1967 book *Capitalism and Underdevelopment in Latin America*, as would seem unbelievable to graduate students only a few years later. I did list classic works of Marx and Engels on primitive society but otherwise reached beyond anthropology only to academic-credentialed Trinidadian politician Eric Williams's 1944 *Capitalism and Slavery* and economist Gunnar Myrdal's 1957 *Rich Lands and Poor*.[54] More broadly, I devoured the 1960s salvos from anthropologists Gerald Berreman, Guillermo Bonfil Batalla, and Gough, and I especially valued anthropologists who were delineating what would later be termed the "capitalist world system." This included Peter Worsley's conceptualization of the Third World and its populist politics, Robert Manners's attention to labor migrant remittances knitting together Caribbean and metropole, Gulliver and van Velsen's studies of African labor migration, and Alvin Wolfe's "Cape to Katanga" detective piece on interlocking directorates in the African mineral industry. Clifford Geertz's counterposing Dutch-colonized Java and never-colonized Japan made a strong impact, even if *Agricultural Involution* (1963) was on Columbia reading lists for its depiction of swidden versus paddy ecologies.[55]

Harris's substantive work resonated with these writings. His *Nature of Cultural Things*, which I read as a poetic of race and inequality, grounded my ethnographic fieldwork in Ghana (and later with the Gray Panthers and in Elmhurst-Corona) in directly observed behavior. Yet by the late 1970s and 1980s, a concern for systematic attention to ongoing behavioral events seemed a minority interest in anthropology. The discipline's ethnographic center of gravity had also strayed from the focus on inequality vigorously pursued in the 1960s. Why? Let me sketch three reasons.

World-System Eclipse

The appearance of sociologist Immanuel Wallerstein's first publication on the "capitalist world system" in 1974 and his books and essays thereafter had the effect of crowding out less bold conceptions, notably those of regional ethnographic analyses by anthropologists (such as Manners, for the Caribbean, or Harris, Gulliver, and van Velsen, for Africa). It also moved attention from behavioral action and outcomes to higher levels of political economic organization and into the past.

All this came as a surprise, as I had attended Wallerstein's "Social Change: The Colonial Situation" course at Columbia in the fall of 1968 and found that his lectures recapitulated the modernization framework of his earlier work[56] and seemed outdated after the Columbia spring 1968 ferment. Wallerstein had been a proponent of what Harris saw as the failed role of mediator between the Columbia administration and occupying students. The 1960s Wallerstein was also noteworthy for State Department and Council on Foreign Relations advisory activities.[57] So the 1970s Wallerstein, no longer at Columbia, appeared like a bolt out of the blue to me. As colleagues began talking about him, I kept asking, "*Immanuel* Wallerstein?" However, I soon joined them.

Critics and emendators of Wallerstein's and also Frank's continuing writings added to the world systems debate and excitement. Anthropologists were thick among them, notably Mintz and Wolf but also others in an emergent "political economy" movement of the 1970s and 1980s.[58] Allied to this development was the 1970s ascent (and 1980s decline) of structural Marxism,[59] with its ceaseless reconsiderations of "modes of production," a target at which Harris, among others, took aim.[60] The microterrains of daily life, where these abstract positions have consequences, were on hold. Even worse for an ethnography of the present, the gaze of anthropological political economy was mainly on the past, as evident in its exemplary monographs.[61]

Modes of Presentation

The rising tide of political economy in the 1970s and 1980s was productive of local and regional book-length studies, many of which framed their ethnographic portraits historically, some with more frame than picture. Sociocultural anthropologists maintained loyalty to the monograph as their exemplary product, and this continues. Thus it was significant that none of the research inspired by *The Nature of Cultural Things* was published in book-length form but appeared as journal articles and essays in edited volumes. This, in part, also reflected the post–World War II shift in anthropology to competitive social sciences funding and anthropology's subsequent methodological sensitivity to systematic fieldwork data in the 1960s. As this trend peaked in the 1970s, it produced its own humanistic and interpretative reaction.

The methodological pioneering that *The Nature of Cultural Things* represented was exciting in its own right, and it was part of a larger ethnographic perspective that included more than Harris and the Columbia studies.[62] Although this work's origin was in substantive issues such as those Harris pursued during the 1950s, the pressure of the times to demonstrate that anthropology was a science—which also affected ethnoscience, psychological anthropology, and other areas of the discipline—reified method. If anthropology made methodological advances, and I think we did, still we did not stress enough the substantive issues we selected to study or produce monographs analyzing these issues.

One consequence of this was the death of network analysis in anthropology. I asked in a 1974 review article, "What Is Network Analysis, and What Is It Good for?" Anthropologists provided too many answers to the first question and too few to the second. Those who saw promise for urban anthropology in Epstein's interaction-based "network" approach presented their work in programmatic, methodological form.[63] By the end of the 1970s, appraisals of network analysis read like inquests. In the 1980s, network analysis had vanished from anthropology as a vehicle of ethnographic inquiry.[64]

Actor to Person to Self to Other

In 1966, Geertz published *Person, Time, and Conduct in Bali.* It was reprinted in his 1973 essay collection *The Interpretation of Cultures*, which had great influence in anthropology and beyond. In this essay (which, curiously, presents a cultural placidity contrasting with the chaotic lived behavior of his Balinese cockfight article), Geertz shifted anthropological attention from the behaving actor to the cultural construction of the person—to the "symbolic structures in terms of which persons are perceived as representatives of certain distinct categories of persons."[65] His thickly descriptive cultural analysis of Balinese "predecessors, contemporaries, consociates, and successors" might have registered as complementary to study of actual Balinese behavioral networks. But in the court of sociocultural anthropology, "the person" won, and "the actor" was soon to retire.

There should be no gainsaying the value of Geertz's conceptualization, even if its ethnographic basis may be contested.[66] Geertz did not bump off the actor. Complicity for this resides far more widely in anthropology. Geertz's approach was ethnographically productive, as can be seen in his own work and that of his students and others.[67] It gained influence during the 1970s as "ideational theories of culture" grew in prominence,[68] and here, Geertz's work had the distinct value of moving culture into performative arenas and out of rigid abodes in cognitive and structural anthropology.[69] Geertz's approach was forthrightly interpretive and did not entail any replicable methodological prescriptions, such as vanquished ethnoscience offered.

It could not be said of Geertz's Indonesia work that he ever forgot that "the subjects of ethnographies are always more important than their authors."[70] But this was not true of a stream of interpretationists who, from the late 1970s onward, insisted that ethnography was autobiographical and proceeded to make it so.[71] In the 1980s, the "self" replaced the "person," and in those Reagan go-go years, too often this became the ethnographer's own self, and the actor or person (in truth, we need both) became "the Other." As one who entered anthropology in the 1960s, I continue to feel uncomfortable with this terminology. The phrase "the Other" retains for me an alienating, unfathomable quality that continual reading of it does not diminish. It is also a politically dangerous reading of the history and practice of ethnography to sharply dichotomize self and other. Much more of this history has been written by "Others" than current textbooks admit (see Chapter 5).

Where Next?

In the 1990s, the mood in sociocultural anthropology was often described as dispirited, contentious, in malaise. "Interpretationism has gone too far." "The Other and his or her native point of view seem more remote than ever." "Method and evidence have been forgotten." "We need practice—no, we need process." "World-system political economy leaves no scope for individual agency."[72]

There was cause for optimism in the attention to agency. Ulf Hannerz found here concern with "variations in the kind and degree of consciousness connected to actions of individuals in society, and the related variations in the degree of freedom to choose lines of action."[73] We were on the way to revivifying the actor and restoring ethnographic focus to both interpreting webs of significance and connecting sequences of action in observable events. I appreciated Barth's reminder that material causality, interaction, and intentions (or agency) are coexisting constituents of events and that "interplay" and "variance" among them, as well as an "outcome," are inherent aspects of events.[74]

But there is a second type of agency that I wish to consider. This is the autobiographical agency exerted by the anthropologist as social theorist and ethnographer. It is the agency exerted in choosing a problem; in according significance to certain events, communications, and persons during fieldwork; in imparting direction and purpose to what one writes; and in defining, engaging, and provoking one's audiences and readerships. This is a matter less for anthropology than for each anthropologist, a sorting through of the critical and political values that motivate us.

Meaning in history and the deployment of theory arise from conviction that certain events are more significant than others. Within the vast human behavior stream, amid the unceasing rush and interconnection of event upon event, are those events that "affect the lives of enough people [to] shift the shape of society at large." The cause of anthropology's malaise and contentiousness may be political at root. "The failure to confront the meaningful particular is a reflection of academic pathology, of theory which generalizes all human responsibility out of existence, and more seriously in our presently complicated world, helps prevent us from understanding the critical and contingent nature of certain sequences of events."[75]

"Meaning" for anthropologists must always be double-edged. Meaning is not only what is in people's heads, the native point of view anthropology has long sought to represent. Meaning is also what we put into our own heads, and those of our publics, by the significance we accord to certain actors, beliefs, opinions, events, and locations and not to others. If we wish to make ethnography meaningful in this second social and political sense, we must give continuing attention to the material, behavioral, unequal, and countable, not to displace emic but to preserve etic. We need to give attention in debates about ethnography to a world of violence and its correlates of morbidity, mortality, displacement, and hunger; to the everyday consequences of global economic dominance; to migration and community disorganization produced by disinvestment and capital relocation; to political disenfranchisement via corporate decision making and political influence;

to racial and ethnic oppression; to commoditization of sexuality, maternal care, child labor, and body parts.

The way out of anthropology's malaise, I believe, lies not in a horizontal melding of political economy and symbolic-interpretive anthropology, as some advocate.[76] Rather, we need to think vertically, as Harris did in *The Nature of Cultural Things*. We need to weave together our most expansive world-system analyses with detailed attention to ongoing human action and interaction. We need to do this without remaining aloof from the great issues of our times and with attention to culture—in its cognitive, symbolic, affective, performative, ideological, and oppositional manifestations—all the way up and down.

That is the nature of cultural things, and there lies our handle on agency, both that of the actors and our own. The transition anthropology went through in the 1960s gave us a new, less-pleasant world but also gave us the actor capable of making history. After all, the point is not only to understand the world but to be enabled to change it in a more humane direction.

Postscript

Marvin Harris died in 2001. For his own view of his career, see his 1994 "Intellectual Roots" statement.[77] See also the obituary published in *American Anthropologist*,[78] which focuses on "cultural materialism," the theoretical approach he advocated from 1968 onward.[79]

Chapter 11

Keeping Ethnography Alive in an Urbanizing World

My initial attraction to ethnography was romantic. The first book I read in my first cultural anthropology course in 1964 was Bronislaw Malinowski's *Argonauts of the Western Pacific* (1922). I was hooked. I realized I could travel via ethnographies to places I would never go, and before my undergraduate years were out, I had encountered *A Chinese Village* (1945), *A Serbian Village* (1958), *Life in a Mexican Village* (1951), *Suye Mura: A Japanese Village* (1939), *A Village on the Border* (1957), and *A Village That Chose Progress* (1950).[1] I also soon discovered ethnographies of places closer to home: *Middletown* (1929), *Yankee City* (1963), *Deep South* (1941), and *Soulside* (1969).[2] These ethnographies connected my romance with anthropology to my growing consciousness of racial and political inequalities.

Not all anthropology was done in villages, I now understood, but my first fieldwork was. In 1965, I spent two months in a Brazilian fishing village on the Bahia coast. This research intensified my interest in race, as I studied the complex vocabulary of terms Brazilians used to describe varying combinations of skin color, hair form, and facial features that centuries of black, white, and Native American mixing had produced. This study was set within the ethnoscience paradigm of cognitive anthropology, then a major theoretical approach. Using an interview instrument (thirty-six line drawings of varying combinations of skin color, hair form, and facial features, designed by Marvin Harris) and my own questionnaire, I attempted to isolate and record "culture," seen as abstract concepts and components of meaning existing in people's heads. I did not, nor did anthropology in general, then appreciate that culture simultaneously has not only cognitive but also perceptual, evaluative, affective, performative, ideological, and oppositional manifestations. Still, from my conversations in halting Portuguese with village residents—unfortunately understood by me as less important than the "real science" of instrument and questionnaire—I learned that social context always mattered. I concluded,

> The expression of the cognitive classification is altered by environmental (situational, sociological) variables which are essential for an understanding of why any term is actually uttered. Such variables would include at least the economic class, the dress, personality, education, and relation of the referrant to the speaker; the presence of other actors and their relations to the speaker and referrant; and contexts of speech, such as gossip, insult, joking, showing affection, maintenance of equality or of differential social status, or pointing out the referrant in a group.[3]

As my graduate education proceeded, I began to differentiate contrasting orientations of cultural and social anthropology—of the focus on meaning contained in people's heads versus meanings constructed from social arrangements and speech in action. My drift toward social anthropology was also propelled by several politically attuned ethnographies: *Bantu Bureaucracy* (1956), *Political Leadership Among Swat Pathans* (1959), *Politics in an Urban African Community* (1958), *Reaction to Conquest* (1936), *Caste and the Economic Frontier* (1957), *Tribal Cohesion in a Money Economy* (1958), and *The Politics of Kinship* (1964).[4]

Cultural anthropology in the United States was fathered by Franz Boas. His fieldwork methods progressively retreated from the participant observation of *The Central Eskimo* (1888)—which I enjoyed reading as a graduate student—to the transcription of texts produced by seated Kwakwaka'wakw (Kwakiutl) informants removed from contexts of daily behavior.[5] In essence, this was the method I used in my Brazil fieldwork, even though it was supervised by my Columbia University advisor Marvin Harris, who opposed the cognitive anthropology movement then flourishing. He advocated a radical behavioral method, which I saw as intersecting with network analysis emanating from Manchester social anthropologists, whose work I admired and encountered firsthand from Jaap van Velsen, a student of Max Gluckman and a visiting professor at Columbia in 1968.[6]

My 1969–1971 dissertation fieldwork combined romance and political consciousness, cultural and social anthropology. I traveled to Ghana in West Africa and studied ethnic relations among residents of a city block in the capital, Accra. I used interviews with forty informants to record detailed accounts of interaction during two workdays and a weekend, but I grounded this network study in neighborhood residence over 18 months, participant observation in locations people traveled to throughout the city and in their hometowns, and everyday conversations that found their way into my fieldnotes.

Thus, I can trace my cultural anthropological lineage through Harris to the Columbia tradition and Boas. I can also trace my social anthropological lineage through van Velsen to Gluckman's Manchester school and to Malinowski. Over the years, the Malinowski side has won out, and perhaps my original *Argonauts* conversion experience explains this. In later work among Gray Panther activists and in Elmhurst-Corona, Queens, I favored participant observation over interviews and naturally occurring speech in action over questionnaire and instrument-mediated quests for culture. In Accra, with the Gray Panthers, and in Elmhurst-Corona, as I met people and my face became familiar, they told me about events, other persons and groups, and themselves, much as Doc told *Street Corner Society* ethnographer William Whyte that people would.

Dangers of Interviews

Interviews, of course, are an indispensable part of fieldwork, and we learn things through them that we can learn in no other way. Anthropology's array of interview methods (Chapter 4) allows us to extend our ethnographic reach in time and space; to learn about events we cannot observe; and, with careful use, to illuminate larger issues that originate in fieldwork observations. Ethnography's great strength is that we generate from our fieldwork the interview questions we ask. In Ghana, with the Gray Panthers, and in Elmhurst-Corona, I postponed formal interviews until I had substantial participant-observation knowledge and had determined therefrom what questions to ask. As fieldworking anthropologists, we are able to maximize the validity of our interview-based research in ways that researchers formulating questions in offices or laboratories—removed from cultural realities—simply cannot.

But even after intensive ethnographic knowledge is amassed, and local theories of significance formulated, interviewing must be conducted with care. As Fredrik Barth explains about his New Guinea fieldwork among the Baktaman: "My field procedure was to rely very heavily on observation of spontaneous, unelicited word and act. I paid particular attention to this in Baktaman questions and explanations to each other—in men's houses, in the fellowship of hunting and working, during initiations and other rites. Only secondarily, and with much reticence, did I ask my own questions, and then only when they seemed cast in a native pattern and received easy and natural response."[7]

The dangers of relying too much on interviews and dialogue and not enough on preparatory and continuing participant observation are seen by Barth as "problems of observer effect and influence."

> The relationships that are developed with friends in the field are inevitably based on reciprocity and compatible learning, and through this it is easy, and perhaps common, to launch "informants" in intellectual careers as analysts of their own society. In this capacity they can naturally provide a number of excellent insights—but these insights can *not* be used as data on the contents of their cultural tradition. And once this process is launched, it becomes impossible for the anthropologist to tell which items are inherent in the tradition he is studying, and which represent the feedback of his own activity.[8]

Years ago, I reviewed a paper submitted to a leading anthropological journal. It concerned an Afro-Brazilian religious sect and described the group's rich ideology, cosmology, and interpretation of its African and colonial-era cultural past. The source of the data was a set of lengthy interviews between the anthropologist and one informant. I wondered how much of this material ever surfaced in the sect's ordinary ritual events or might be heard in conversations among sect members themselves. Here was an example of Barth's "observer effect" problem: I had no way of knowing whether this was the sect's existing culture or, instead, the product of dialogue between ethnographer and chosen informant. How much was culturally valid, and how much had been elaborated or emerged dialogically between them? As Barth warns, "My strong suspicion is that the bodies of native explanation that we find in anthropological literature are often created as an artefact of the anthropologist's activity."[9]

Interviews are problematic for other reasons as well (see Chapter 4). So let me pose a problem for anthropology looking forward: How do we preserve wide-ranging ethnography and not retreat to interviews alone in the dense and increasingly enormous cities of our urbanizing world?

From Villages to Cities

Today, more than half the world's seven billion people live in cities. Twenty-one urban agglomerations contain more than ten million people each, scores of others house millions, and during the current century, the proportion of city dwellers will slope upward to two-thirds or more. We may not be running out of villages as much as we are running over them: numerous once-rural areas are being absorbed into vast urbanized regions. Many anthropologists with no special interest in urbanism already do fieldwork in cities, and more will follow.

In the romantic days of village ethnographies, we maintained the myth of holistic study. Certainly it is possible in many villages for a single ethnographer to keep track of nearly everything going on within the settlement's perimeter. Margaret Mead capitalized upon this in her exhaustive study of the New Guinea village of Alitoa, where every day, even with an injured leg, she could observe virtually all 212 residents of this mountain-top settlement.[10] In Sitio, the Brazilian fishing village I studied, I could travel rapidly throughout this beachside settlement. However, both Mead and I were well aware of movement of people, goods, and ideas in and out of these villages.[11] During the 1960s, these movements became an intrinsic part of village studies, and we saw documented, for example in Bernard Gallin's *Hsin Hsing, Taiwan: A Chinese Village in Change* (1966), rituals marking the departure of young men (here for military service) and the increasing dependence of households on wages earned by family members in the capital city (here Taipei).

For urban anthropologists, the holistic pretense had died even earlier.[12] In my fieldwork in Accra, I studied eleven residential buildings along one city block, a population of 423 people.[13] Like Mead, I could literally watch people come and go, and through participant observation and interviews I could learn where the block's residents traveled within the city or beyond.

Although the border I drew around these eleven buildings was artificial compared to the discrete perimeters of Alitoa, Sitio, or Hsin Hsing, I was able to do anthropology "in the city" in a manner similar to Mead, Gallin, or other village ethnographers. What was different was that much of my participant observation (as well as the behavior recorded in network interviews) occurred beyond this block—in markets, commercial areas, workplaces, bars, association meeting sites, churches, government offices, transportation hubs, and the rural hometowns to which many Adabraka people regularly traveled.

I knew also that my wide-ranging fieldwork in Accra by itself remained contextually incomplete. As theoreticians of urban anthropology argued, bottom-up ethnographic findings "in the city" needed to be complemented by top-down study "of the city."[14] More pointedly, Anthony Leeds stressed that we need to be not only (1) urban ethnographers but (2) urban historians and political economists, drawing on documentary evidence to understand the city we study and how its specific history affects culture and behavior within our chosen fieldwork locale; also (3) comparative theorists, utilizing insights on urban structure and process at more general, even global, levels. Accordingly, my work on Accra (1) set its extensive contemporary interethnic mixing and multilingualism within (2) the history of its indigenous Gã people and their neighbors and (3) compared it with other third-world cities in similar recent transition from colonialism to neocolonialism.[15]

As realization of these triple duties (compare Chapter 4) sank in, the new danger urban anthropologists faced was that historical contextualization and comparative theorizing might overshadow participant observation. This could lead to ethnographies that might be characterized as "thin description" or "history without people." The ethnographic richness and detail of *Argonauts*, village studies, and Manchester-style political ethnographies, whatever their faults, are qualities we should not wish to sacrifice. So, how might we escape both the first danger, of retreat into interviews alone—the easiest solution to fieldwork "in the city"—and also the second danger, of too much history, political economy, and theory at the expense of ethnography?

I would like to offer some answers that emerged from our team study of Elmhurst-Corona, Queens. I will spotlight in particular several urban settings that proved especially productive for participant observation and might find analogs elsewhere in our urbanizing globe.

Fieldwork in Elmhurst-Corona

My goal was to study a New York City neighborhood in which substantial numbers of white and black Americans and Asian and Latin American immigrants coresided and to recruit a research team that reflected major components of its racial, ethnic, and linguistic diversity. In 1983, Chen Hsiang-shui and I analyzed 1980 U.S. Census data for Queens and quickly settled on Community District 4 (CD4), comprising Elmhurst and Corona. One of fifty-nine community districts in New York City, its 1980 population included forty-six thousand whites, thirteen thousand blacks, nineteen thousand Asians, and fifty-two thousand Latin Americans. Chen began studying the Chinese immigrants, and I, a grandchild of Croatian and Irish immigrants to New York, focused on the whites. By 1987, we were joined by Kyeyoung Park, studying Koreans; Ruby Danta (from Cuba) and Milagros Ricourt (from the Dominican Republic), the diverse Latin Americans; Steven Gregory, the African Americans; and Madhulika Khandelwal, the Indians.

Our New Immigrants and Old Americans Project focused on Jane Jacobs's urban "district-level" perspective rather than village-like studies of sample blocks—on what Anthony Leeds termed "the locality" and others identified as the city "ward" or "quarter"—the larger, named neighborhood in which political groups and leaders organize and maneuver vis-à-vis "the city as a whole." I began with Elmhurst-Corona's Community Board 4, and as I traced links from it into the surrounding political field, my work intersected with team members studying the area's Chinese, Korean, Latin American, African American, and Indian populations.

Each of us conducted interviews in households in CD4 or in neighboring districts into which research extended. Chen, whose one hundred household interviews took place in both Elmhurst and in Flushing in Community District 7, details topics we covered in *Chinatown No More: Taiwan Immigrants in Contemporary New York* (1992). Although he analyzes this household-level data exhaustively,[16] the greater part of his book derives from participant observation, not interviews. His "continuing study of twenty households" involved "many days in stores and homes, talking with household members, helping when they asked for help, eating with them in restaurants and at their houses or [his] home." Nine of these household members are portrayed in the three chapters of his book that discuss workers, small-business proprietors, and professionals.[17] The richest of these portraits is a remarkable twelve-page section titled "Mr. Lou's Candy Store."

Candy stores are an established New York City neighborhood fixture in which newspapers and magazines (now in Spanish, Chinese, English, Italian, etc.), toys, coffee, snacks, batteries, lottery tickets, and other items are sold, and local residents, particularly children, "hang out." These stores are often run by immigrants and may become a stepping stone to a more profitable, less labor-intensive business. At their store, Mr. and Mrs. Lou, both immigrants from Taiwan, began their thirteen-hour days at 6:30 a.m. and remained until 8:00 p.m. each night except Sunday, when they finished by 3:00 p.m. Closed only on Christmas, their store was open 364 days a year.

Chen's account highlights the intensely multiethnic nature of contemporary Elmhurst-Corona life. The Lous bought their store from an Indian owner, and 90 percent of their customers were non-Chinese, many of them Latin Americans, with whom the Lous used their rudimentary business Spanish. An older German American man voluntarily helped collate the Sunday newspaper sections, and they treated him to dinner at Chinese New Year. The landlord of the house they rented nearby was Latin American, as were two successive housekeepers they hired. They also dealt with numerous suppliers and city inspectors, one of whom, an African American woman, ticketed them—unfairly, they felt—for unsatisfactory health conditions at their prepared food counter. Problems with customers who demanded credit or shoplifted items tucked into a newspaper involved people of many ethnic backgrounds, yet their biggest headache was a Chinese man who ran up a $180 bill and then disappeared. They also dealt with a white organized crime figure who pressed them to place a "Joker Poker" video game in the store. The machine was illegal, but given the widespread predilection for gambling among all local ethnic groups,[18] it proved the most profitable aspect of the Lous' business.

Chen also spent many hours at the Reform Church of Newtown, and his participant observation—including "ping-pong ethnography" as a player on the church's team—paid off in a rich analysis of its changing ethnic relations.[19] Like many Elmhurst churches, this one's white population was aging and losing members to suburbanization. To counter this, services in Taiwanese were introduced to attract new numbers, and space was rented to a succession of Korean, Filipino, Tamil, and other immigrant congregations. Several of the renter groups eventually became strong enough to move out and buy their own buildings, but as the white-to-Chinese balance in the Reform Church's own congregation shifted, conflicts arose over whose church it was and whether a Taiwanese pastor should replace the retiring white minister. Eventually he did.

In addition, Chen allocated much intensive fieldwork to meetings and events of five Chinese voluntary associations headquartered in Flushing.[20] He contrasted this organizational arena with classic anthropological studies of hierarchically organized overseas Chinese communities. In Queens, each organization formed its own relationships with white, Korean, and other Chinese groups; with city agency personnel and elected officials; and with each other. His detailed ethnography traces links among overlapping boards of directors and highlights the place of women leaders in several organizations and as school board members and candidates, mayoral honorees, and political party appointees.

The organizational drama culminates in the roles these Chinese associations played in the annual Queens Festival, a two-day event in Flushing Meadows–Corona Park that attracted hundreds of thousands. The Flushing Chinese associations were invited to organize a pavilion (sited next to the Korea, India, and Japan pavilions) in the festival's "Asian Village." Chen showed how, behind the scenes, this indexed the varying strengths and interests of the five associations and their leaders and served to affirm their place in the wider Flushing and Queens County emerging multiethnic political fields.

My own long-term, most often part-time, fieldwork in Elmhurst-Corona occurred between 1983 and 1996. Like other team members, I conducted household interviews, and I included portraits of five white American households in *The Future of Us All.*[21] I also studied three historically white, then multiethnic Protestant churches,[22] and I attended meetings of Community Board 4 and other Elmhurst-Corona civic groups.

The most unanticipated aspect of my fieldwork was the many public ritual events I observed between 1984 and 1996 (Chapter 2). Since Gluckman's "Analysis of a Social Situation in Modern Zululand" (1940), anthropologists have been attuned to secular rituals in complex societies. I recalled his account of black and white South African participation at a bridge-opening ceremony when, in 1985, I attended the dedication of a renovated playground in Corona, my first local ritual event. The white American "chiefs" (the Community Board 4 chairperson and two Democratic Party district leaders) were in attendance, as were higher-level officials (the

Queens borough president and New York City parks commissioner). Following an opening prayer by an Italian American Roman Catholic priest, a chorus of Latin American, Asian, black, and white school children sang the U.S. national anthem and "We Are the World." The African American park leader then gathered her preschool children at the new play equipment, forming a backdrop for ribbon cutting, speeches, and photographs. These children's Latin American, South Asian, and white mothers, elderly Italians from the neighborhood, and uniformed park workers all looked on.

Rituals in CD4 shared features with those elsewhere.[23] They were planned and enacted rather than spontaneous. They marked special occasions or purposes, occurred in central or symbolically transformed locations, and broke the flow of ordinary events with formal behavior, including invocations, speeches, music, processions, dance, and the sharing of food. They sorted and positioned those present into organizers, participants, and audience. And by employing the dramatic qualities of rituals—temporary but memorable focused assemblages, the display of symbols (such as flags and anthems), and orations and exhortations—their organizers communicated messages.

Some rituals reinforced existing social and political arrangements; others presented critical or competing visions. In each ritual, however, overt messages and implicit meanings could differ for organizers, participants, audience members, and those who later read or learned about it.[24] Memorial Day, for example, meant one thing to an elderly white Elmhurst resident whose brother died in World War II. It meant something else to the Latin American or Asian parent of a junior high school bugler playing the military hymn "Taps."

Generating Fieldwork, Contextualization, and Theory from Fieldwork

Fieldwork is hard work. Clifford Geertz speaks of it as "the day in, day out, one step forward, one step back, effort to get genuinely close to a handful of people who have no particular reason to get close to you."[25] It entails repeated listening and observation in the same locations and with the same actors. One or two visits by Chen to Mr. Lou's candy store or the Reform Church of Newtown (let alone one or two interviews) would not have generated the results that repeated participant observation yielded, with each sequence of observed events influencing what to see and listen to in the next. In this regard, I want to stress how fieldwork generates more fieldwork, a point Malinowski often reiterated to his students.

We come to fieldwork with a set of significant theories that play a strong part in molding what we hear and observe in events, in shaping the "there" we find there. But we are also confronted by what M. N. Srinivas, A. M. Shah, and E. A. Ramaswamy term "the grain of the field": the ongoing events and commentaries of our informants that lead to terrain-specific theories of significance, which in turn mold what we hear and observe.[26] Both kinds of theories swirl and mix in our heads and contribute to our decisions about when to be where, with whom, observing and listening to what.

My repeated participant observation at political meetings exposed two patterns that prior significant theories (and my initial research proposal) did not anticipate. First, I saw numbers of women leaders enter and, by the later 1980s, reshape the Elmhurst-Corona political field. They also established more lasting linkages across ethnic and racial lines than did male leaders. Second, I watched what in 1983 had been an overwhelmingly white community board add Asian and include more Latin American and black members. By the 1990s, the neighborhood's immigrant majority remained numerically underrepresented, but blacks, like whites, were now overrepresented. I well remember when the first female CB4 chairperson was elected, when the first Chinese, Korean, and Indian members joined, when the Latin American membership doubled and then stabilized, and when the African American membership doubled and then doubled again.

Fieldwork also generates a search for contextualization—the particular seams of history and political economy "of the city" that illuminate ethnographic work "in the city." From early in my fieldwork, I repeatedly heard the phrase "quality of life" when neighborhood leaders and residents discussed "problems that are important to us." Like Malinowski's quest to understand the meaning of "kula," I had to understand what "quality of life" meant, not to academics, politicians, or the press, but to the people of Elmhurst-Corona. In my fieldnotes, I carefully catalogued the neighborhood's "quality of life" complaints: school crowding, housing code violations, street-level drug sales, lack of youth recreation facilities, dissatisfaction with police response, and others.[27]

To contextualize and explain why it was *these* specific problems, and why these problems *now*, I turned to newspaper clipping files, policy studies, and analyses from economics, political science, history, and sociology. The drug sales that residents bemoaned and I could observe in progress I placed within the wider organization of cocaine and other drug importing and distribution.[28] Most other quality-of-life problems, including the shrunken police ranks pursuing drug sellers, were traceable to the city's 1975 fiscal crisis and ensuing budget cuts by successive mayors. I remember my "Eureka!" experience when this larger explanation for overcrowded schools, diminished numbers of building inspectors, curtailed youth programs, and other specific quality-of-life complaints dawned on me, something that then seemed obvious.

Similarly, rising numbers of street vendors, long-distance telephone hustlers, subway musicians, unlicensed transportation providers, and beverage-can scavengers in Elmhurst-Corona, as well as in the rest of the city, led me to research the size and dynamics of New York's underground economy and its relation to the city's "speculative-electronic" and "real" economies.[29] This in turn put in sharper perspective the continuing city tax breaks to owners of Wall Street and midtown office buildings and the ways in which electronic and digital technologies were transforming the financial sector and rendering city policies to hold it in New York both more expensive and less likely to work.[30] These municipal expenditures, of course, further worsened "quality of life" in Elmhurst-Corona's schools, parks, streets, housing stock, subways, and hospital. And people organized to resist.

My initial understanding of New York's land-use policies and its "permanent government" derived from political economic analyses I read long before beginning fieldwork.[31] But these analyses came alive for me more vividly as my ethnographic experience deepened. My book obscures this dialectical "context of discovery" by presenting New York City political economy first and Elmhurst-Corona quality-of-life issues second. As often happens, this transforms an inductive fieldwork-contextualization back-and-forth process into a straightforward deductive and explanatory "context of presentation."[32]

Lastly, fieldwork generates comparative theory. Our research in Elmhurst-Corona addressed both popular and scholarly conceptions of ethnic and racial "balkanization" in what some call "the disuniting of America." From Mr. Lou's candy store to historically white and now rainbow churches to ties across lines of race and ethnicity among local political or small business leaders, we documented multiethnic and multiracial settings that could be fruitful locations for fieldwork in other globalizing cities.

On the other hand, we also documented creation of ethnically homogeneous Chinese, Korean, Spanish-language (although pan–Latin American), and South Asian houses of worship, as well as persisting African American housing segregation. Obviously, we need and welcome comparative ethnographic testing elsewhere of our fieldwork discoveries, and in this regard, we point to commercial locations and interactions, houses of worship, secular rituals, and local political fields and arenas as prime sites for future urban ethnography globally.

At a more general theoretical level, in *Transnational Connections* (1996), Ulf Hannerz advises we pay particular attention to four "organizational frameworks" in which cultural production arises in the contemporary world: *form of life*, which comprehends everyday patterns of work, social reproduction, neighboring, and recreation and tends toward stability unless affected by the other three frameworks—*market*, *state*, and *movement*.[33] My fieldwork in Accra and Chen's and my household interviews in Queens concerned urban Ghanaian, Taiwan immigrant, and "outer-borough white ethnic" forms of life. The market, of course, produces the flows of migration that brought these groups to these cities, and our Queens work on commercial settings and on housing market forces (integrative for whites and immigrants but not for African Americans) indicates how forms of life may undergo market-generated change.

The state, and more specifically New York's "permanent government" and its successive city hall regimes, produces cultural ideologies—mayors Edward Koch's "world city," David Dinkins's "gorgeous mosaic," Rudolf Giuliani's "Police Strategy No. 5"—that influence how Elmhurst-Corona residents see their city and themselves.[34] But against this, and also against budget cuts that assault their cognized "quality of life," they organize (create movements) to press for more schools, youth programs, building inspectors, and "cops on the beat" and against upscale housing, commercial overdevelopment, and privatization of public parks and hospitals.

My participatory research with the Gray Panthers concerned a multilocal and national social movement.[35] The wellsprings of movements are found in the political actions of individuals, in this case, founder Maggie Kuhn, who, on facing mandatory retirement at age 65, organized others in the same situation to fight this inequity. In Elmhurst-Corona, movements began when white block association leaders mobilized both established residents and new immigrant neighbors to preserve "quality of life," when Asian small business owners built ties with white, Latin American, and

Caribbean business associations to fight commercial rent increases and city-subsidized corporate expansion, when white and Chinese residents struggled to increase hours of service at their local library, and when black tenants and Korean merchants met together to contain racial tensions. Political movements like these, responding to market and state forces, destabilized and reconfigured everyday forms of life.

Fieldwork enables us to advance and extend theory. My sense of intellectual engagement rises when fieldwork transforms a set of theoretical concepts into a dynamic field of ideas within which observable consequences and new fieldwork hypotheses are generated. For those committed to a continuing interplay between bottom-up and top-down anthropological perspectives, the vast, ongoing expansion of urban space that the twenty-first century portends will be fertile soil for ethnography. Countless human beings will leave or be displaced from familiar places and create attachments to new ones. The social, symbolic, and political processes involved in this culturalization and deculturalization of space and place[36] offer a vital future for ethnography.

Chapter 12

Going Public: Responsibilities and Strategies in the Aftermath of Ethnography

Engaging the public sphere is central to contemporary anthropology's agenda.[1] Exhortations to do so are plentiful. Individual examples are readily identifiable. Yet analyses of how public engagement actually works are few. How may we disaggregate "the public sphere" into the actual pathways of audiences, sites, media, and roles that anthropologists encounter and navigate? And how do contemporary forays into action, advocacy, applied, popular, or public interest anthropology articulate with a disciplinary history of concern about ethical and professional responsibilities to the people we study and to "society at large?"

To unravel these questions, let us begin with an insight from Sandra Wallman: "It may be helpful to think of an anthropological enterprise as composed of stages in the movement of information. Collecting information [is] the first stage; then there's the writing-up of the information; and a third stage is 'applying' the information when asked to do so—these three stages are all within the purview of the most cautious and traditional academic anthropology. [In] crossing over [into advocacy] one may [also] push the inference of the information when not asked: 'Listen, I've found this out and you people should know about it!' "[2]

Using Wallman's framework, an ethnographer confronts one cluster of responsibilities while doing fieldwork, a second during the writing process, and a third in the aftermath of fieldwork and publication. This ensemble of responsibilities is addressed in the Society for Applied Anthropology's Statement of Ethical and Professional Responsibilities (available on the society's sfaa.net website).[3] The statement defines our responsibilities to the peoples we study, the communities affected by our work, our professional colleagues, our students and fieldwork team members, and our research sponsors. All of these may pertain in each of Wallman's three stages of an anthropological enterprise. The final set of defined responsibilities, however, applies solely during the third, postfieldwork and postwriting, stage: "To society as a whole we owe the benefit of our special knowledge and skills in interpreting sociocultural systems. We should communicate our understandings of human life to the society at large."[4]

Lionizing Boas?

Communicating anthropological findings and perspectives to "society at large" is not a new development, and Franz Boas, whose career spanned the 1880s to the 1940s, has been lauded as the discipline's foundational practitioner of such public engagement.[5] Boas was a fascinating figure, and understanding his work, career, and ideas remains an enduring task for contemporary anthropology.[6] Yet although Native American peoples were the subjects of Boas's and most of his Columbia students' fieldwork, his scholarly and popular writings dealt scarcely at all with the contemporary conditions or experiential realities Native Americans faced. The life of the Indians of the Northwest Coast during his 1886–1900 fieldwork years included logging camps, migrant labor, salmon cannery employment, depopulation, colonial rule, and the impact of the fur trade and gold rush. Yet aside from a reference in 1894 to European-introduced diseases and a brief defense of the legally banned potlatch in 1899,[7] these contemporary realities found mention only in his private letters, not his voluminous publications on the Kwakwaka'wakw (Kwakiutl) and other Northwest Coast peoples. Instead, readers learned about a vaguely past-time Indian culture, one without any individual Indians or any sense of how the actual world Northwest Coast people inhabited during Boas's day "appears to the Indian himself."[8]

This anthropological salvage mission—reconstructing an ethnographic present—was what he taught his first generation of students, and they remained resistant to scholarly or public engagement with issues of contemporary Native American life.[9] Only with Paul Radin's *Autobiography of a Winnebago Indian* (1920) did Boasian anthropology at last produce a "native's point of view" that included contemporary realities the book's subject himself experienced: craft sales to whites, farm and railroad wage labor, "Wild West" show employment, federal annuity payments, alcoholism, attacks from whites, imprisonment, and conversion to the Christian-influenced, pan–Native American peyote religion.

Boas's commitment to the scientific goal of salvaging culture as he understood it was more important than the life circumstances of his informants. This may also be gauged by his treatment of father and son Qisuk and Minik, two of six Polar Inuit transported to New York City in 1897 by explorer Robert Peary in fulfillment of Boas's request "to bring back an Eskimo."[10] Boas had done fieldwork in 1883–1884 with the Baffinland Inuit, south of the Polar group, and he continued to correspond with whaling captains and a missionary, whose materials he edited for publication by the American Museum of Natural History where he was a curator. He arranged to house the six Polar Inuit men in the museum, but, busy with other tasks, he assigned his student Alfred Kroeber to work with them. The men supplied Kroeber with enough information on their language and culture for three publications.

Within eight months, four had died of tuberculosis. Boas staged a mock funeral for Qisuk and lied to Minik about what he did with his father's body, which in fact was autopsied and accessioned to the museum's collections. When Minik later discovered what had happened, he asked for the remains so he could bury them, but they stayed in the museum. Boas defended his actions in the press, stating that the fake burial was conducted "to appease the boy, and keep him from discovering that his father's body had been chopped up and bones placed in the collection of the institution." Only in 1993 were they repatriated for burial in Greenland.[11]

Although he did not conduct research with African Americans, Boas was outspoken in denouncing the unfounded white presumption of black inferiority. In 1906, he asked industrialist-philanthropist Andrew Carnegie to fund an "African Institute" to focus on "scientific study of this civilization," "the anatomy of the Negro," and "the Negro race in this country."[12] Although Carnegie turned him down, Boas pursued this research agenda over a three-decade period. He produced popular and scholarly contributions, as did his collaborators Elsie Clews Parsons, Melville Herskovits, Zora Neale Hurston, and Otto Klineberg.[13] Boas undoubtedly was a liberal in his time in terms of prevailing white attitudes toward Africans and black Americans, yet what he advocated publicly as a solution to "the Negro problem" in the United States was their disappearance via miscegenation between white men and black women (see Chapter 8).

The point of critically appraising his work is "neither to praise Boas nor to damn him."[14] Rather, it is to understand how his postfieldwork actions and omissions within "society at large" help us frame current ideas about responsibilities to the peoples and communities we study and also to a "society as a whole" that includes both them and their ethnographers.[15] In terms of a publicly engaged anthropology in relation to living Native Americans, Boas's record was minuscule.[16] In relation to African Americans, it was mixed, and perhaps anthropology is fortunate that he was not more successful in publicizing his recipe for racial harmony.

An Alternative Genealogy

Measured against the SfAA Statement of Ethical and Professional Responsibilities, Boas did not "communicate to society at large" any anthropological understanding of the contemporary situation of the Native Americans he and his students studied, and what he advocated for African Americans failed to convey "respect for their dignity, integrity, and worth" or to affirm the "continued existence of a diversity of human communities." In neither case did he seriously question unequal power relationships between his own white North American society and the peoples he studied and wrote about. But before Boas and since Boas, other anthropologists did and have acted differently, both in writings and in public actions that "spoke truth to power" on behalf of the peoples they studied.

Morgan on Seneca Land and Custer's Last Stand

In the 1830s, the owners of the Ogden Land Company in upstate New York persuaded Congress to purchase reservation land in Wisconsin for "removal" of the Seneca, one of the six Iroquois nations. Ogden agents then began bribing Seneca chiefs to sell them rights to their valuable tribal land near Buffalo, New York. A number of chiefs complied, but most Seneca refused to move, and a national controversy resulted. In 1846, Lewis Henry Morgan traveled to Washington, D.C. to deliver to the president and U.S. Senate a memorial from several hundred white Upstate New York supporters of the Seneca resisters. The case dragged on until 1857, when Congress appropriated funds for the Seneca to buy back their land from Ogden.[17]

Morgan's involvement with the Iroquois eventuated in his book, *The League of the Ho-de-no-sau-nee, or Iroquois*, anthropology's first ethnography, published in 1851. In the book's final chapter, concerning contemporary issues and the "Future Destiny of the Indian," he wrote,

> Our Indian relations, from the foundation of the Republic to the present moment, have been administered with reference to the ultimate advantage of the government itself; in all prominent negotiations the profit has been on the side of the government, and the loss on that of the Indian. In addition to this, instances of sharp-sighted diplomacy, of ungenerous coercion, and of grievous injustice, are to be found in the journal of our Indian transactions—a perpetual stigma upon the escutcheon of our Republic. If references are demanded the reader may turn to the Seminoles, or the Georgia Cherokee treaty, or to the more recent treaties with the Iroquois themselves, in which the government bartered away its integrity, to minister to the rapacious demands of the Ogden Land Company.[18]

Years later, following the Sioux defeat of General George Armstrong Custer at the Little Big Horn in 1876, Morgan, now a respected scientist and national figure, again castigated his government's Indian policy. In the national magazine *The Nation*, he wrote: "Who shall blame the Sioux for defending themselves, their wives and children, when attacked in their own encampment and threatened with destruction? Before the summer is over we may expect to hear of the destruction of the great body of these unreasoning and unreasonable Indians, who refuse to treat for the surrender of their lands upon terms they do not approve, and whose extermination may be regarded by some as a merited punishment. The good name of our country cannot bear many wars of this description."[19]

Other of Morgan's views and actions with respect to Native Americans and African Americans are objectionable by today's professional standards.[20] We are likely to be disappointed if we make formative anthropological figures such as Morgan or Boas into unblemished disciplinary paragons. We need, rather, to be aware of their complexity, drawing from their actions, or inaction, lessons for contemporary practice.

Cushing on a Land Grab at Zuni

While conducting his 1879–1884 fieldwork at Zuni Pueblo for the Bureau of American Ethnology,[21] in 1882, Frank Hamilton Cushing tangled with U.S. Senator John Logan of Illinois after discovering that the legislator's son-in-law had registered a claim to the Zunis' Nutria spring and surrounding irrigated farmland. Logan had learned that this tract was mistakenly omitted from the government's official demarcation of Zuni boundaries five years earlier, and he passed the information to his daughter's husband. Cushing knew the Zunis had farmed the eleven hundred–acre parcel for centuries, and he briefed a journalist friend about the matter.

Newspaper reports soon appeared accusing Senator Logan of "disreputable land transactions." Logan was outraged and retaliated by pressuring BAE director John Wesley Powell to recall Cushing to Washington or lose Congressional financial support. Powell complied. This ended Cushing's fieldwork at the pueblo. It was not until 1891 that the Nutria claim was resolved in the Zunis' favor.[22]

Wilson on the Northern Rhodesia Mining Industry

In 1938, the Malinowski-trained fieldworker Godfrey Wilson undertook applied anthropological research in the Northern Rhodesian (now Zambian) mining community Broken Hill (now Kabwe). Six striking African miners had been killed by police in this British colony in 1935, and at the government's request, the mining companies consented to provide funds for background research about their African labor force. Granted permission to work at only one mine, Wilson collected data on the workers' migration patterns, budgets, and social life. After further strikes in 1940 and the killing of seventeen black miners by colonial troops, Wilson was ordered to suspend and then end his fieldwork. His 1941–1942 report, an exemplary ethnography of the present, hardly pleased its financial sponsors.

> Most of the men come to town in their sixteenth year, to participate in the industrial revolution which is reshaping their world, and spend the next twenty years or so mainly in the towns. When they marry they either do so in town or bring wives from the country to live in town with them. The rest of the population, however, cannot generally follow owing to the low urban wages, the absence of light

> work, the absence of pensions and the absence of adequate accommodation. There is thus a disproportionate number of able-bodied young men in town and disproportionate number of women, children, old people, and cripples in the country. The withdrawal of young men from the rural areas destroys the balance of the old primitive agricultural systems, without creating a new market sufficient to make any general revolution in agricultural methods possible. Of the small market for agricultural produce, moreover, a large part is already occupied by immigrant European farmers employing unskilled African labour at low wages. The distant rural areas are thus left poor and hungry; their poverty drives to town all the men who can possibly find a living there; and this, in its turn, keeps urban wages low.[23]

The mine management and white settlers already had been disturbed that Wilson and his wife Monica (née Hunter), also an anthropologist, socialized with Africans and that Godfrey was a pacifist opposed to fighting in World War II. Under pressure, he resigned from his research position in 1941. He then served as a combat ambulance corps volunteer until he committed suicide later during the war.[24]

Goldschmidt on California Agriculture

Walter Goldschmidt's ten months of fieldwork in California's Central Valley in the early 1940s uncovered the deleterious social impact of large-scale, industrialized food production. He found that class and ethnic division were more pronounced in the corporate-controlled, mechanized production setting, and more social interaction and stronger community ties existed where family farms prevailed. As a second, comparative phase of his research was getting underway, California agribusiness interests began attacking him and his work, enlisting a member of Congress, major California newspapers, and anti–New Deal radio commentator Fulton Lewis. Having received a PhD degree for his study of one community in 1940 and then preparing to test his findings in two others, Goldschmidt found himself vilified and labeled a communist. Ironically, Goldschmidt had been recommended by his University of California professor, Alfred Kroeber, for a U.S. Department of Agriculture research appointment with "the dubious compliment that I was 'not the reformer type.'"[25]

Goldschmidt's initial study, *As You Sow*, a classic ethnography of the present, was published commercially by the Free Press in 1947. Publication of *Agribusiness and the Rural Community*, his comparative follow-up research completed in 1944, was suppressed at agribusiness's behest by the U.S. secretary of agriculture, whose department had funded it. It was issued in December 1946 by the Senate Small Business Committee under the auspices of its chair, a liberal Montana Democrat who feared further delay would doom it after a newly elected Republican-majority Congress took power in 1947. That year, the valuable series of rural ethnographic studies sponsored by the U.S. Bureau of Agricultural Economics since the 1930s ended via an explicit provision in the Department of Agriculture appropriation to discontinue funding.

Years later, in the mid-1970s, Goldschmidt reflected that agribusiness continued to dominate U.S. food production and that the negative social consequences he had documented and predicted would worsen in fact had done so, abetted by proagribusiness government policies and subsidies.[26]

Modes of Advocacy

At its best, traditional ethnography has embodied the humanistic goal of "broadening human understanding" by "persuading audiences that 'other [non-Western or nonmainstream] cultures' make sense in the light of 'other' premises."[27] In fulfilling this mission, ethnographers as "interpreters of cultural differences" seek to demonstrate "the relation of present action to a body of values initiated in the past."[28] The classic Iroquois and Zuni ethnographies of Morgan and Cushing helped initiate and well exemplify this orientation.

In contrast to traditional ethnography, an advocacy orientation focuses on the past and present in relation to the future. As Peter Harries-Jones puts it, advocacy anthropology re-envisions "culture" dynamically—as a human group's "capacity for action"—and recasts "society" fluidly—as "what [a group] makes itself to be."[29] Embracing a "concern with the outcome," the advocacy approach thus begins with ethnographies of the present. But it also implicates the ethnographer in "putting knowledge to use" by, at a minimum, "helping shape the way people view themselves in relation to issues" and, more expansively, by helping to "strengthen the representation of economically and politically marginal groups who have been denied a voice in societal design and action in the past."[30] The Broken Hill and California Central Valley ethnographies of Wilson and Goldschmidt exemplify this orientation.[31]

For some anthropologists, advocacy occurs mainly during fieldwork, with advocacy goals determining research practice.[32] This approach, termed "participatory action research" by William Foote Whyte and labeled simply "advocacy anthropology" by John van Willigen, was first well described in the 1970s by Stephen and Jean Schensul and Sue-Ellen Jacobs.[33] For other anthropologists, advocacy takes place primarily beyond the immediate research setting in efforts to engage public audiences and to influence power holders.[34] Sometimes this occurs during the fieldwork stage (as with Morgan and the Seneca or Cushing at Zuni), but more often, it follows in the postfieldwork and postwriting stages (as with Wilson and Goldschmidt).

During 1983–1996, I directed a long-term team research project on relations between established white and newcomer black, Asian, and Latin American residents in the Elmhurst-Corona neighborhood in Queens, New York City (see Chapters 1–3).[35] My choice of topic and setting involved ethnographic interests in ethnic relations and political activism from previous fieldwork in Ghana and with the Gray Panthers, as well as personal considerations as a "citizen"[36]: I am a lifelong New Yorker; lived part of my childhood in Queens; formed my political and professional anthropological outlook in the 1960s; and since 1972, have taught increasingly diverse students at Queens College, part of the public City University of New York.

My research proposed to identify factors that promoted or impeded interracial and U.S.-born/immigrant interaction, cooperation, and political efficacy in this complex Queens setting, one that mirrored larger transformations in U.S. society. It was funded by the National Science Foundation and the Ford Foundation. Ford later adopted our team approach as a model for a national research project on immigration and racial change in six other U.S. cities.[37] Our work clearly was "policy relevant research"[38] aimed at understanding the present in relation to the future. The conclusion to my book *The Future of Us All* consists of "lessons that may be drawn from the Elmhurst-Corona story."[39]

During our fieldwork, all team members attempted to accommodate requests from local community groups and leaders, something I saw as part of our ethical and professional responsibilities. For me, this included speaking invitations from the local Community Board, a civic association, two branch libraries, and three senior centers, as well as invited membership in an African American–led "Community Task Force" formed after an incident of black-Korean conflict at a local supermarket.[40] I also wrote short pieces for Elmhurst and Queens newspapers and the Queens branch of the Chinatown Planning Council and accepted similar speaking and writing requests in other Queens neighborhoods and at Queens College.[41]

In 1986, our team conducted a six-month applied research project for the Elmhurst Economic Development Corporation, under which we contracted to survey and produce a report on the several hundred businesses along that neighborhood's commercial streets. We later extended the survey to Corona, with sponsorship by the Corona Community Development Corporation. During 1987–1990 I served as founding director of the Asian/American Center at Queens College, where my research team became staff members. There we initiated a free service funded by the Queens borough president to translate documents for community organizations and government agencies into Chinese, Korean, Spanish, and Hindi.

These instances of fieldwork reciprocity and applied activities did not transform my Elmhurst-Corona fieldwork overall into participatory action research or advocacy anthropology. My research stance remained primarily "critic and scholar in the academic world,"[42] observing and analyzing rather than participating in advocacy, as I had during 1977–1978 at the Berkeley Gray Panthers Over 60 Health Clinic.[43] Moreover, unlike the politically disempowered Iroquois, Zuni, Northern Rhodesian miners, or California agricultural workers, Elmhurst-Corona's civic activists did not need an anthropologist ally to speak for them in the wider political arena. They spoke for themselves, using skills and organization that it was my job to study and describe. My later postfieldwork advocacy role was primarily "helping shape the way people view themselves in relation to issues." This included people in the local community and in the wider "public sphere" of "society at large."

The Aftermath of an Ethnography

Although I desired to produce a fieldwork-based ethnography within disciplinary traditions I value, my intended audiences while writing *The Future of Us All* were, first, the white, black, Latin American, and Asian civic activists the book is about and, second, other Elmhurst-Corona, Queens, and

New York City residents. I wanted to portray the local "wardens"[44] I studied to themselves, each other, and their neighbors and to provide what I as author saw as the relevant historical, demographic, economic, and political context. Accordingly I tried to write readable prose, maintain narrative flow, and subordinate academic cross-discussion.

I did include in the text ideas and concepts I wanted all my readers to grasp (from Jane Jacobs, Max Gluckman, Anthony Leeds, Fernand Braudel, Jack Newfield and Paul DuBrul, Robert Fitch, and others), because I found them important to my arguments. For academic readers, I placed in endnotes a Victor Turner–F. G. Bailey–J. Clyde Mitchell Manchester political anthropology thread; David Kertzer, Sally Falk Moore and Barbara Myerhoff, Judith Irvine, Edward Schieffelin, Talal Asad, Maurice Bloch, and Mary Douglas on ritual; Cheryl Townsend Gilkes and Karen Sacks on female activists; and scholarly commentary on "civil society," theories of community organizing, U.S. versus Western European political economies, and debates over the burdens or benefits of immigration.

Overall, my aim was to avoid in the body of the book the "parade of social theory"[45] found in much contemporary anthropology and to employ no more theory than I needed to organize and tell my story. Gratifyingly, the book was well received and reviewed by academic colleagues. In 1999, it was awarded the Anthony Leeds prize by the Society for Urban, National, and Transnational/Global Anthropology, the Prize for Distinguished Achievement in the Critical Study of North America by the Society for the Anthropology of North America, and a Commendation for Excellence in Ethnographic Writing by the Society for Humanistic Anthropology. In 2002, it won the prestigious J. I. Staley Prize of the School of American (now Advanced) Research in Santa Fe, New Mexico.

Going Public

As my book neared completion, I began to think about the impending third stage of this anthropological enterprise. As Wallman observes, "Today it is very difficult to say 'O.K., now I've done the job and what other people decide to do with the material is not my problem.' The difference is particularly true when the anthropologist is working in his or her own culture. Your material by itself is 'active.' *What you do with what you find is the new issue.*"[46]

Understanding this in terms of ethical and professional responsibilities, not merely selling books, I began to formulate strategies with which to engage Elmhurst-Corona residents as well as wider audiences in "rethinking the way questions are asked, the way issues are defined."[47] This proved to involve more time and harder work than I anticipated. Other anthropologists have had similar experiences,[48] and sharing our stories may be useful to still others planning "third stage" activities. In this spirit, rather than adding to theoretical debate about "public interest anthropology," I adopt here an ethnographic approach and discuss the audiences, sites, media, and roles I encountered and what I learned from them.

People and Community Studied: Elmhurst-Corona

In 1996, I asked a dozen Elmhurst-Corona civic leaders to read drafts of my book's sections or chapters in which they appeared. As John Barnes has observed, "The book or report that follows the inquiry may well become an authoritative document that can be appealed to in future struggles and negotiations. Hence it is only fair that the citizens should be associated with the writing of the report, even if only to provide them with an opportunity to repudiate it."[49] Several gave detailed responses, including corrections and additional information.[50] All had positive reactions except Rose Rothschild, the Community Board's district manager. She told me that the chapter on quality of life issues[51] put the area in a bad light, and I countered that it covered the same topics as did her own annual District Needs statements.[52] She also objected that the chapter that was focused on her activities as district manager[53] identified as "allies" people she thought of as "friends" and presented her leadership as "manipulation," a word I did not use. In contrast, several of her supporters commended me for my portrayal of her skills and range of operation and validated my description of her critical leadership during the 1980s and 1990s.

I have tried to understand her response, particularly because my account was based on public activities and not interviews or confidential data. My guess is that she was surprised by the level of detail in my description of how she navigated among the neighborhood's diverse groups and interests. As Barnes notes, "a community study, focusing on local politics, if it has any success at all, will bring to light and record in cold print actions and relations that previously may have been obscure or hidden or preserved only in the ambiguous medium of oral tradition."[54]

Among other readers, Seung Ha Hong, a founder of the Korean American Association of Mid-Queens, told me, "You touched not only my heart, but my soul." He explained that my chapter brought back to him the suffering experienced by Koreans in the two police brutality cases that led to the formation of his association. He then told me that Sung Jin Chun, to whom I had also sent the chapter, had read aloud from it at their last meeting so that the more recent members could hear "the real history of the organization, which you, Professor Sanjek," had recorded. Haydee Zambrana of the pan-Latino *Ciudadanos Conscientes de Queens*/Concerned Citizens of Queens told me she enjoyed reading not only about her own organization but also about the white American and Korean activists discussed in the same chapter, people she knew but now knew more about.

When the book was published in 1998, I delivered or mailed sixty copies to Elmhurst-Corona civic activists, residents, and city agency personnel whom I had encountered in my fieldwork. Rothschild sent a short note expressing disappointment with the book. Other responses were more appreciative. Al Blake, a Lefrak City leader, told me that he read the book "cover to cover," and if there was anything he could do to help, "just ask," which I later did. Louisa Chan told the audience at an Elmhurst Library event that she had placed it by her nightstand to read when she wanted to fall asleep but when she picked it up, "This book is so interesting that it kept me awake." I realized, of course, that it was a long book, and I made sure the index was sufficiently detailed, so people could locate themselves.

The Elmhurst-Corona forum where I would most have welcomed dialogue, Community Board 4, was closed because of Rothschild's response. I did, however, give copies to many current and former Community Board members, several of whom shared their reactions. Lucy Schilero, who led the neighborhood's most active civic association, the Coalition of United Residents for a Safer Community, presented me with a plaque honoring the book at her organization's meeting two months after it was published. At this event, I discovered that several of her group's members had already read parts of it. So had Sergeant Pete Petrone of the 110th Police Precinct, who was also honored that night. He thanked me for sending a copy, saying he never thought that what he did was important enough to write about. Schilero told me that the parts of the book in which Sgt. Petrone was portrayed had been read aloud in the precinct house and elicited some good-natured ribbing by fellow officers.

In 1999, I was invited to speak at the Elmhurst and Corona branch libraries and in 2000, to Elmhurst teachers on Newtown High School Staff Development Day. For these talks, I used an outline that began with a brief description of participant observation and the neighborhood settings I studied—the community board, civic, block, and tenant associations, the small business sector, houses of worship, and public festivals and events. I then discussed five things that brought old and new residents together: concern for quality-of-life issues, such as school overcrowding and police indifference; revived and new public rituals; a decade-long citywide small business movement; diverse religious congregations; and the efforts of women leaders. I also discussed two things that divided local residents: the persistence of housing segregation, which affected African Americans but not Latin American or Asian immigrants, and the city, state, and Congressional electoral redistricting in 1990 that fragmented along racial lines local civic activists who otherwise had learned to work together. I made these presentations informally and enjoyed both the predictable and the unexpected questions that followed.

Society at Large: Queens

I used this same outline for other talks I gave in Queens during 1999–2001. These included rewarding discussions with African American and racially diverse audiences at branch libraries in East Elmhurst and North Corona; several dozen branch managers at a Queensborough Public Library conference; audiences at two bookstores, where neighborhood leaders featured in my book were present; a forum attended by public and private social service agency personnel; and a Democratic Party club in Jackson Heights. At the Woodhaven Cultural and Historical Society, a mainly white senior citizens group, I had anticipated agitation about immigrants and blacks moving into a formerly white neighborhood like theirs. Instead, I received rapt attention and polite response. This contrasted with racist and anti-immigrant remarks from several members of a white senior citizens community audience at Queens College. I also spoke about demographic and housing market change in Queens to a group of Asian American activists and service providers at a workshop on the 2000 U.S. Census. In all, I addressed about four hundred persons at these Elmhurst-Corona and Queens venues.

To the dozen academic audiences I also addressed during 1998–2000, I read a different paper, which summarized the book (Chapter 1). My experiences with community and academic groups validated Penny Van Esterik's suggestion that "we broaden our style of communicating in written and oral [forms] for different audiences [by] adopting a dual writing style: writing first to meet the scholarly standards of anthropology, and then summarizing the main points so that the arguments and evidence are readily available for advocacy groups and concerned individuals."[55]

I reached countless other Queens residents through media coverage. Five months before my book was published, a story in *Newsday*, a New York metropolitan area paper with extensive Queens coverage, quoted me on civic campaigns for downzoning and against megastores and also mentioned my forthcoming book.[56] Another *Newsday* reporter interviewed me for a cover story in its "Queens Life" Sunday section, which appeared the week my book was published. We met in Elmhurst, where I was able to show her and a photographer the locations of activities I wrote about. Two similar features in Queens weekly newspapers soon followed.[57]

As a result of these stories, I became a source of quotes for *Newsday* reporters and was featured in a *Newsday* person-of-the-day "Queens Profile." I also became a source for *Daily News*, *New York Times*, *Flushing Times*, and *Village Voice* reporters, sometimes quoted and otherwise used on background. Their stories were more or less related to my Elmhurst-Corona research and included coverage of ethnic conflict and cooperation in other Queens neighborhoods, results of the 2000 Census, interracial marriage, a public school siting controversy, and diversity in religious congregations.

Probably the largest Queens audiences I reached were on three half-hour cable television programs. The first focused on Corona artist Carmela George's paintings of stores, streets, and people in mainly Italian Corona Heights during the 1970s, just before new immigrants began to arrive. This program aired four times in 1997 and was later rebroadcast. I also appeared in two other programs, both in 2000. In one, Jyoti Thottam, a newspaper reporter, interviewed me about my book. In the second, I again interviewed Carmela George, who was also a block association leader I had written about in *The Future of Us All*, with two of her neighbors concerning their street, which had been featured as the city's most racially mixed block in a *Daily News* newspaper series.[58] Again, both programs aired numerous times, and all three were produced by George's son, Richard George.

Society at Large: New York City

During 1999, I accepted several speaking invitations in Manhattan arranged by people who had read or knew about my book, including staff members at the Citizens Committee for New York and the New York Association for New Americans, two philanthropic and service organizations concerned with city neighborhoods and immigrants. I made four presentations in one weekend at the American Museum of Natural History, mainly to drop-in audiences already visiting the museum. I also spoke about Chinese settlement patterns and neighborhood involvement in Queens at the Museum of Chinese in the Americas in Chinatown. In all, these Manhattan audiences together totaled perhaps two hundred.

Upon publication, I sent copies of my book, with the *Newsday* "Queens Life" feature story, to fourteen prominent New York City journalists and editors. Two responded. David Gonzalez, a *New York Times* columnist, read the book and called me, and we drove from Manhattan to Elmhurst. Our walking tour there ended at the Elmhurst Library, where, as usual, every seat was taken, and there was a long line at the book checkout desk. He wrote a wonderful column that captured the feel of the neighborhood, as well as my critique of city tax and development policies favoring Manhattan real estate interests at the expense of neighborhood services like libraries. I later quoted Gonzalez's column in my testimony supporting expanded library hours at a hearing of the New York State Assembly Committee on Libraries, an appearance arranged by a Queensborough Public Library official who had attended my Elmhurst library talk. Gonzales and I met again in Elmhurst at a memorial service for Olga Conway, a longtime resident who was a volunteer cultivator of the library's garden. I had introduced him to her on our first visit, and he published another sensitive column about her passing.[59] My work also received coverage in several New York City Asian-language newspapers, following press conferences at Queens College and at the Museum of Chinese in the Americas. This included the Chinese newspapers *Asian American Times*, *China Press*, *Ming Pao Daily News*, *Sing Tao Daily*, and *World Journal*, as well as the *Korea Times*.

The second prominent New York media figure who contacted me was Brian Lehrer, host of a weekday program broadcast on National Public Radio affiliate WNYC. After reading my book, he invited me to be a guest in 1998, and his well-prepared questions, generous half-hour time slot, and listener call-in responses made for a satisfying experience. I returned in 1999, this time, at Lehrer's suggestion, with two of the civic activists I had written about, Al Blake and Lucy Schilero. In 2001, I again was a guest for a short segment on immigration issues. Two other New York talk radio programs I did reached smaller audiences: "Crossing Wall Street," on WBAI, hosted by economist Bob Fitch, whose writings on New York City featured prominently in my book, and "The Communiqué," on WNYE, moderated by Bill Henning, a Communications Workers of America labor leader, on which I was paired with progressive urban planner Ron Schiffman.

My citywide television exposure was limited to a brief comment for an NY1 (a cable news channel) news report on Lefrak City. I declined to appear in a Newscenter 4 (NBC's channel 4 news show in New York) story about how immigrants in New York did not celebrate the Fourth of July. I told the reporter I did not believe this was true, pointing out that during the 1980s and early 1990s, thousands of Latin American Queens residents attended the Corona Fourth of July fireworks display I wrote about in my book (see Chapter 2). I countered that a better story would be how New Yorkers were reacting three years later to Mayor Rudolph Giuliani's 1996 "zero tolerance" ban on neighborhood fireworks, but Newscenter 4 had no interest in that. I turned down a CNN request to criticize the latest development in city school politics in front of Corona's severely overcrowded PS19 on a day Senator Hillary Clinton visited the school.

In general, I resisted becoming a know-it-all expert for the media, and if I could suggest a more knowledgeable anthropologist, I did. When a *Newsday* reporter, for example, asked for a comment about Romanian gypsies in Ridgewood, Queens, I directed her to David Kideckel, who had done fieldwork in Romania, and he became the source quoted in her story.[60]

Society at Large: The National Level

The month my book was published, I was quoted in a brief "Geographica" feature about Elmhurst in *National Geographic*, which has a world circulation of 21 million.[61] Several media contacts resulted from this, perhaps including the Associated Press (AP) news service writer assigned to interview me in 1999. We met in Elmhurst on the day PS89 held its annual multicultural street parade (see Chapter 3), and an AP photographer accompanying her took pictures that appeared with her story in the Queens edition of the *Daily News*[62] as well as in the *Boston Globe* and in newspapers in Ithaca, New York; Newton, New Jersey; Orlando, Florida; San Juan, Puerto Rico; Canton, Ohio; Springfield, Ohio; Sturgis, Michigan; Watertown, Wisconsin; Hibbing, Minnesota; Brookhaven, Missouri; McCurtain, Oklahoma; and Casa Grande, Arizona.

This coverage impressed upon me that Queens' ethnic and racial transition was of interest widely across the United States. Reinforcing this, a reporter for the Hamtramck, Michigan *Citizen* discovered my book, interviewed me by phone, wrote a story about Elmhurst-Corona, arranged to visit for a walking tour in Queens, and then published two more stories and an editorial. The *National Geographic* feature also resulted in correspondence with the eminent and Elmhurst-reared New Deal historian William E. Leuchtenberg. His essay "Queens," in his edited volume *American Places* (2000), drew on my book, and he mentioned it again in a 2001 article in *Newsweek*.[63]

I also reached nationwide audiences on three National Public Radio (NPR) programs. In 1997, sociologist Sylvia Pedraza and I were guests for a call-in show about immigration on NPR's "Talk of the Nation," hosted by Ray Suarez. In 1999, again because of the *National Geographic* feature, I was contacted by Marco Werman of the news program "The World," and we toured South Asian, Latin American, and Chinese music CD shops in Elmhurst, Jackson Heights, and Flushing. Two radio features with music and street sounds, plus my commentary on immigration in Queens, were broadcast by Werman and later repeated.

An appearance on NPR's "All Things Considered" with host Noah Adams in 1999 resulted in my largest audience of all. It was preceded over a couple of weeks by constantly changing telephone instructions from Adams's assistant about what to schedule in Queens. Then, unbeknownst to me, at the last minute, the assistant requested that the Queens College press office produce two students of immigrant background for Adams to interview. I knew neither student, and their Filipino and Trinidadian ethnicities were not well represented in Elmhurst-Corona. Most of Adams's tape-recorded interview with me was conducted as the assistant drove us through Queens streets, and I tried to give directions and answer Adams's questions at the same time. We wound up at Shaheen's, a South Asian restaurant run by my friend Tariq Hamid, whom Adams also interviewed. Although Adams certainly had read my book, under these circumstances I felt pressed to present my findings within a format over which I had much less input than in previous press encounters. Even less satisfactory were short on-air telephone interviews for the Australian Broadcasting Corporation's "Breakfast" program and the BBC's "Outlook," where I struggled to compress my fieldwork results into brief sound bites.

Society at Large: Religion and Politics

The most unexpected public responses came from the world of religion. I had discussed Elmhurst-Corona houses of worship in my book and stressed the role of local churches in bringing together diverse residents. A friend gave my book to her minister, Rev. Bruce Southworth of the Unitarian Universalist Community Church of New York in Manhattan, and after reading it, he delivered a sermon titled "The Future of Us All." I read it in its printed version and thought he well summarized my work and conclusions, but what struck him most was what he identified as the book's "theological subtext, one powerfully resonant with our faith. [Sanjek] declares firmly, clearly, cogently, 'Nothing is impossible if we believe people can change.'" That is how I ended the book, referring to changes I had observed in some white American residents who, over time, moved from suspicion and resistance to newcomers to cooperation and common effort with them.

On the Internet, I discovered two other religious notices. A thoughtful review of the book was posted on the webpage of the Witherspoon Society, a liberal Presbyterian group. And a section titled "The Future of Us All" was included in "Charting a Course for Participation in Mission," the 2001 John Cardinal Dearden Lecture, which had been delivered at Catholic University in Washington, D.C., by Cardinal Roger Mahoney, Archbishop of Los Angeles. His discussion highlighted my book's conclusion that a diverse society must purposefully ensure that organizations and political alliances are color full, or inclusive, rather than color blind, professing that individuals can somehow choose to bypass or ignore the racial categories of past and present U.S. society.[64]

Finally, my book led to working with two politicians. Sal Albanese, a former City Council member from Brooklyn, ran for mayor in 1997 and received 26 percent of the vote in the Democratic primary. His campaign message and economic policies resonated with what I had learned from my fieldwork and with analyses and recommendations in my book. In 1998, I sent him a copy, we met over breakfast, and at his invitation, I worked in his second mayoral primary campaign during 1999 and 2000 until fund-raising proved insufficient and he could not continue. Here I veered into what was perhaps a fourth stage of my Elmhurst-Corona experience: as a policy advisor and campaign worker, I now was functioning in what Susan Wright terms a "no longer anthropologist" role.[65]

During 2001–2003, I served as an advisor to Queens Borough President Helen Marshall's "Queens General Assembly" project. I knew Marshall, who had represented Corona in the State Assembly and City Council, from my fieldwork. An African American, she had declared of her district, "You've got to be able to pick up black votes, Hispanic votes, and white votes to win," which she did.[66] I had sent her a copy of my book, and she attended my East Elmhurst library talk. After she was elected borough president, I was recruited by her staffer Susie Tanenbaum, my former student, who had studied New York subway music.[67] Marshall had given Susie the task of convening a group of forty ethnic and community leaders of white, black, Latin American, and Asian background and also diverse religions to meet monthly and advise her on multicultural issues. I made recommendations of people I knew from my fieldwork and served as a sounding board and discussion leader over a two-year period. In 2007, I returned as guest speaker at Borough President Marshall's annual reception for her General Assembly and Immigration Task Force, and my remarks, "Cultural Diversity in Queens, from Then to Now," were posted on her Internet home page.[68]

Overall, the postfieldwork, postwriting stage of my Elmhurst-Corona anthropological enterprise was much busier, and I became more "publicly engaged," than I ever expected. I felt most comfortable speaking before Queens and New York City audiences and especially enjoyed dialogue with "first responders" to changes I wrote about—librarians, teachers, and service agency staff. The public forums at libraries, museums, and bookstores brought me into contact with hundreds of ordinary New Yorkers, some of whom had even read my book, and allowed me to share my research findings beyond the academic world. Here, and especially with the press, I learned indeed that "your material by itself is 'active.'" With journalists, I preferred face-to-face interactions, and especially those where we were able to meet "on the ground" in Elmhurst-Corona. In radio news and talk show interviews, I found program length and clarity of format were what mattered: when time was very short or the program's direction uncertain, I experienced difficulty in conveying my message. Print and broadcast media certainly allowed me to reach larger segments of "society at large" yet without the stimulation of response and feedback that live audiences offered.

Strategies for Public Engagement

Few anthropologists face the retaliation Cushing encountered when he decided to publicize the theft of Zuni land occurring in front of him or the antagonism to their research that Wilson and Goldschmidt received. Still, in less dramatic ways, when anthropologists communicate with audiences beyond their disciplinary colleagues and students, they engage some segment of "the public sphere" or "society as a whole." Whether in participatory action research or in postfieldwork "third stage" activities like mine in Queens, anthropologists develop advocacy strategies utilizing what Anthony Leeds terms our "lubricatory power" as information purveyors.[69]

These activities, I believe, have a deep disciplinary history and are far more common than recent exhortations to embrace a new public-interest anthropology suggest.[70] The audiences, sites, media, and roles are many, and my experiences no doubt resemble those of numerous colleagues. A small number of anthropologists may be guests on television news or interview shows, be published in the *New York Times*, or blog on the Huffington Post, but between such high-profile venues and the study or classroom lies a vast territory, which includes the following:

1. Writing books that can be read by nonanthropologists and nonacademics. This requires a prose style that is reader friendly and avoids the theory parade and abstract language ("*American Ethnologist* baroque") found particularly in anthropological journals.[71] There is useful discussion of this in Jeremy MacClancy and Chris McDonaugh's edited volume *Popularizing Anthropology* and in Jeremy Sabloff's 1998 Distinguished Lecture in Archeology, "Communication and the Future of American Archeology." This also involves writing in ways the subjects of our work can read, since today we should assume they will.[72]
2. Making deliberate effort to disseminate what we learn to various publics and leaders, not assuming they will discover it on their own. "Research is not necessarily used," John van Willigen cautions,

"utilization does not just happen. It has to be worked on."[73] First, we should let our colleagues know about our work by publishing articles in journals and sending them book flyers and article reprints, PDFs, and links. Beyond anthropology, our work—or better, concise information about it—can be disseminated to newspaper reporters and editors, radio talk show hosts, book review editors of nonacademic publications, bookstore managers, organization leaders, and government officials and their staffs. Everything matters, moreover, in creating "buzz" about a book or research finding: notifying alumni magazines, professional newsletters, and home institution press offices and sending excerpts to the *Chronicle of Higher Education* and other publications. I never discovered how *National Geographic* and AP writers, or Cardinal Mahoney, learned about my book, but whatever the channels, I am glad they did.

3. Writing articles and letters in nonacademic publications to influence public awareness and policy. Morgan's criticism of Custer's debacle in *The Nation* was an early example, and op-ed columns today are an important venue, about which William Beeman provides excellent advice.[74] The Internet opens even greater potential for public commentary.
4. Public speaking about our work and about anthropological perspectives on current issues. This includes forums at our own and other institutions; guest class lectures; teach-ins; and talks at public libraries, political party clubs, museums, local historical societies, senior centers, philanthropy committees, public school staff development days, bookstores, civic associations, and organization staff meetings. Donald Stull and Michael Broadway provide rich discussion of the extensive consultations and forums their research team colleagues conducted in communities affected by meat and poultry processing plants.[75]
5. Appearing on radio and television talk shows, debates, and documentaries.
6. Testifying at government hearings, commissions, and community-sponsored forums.
7. Working as a "source" with reporters to provide background information, like Cushing on the attempted Zuni landgrab or James Spradley on public treatment of alcoholics.[76] Sometimes this includes being mentioned in the story and sometimes not.

8. Consulting and conducting applied research for organizations.[77]
9. Being an expert witness. This is a complex area, with many roles and audiences.[78]
10. Being prepared to assume various "anthropologist no longer" roles, including working in private firms, NGOs, or government agencies, as well as in citizen activism, electoral campaigns, or political administrations.

Conclusion

In November 1999, as I entered the Flushing subway station, a man stopped me. He said, "You wrote the book, right—I know you—about Seung Ha Hong and Sung Jin Chun and the Mid-Queens Korean Association. Professor Sanjek, right? I've underlined, but haven't read it all. I'm John Park, and I'm having a fundraising event for my organization, Korean American Community Empowerment Council, in Jackson Heights. I'd like you to come, as my guest. Give me your card, or [tell me] how can I get in touch with you. You are our mentor."

More scribe than mentor, I think, but hey!—being recognized on the streets of Queens because my ethnography has entered its public life—that is the kind of engaged anthropologist I am happy to be.

Notes

Preface

1. For parallel journeys, see Fienup-Riordan 2000; Hannerz 2010; Shokeid 2007, 2009. See also Clifford 2003:1–22; Hart 2008; Jacobs 1996; Peterson 2000.

2. For comparable treatments see Jackson 1997a, b, c, d; Shokeid 2001.

3. Salzman 1994; see also Rosaldo 1989:30–32.

4. Tedlock 1995. Margaret Hall Warner's biography of husband W. Lloyd Warner includes much revealing exposition of her backstage role in his professional life: e.g., "I typed all of Lloyd's field notes" (Warner 1988:81).

5. Baker 2007. I thank Ulf Hannerz for this reference.

6. Sanjek 1969a, 1995, and Chapter 10, this volume.

7. Sanjek 1982c, 1998a; Sanjek and Colen 1990b.

8. Sanjek 1982a, 1982c, 1983, 1998a, 2009; Sanjek and Sanjek 1976; Sanjek and Colen 1990a.

9. Clifford 1983; Marcus and Cushman 1982.

10. Sanjek 1990a:xi.

11. Besteman 2010; Lamphere 2004; Lassiter 2005.

12. Burrell 2012; Coleman 2010; Constable 2003; Miller and Slater 2000.

13. Hannerz 2010:40. Compare Miller 1995:17–18 on "third way" anthropology.

14. Gay y Blasco and Wardle 2007; Halstead et al. 2008; Melhuus et al. 2010; Okely 2012. For an alternative view of ethnography in contemporary anthropology, see Marcus 2006; I thank Moshe Shokeid for this reference, and concur with his response to it in Shokeid 2007. See also Marcus 2009.

15. The panel papers by Charles Keil, Steven Feld, Thomas Porcello, Brett Williams, Roger Sanjek, and Kyra Gaunt were published in *City & Society* 14, no. 1 (2000): 37–146.

16. See Gibson 1988, for example, who does ask.

17. Gregory and Sanjek 1994.

18. Howells 1959; White 1951, 1953.

19. Wells 2002; see also references in Chapter 9 endnotes in this volume.

20. Darnell 2001:24.

21. Barnes 1977.

22. Okely 2008.

23. See also Okely 2012:142–144.

24. Bond and Johnson later contributed essays to my edited volume *Fieldnotes*.

25. Barth 1967a.

26. See also the Queens-based ethnographies of Guo 2000 and Tanenbaum 1995.

27. Stull and Broadway 2004.

Chapter 1

This essay is based on Color-Full before Color-Blind: The Emergence of Multiracial Neighborhood Politics in Queens, New York City, *American Anthropologist* 102, no. 4 (2000): 762–772. It is reprinted by permission of the *American Anthropologist*. Copyright 2000 American Anthropological Association.

1. Logan and Stultz 2011; Penny 2008.

2. Frey 1995.

3. Falcon 1985.

4. Salvo et al. 1992:4. In 2010, the area was 52 percent Latin American, 33 percent Asian, 7 percent white, 5 percent black, and 2 percent biracial or multiracial. For a broader demographic view of such U.S. "global neighborhoods," see Logan and Zhang 2010.

5. Chen 1992; Gregory 1998; Khandelwal 2002; Park 1997; Ricourt and Danta 2003; Sanjek 1998a.

6. Guinier 1994:6.

7. Swartz 1968. As Victor Turner (1974) phrases it, "the arena is a scene for the making of a decision. The field [is] the totality of coexisting entities, channels of communication, [and] ideological views about the desirability or undesirability of the extant stratification [of power. Anthropologists] are interested in concatenations of events, relationships, [and] groups which bring actors into field relationships with one another and form nodes of intersection between [arenas and] fields" (pp. 102, 126–41).

8. Jacobs 1961:117–134.

9. Sanjek 1990e:210–213, 243–247; see also Chapter 4, this volume.

10. For overviews of housing discrimination see Massey and Denton 1993; Yinger 1995.

11. Pecorella 1994:3.

12. All quotations in this chapter are from fieldnotes and documents cited in Sanjek 1998a.

13. Sanjek 1998a:74.

14. Bailey 1968:281.

15. Newfield and DuBrul 1977.

16. Gans 1988:111.

17. Chodorow 1974; Tannen 1990:227; Kaplan 1982:545–547; Hardy-Fanta 1993:13, 191.

18. Mitchell 1966:51–56.
19. Compare Gilkes 1980, 1988; Sacks 1988:121–122, 132–133.
20. Katznelson 1981.
21. Salins 1993:168, 171.
22. Leeds 1994.
23. Bailey 1971:7, 13–15, 24.
24. West 1993:6.
25. Sanjek 1994a, 1994b.

Chapter 2

Copyright for this chapter is held by Roger Sanjek and The Swedish Immigration Institute and Museum. The chapter is based on The Organization of Festivals and Ceremonies among Americans and Immigrants in Queens, New York, in *To Make the World Safe for Diversity: Towards an Understanding of Multi-Cultural Societies*, ed. Åke Daun, Billy Ehn, and Barbro Klein, 123–143 (Stockholm: The Swedish Immigration Institute and Museum, 1992).

1. Gans 1962.
2. Gluckman 1940.
3. Sanjek 1990d.
4. Cohen 1980; Errington 1987; Grimes 1976; Kasinitz and Freidenberg-Herbstein 1987; Leis 1977; Myerhoff and Mongulla 1986; Warner 1962.
5. Fortes 1936.
6. Evans-Pritchard 1937, 1956; Turner 1967; Tambiah 1970, 1985; Barth 1987.
7. Weingrod 1990 uses "ceremony of ethnic renewal" to categorize such events.
8. Sacks 1988.
9. Chen 1992
10. Kertzer 1988.
11. Like those of Embree 1939; Tambiah 1970; Turner 1967.
12. Clifford 1988:95; Geertz 1988:132.
13. Tambiah 1985:13.
14. Barth 1987:23.
15. Park 1989, 1997.
16. Chen 1992.
17. Khandelwal 2002.
18. Ricourt and Danta 2003.
19. Gregory 1992, 1994, 1998.

Chapter 3

The original version of this chapter is What Ethnographies Leave Out, *Xcp: Cross-Cultural Poetics* 3 (1998): 103–115. Copyright is held by *Xcp: Cross-Cultural Poetics*.

1. Mead 1969:xvi; 1976:3–4.
2. Mead 1976:3.

3. Smith 1959:54. Though utilizing "data" of a very different kind, "the Manchester code of ethnographic work" that Shokeid (2007:308) encountered in the 1960s was similarly, or professed to be, hypothesis resistant: "It was part of the prevailing ethos that an innovative sociological idea would inevitably emerge from high-quality ethnographic data."

4. Ottenberg 1996; Sanjek 1990d.

5. Sanjek 1996a, 1997; Emerson et al. 1995; see also Chapter 4, this volume.

6. Srinivas 1976:xiv.

7. Rubinstein 1991; Sanjek 1994c; Tax 1951.

8. On "using" fieldnotes, see Agar 1986:178–179. For a particularly vivid and effective use of direct fieldnote observations, see Southall 1969:233–243.

9. See Sanjek 1988.

10. A portrait of these two sisters is found in Sanjek 1998a:230–232.

11. See Ricourt and Danta 2003.

12. Compare "He Looked beyond My Fault" on Andrae Crouch and the Disciples, *"Live" at Carnegie Hall*, Light Records, 1973.

13. Chen 1992; Gregory 1998; Ricourt and Danta 2003.

Chapter 4

Earlier versions of portions of this chapter appeared as Ethnography, in *Encyclopedia of Social and Cultural Anthropology*, ed. Alan Barnard and Jonathan Spencer, 193–198; 2d ed., 243–249 (London: Routledge, 1996, 2010), copyright Routledge; and as Field Observational Research in Anthropology and Sociology, in *International Encyclopedia of the Social and Behavioral Sciences*, ed. Neil Smelser and Paul Baltes, 8: 5620–5625 (Oxford: Pergamon; Amsterdam: Elsevier, 2001).

1. On "context," see also Wallman 1997.

2. Sanjek 1990e:189–192.

3. Sanjek 1990e:193–203.

4. Sanjek 1990e:203–207.

5. Malinowski 1922:1–25.

6. Sanjek 1990e:207–215.

7. Sanjek 1990e:215–226.

8. Madge 1962.

9. Madge 1962.

10. Burgess 1984.

11. Agar 1980; see also Okely 2012.

12. With some hesitation, Clifford Geertz (1995:119–120) compares fieldwork to a chess game: "traditionalized positional moves . . . as one gets settled, finds people to work with . . . ; harder-to-standardize combinations of the middle game when one launches probes in all sorts of directions and tries . . . to relate them to one another; and . . . more formalized mopping up procedures of the . . . end game."

13. Richards 1939a.

14. Whyte 1955:303.
15. Johnson 1978.
16. Bernard et al. 1984; Briggs 1986; see also Okely 2012:17, 83–85.
17. Ottenberg 1990.
18. Mead 1977.
19. Lederman 1990.
20. Clifford 1983; Geertz 1988; Marcus and Cushman 1982.
21. Anglin 1979:49.

Chapter 5

This chapter is based on Anthropology's Hidden Colonialism: Assistants and Their Ethnographers, *Anthropology Today* 9, no. 2 (1993): 13–18. John Wiley & Sons Ltd.

1. See Crick 1992:177.
2. Malinowski 1967:9–10. See also Young 2004.
3. Sanjek 1990e:203–215.
4. Williams 1939; Belshaw 1951, see also 1957; Shelley 1978; compare Ova 1925.
5. Bulmer and Majnep 1977; Keesing 1978; Strathern 1979.
6. Sanjek 1990e:195–203. See also Berman 1996, 2001; Jacknis 2002b; Suttles 1991.
7. Spier 1928:83.
8. Osgood 1940:50–55, 1958:4–5, 1959. Fienup-Riordan's collaboration with Alaskan Native Yup'ik elders in several volumes (1996, 2005a, 2005b, 2007; Barker and Fienup-Riordan with John 2010) surpasses both Boas and Osgood.
9. Liberty 1976, 1978b; Parks 1978, 1981. See also Bailey 1995; Mark 1982, 1988.
10. Compare the frontispiece in Liberty 1976, and Liberty 1978a:44. See also Bailey 1994, 1995; Sanjek 1994c.
11. Linton and Wagley 1971:25; Linton 1923, 1926; Parks 1978:87.
12. Sanjek 1990e:195–203.
13. Sanjek 1990e:215–235.
14. Mead 1977:238. See also Jensen and Suranyi 1992; Sullivan 1999.
15. Geertz 1972.
16. Geertz 1960:383–385; see also Geertz 1961:161–171.
17. Redfield 1930; Stocking 1989:229–235.
18. Redfield and Villa Rojas 1934; Villa Rojas 1945. See also Bricker and Vogt 1998.
19. Rubinstein 1991; Sanjek 1994d; Stocking 1989:229–235; Tax 1979.
20. Bunzel 1952:v–xxiii; Sanjek 1993; Wagley 1949:122–137, 1983.
21. Lewis 1950, 1951, 1964; Sexton 1981, 1985, 1992; Vogt 1965. See also Vogt 1994:108–109, 265–266, 283–284, 303, 308, 315, 321, 359–360.
22. Thornton 1983; compare Owusu 1976.
23. See, however, Jabavu (1934), a chapter on "Bantu Grievances" that editor Isaac Schapera included alongside contributions from white authors in a volume on South Africa. See as well Matthews and Wilson 1981.

24. Quartey-Papafio 1910, 1911, 1913, 1914, 1920.

25. Brown 1973, 1979; Epstein 1958, 1959, 1961, 1981; Mitchell 1956, 1965. See also Barnes 1996; Schumaker 2001; and see Banks 2008.

26. Mafeje 1971, 1975, 1976, 1978; Owusu 1970, 1976, 1978; Wilson and Mafeje 1963.

27. Obbo 1980, 1990.

28. Kelly 1985.

29. Whyte 1955. See also Adler and Adler 1992; Whyte 1993.

30. See Spicer et al. 1969.

31. Suzuki 1981; Starn 1986. See also Nishimoto 1995; Hirabayashi 1999.

32. Later published as Yatsushiro 1978.

33. Ichioka 1989:25.

34. Yanagisako 1985.

35. Miyakawa 1979; Okubo 1946; Sone 1953; Uchida 1982. See also Ichioka 1989.

36. Sanjek 1990b:40.

37. Bond 1988; Sanjek 1990d:408–409.

38. Alvarez 1994. The 2010 report of the American Anthropological Association's Commission on Race and Racism in Anthropology contains no more recent employment figures.

39. In this regard, see Baker 1998; Darnell 2001:17–20; Harrison and Harrison 1998.

Chapter 6

This chapter is based on The Ethnographic Present, *Man: The Journal of the Royal Anthropological Institute* 26 (1991): 609–628. John Wiley & Sons Ltd.

1. Rapport 1989:26.

2. Clifford 1983, 1988; Clifford and Marcus 1986; Marcus and Cushman 1982; Marcus and Fischer 1986.

3. See Barth 1989; Beidelman 1989; Birth 1990; Caplan 1988; Fardon 1990; Geertz 1988; Jackson 1987; Kapferer 1988; Leach 1989; Mascia-Lees et al. 1989; Sangren 1988; Shokeid 1988; Spencer 1989; Strathern 1987a, 1987b; Whitten 1988. In my opinion, Clifford 1983 and Marcus and Cushman 1982 are lasting contributions, raising useful points for doing and writing ethnography. For other discussion of the textualist enterprise see Sanjek 1990a:36–37, 236–237, 254–255, 329n, 404–409, and essays of my fellow contributors to *Fieldnotes.*

4. Sanjek 1990a.

5. Fardon 1990; Ingold 1989.

6. Appadurai 1986.

7. Fardon 1990:16, 23.

8. Lutkehaus 1990; Smith 1990.

9. Fardon 1990:22, 24.

10. McKnight 1990; James 1990.

11. Parkin 1990.

12. Fardon 1990:26.

13. Parkin 1990:182.

14. Kapferer 1990:286; Gilsenan 1990:238.

15. Ingold 1989:4, 6, 28; compare Diamond 1964d:38–40.

16. Ingold 1989:11–12, 16, 19, 29; Holy and Stuchlik 1983.

17. Ingold 1989:20, 23; see Okely 1987.

18. Ingold 1989: 4–6, 19, 25–29, 30–34.

19. Sanjek 1990d:393–395.

20. Ingold 1989:29; compare Sanjek 1990d:398n.

21. Ingold 1989:5.

22. On its lineage, see Burton 1988.

23. Fabian 1983:80; McKnight 1990:58.

24. See Diamond 1964d:37.

25. There are, of course, studies of past cultures written in the present tense by anthropologists that involve no such pretense—compare Carmack 1972; Hudson 1973; Sturtevant 1968. Richard Henderson, for example, is explicit (1972:106, 230n) that his portrayal of Onitsha society is a reconstruction datable to "just prior to 1880." Rather than being a selective projection of current conditions into the past, this work triangulates ethnographic study of Onitsha institutions, oral traditions and memories, and documentary sources. In other publications (Henderson 1976), the ethnography of Onitsha's present is given due attention.

26. Parkin 1990 refers to Asad 1973. I would add, as roughly contemporaneous, Africa Research Group 1969; Berreman 1968, 1969; Bonfil Batalla 1966; Condominas 1973; Frank 1975; Gough 1968a, 1968b; Hymes 1972a; Manners 1956; Onwuachi and Wolfe 1966; Stauder 1974; Wolf and Jorgensen 1970. I also consider post-1970s feminism a valuable "critique" that orients us toward more valid and politically relevant ethnographic practice; see Caplan 1988; Colen and Sanjek 1990a, 1990b; Mascia-Lees et al. 1989; Sanjek 1982b, 1983, 1990c; Strathern 1987a; M. Wolf 1990. Both these critical currents establish an agenda and vocabulary of "ethics" different from that of postmodernist anthropology, on which see Birth 1990; Sangren 1988.

27. McKnight 1990:50–51.

28. Malinowski 1935, vol. 1:479–481.

29. Sanjek 1990a:103–105, 197–201.

30. This remains the case in symbolic anthropology in the view of Roger Keesing (1987); see also Hatch in Strathern 1987b:272.

31. Thornton 1983:508, 513; compare Goody 1957; Southall 1971.

32. Henige 1973, 1974, 1982.

33. Henige 1982:409.

34. Compare Henige 1982.

35. Fabian 1983:74, 76.

36. Fabian 1983:84–85.

37. Fabian 1983:45–50.

38. Fabian 1971, 1978, 1986.

39. Fabian 1983:35, 154, 156.

40. This sweeping overview obviously simplifies. I do so in order to situate *current* anthropological attitudes to the past in relation to the ethnographic method. My brief characterization of anthropology's changing attitudes to history, however, accords with Peel's (1987) persuasive analysis of interest in comparison through anthropology's history. His comparative Mode I (universal history) fits with the nineteenth-century evolutionist's active attitude toward the past and with White's neoevolutionism; Mode II (branching histories) with some strains of Boasian historical reconstruction (but see Hudson 1973:117–118), and Stewardian neoevolutionism; Mode III (universals and laws) with the passive historical attitudes of functionalism, configurationalism, structuralism, and scientism; Mode IV (regional comparison) with other strains of Boasian-influenced American anthropology and with work by some figures who operated primarily within Mode III; and Mode V (comparison of historical sequences) with many current attitudes to history. On anthropology and history, I find helpful Appadurai 1981; Carmack 1972; Cohn 1980; Diamond 1964d; Hudson 1973; Peel 1984, 1987; Sahlins 1985; Smith 1989; Sturtevant 1968. See also Des Chene 1997.

41. Moore 1987.

42. Ghani 1987:364–365.

43. Dirks 1979, 1989.

44. Dirks 1989:63.

45. See also Quigley 1997.

46. Ortner 1984:141–144, 158–159; Roseberry 1988.

47. In Ingold 1989:5.

48. Moore 1987: 727.

49. Moore 1987:728–729; Ortner 1984.

50. Hymes 1972b:14.

51. Ortner 1984:159.

52. Moore 1987:730–731.

53. Sanjek 1990e:187–270.

54. Stocking 1985.

55. Sanjek 1990e:237–243, 248–252.

56. Sanjek 1990a:110–111, 242–243, 329n.

57. Compare Parkin 1990:183–184.

58. Fabian 1983:30–31, 33, 60, 73, 87–92, 119–120, 148.

59. Compare Young 1984:10, 23–25.

60. Sharpe 1984:29.

61. Barth 1989:134; Moore 1987:730; Parkin 1990:194, 200.

62. Compare Jonathan Friedman in Keesing 1987:170.

63. See Sanjek 1990a: 247, 405–406.

64. Fabian 1983:67, 92–93, 105–141.

65. Sanjek 1990a:100–108, 395–398.

66. Fabian 1983:92–93, 106–107, 116–118, versus Fabian 1971, 1978.

67. Fabian 1983:118; compare Fenton 1987.

68. Fabian 1983: 108, 122–123.

69. Barth 1989:134, 141; Sanjek 1990a:174–176.

70. Compare Spencer et al. in Ingold 1990:23, 29–31.

71. Leeds 1976.

72. Sahlins 1978, 1985; Stannard 1989.

73. Moore 1987; E. Wolf 1990.

74. Compare Moore 1987:730.

75. Sanjek 1990e:187–270

76. Sanjek 1990a:92–121, 385–418.

77. Ingold 1989:23.

78. Sanjek 1990a:110, 243n, 254, 400.

79. Langness and Frank 1978; Sanjek 1990a:108–111, 189–195.

80. Mascia-Lees et al. 1989:7n–8n; van Maanen 1988.

81. Parkin 1990:183.

82. James 1990:127.

83. Pelto 1970:42; Sanjek 1990d:394–395.

84. Sanjek 1982a, 1987a.

85. See also Cohn 1980:201.

86. I agree with Darnell (2001:320) that "we must retain the possibility of finding one interpretation to be a good one and another execrable, epistemologically as well as anecdotally."

87. Pelto 1970:41–44; Sanjek 1990d:393–404.

88. Fardon 1990:19–20.

89. Haekel 1970; Naroll 1970.

90. Sanjek 1990d:393–404.

91. Curtin 1968.

92. Sturtevant 1968:460–461.

93. Naroll 1970:928.

94. See Clifford 1988:189–251. The debate in Ingold 1990 is relevant to this argument.

95. Stocking 1966.

96. Geertz 1988:132.

97. See Geertz 1995:42–44.

98. Compare Lederman (2005:64) on the "considerable . . . energy [over the past generation] to unmaking an older culture idea in favor of a concept of cultural practice as discursive, enacted, contested, historical, and unbounded." See also Malkki 1997; Ortner 2006:11–18, 50–53, 112–114; Strauss and Quinn 1994; Yanagisako 2002.

99. Goody 1957; Southall 1971; Wolf 1982:19, 1988. Linguists have long been attuned to such processes, and the import of several key writings is to rethink human history in multilingual terms—see Emeneau 1956; Hill 1978; Reinicke 1938; Sherzer and Bauman 1972.

100. Appadurai 1981; Barth 1989; Cohn 1980; Comaroff 1984; Geertz 1988:129–149; Hannerz 1987a, 1987b, 1989; Moore 1987; Peel 1984, 1987; Smith 1989. Yengoyan (1986) is perhaps more doubtful about the word "culture" than these others, but the thrust of his argument is in line with this wider view. He and Smith (1989) also situate the new view of culture in relation to "ideology," as does Roger Keesing (1987) in a thoughtful examination of the relationship between these concepts.

101. Clifford 1988, especially Chapter 10.

102. Ingold 1990; E. Wolf 1990.

103. Geertz 1988:147.

104. Compare Hannerz 1989:205; Mintz 1985:xxvii–viii.

105. Cowlishaw 1988; de Waal 1989; Hopper 1988; Williams 1988.

106. Parkin 1990:200.

107. Sanjek 1990a:407–413.

108. Sanjek 1990a:38–41, 407–409.

Chapter 7

An earlier version of this chapter originally appeared as Worth Holding Onto: The Participatory Discrepancies of Political Activism, *City & Society* 14, no. 1 (2002): 103–117, published by the American Anthropological Association, and is reprinted with permission. The copyright holder is the American Anthropological Association.

1. Kasinitz 1999.

2. Sanjek 1998a, 2009.

3. Sanjek 1998a:259, 415.

4. See Merriam 1965, 1973 for examples.

5. See also Keil 1979; Keil et al. 1992; and Keil's essays and dialogues in Keil and Feld 1994. For similar moves in the study of African art, see Thompson 1974; Ottenberg 1975.

6. Keil and Feld 1994:20, 159–160, 161–162.

7. Keil and Feld 1994:20, 24, 109, 129, 167; compare Chernoff 1979:117, 158; see also Keil 1966; Keil et al. 1992.

8. Keil and Feld 1994:23, 98–101, 190.

9. Keil and Feld 1994:22, 97–98, 122–123, 170.

10. Leeds 1994; Sanjek 1998a:12–13.

11. Although I attended three DSCU meetings in December 1970 and March and April 1971 and traveled with members to their 1971 Easter gathering and dance in Dzodze, the meetings and festivities were conducted in Ewe, which I did not understand. I was permitted, however, to photocopy a hundred and sixty single-spaced pages

of extraordinarily detailed DSCU minutes in English, covering thirty-seven meetings. The starting point for studies of African hometown societies is Ottenberg 1955.

12. Keil et al. 1992:5.

13. Sanjek 2009:115–126.

14. Feld in Keil and Feld 1994:146.

15. Chernoff 1979.

16. Kuhn et al. 1991:221.

17. The New York network revived under new leadership in 2003; see Sanjek 2009.

18. Keil and Feld 1994:111.

19. Roberts 1972:28.

20. Chernoff 1979:153, 162.

21. Crafts et al. 1993:210.

22. Clark and Anderson 1967:428.

23. Clark and Anderson 1967:319.

24. Diamond 1964a, 1964b, 1967.

25. Keil 1966; Keil et al. 1992.

Chapter 8

An earlier version of this chapter originally appeared as Intermarriage and the Future of Races in America, in *Race*, ed. Steven Gregory and Roger Sanjek, 103–130 (New Brunswick: Rutgers University Press, 1994).

1. Jordan 1968; Spickard 1989:235–342; Washington 1970; Williamson 1980.

2. Lieberson 1980:253–291; Massey and Denton 1993; O'Hare et al. 1991:19.

3. Drake and Cayton 1962:195; Racial Segregation 1991.

4. Alba 1990:12–13; Collins 1985; O'Hare and Felt 1991:12; Spickard 1989:280; Spigner 1990.

5. Davis et al. 1941:24–38; Drake and Cayton 1962:116–136, 556–557, 638; Powdermaker 1939; Washington 1970; Williamson 1980.

6. Quoted in Spickard 1989:299. In a 1991 National Opinion Research Center poll, nearly two-thirds of African American respondents said that they would neither favor nor oppose the marriage of a relative to someone of a different race (Wilkerson 1991).

7. Washington 1970:69–97.

8. Washington 1970:4–7, 114, 131–139, 153–155, 173–179, 187.

9. Boas 1945:80–81; compare Washington 1970:5.

10. Boas 1974:327–328.

11. Washington 1970:154, 177; see also Hyatt 1990:89–91.

12. Spigner 1990; Wilkerson 1991; Williamson 1980:189.

13. Collins 1985; Heer 1980; Spickard 1989:306.

14. O'Hare and Felt 1991:12.

15. Lieberson and Waters 1988:18; Jaimes 1992; Johnson 1991. For instances, see Alba 1990:32–34, 47–48, 138, 340, 342; Waters 1990:14, 61, 92.

16. Collins 1985; Gonzalez 1992; compare Alba and Golden 1986.

17. See Lieberson and Waters 1988:169.

18. Johnson 1991.

19. See Jordan 1968:89–91, 162–163, 217–228, 239–242, 477–481.

20. See Jordan 1968:102, 143, 254.

21. Colford 1987; Omi and Winant 1986:64–65; Waters 1990:2–3, 76.

22. Goodfriend 1992.

23. See Gans 1979; Waters 1990.

24. Alba 1990; Draschler 1921; Waters 1990.

25. Riker 1852:335.

26. Ernst 1949:295.

27. Draschler 1921:91, 175.

28. Gordon 1964.

29. Stuckert 1964.

30. Harris 1964b:56–57; Lieberson and Waters 1988:169; Omi and Winant 1986:57; Spickard 1989:331.

31. See Waters 1990:18–19, 167. Essays by Daniels, Gibbs and Hines, and Hall in Root 1992b discuss "biracial," "black-Japanese," "interracial," and "mixed" self-identifications by person with one black and one white or Asian parent.

32. Forbes 1990.

33. Compare O'Hare 1992:6–7.

34. See Murguia and Martinelli 1991; Nakashima 1992:162; Omi and Winant 1986; Waters 1990:99, 101, 109–110, 156–168.

35. See Alba 1990:311; Bonacich 1972:548; Light 1981; Spickard 1989:9–10.

36. Omi and Winant 1986:166; Ringer 1983; Spickard 1989:235.

37. Glazer and Moynihan 1963; Handlin 1959; Kristol 1966.

38. Banton 1983; Kilson 1975; Sanjek 1994a.

39. Bachman 1969:6–7, 11; Rink 1986:33–36, 42.

40. Padilla 1958; Rivera 1982; Thomas 1967.

41. Dominguez 1973.

42. Draschler 1921; Ernst 1949; McCabe 1872:734–737; Tchen 1990.

43. Daniels 1962; Galarza 1972; Gamio 1930, 1931; Ichioka 1988; Montejano 1987; Ringer 1983; Spickard 1989:36; Tchen 1984; Zavella 1994.

44. Leonetti and Newell-Morris 1982:25; compare Kikumura and Kitano 1973 on Los Angeles and California; Spickard 1989:25–120; Tinker 1973 on Fresno.

45. Yuan 1980:185.

46. Kitano et al. 1984:181.

47. Sung 1990:11–12.

48. Calculated from Lee and Yamanaka 1990:291.

49. Mittelback and Moore 1968:51–53, 58; Schoen et al. 1978:362–363.

50. Fernandez and Holscher 1983:299–300.

51. Cazares et al. 1984; Murguia and Frisbee 1979:384–385.

52. Falcon 1993:12; Sung 1990:18.

53. Sung 1990:18.

54. Fitzpatrick and Gurak 1979:34.

55. Falcon 1993:18.

56. Fitzpatrick and Gurak 1979:34.

57. Lee and Yamanaka 1990:291.

58. I have calculated these rates from tables in Draschler 1921; additionally, six of ten Indian, Korean, and Filipino spouses married whites. Schwartz (1951) traces the declining interracial marriage rate for New York Chinese men from 55 percent early in the twentieth century through the 1920s, to 20 percent by the late 1930s. See also Posadas 1981 on high intermarriage rates among Filipino men in Chicago during the 1920s.

59. Lee and Yamanaka 1990:291; O'Hare 1992:14; O'Hare et al. 1991:19.

60. Alba and Golden 1986; Fitzpatrick and Gurak 1979:1–12; Heer 1980; Hirschman 1983; Merton 1941; Spickard 1989:6–9, 361–369.

61. Alba 1990; Alba and Golden 1986; Draschler 1921; Goodfriend 1992; Lieberson 1985; Lieberson and Waters 1988; Waters 1990.

62. Calculated from Spigner 1990:215.

63. This projection was later affirmed: based on statistical analyses of U.S. population data, Goldstein 1999 estimated that 15 percent of whites have a close affinal relative of a different race, as do 36 percent of blacks and 85 percent of Asians.

64. See Benson 1981. See also chapters by Gibbs and Hines, Hall, Mass, and Nakashima in Root 1992b.

65. Glazer and Moynihan 1963; Kilson 1975; Omi and Winant 1986:38–51, 89–135.

66. Fitch 1989, 1991.

67. Marable 1990.

68. Falcon 1988.

69. Calculated from Spigner 1990:215.

70. See Alba 1990:9–10, 312; Bouvier and Briggs 1988:82–83; Heer 1980:521; Hirschman 1983.

71. See Posadas 1981; Salgado de Snyder and Padilla 1982; Spickard 1989:109–117, 149–151, 367, 408; Sung 1990:100–115; Valle 1991:79; articles by Bradshaw, Mass, and Nakashima in Root 1992b.

72. Atkins 1991; Campos Rajs 1991; Spickard 1989:338–339, 376; articles by Daniel and Fernandez in Root 1992b.

73. O'Hare 1992:14; articles by Daniel, Hall, Root, and Thornton in Root 1992b.

74. And by Washington 1970; but see Wilkerson 1991.

75. Kich 1992:317; Hall 1992:326.

76. See Padilla 1958; Rodriguez 1989; Sanjek 1971; Zavella 1994.

77. Rodriguez 1989.

78. Kerr 1991.

79. Marable 1990; see also Omi and Winant 1986:142–143.

80. Telsch 1988; article by Valverde in Root 1992b; Walt 1988; Wheeler 1993; Tarmann 2003.

81. Wilkerson 1991

82. Banton 1983:397; see also Kilson 1975:236–237; Waters 1990:167.

83. Alba 1990:268–270; Farley and Allen 1987; Massey and Denton 1993; O'Hare et al. 1991; Stafford 1985.

84. Logan and Stults 2011.

85. Lee and Edmonston 2005; Passel et al. 2010.

86. Passel et al. 2010:26–30.

87. Goldstein 1999:403; Lee and Edmonston 2005:30.

Chapter 9

Copyright for this chapter is held by Global Networks Partnership and Blackwell Publishing Ltd., 2033. The chapter is based on Rethinking Migration, Ancient to Future, *Global Networks* 3, no. 3 (2003): 315–336.

1. Appadurai 1996; Basch et al. 1994; Bestor 2004; Bhachu 2004; Clifford 1997; Hannerz 1987a, 1987b, 1993, 1996, 1998; Hansen 2000; Marcus 1995; Watson 1997.

2. Appadurai 1996:2, 4, 9.

3. Suarez-Orozco 2000:1–2.

4. Brettell 2000; Eades 1987; Foner et al. 2001; Glick Schiller et al. 1992; Gmelch 1980; Hannerz 1998:240–241; Kearney 1986; Mahler 1998; Suarez-Orozco 2000; Watson 1977a.

5. Sanjek 1998a:61–82, 134, 293, 386–389. See also A Year of Crises 2012.

6. Mahler 1999; Malkki 1995; Smith 1998a, 1998b.

7. Hagan 1994; Holtzman 2000; Laguerre 1984:33–48; Lessinger 1992; Stepick 1998.

8. See Brettell 2000; Eades 1987.

9. Foster 1991; Malkki 1995; Nagengast 1994; Rosaldo 1994.

10. Rosaldo 1994:402.

11. Conklin and Lourie 1983; Hu-DeHart 1994; Suarez-Orozco 2000.

12. Gordon 1964.

13. Hirschman 1983.

14. See, for example, Alba and Nee 1997; Foner 2000; Foner et al. 2001; Suarez-Orozco 2000.

15. Hu-DeHart 1994; Nagengast 1994; Ringer 1983.

16. See Marks 1974.

17. Du Bois 1903; Robinson 2000; Williams 1997.

18. See Flores 1985; Jaimes 1992; Trask 1996; Zavella 1994.

19. Zavella 1994:203.

20. Trask 1996:906.

21. Park 1997.

22. Basch et al. 1994; Manners 1965; Philpott 1977.

23. Chavez 2001.

24. Sanjek 1998a:70–75.

25. Rosaldo 1994:403.

26. Trask 1996: 906.

27. Hannerz 1993:385.

28. Foner et al. 2001:10; Suarez-Orozco 2000:24.

29. Foster 1991:238, 241.

30. Hannerz 1996:6–9, 1998:250–251.

31. Kroeber 1946:9.

32. Adams et al. 1978; Vincent 1991; see also McNeill 1979.

33. Kroeber 1946:9, quoting Lowie 1937:236.

34. See Snow 2009 and Earle et al. 2011 for compatible approaches.

35. Gibson 1988; Lamphere 1992; Lamphere et al. 1994; Sanjek 1998a.

36. Sahlins 1961.

37. Cavalli-Sforza and Cavalli-Sforza 1995; Jablonski 2002; Renfrew 1992; Sussman 1993. For more recent dates and interpretations, see Anderson et al. 2010; Mellars et al. 2007; Meltzer 2009; Peregrine et al. 2009; Pringle 2011; Schurr 2004.

38. Dumond 1987.

39. See in particular Cavalli-Sforza and Cavalli-Sforza 1995.

40. Hill 1978; Owen 1965.

41. Aiello 1993; Frayer et al. 1993.

42. Greenberg 1987; Nichols 1997.

43. Sherzer and Bauman 1972; Emeneau 1956; Matisoff 1991.

44. Ammerman and Cavalli-Sforza 1971; Cavalli-Sforza and Cavalli-Sforza 1995.

45. Bellwood 2001; Evett 1973; Hill 2001; Renfrew 1992. See also Bellwood 2005; Bellwood and Renfrew 2002; Richards 2003.

46. Turnbull 1963.

47. Kirch 2000; see Terrell 1986 for a perspective stressing intercultural reticulation.

48. Phillipson 1977; Sutton 1974.

49. Kopytoff 1987; Vansina 1990.

50. Barth 1961; McNeill 1979; Stenning 1957.

51. Casagrande et al. 1964; Cohen 1968; Hill 1970b:30–52; Stenning 1957; Watson 1977b.

52. Stenning 1957.

53. Kopytoff 1987; Meggitt 1977; Schapera 1952; Southall 1988.

54. Compare Piot 1999 on Kabre origins.

55. Aptheker 1939; Kent 1965; Price 1983.

56. Abusharaf 2002.

57. Chaliand and Rageau 1995; Cohen 1997; Wirth 1928.

58. Malkki 1995.

59. Abusharaf 2002; Basch et al. 1994; Holtzman 2000; Mahler 1995; Stepick 1998.

60. Khosravi 2010.

61. A Year of Crises 2012.

62. Cohen 1997:2.

63. Cohen 1997:66–81; compare Chaliand and Rageau 1995:xiii.

64. Bogoras 1904–1909:53–69, 680–733; Anthony 1990:902–903; Brown 1994; Casagrande et al. 1964:284; Takakura 1960.

65. Elphick 1977; Hodder and Hassall 1971; Lamley 1981; McLeod 1967; Sahlins 1992; Wilks 1975.

66. Arhin 1967; Barnes 1954; Law 1977; Omer-Cooper 1966.

67. Legassick 1996.

68. Johnson 1966; Rowe 1946:269–270; Wilks 1975:83–86.

69. Arensberg 1937; McLeod 1967.

70. Curtin 1969; Drake 1990:227–303; Lovejoy 1982.

71. Curtin 1967.

72. Davis 1985.

73. Stannard 1992; Thornton 1987.

74. Miyakawa 1979; Nishimoto 1995; Okubo 1946; Sone 1953; Uchida 1982; Weglyn 1976.

75. Chaliand and Rageau 1995.

76. Hannerz 1998:241.

77. Cohen 1969; Duany 2000; Hendricks 1974; Lynn 1992.

78. Basch et al. 1994:207–208.

79. Hannerz 1998:241.

80. Clifford 1997:244–277.

81. Anthony 1990:897–898.

82. Curtin 1984.

83. See also Hill 1966.

84. See also Wheatley 1975.

85. Cohen 1997:21.

86. Chaliand and Rageau 1995:7–28; Clifford 1997:273–274; Cohen 1997:4–15; Ghosh 1992; Kautsky 1925:242–273; Wirth 1928:11–27.

87. Wirth 1928:15.

88. Lovejoy 1978, 1980; Lovejoy and Baier 1975; Sutton 1979; Wilks 1968, 1982.

89. Dike and Ekejiuba 1990; Ottenberg 1958.

90. Lynn 1984, 1992.

91. Garlick 1967.

92. Lamphere 1987:47–64; McNeill 1979.

93. Anthony 1990:898.

94. Richards 1939.

95. Engels 1892.

96. Chaliand and Rageau 1995:159.

97. Arensberg 1937:86.

98. Crew 1987; Kiser 1932.

99. Du Bois 1899.

100. Lamphere 1987:64–91.

101. Thomas and Znaniecki 1984; Zorbaugh 1929.

102. Gamio 1930, 1931.

103. Hunter 1936; Marcus 1995, in which it is not cited.

104. Benedict 1961; Cohen 1997:57–66; Dotson and Dotson 1968; Jayawardena 1963; Klass 1961; Kuper 1960; Leonard 1992; Mayer 1961; Morris 1968.

105. Ballard and Ballard 1977; Desai 1963; Fisher 1980.

106. Bhachu 1985; Gibson 1988; Khandelwal 2002.

107. Bhachu 2004; Ghosh 1989; Lessinger 1992.

108. Chaliand and Rageau 1995:125–143; Freedman 1957; Nee and DeBary Nee 1973; Siu 1987; Skinner 1957; T'ien 1953; Willmott 1970; Wu 1982.

109. Chen 1992; Guo 2000; Ong 1992; Oxfeld 1993; Watson 1975, 1977b; Wong 1982.

110. Manners 1965.

111. Watson 1977a:2.

112. Palmer 1977; Philpott 1977.

113. Basch et al. 1994; Rhoades 1980; Wiest 1973.

114. Basch et al. 1994; Hagan 1994; Mahler 1998, 1999; Smith 1998a, 1998b.

115. Basch et al. 1994:128.

116. Basch et al. 1994:179.

117. Compare Kopytoff 1987.

118. Lozano 1984.

119. Boadi-Siaw 1982; Fraenkel 1964; Porter 1963; Ralston 1969. On continuing Brazil–West Africa links, see Matory 2005.

120. Chaliand and Rageau 1995:52–54.

121. Deshen and Shokeid 1974; Shokeid 1971; Weingrod 1990.

122. Hannerz 1993:384.

123. Appadurai 1996.

124. Hannerz 1987, 1996.

Chapter 10

This chapter is based on Politics, Theory, and the Nature of Cultural Things, in *Science, Materialism, and the Study of Culture*, ed. Martin F. Murphy and Maxine L. Margolis, chapter 3, pp. 39–61 (Gainesville: University Press of Florida, 1995). Reprinted by permission of the University Press of Florida.

1. Clifford 1986; Fabian 1983; Okely and Callaway 1992.

2. Compare Okely 1992; Wolcott 1990:61.

3. This is strongly evident in the autobiographical "Intellectual Roots" statements by the contributors to Borofsky 1994.

4. Sanjek 1971.

5. Leach 1984. On Columbia in the 1970s, see Lederman 2005:61–64.

6. Okely 1992:8.

7. Stocking 1991. See Collins 1997 on the late 1950s–early 1960s American anthropological scene soon to fracture.

8. Fried 1966; Southall 1970; Silverman 1965; Skinner 1964; Leeds 1964; Srinivas and Beteille 1964.

9. Bonfil Battalla 1966; Gough 1968a, 1968b; Manners 1965; Onwuachi and Wolfe 1966; Wolf 1969; Worsley 1964.

10. Deloria 1969; Leacock 1969; Liebow 1967; Nader 1972; Valentine 1968.

11. Davis et al. 1941; Dennis et al. 1956; Epstein 1956; Gluckman 1940; Manners 1956; Murphy and Steward 1956; Schapera 1928; Wilson 1941–1942; Wilson and Wilson 1945; Wolf and Mintz 1957. On Godfrey Wilson, Gluckman, and the Southern Africa–Manchester story, see Brown 1973, 1979; Gluckman 1975. On Allison Davis and African American ethnography, see Bond 1988; Drake 1980.

12. Goldfrank 1978:114–124; Landes 1970; Mead 1959:341–422; compare Murphy 1991:70–72, 75.

13. Ghani 1987:355; Murphy 1991:72–74; Sieber 1994.

14. Frank 1966, 1967; Wallerstein 1974; Wolf 1982; compare Roseberry 1988, 1989; Vincent 1986.

15. Gulliver 1985:49; Asad 1973; Berreman 1968; Gough 1968b.

16. Wolf and Jorgensen 1970.

17. Ghani 1987:353.

18. Sanjek 1982a, 1984, 1987a, 2009.

19. Firth 1972, 1975; compare Roseberry 1988:161.

20. Roseberry 1988; see also Roseberry 1989, which barely mentions the impact of the Vietnam War on anthropology.

21. Harris 1974, 1977, 1989.

22. Harris 1952.

23. Harris 1956, 1959a, 1962, 1967a, 1968b.

24. Harris 1964c, 1970; Harris and Kottak 1963. See also Sanjek 1971.

25. Wagley and Harris 1958.

26. Harris 1964b.

27. Harris 1958:34, 36.

28. Harris 1958:1.

29. Harris 1959b.

30. Harris 1966b. See also Mondlane 1969.

31. Harris 1965, 1966a.

32. Harris 1967b.

33. See Berreman 1968:391; Sahlins 2000:205–217.

34. Compare Wolf 1969:ix–xv.

35. Fried et al. 1968:ix–xix.

36. Harris 1968a.

37. Harris 1964a:129.

38. Compare Ortner 2006:2–3.

39. Harris 1968d, 1975, 1976, 1979, 1980, 1990a, 1990b, 1990c. In *Theories of Culture in Postmodern Times* (Harris 1999:31–64), he reprises and updates viewpoints presented in *The Nature of Cultural Things.*

40. Schein and Diamond 1966:1.

41. Dehavenon and Harris 1975; Harris 1968c, 1969, 1971, 1975; Sanjek 1969b.

42. Harris 1975. See also Johnson 1978:113–115.

43. Sanjek 1977, 1982b.

44. Epstein 1961; Sanjek 1972, 1978.

45. Sanjek 1982b, 1983, 1990c; Sanjek and Sanjek 1976.

46. Johnson 1980:364–365.

47. Johnson 1975, 1977, 1978:87–92, 106–110; A. Johnson and O. Johnson 1990; O. Johnson and A. Johnson 1975. See also Johnson 2003.

48. Barth 1967b; Epstein 1961; Firth 1954, 1955; Leach 1961; van Velsen 1967.

49. Gough 1968a, 1968b.

50. Baran 1957; Baran and Sweezy 1966; Magdoff 1969.

51. Frank 1966, n.d.a, n.d.b.

52. Fitch and Oppenheimer 1966.

53. Horowitz 1967a, 1967b, 1969.

54. Williams 1944; Myrdal 1957.

55. Berreman 1968; Bonfil Batalla 1966; Gough 1968a, 1968b; Worsley 1964; Manners 1965; Gulliver 1955; van Velsen 1961; Wolfe 1963; Geertz 1963.

56. Wallerstein 1961.

57. Africa Research Group 1969.

58. Mintz 1977, 1985; Wolf 1982; Ortner 1984; Roseberry 1988, 1989; Vincent 1986.

59. Compare Murphy 1991:79–80.

60. Harris 1979.

61. Sanjek 1991. See also Chapter 6 in the current volume; Ortner 1984; Roseberry 1988, 1989:33–37.

62. Johnson 1978; Pelto 1970. See also Barth 1978; Boissevain 1979; Hannerz 1976, 1980, 1990; Leacock 1969; Leeds 1964; Ortner 1984:144–145; Skinner 1964.

63. Barth 1978; Hannerz 1976; Sanjek 1974, 1978.

64. Boissevain 1979; Hannerz 1980, 1992; Sanjek 1996b.

65. Geertz 1973:363.

66. Barth 1989.

67. See Johnson 1987; Marcus and Fischer 1986; Ortner 1984.

68. Keesing 1974.

69. Geertz 1973:17, 20–21, 30, 45.

70. Smith 1990:369.

71. See Geertz 1995:120 on this "rumination and self-inspection" turn. See also Darnell 2001:279; Shokeid 2009:24.

72. Compare Lederman 2005:49–54.

73. Hannerz 1990:29.

74. Barth 1989:134.

75. Diamond 1964d:41–42.

76. Marcus and Fischer 1986; see Barth 1989:141.

77. Borofsky 1994:75–76.

78. Margolis and Kottak 2003.

79. Harris 1968d, 1974, 1977, 1979, 1989, 1999.

Chapter 11

An earlier version of this chapter appeared in, and is reprinted by permission of, *Human Organization*. Keeping Ethnography Alive in an Urbanizing World, *Human Organization* 59 (2000): 280–288.

1. Embree 1939; Frankenberg 1957; Halpern 1958; Lewis 1951; Redfield 1950; Yang 1945.

2. Davis et al. 1941; Hannerz 1969; Lynd and Lynd 1929; Warner 1963.

3. Sanjek 1971:1128. Holy and Stuchlik (1983:60–68) criticize Harris and Sanjek's work, but see the superb, unpublished 1978 dissertation by Blanco, especially pp. 60–63.

4. Bailey 1957; Barth 1959; Epstein 1958; Fallers 1956; Hunter 1936; Watson 1958; van Velsen 1964.

5. Sanjek 1990e:193–203.

6. Sanjek 1978, 1995.

7. Barth 1975:226.

8. Barth 1975:225.

9. Barth 1975:226.

10. Sanjek 1990e:222–224. See Dobrin and Bashkow 2006, 2010 for reassessment of Mead's Alitoa fieldwork.

11. Mead 1938.

12. Hunter 1936; Whyte 1955.

13. Sanjek 1972, 1977, 1978, 1982c, 1983, 1990c; Sanjek and Sanjek 1976.

14. Fox 1977; Leeds 1994.

15. Sanjek 1972, 1977, 1982c.

16. Chen 1992:45, 51–90.

17. Chen 1992:46, 91–143.

18. Sanjek 1998a:193–196.

19. Chen 1992:163–181.

20. Chen 1992:183–245.

21. Sanjek 1998a:230–238.

22. Sanjek 1989b, 1998a:337–341, 1998b:100–105.

23. Bloch 1974; Irvine 1979; Moore and Myerhoff 1977. See also Ikeda 1998; Rodriguez 2006.

24. Compare Schieffelin 1993:293.

25. Geertz 1995:81.

26. Srinivas et al. 1979:8.

27. Sanjek 1998a:156–164, 185–212.

28. Sanjek 1998a:196–202.

29. Sanjek 1998a:119–140.

30. Sanjek 1998a:379–385.

31. Fitch 1976; Newfield and DuBrul 1977.

32. See Plath 1990.

33. Hannerz 1996:65–78.

34. Sanjek 1998a:141–164.

35. Sanjek 2009.

36. Rodman 1992.

Chapter 12

An earlier version of this chapter appeared in, and is reprinted by permission of, *Human Organization*. Going Public: Responsibilities and Strategies in the Aftermath of Ethnography, *Human Organization* 63, no. 4 (2004): 444–456.

1. Ahmed and Shore 1995; MacClancy and McDonaugh 1996; Peacock 1997; Sabloff 1998; Sanday 2003; and see *Anthropology News*, published by the American Anthropological Association, and *Anthropology Today*, published by the Royal Anthropological Institute.

2. Wallman 1985a:80–81.

3. Society for Applied Anthropology n.d. See also van Willigen 1986:52–54.

4. Society for Applied Anthropology n.d.

5. Lewis 2001; Pierpont 2004; Sanday 2003.

6. Sanjek 1996a.

7. Stocking 1974:105–107, 224–225.

8. Sanjek 1990e:193–203; compare Briggs and Bauman 1999:501–506.

9. Goldschmidt 2000; Jacknis 2002a.

10. Jacknis 2002a:522.

11. Thomas 2000:77–83, 218–219.

12. Stocking 1974:316–318.

13. Baker 1998; Boas 1945:54–81; Pierpoint 2004:60; Stocking 1979.

14. Briggs and Bauman 1999:481.

15. Barnes 1977.

16. There is a one-page item, "Making the Red Faces White," in *World Outlook* 4(1), 1918, and a 1924 "Letter on the Laws against the Potlatch," published in *Bulletin* 3, Eastern Association on Indian Affairs, neither of which I have seen.

17. Resek 1960:28–44.

18. Morgan 1851:458.

19. Resek 1960:145; compare Thomas 2000:259–260.

20. Baker 1998:43–45; Thomas 2000:48–49.

21. Cushing 1883, 1920.

22. Green 1990.

23. Wilson 1942:79–80.

24. Brown 1973; Wilson 1977.

25. Goldschmidt 2000:804.

26. Goldschmidt 1978.

27. Paine 1985b:xiv; Singer 1990:549. See also Paine 1985a.

28. Harries-Jones 1985:239; Van Esterik 1985:60.

29. Harries-Jones 1985:237.

30. Hymes 1972b:14; Schensul and Schensul 1978:122; Singer 1990:548; Van Esterik 1985:61–62.

31. Compare Barnes 1977:47.

32. Sanjek 1987.

33. Jacobs 1974a, 1974b, 1979; Schensul 1973, 1974; Schensul and Schensul 1978; van Willigen 1986; Whyte 1997:109–121.

34. Van Esterik 1985.

35. See Chen 1992; Gregory 1998; Khandelwal 2002; Park 1997; Ricourt and Danta 2002; Sanjek 1998a.

36. Barnes 1977:4; Van Esterik 1985:63.

37. Philadelphia; Miami; Chicago; Garden City, Kansas; Houston; and Monterey Park, California. See Erickson and Stull 1998; Erdmans 1998; Goode and Schneider 1994; Hagan 1994; Horton 1995; Lamphere 1992; Lamphere et al. 1994; Pardo 1998; Saito 1998; Stull 1990, 1994; Stull et al. 1990; Stull and Broadway 2004.

38. van Willigen 1986:143–154.

39. Sanjek 1998a:367–393.

40. Sanjek 1998a:348–355.

41. Sanjek 1987b, 1987c, 1987d, 1989a; Sanjek and Chen 1986. At the Conference on 350 Years of Life in Queens, held April 16, 1988, at Queens College and sponsored by the Queens Historical Society, the borough historian, and Queens College, I gave the keynote address, titled The People of Queens from Now to Then (Sanjek 1988).

42. Hymes 1972b:26.

43. Sanjek 1987a, 2009.

44. Sanjek 1998a:258.

45. Firth 1952:vi.

46. Wallman 1985:219.

47. Van Esterik 1985:61.

48. Well described in Stull and Broadway 2004.

49. Barnes 1977:9.

50. Compare Brettell 1993:11, 21.
51. Sanjek 1998a:185–212.
52. Rothschild 1993, 1996.
53. Sanjek1998a:300–331.
54. Barnes 1977:10.
55. Van Esterik 1985:75.
56. Bazzi 1998.
57. Wax 1998; Tenzer 1999; Thottam 1999.
58. O'Shaughnessy et al. 1999.
59. Gonzalez 1999a, 1999b.
60. Wax 1999; Kideckel 1993.
61. All the World 1998.
62. Gardner 1999.
63. Leuchtenberg 2001.
64. Southworth 1998–1999; Teselle 2000; Mahoney 2001.
65. Wright 1995:66–67.
66. Sanjek 1998a:362.
67. Tanenbaum 1995.
68. Sanjek 2007.
69. Leeds 1994; Sanjek 1998a:12–13.
70. Compare Singer 2000.
71. See Benthall 1995:5–6.
72. Brettell 1993; MacClancy and McDonaugh 1996; Sabloff 1998.
73. Van Willigen 1986:154.
74. Beeman 1987.
75. Stull and Broadway 2004:117–144.
76. Spradley 1976.
77. For an excellent case study, see Stull and Broadway 2004:82–98.
78. See Good 2003; Kiste 1976; Layton 1985; Sanday 2003.

Acknowledgments

1. For brief autobiographical accounts of the impact of the 1960s on anthropologists Sylvia Yanagisako and Nancy Scheper-Hughes, see Borofsky 1994:200–201, 240–242.
2. Sanjek 1982a.
3. Colen and Sanjek 1990a, 1990b; Sanjek and Colen 1990a, 1990b.
4. Sanjek 1987a, 2009.

References

Abusharaf, Rogaia. 2002. *Wanderings: Sudanese Peoples in North America*. Ithaca, N.Y.: Cornell University Press.

Adams, William Y., Dennis Van Gerven, and Richard Levy. 1978. The Retreat from Migrationism. *Annual Review of Anthropology* 7:483–532.

Adler, Peter, and Patti Adler, eds. 1992. Special Issue: *Street Corner Society* Revisited. *Journal of Contemporary Ethnography* 21(1):3–132.

Africa Research Group. 1969. *African Studies in America: The Extended Family. A Tribal Analysis of U.S. Africanists: Who They Are; Why to Fight Them*. Cambridge, Mass.: Africa Research Group.

Agar, Michael. 1980. *The Professional Stranger: An Informal Introduction to Ethnography*. New York: Academic Press.

———. 1986. *Independents Declared: The Dilemmas of Independent Trucking*. Washington, D.C.: Smithsonian Institution Press.

Ahmed, Akbar, and Cris Shore. 1995. Introduction: Is Anthropology Relevant to the Contemporary World? In *The Future of Anthropology: Its Relevance to the Contemporary World*, ed. Ahmed Akbar and Cris Shore, 12–45. London: Athlone Press.

Aiello, Leslie. 1993. The Fossil Evidence for Modern Human Origins in Africa: A Revised View. *American Anthropologist* 95:73–96.

Alba, Richard. 1990. *Ethnic Identity: The Transformation of White America*. New Haven, Conn.: Yale University Press.

———, and Reid Golden. 1986. Patterns of Ethnic Marriage in the United States. *Social Forces* 65:202–223.

———, and Victor Nee. 1997. Rethinking Assimilation Theory for a New Era of Immigration. *International Migration Review* 31:826–874.

All the World Comes to Queens. 1998. *National Geographic*, September, preceding p. 1.

Alvarez, Robert R., Jr. 1994. Sifting and Shifting: The Recruitment of Minorities into the Academy. In Gregory and Sanjek eds., 257–269.

Ammerman, A. J., and L. L. Cavalli–Sforza. 1971. Measuring the Rate of Spread of Early Farming in Europe. *Man* 6:674–688.

Anderson, Atholl, James Barrett, and Katherine Boyle, ed. 2010. *The Global Origins and Development of Seafaring*. Cambridge, U.K.: McDonald Institute for Archaeological Research.

Anglin, Andrew. 1979. Analytic and Folk Models: The Tallensi Case. In *Segmentary Lineage Systems Reconsidered*, ed. Ladislav Holy, 49–67. Belfast, Ireland: Department of Social Anthropology, The Queen's University of Belfast.

Anthony, David. 1990. Migration in Archeology: The Baby and the Bathwater. *American Anthropologist* 92:895–914.

Appadurai, Arjun. 1981. The Past as a Scarce Resource. *Man* 16:201–219.

———. 1986. Theory in Anthropology: Center and Periphery. *Comparative Studies in Society and History* 28:356–361.

———. 1996. *Modernity at Large: Cultural Dimensions of Globalization.* Minneapolis: University of Minnesota Press.

Aptheker, Herbert. 1939. Maroons Within the Present Limits of the United States. *Journal of Negro History* 24:167–184.

Arensberg, Conrad. 1937. *The Irish Countryman: An Anthropological Study.* Cambridge, Mass.: Harvard University Press.

Arhin, Kwame. 1967. Financing the Ashanti Expansion (1700–1820). *Africa* 37:283–290.

Asad, Talal, ed. 1973. *Anthropology and the Colonial Encounter.* London: Ithaca Press.

Atkins, Elizabeth. 1991. When Life Simply Isn't Black or White. *New York Times*, June 5, C1.

Bachman, Van Cleaf. 1969. *Peltries or Plantations: The Economic Policies of the Dutch West India Company in New Netherland, 1623–1639.* Baltimore: Johns Hopkins University Press.

Bailey, F. G. 1957. *Caste and the Economic Frontier: A Village in Highland Orissa.* Manchester, U.K.: Manchester University Press.

———. 1968. Parapolitical Systems. In *Local-Level Politics*, ed. Marc Swartz, 281–294. Chicago: Aldine.

———. 1971. Gifts and Poisons. In *Gifts and Poison: The Politics of Reputation*, ed. F. G. Bailey, 1–25. Oxford: Basil Blackwell.

Bailey, Garrick. 1994. Francis La Flesche, Anthropologist. *Anthropology Newsletter* 35(9):2.

———. 1995. *The Osage and the Invisible World: From the Works of Francis La Flesche.* Norman: University of Oklahoma Press.

Baker, Hugh. 2007. The "Backroom Boys" of Hong Kong Anthropology: Fieldworkers and Their Friends. *Asian Anthropology* 6:1–27.

Baker, Lee. 1998. *From Savage to Negro: Anthropology and the Construction of Race, 1896–1954.* Berkeley: University of California Press.

Ballard, Roger, and Catherine Ballard. 1977. The Sikhs: The Development of South Asian Settlements in Britain. In Watson ed., 21–56.

Bank, Andrew. 2008. The "Intimate Politics" of Fieldwork: Monica Hunter and Her African Assistants, Pondoland and the Eastern Cape, 1931–32. *Journal of Southern African Studies* 34:557–574.

Banton, Michael. 1983. *Racial and Ethnic Competition*. Cambridge: Cambridge University Press.

Baran, Paul. 1957. *The Political Economy of Growth*. New York: Monthly Review Press.

———, and Paul Sweezy. 1966. *Monopoly Capital: An Essay on the American Economic and Political Order*. New York: Monthly Review Press.

Barker, James, and Ann Fienup-Riordan with Theresa Arevgaq John. 2010. Yupiit Yuraryarait: *Yup'ik Ways of Dancing*. Fairbanks: University of Alaska Press.

Barnard, Alan, and Jonathan Spencer, eds. 1996. *Encyclopedia of Social and Cultural Anthropology*. London: Routledge.

———, eds. 2010. *Encyclopedia of Social and Cultural Anthropology*. 2d ed. London: Routledge.

Barnes, J. A. 1954. *Politics in a Changing Society: A Political History of the Fort Jameson Ngoni*. Manchester, U.K.: Manchester University Press.

———. 1977. *The Ethics of Inquiry in Social Science*. Delhi: Oxford University Press.

———. 1996. Obituary: Matshakaza Blackson Lukhero. *Anthropology Today* 12(3):24.

Barth, Fredrik. 1959. *Political Leadership Among Swat Pathans*. London: Athlone Press.

———. 1961. *Nomads of South Persia: The Basseri Tribe of the Khamseh Confederacy*. Oslo: Oslo University Press.

———. 1967a. Economic Spheres in Darfur. In *Themes in Economic Anthropology*, ed. Raymond Firth, 149–174. London: Tavistock.

———. 1967b. On the Study of Social Change. *American Anthropologist* 69:661–669.

———. 1975. *Ritual and Knowledge among the Baktaman of New Guinea*. New Haven, Conn.: Yale University Press.

———. 1978. Scale and Network in Urban Western Society. In *Scale and Social Organization*, ed. Fredrik Barth, 163–183. Oslo: Universitetsforlaget.

———. 1987. *Cosmologies in the Making: A Generative Approach to Cultural Variation in Inner New Guinea*. Cambridge: Cambridge University Press.

———. 1989. The Analysis of Culture in Complex Societies. *Ethnos* 54:120–142.

Basch, Linda, Nina Glick Schiller, and Cristina Szanton Blanc. 1994. *Nations Unbound: Transnational Projects, Postcolonial Predicaments, and Deterritorialized Nation-states*. Basel: Gordon & Breach.

Bazzi, Mohamad. 1998. Queens' Civic Lesson: New Strength in Numbers. *Newsday*, May 4, A27.

Beeman, William. 1987. Anthropology and the Print Media. *Anthropology Today* 3(3):2–4.

Behar, Ruth, and Deborah Gordon, eds. 1995. *Women Writing Culture*. Berkeley: University of California Press.

Beidelman, T. O. 1989. Review of Clifford, *The Predicament of Culture*. *Anthropos* 84:263–267.

Bellwood, Peter. 2001. Early Agriculturalist Population Diasporas? Farming, Languages, and Genes. *Annual Review of Anthropology* 30:181–207.

———. 2005. *First Farmers: The Origins of Agricultural Societies.* Malden, Mass.: Blackwell.

———, and Colin Renfrew, ed. 2002. *Examining the Farming/Language Dispersal Hypothesis.* Cambridge, U.K.: McDonald Institute for Archaeological Research.

Belshaw, Cyril. 1951. The Last Years of Ahuia Ova. *Man* 51:131–132.

———. 1957. *The Great Village: The Economic and Social Welfare of Hanuabada, an Urban Community in Papua.* London: Routledge & Kegan Paul.

Benedict, Burton. 1961. *Indians in a Plural Society: A Report on Mauritius.* London: Her Majesty's Stationery Office.

Benson, Susan. 1981. *Ambiguous Ethnicity: Interracial Families in London.* Cambridge: Cambridge University Press.

Benthall, Jonathan. 1995. From Self-Applause Through Self-Criticism to Self-Confidence. In Ahmed and Shore eds., 1–11.

Berman, Judith. 1996. "The Culture as It Appears to the Indian Himself": Boas, George Hunt, and the Methods of Ethnography. *History of Anthropology* 8:215–256.

———. 2001. Unpublished Materials of Franz Boas and George Hunt: A Record of 45 Years of Collaboration. In *Gateways: Exploring the Legacy of the Jesup North Pacific Expedition, 1897–1902,* ed. Igor Krupnik and William Fitzhugh, 181–213. Washington, D.C.: Smithsonian Institution.

Bernard, H. Russell, ed. 1998. *Handbook of Methods in Cultural Anthropology.* Walnut Creek, Calif.: AltaMira.

———, Peter Killworth, David Kronenfeld, and Lee Sailer. 1984. The Problem of Informant Accuracy: The Validity of Retrospective Data. *Annual Review of Anthropology* 13:495–517.

Berreman, Gerald. 1968. Is Anthropology Alive? Social Responsibility in Social Anthropology. *Current Anthropology* 9:391–396.

———. 1969. Academic Colonialism: Not So Innocent Abroad. *Nation,* November 10, 505–508.

Besteman, Catherine. 2010. In and Out of the Academy: Policy and the Case for a Strategic Anthropology. *Human Organization* 69:407–417.

Bestor, Theodore. 2004. *Tsukiji: The Fish Market at the Center of the World.* Berkeley: University of California Press.

Bhachu, Parminder. 1985. *Twice Migrants: East African Sikh Settlers in Britain.* London: Tavistock.

———. 2004. *Dangerous Designs: Asian Women Fashion the Diaspora Economies.* London: Routledge.

Birth, Kevin. 1990. Reading and the Righting of Writing Ethnographies. *American Ethnologist* 17:549–557.

Blanco, Merida. 1978. *Race and Face Among the Poor: The Language of Color in a Brazilian Bairro.* PhD dissertation, Department of Anthropology, Stanford University.

Bloch, Maurice. 1974. Symbols, Song, Dance and Features of Articulation: Is Religion an Extreme Form of Traditional Authority? *European Journal of Sociology* 15:55–81.

Boadi-Siaw, S. Y. 1982. Brazilian Returnees of West Africa. In *Global Dimensions of the African Diaspora*, ed. Joseph Harris, 291–308. Washington, D.C.: Howard University Press.

Boas, Franz. 1888 [1964]. *The Central Eskimo*. Lincoln: University of Nebraska Press.

———. 1945. *Race and Democratic Society*. New York: J. J. Augustin.

———. 1974. Race Problems in America. In *The Shaping of American Anthropology, 1883–1911: A Franz Boas Reader*, ed. George W. Stocking, Jr., 318–330. Chicago: University of Chicago Press.

Bogoras, Waldemar. 1904–1909. *The Chukchee*. New York: Johnson Reprint Corporation.

Boissevain, Jeremy. 1979. Network Analysis: A Reappraisal. *Current Anthropology* 20:392–394.

Bonacich, Edna. 1972. A Theory of Ethnic Antagonism: The Split Labor Market. *American Sociological Review* 37:547–559.

Bond, George C. 1988. A Social Portrait of John Gibbs St. Clair Drake: An American Anthropologist. *American Ethnologist* 15:762–781.

Bonfil Batalla, Guillermo. 1966. Conservative Thought in Applied Anthropology: A Critique. *Human Organization* 25:89–92.

Borofsky, Robert, ed. 1994. *Assessing Cultural Anthropology*. New York: McGraw Hill.

Bouvier, Leon, and Vernon M. Briggs, Jr. 1988. *The Population and Labor Force of New York: 1990–2050*. Washington, D.C.: Population Reference Bureau.

Brettell, Caroline. 1993. Introduction: Fieldwork, Text, and Audience. In *When They Read What We Write: The Politics of Ethnography*, ed. Caroline Bretell, 1–24. Westport, Conn.: Bergin & Garvey.

———. 2000. Theorizing Migration in Anthropology: The Social Construction of Networks, Identities, Communities, and Globalscapes. In *Migration Theory: Talking Cross Disciplines*, ed. Caroline Brettell and J. Hollifield, 97–135. New York: Routledge.

Bricker, Victoria, and Evon Vogt. 1998. Alfonso Villa Rojas (1906–1998). *American Anthropologist* 100:994–998.

Briggs, Charles. 1986. *Learning How to Ask: A Sociolinguistic Appraisal of the Role of the Interview in Social Science Research*. New York: Cambridge University.

———, and Richard Bauman. 1999. "The Foundation of All Future Researches": Franz Boas, George Hunt, Native American Texts, and the Construction of Modernity. *American Quarterly* 51:479–528.

Brown, Jennifer S. H. 1994. Fur Trade as Centrifuge: Familial Dispersal and Offspring Identity in Two Company Contexts. In *North American Indian Anthropology: Essays on Society and Culture*, ed. Raymond DeMallie and Alfonso Ortiz, 197–219. Norman: University of Oklahoma Press.

Brown, Richard. 1973. Anthropology and Colonial Rule: Godfrey Wilson and the Rhodes-Livingstone Institute, Northern Rhodesia. In Asad ed., 173–197.

———. 1979. Passages in the Life of a White Anthropologist: Max Gluckman in Northern Rhodesia. *Journal of African History* 20:525–541.

Bulmer, Ralph, and Saem Majnep. 1977. *Birds of My Kalam Country*. Auckland: Oxford University Press.

Bunzel, Ruth. 1952. *Chichicastenango: A Guatemalan Village*. Locust Valley, N.Y.: J. J. Augustin.

Burgess, Robert. 1984. *In the Field: An Introduction to Field Research*. London: George Allen and Unwin.

Burrell, Jenna. 2012. *Invisible Users: Youth in the Internet Cafes of Urban Ghana*. Cambridge, Mass.: MIT Press.

Burton, John. 1988. Shadows at Twilight: A Note on History and the Ethnographic Present. *Proceedings of the American Philosophical Society* 132:420–433.

Campos Rajs, Elizabeth. 1991. Pros, Cons of Ethnic Labels: Standard Categories Don't Fit Multiethnic Population. *UC Focus*, May/June, 1, 8.

Caplan, Patricia. 1988. Engendering Knowledge: The Politics of Ethnography. *Anthropology Today* 4(5):8–12, 4(6):14–17.

Carmack, Robert. 1972. Ethnohistory: A Review of Its Development, Definitions, Methods, and Aims. *Annual Review of Anthropology* 1:227–246.

Casagrande, Joseph, Stephen Thompson, and Philip Young. 1964. Colonization as a Research Frontier: The Ecuadorian Case. In *Process and Pattern in Culture: Essays in Honor of Julian H. Steward*, ed. Robert Manners, 281–325. Chicago: Aldine.

Cavalli-Sforza, Luigi Luca, and Francesco Cavalli-Sforza. 1995. *The Great Human Diasporas: The History of Diversity and Evolution*. Cambridge, Mass.: Perseus.

Cazares, Ralph B., Edward Murguia, and W. Parker Frisbie. 1984. Mexican American Intermarriage in a Nonmetropolitan Context. *Social Science Quarterly* 65:626–634.

Chaliand, Gerard, and Jean-Pierre Rageau. 1995. *The Penguin Atlas of Diasporas*. New York: Viking.

Chavez, Leo. 2001. *Covering Immigration: Popular Images and the Politics of the Nation*. Berkeley: University of California Press.

Chen, Hsiang-shui. 1992. *Chinatown No More: Taiwan Immigrants in Contemporary New York*. Ithaca, N.Y.: Cornell University Press.

Chernoff, John Miller. 1979. *African Rhythm and African Sensibility: Aesthetics and Social Action in African Musical Idioms*. Chicago: University of Chicago Press.

Chodorow, Nancy. 1974. Family Structure and Feminine Personality. In *Woman, Culture, and Society*, ed. Michelle Rosaldo and Louise Lamphere, 43–66. Stanford: Stanford University Press.

Clark, Margaret, and Barbara Gallatin Anderson. 1967. *Culture and Aging: An Anthropological Study of Older Americans*. Springfield, Ill.: Charles C Thomas.

Clifford, James. 1983. On Ethnographic Authority. *Representations* 1(2):118–46.

———. 1986. Introduction: Partial Truths. In Clifford and Marcus eds., 1–26.

———. 1988. *The Predicament of Culture: Twentieth-Century Ethnography, Literature, and Art*. Cambridge, Mass.: Harvard University Press.

———. 1997. *Routes: Travel and Translation in the Late Twentieth Century*. Cambridge, Mass.: Harvard University Press.

———. 2003. *On the Edges of Anthropology (Interviews)*. Chicago: Prickly Paradigm Press.

———. and George Marcus, eds. 1986. *Writing Culture: The Poetics and Politics of Ethnography*. Berkeley: University of California Press.

Cohen, Abner. 1969. *Custom and Politics in Urban Africa: A Study of Hausa Migrants in Yoruba Towns*. London: Routledge and Kegan Paul.

———. 1980. Drama and Politics in the Development of a London Carnival. *Man* 15:65–87.

Cohen, Myron. 1968. The Hakka or "Guest People": Dialect as a Sociocultural Variable in Southwestern China. *Ethnohistory* 15:237–292.

Cohen, Robin. 1997. *Global Diasporas: An Introduction*. Seattle: University of Washington Press.

Cohn, Bernard S. 1980. History and Anthropology: The State of Play. *Comparative Studies in Society and History* 22:198–221.

Coleman, E. Gabriella. 2010. Ethnographic Approaches to Digital Media. *Annual Review of Anthropology* 39:487–505.

Colen, Shellee, and Roger Sanjek. 1990a. At Work in Homes I: Orientations. In Sanjek and Colen eds., 1–13.

———. 1990b. At Work in Homes II: Directions. In Sanjek and Colen eds., 176–188.

Colford, Paul. 1987. An Inside Look at the Klan. *Newsday*, February 18, Part 2, 1.

Collins, Glenn. 1985. A New Look at Intermarriage in the U.S. *New York Times*, February 11, C13.

Collins, Jane. 1997. The Waxing and Waning of "Subfields" in North American Sociocultural Anthropology. In Gupta and Ferguson ed., 117–130.

Comaroff, John. 1984. The Closed Society and Its Critics: Historical Transformations in African Ethnography. *American Ethnologist* 11:571–583.

Condominas, Georges. 1973. Ethics and Comfort: An Ethnographer's View of His Profession. *Annual Report 1972*, 1–17. Washington, D.C.: American Anthropological Association.

Conklin, Nancy, and Margaret Lourie. 1983. *A Host of Tongues: Language Communities in the United States*. New York: Free Press.

Constable, Nicole. 2003. *Romance on a Global Stage: Pen Pals, Virtual Ethnography, and "Mail Order" Marriages*. Berkeley: University of California Press.

Cowlishaw, Gillian. 1988. *Black, White or Brindle: Race in Rural Australia*. Cambridge: Cambridge University Press.

Crafts, Susan, Daniel Cavicchi, and Charles Keil. 1993. *My Music*. Hanover, N.H.: University Press of New England.

Crew, Spencer. 1987. *Field to Factory: Afro-American Migration 1915–1940.* Washington, D.C.: Smithsonian Institution.

Crick, Malcolm. 1992. Ali and Me: An Essay in Street-Corner Anthropology. In Okely and Callaway, eds., 175–192. London: Routledge.

Crosby, Alfred. 1986. *Ecological Imperialism: The Biological Expansion of Europe, 900–1900.* Cambridge: Cambridge University Press.

Curtin, Philip, ed. 1967. *Africa Remembered: Narratives by West Africans from the Era of the Slave Trade.* Madison: University of Wisconsin Press.

———. 1968. Field Techniques for Collecting and Processing Oral Data. *Journal of African History* 9:367–385.

———. 1969. *The African Slave Trade: A Census.* Madison: University of Wisconsin Press.

———. 1984. *Cross-cultural Trade in World History.* Cambridge: Cambridge University Press.

Cushing, Frank Hamilton. 1883 [1988]. *Zuñi Fetiches.* Las Vegas, Nev.: KC Publications.

———. 1920 [1974]. *Zuñi Breadstuff.* New York: Museum of the American Indian.

Daniels, Roger. 1962. *The Politics of Prejudice: The Anti-Japanese Movement in California and the Struggle for Japanese Exclusion.* New York: Atheneum.

Darnell, Regna. 2001. *Invisible Genealogies: A History of Americanist Anthropology.* Lincoln: University of Nebraska Press.

———, ed. 2002. *American Anthropology, 1971–1995: Papers from the* American Anthropologist. Lincoln: University of Nebraska Press.

Davis, Allison, Burleigh Gardner, and Mary Gardner. 1941. *Deep South: A Social Anthropological Study of Caste and Class.* Chicago: University of Chicago Press.

Davis, T. J. 1985. *A Rumor of Revolt: The "Great Negro Plot" in Colonial New York.* Amherst: University of Massachusetts Press.

Dehavenon, Anna Lou, and Marvin Harris. 1975. Hierarchical Behavior in Domestic Groups: A Videotape Analysis. Manuscript, photocopy.

Deloria, Vine, Jr. 1969. *Custer Died for Your Sins: An Indian Manifesto.* New York: Macmillan.

Dennis, Norman, Fernando Henriques, and Clifford Slaughter. 1956. *Coal Is Our Life: An Analysis of a Yorkshire Mining Community.* London: Tavistock.

Desai, Rashmi. 1963. *Indian Immigrants in Britain.* London: Oxford University Press.

Des Chene, Mary. 1997. Locating the Past. In Gupta and Ferguson eds., 66–85.

Deshen, Shlomo, and Moshe Shokeid. 1974. *The Predicament of Homecoming: Cultural and Social Life of North African Immigrants in Israel.* Ithaca, N.Y.: Cornell University Press.

de Waal, Alexander. 1989. *Famine That Kills: Dar Fur, Sudan, 1984–1985.* Oxford: Oxford University Press.

Diamond, Stanley. 1964a. Introduction: The Uses of the Primitive. In Diamond ed., v–xxix.

———. 1964b. Plato and the Definition of the Primitive. In Diamond ed., 170–193.

———, ed. 1964c. *Primitive Views of the World: Essays from Culture in History.* New York: Columbia University Press.

———. 1964d. What History *Is.* In *Process and Pattern in Culture: Essays in Honor of Julian H. Steward,* ed. Robert Manners, 29–46. Chicago: Aldine.

———. 1967. The Anaguta of Nigeria: Suburban Primitives. In *Contemporary Change in Traditional Societies I: Introduction and African Tribes,* ed. Julian Steward, 361–505. Urbana: University of Illinois Press.

Dike, Kenneth Onwuka, and Felicia Ekejiuba. 1990. *The Aro of South-eastern Nigeria, 1650–1980: A Study of Socio-economic Formation and Transformation in Nigeria.* Ibadan: Ibadan University Press.

Dirks, Nicholas. 1979. The Structure and Meaning of Political Relations in a South Indian Little Kingdom. *Contributions to Indian Sociology* 13:169–206.

———. 1989. The Original Caste: Power, History and Hierarchy in South Asia. *Contributions to Indian Sociology* 23:59–78.

Dobrin, Lise, and Ira Bashkow. 2006. "Pigs for Dance Songs": Reo Fortune's Empathetic Ethnography of the Arapesh Roads. *Histories of Anthropology Annual* 2:123–154.

———. 2010. "The Truth in Anthropology Does Not Travel First Class": Reo Fortune's Fateful Encounter with Margaret Mead. *Histories of Anthropology Annual* 6:66–128.

Dominguez, Virginia. 1973. Spanish-Speaking Caribbeans in New York: "The Middle Race." *Interamerican Review* 3(2):135–143.

Dotson, Floyd, and Lillian Dotson. 1968. *The Indian Minority of Zambia, Rhodesia, and Malawi.* New Haven, Conn.: Yale University Press.

Drake, St. Clair. 1980. Anthropology and the Black Experience. *Black Scholar* 11(7):2–31.

———. 1990. *Black Folk Here and There: An Essay in History and Anthropology.* Vol. 2. Los Angeles: Center for Afro-American Studies, University of California.

———, and Horace Cayton. 1962. *Black Metropolis: A Study of Negro Life in a Northern City.* Revised and enlarged ed. New York: Harper.

Draschler, Julius. 1921. *Intermarriage in New York City: A Statistical Study of the Amalgamation of European Peoples.* New York: AMS.

Duany, Jorge. 2000. Nation on the Move: The Construction of Cultural Identities in Puerto Rico and the Diaspora. *American Ethnologist* 27:5–30.

Du Bois, W. E. B. 1899 [1967]. *The Philadelphia Negro: A Social Study.* New York: Schocken.

———. 1903 [1990]. *The Souls of Black Folk.* New York: Vintage.

Dumond, Don. 1987. A Re-examination of Eskimo-Aleut Prehistory. *American Anthropologist* 89:32–56.

Dyk, Walter. 1938. *Son of Old Man Hat: A Navaho Autobiography.* Lincoln: University of Nebraska Press.

Eades, Jeremy, ed. 1987 *Migrants, Workers, and the Social Order.* London: Tavistock.

Earle, Timothy, Clive Gamble, and Hendrik Poinar. 2011. Migration. In *Deep History: The Architecture of Past and Present*, ed. Andrew Shryock and Daniel Smail, 191–218. Berkeley: University of California Press.

Elphick, Richard. 1977. *Kraal and Castle: Khoikhoi and the Founding of White South Africa*. New Haven, Conn.: Yale University Press.

Embree, John. 1939. *Suye Mura: A Japanese Village*. Chicago: University of Chicago Press.

Emeneau, Murray. 1956. India as a Linguistic Area. *Language* 32:3–16.

Emerson, Robert, Rachel Fretz, and Linda Shaw. 1995. *Writing Ethnographic Fieldnotes*. Chicago: University of Chicago Press.

Engels, Frederick. 1892 [1969]. *The Condition of the Working Class in England*. London: Panther.

Epstein, A. L. 1956. An Outline of the Political Structure of an African Urban Community on the Copperbelt of Northern Rhodesia. In *Social Implications of Industrialization and Urbanization in Africa South of the Sahara*, ed. Daryll Forde, 711–724. Paris: UNESCO.

———. 1958. *Politics in an Urban African Community*. Manchester, U.K.: Manchester University Press.

———. 1959. Linguistic Innovation and Culture on the Copperbelt. *Southwestern Journal of Anthropology* 15:235–253.

———. 1961. The Network and Urban Social Organization. *Rhodes-Livingstone Institute Journal* 29:28–62.

———. 1981. *Urbanization and Kinship: The Domestic Domain on the Copperbelt of Zambia 1950–1956*. New York: Academic Press.

Erdmans, Mary. 1998. *Opposite Poles: Immigrants and Ethnics in Polish Chicago, 1976–1990*. University Park: Pennsylvania State University Press.

Erickson, Ken, and Donald Stull. 1998. *Doing Team Ethnography: Warnings and Advice*. Thousand Oaks, Calif.: Sage.

Ernst, Robert. 1949. *Immigrant Life in New York City, 1825–1863*. Port Washington, N.Y.: Friedman.

Errington, Frederick. 1987. Reflexivity Deflected: The Festival of Nations as an American Cultural Performance. *American Ethnologist* 14:654–667.

Evans-Pritchard, E. E. 1937. *Witchcraft, Oracles and Magic Among the Azande*. Oxford: Oxford University Press.

———. 1940. *The Nuer*. Oxford: Oxford University Press.

———. 1956. *Nuer Religion*. Oxford: Oxford University Press.

Evett, Daniel. 1973. Early Farming in Europe. *Man* 8:475–476.

Fabian, Johannes. 1971. *Jamaa: A Charismatic Movement in Katanga*. Evanston, Ill.: Northwestern University Press.

———. 1978. Popular Culture in Africa: Findings and Conjectures. *Africa* 48:315–334.

———. 1983. *Time and the Other: How Anthropology Makes Its Object*. New York: Columbia University Press.

———. 1986. *Language and Colonial Power: The Appropriation of Swahili in the Former Belgian Congo 1880–1938.* Cambridge: Cambridge University Press.

Falcon, Angelo. 1985. Puerto Rican and Black Electoral Politics in NYC in the "Decade of the Hispanic." *Hunter College Centro de Estudios Puertorriqueños Newsletter,* June, 7–10, 23.

———. 1988. Black and Latino Politics in New York City: Race and Ethnicity in a Changing Urban Context. In *Latinos and the Political System,* ed. F. Chris Garcia, 171–194. Notre Dame, Ind.: Notre Dame University Press.

———. 1993. The Puerto Rican Community: A Status Report. *Dialogo: Newsletter of the National Puerto Rican Policy Network* 7:1, 5, 10–13.

Fallers, Lloyd. 1956. *Bantu Bureaucracy: A Century of Political Evolution Among the Basoga of Uganda.* Chicago: University of Chicago Press.

Fardon, Richard, ed. 1990. *Localizing Strategies: Regional Traditions of Ethnographic Writing.* Washington, D.C.: Smithsonian Institution Press.

Farley, Reynolds, and Walter R. Allen. 1987. *The Color Line and the Quality of Life in America.* New York: Russell Sage.

Fenton, William. 1987. *The False Faces of the Iroquois.* Norman: University of Oklahoma Press.

Fernandez, Celestino, and Louis Holscher. 1983. Chicano-Anglo Intermarriage in Arizona. *Hispanic Journal of the Behavioral Sciences* 5:291–304.

Field, M. J. 1937. *Religion and Medicine of the Gã People.* London: Oxford University Press.

———. 1940. *Social Organization of the Gã People.* London: Crown Agents.

Fienup-Riordan, Ann. 1996. *The Living Tradition of Yup'ik Masks:* Agayulitararut *(Our Way of Making Prayer).* Seattle: University of Washington Press.

———. 2000. *Hunting Tradition in a Changing World: Yup'ik Lives in Alaska Today.* New Brunswick, N.J.: Rutgers University Press.

———. 2005a. *Wise Words of the Yup'ik People: We Talk to You Because We Love You.* Lincoln: University of Nebraska Press.

———. 2005b. *Yup'ik Elders at the Ethnologisches Museum Berlin: Fieldwork Turned on Its Head.* Seattle: University of Washington Press.

———. 2007. Yuungaqpiallerput/*The Way We Genuinely Live: Masterworks of Yup'ik Science and Survival.* Seattle: University of Washington Press.

Firth, Raymond. 1952. Preface. In Adrian Mayer, *Land and Society in Malabar.* Bombay: Oxford University Press.

———. 1954. Social Organization and Social Change. *Journal of the Royal Anthropological Institute* 84:1–20.

———. 1955. Some Principles of Social Organization. *Journal of the Royal Anthropological Institute* 85:1–180.

———. 1972. *The Skeptical Anthropologist? Social Anthropology and Marxist Views on Society.* London: British Academy.

———. 1975. The Skeptical Anthropologist? Social Anthropology and Marxist Views on Society. In *Marxist Analysis and Social Anthropology*, ed. Maurice Bloch, 29–60. London: Malaby.

Fisher, Maxine. 1980. *The Indians of New York City: A Study of Immigrants from India*. Columbia, Mo.: South Asian Books.

Fitch, Robert. 1976. Planning New York. In *The Fiscal Crisis of American Cities*, ed. Roger Alcaly and David Mermelstein, 246–284. New York: Vintage.

———. 1989. Foundations and the Charter: Making New York Safe for Plutocracy. *Nation*, December 11, 709–714.

———. 1991. Mauling the Mosaic: Redistricting Was Meant to Boost Minorities; It Ended Up Preserving White Power. *Village Voice*, June 18, 11–15.

———, and Mary Oppenheimer. 1966. *Ghana: End of an Illusion*. New York: Monthly Review Press.

Fitzpatrick, Joseph, and Douglas Gurak. 1979. *Hispanic Intermarriage in New York City: 1975*. New York: Hispanic Research Center, Fordham University.

Flores, Juan. 1985. "Que Assimilated, Brother, Yo Soy Asimilao": The Structuring of Puerto Rican Identity in the U.S. *Journal of Ethnic Studies* 13(3):1–16.

Foner, Nancy. 2000. *From Ellis Island to JFK: New York's Two Great Waves of Immigration*. New Haven, Conn.: Yale University Press

———, Ruben Rumbaut, and Steven Gold. 2001. Immigration and Immigration Research in the United States. In *Immigration Research for a New Century: Multidisciplinary Perspectives*, ed. Nancy Foner, Ruben Rumbaut, and Steven Gold, 1–19. New York: Russell Sage Foundation.

Forbes, Jack D. 1990. Undercounting Native Americans: The 1980 Census and the Manipulation of Racial Identity in the United States. *Wicazo Sa Review* 6:2–26.

Ford, Clellan. 1941. *Smoke from Their Fires: The Life of a Kwakiutl Chief*. New Haven, Conn.: Yale University Press.

Fortes, Meyer. 1936. Ritual Festivals and Social Cohesion in the Hinterland of the Gold Coast. *American Anthropologist* 38:590–604.

Foster, Robert. 1991. Making National Cultures in the Global Ecumene. *Annual Review of Anthropology* 20:235–260.

Fox, Richard. 1977. *Urban Anthropology: Cities in Their Cultural Setting*. Englewood Cliffs, N.J.: Prentice Hall.

Fraenkel, Merran. 1964. *Tribe and Class in Monrovia*. London: Oxford University Press.

Frank, Andre Gunder. 1966. The Development of Underdevelopment. *Monthly Review* 18(4):17–21.

———. 1967. *Capitalism and Underdevelopment in Latin America: Historical Studies of Chile and Brazil*. New York: Monthly Review Press.

———. 1975. Anthropology = Ideology, Applied Anthropology = Politics. *Race and Culture* 17:57–68.

———. n.d.a. *Hunger*. Ann Arbor, Mich.: Radical Education Project.

———. n.d.b. *Rostow's Stages of Economic Growth through Escalation to Nuclear Destruction*. Ann Arbor, Mich.: Radical Education Project.

Frankenberg, Ronald. 1957. *Village on the Border: A Social Study of Religion, Politics and Football in a North Wales Community*. London: Cohen & West.

Frayer, David, Milford Wolpoff, Alan Thorne, Fred Smith, and Geoffrey Pope. 1993. Theories of Modern Human Origins: The Paleontological Test. *American Anthropologist* 95:14–50.

Freedman, Maurice. 1957. *Chinese Family and Marriage in Singapore*. London: Her Majesty's Stationery Office.

Frey, William. 1995. The New Geography of Population Shifts. In *State of the Union*. Vol. 2, ed. Reynolds Farley, 271–336. New York: Russell Sage.

Fried, Morton. 1966. On the Concepts "Tribe" and "Tribal Society." *Transactions of the New York Academy of Sciences* 28:527–540.

———, Marvin Harris, and Robert Murphy, eds. 1968. *War: The Anthropology of Armed Conflict and Aggression*. New York: Natural History Press.

Galarza, Ernesto. 1972. Mexicans in the Southwest: A Culture in Process. In *Plural Society in the Southwest*, ed. Edward Spicer and Raymond Thompson, 261–297. Albuquerque: University of New Mexico Press.

Gallin, Bernard. 1966. *Hsin Hsing, Taiwan: A Chinese Village in Change*. Berkeley: University of California Press.

Gamio, Manuel. 1930. *Mexican Immigration to the United States: A Study of Human Migration and Adjustment*. New York: Dover.

———. 1931. *The Mexican Immigrant: His Life-Story*. New York: Dover.

Gans, Herbert. 1962. Urbanism and Suburbanism as Ways of Life: A Re-Evaluation of Some Definitions. In *Human Behavior and Social Processes*, ed. Arnold Rose, 635–648. Boston: Houghton Mifflin.

———. 1979. Symbolic Ethnicity: The Future of Ethnic Groups and Cultures in America. *Ethnic and Racial Studies* 2:1–20.

———. 1988. *Middle American Individualism: Political Participation and Liberal Democracy*. New York: Oxford University Press.

Gardner, Beth. 1999. Our World in Working Model. *Daily News*, July 22, Queens section, 3.

Garlick, Peter. 1967. The Development of Kwahu Business Enterprise in Ghana Since 1874. *Journal of African History* 8:463–480.

Gay y Blasco, Paloma, and Huon Wardle. 2007. *How to Read Ethnography*. London: Routledge.

Geertz, Clifford. 1960. *The Religion of Java*. New York: Free Press.

———. 1963. *Agricultural Involution: The Process of Ecological Change in Indonesia*. Berkeley: University of California Press.

———. 1966. *Person, Time and Conduct in Bali: An Essay in Cultural Analysis*. New Haven, Conn.: Yale Southeast Asia Program.

———. 1972. Deep Play: Notes on the Balinese Cock Fight. *Daedalus* 101:1–37.

———. 1973. *The Interpretation of Cultures*. New York: Basic Books.

———. 1980. *Negara: The Theatre State in 19th Century Bali*. Princeton, N.J.: Princeton University Press.

———. 1988. *Works and Lives: The Anthropologist as Author*. Stanford, Calif.: Stanford University Press.

———. 1995. *After the Fact: Two Countries, Four Decades, One Anthropologist*. Cambridge, Mass.: Harvard University Press.

Geertz, Hildred. 1961. *The Javanese Family*. New York: Free Press.

Ghani, Ashraf. 1987. A Conversation with Eric Wolf. *American Ethnologist* 14:346–366.

Ghosh, Amitav. 1989. The Diaspora in Indian Culture. *Public Culture* 2:73–78.

———. 1992. *In an Antique Land*. New York: Vintage.

Gibson, Margaret. 1988. *Accommodation without Assimilation: Sikh Immigrants in an American High School*. Ithaca, N.Y.: Cornell University Press.

Gilkes, Cheryl Townsend. 1980. "Holding Back the Ocean with a Broom": Black Women and Community Work. In *The Black Woman*, ed. La Frances Rodgers-Rose, 217–231. Beverly Hills, Calif.: Sage.

———. 1988. Building in Many Places: Multiple Commitments and Ideologies in Black Women's Community Work. In *Women and the Politics of Empowerment*, ed. Ann Bookman and Sandra Morgen, 53–76. Philadelphia: Temple University Press.

Gilsenan, Michael. 1990. Very Like a Camel: The Appearance of an Anthropologist's Middle East. In Fardon ed., 222–239.

Glazer, Nathan, and Daniel P. Moynihan. 1963. *Beyond the Melting Pot: The Negroes, Puerto Ricans, Jews, Italians, and Irish of New York City*. Cambridge, Mass.: MIT Press.

Glick Schiller, Nina, Linda Basch, and Cristina Blanc-Szanton, eds. 1992. *Towards a Transnational Perspective on Migration: Race, Class, Ethnicity, and Nationalism Reconsidered*. New York: New York Academy of Sciences.

Gluckman, Max. 1940. Analysis of a Social Situation in Modern Zululand. *Bantu Studies* 14:1–30.

———. 1975. Anthropology and Apartheid: The Work of South African Anthropologists. In *Studies in African Social Anthropology*, ed. Meyer Fortes and Sheila Patterson, 21–39. London: Academic Press.

Gmelch, George. 1980. Return Migration. *Annual Review of Anthropology* 9:135–159.

Goldfrank, Esther. 1978. *Notes on an Undirected Life: As One Anthropologist Tells It*. Flushing, N.Y.: Queens College Press.

Goldschmidt, Walter. 1946, 1947 [1978]. *As You Sow: Three Studies in the Social Consequences of Agribusiness*. Montclair, N.J.: Allanheld, Osmun.

———. 2000. A Perspective on Anthropology. *American Anthropologist* 102:789–807.

Goldstein, Joshua. 1999. Kinship Networks That Cross Racial Lines: The Exception or the Rule? *Demography* 36(3):399–407.

Gonzalez, David. 1999a. Neighborhood Is the Source of Real Capital. *New York Times*, January 6, M1.

———. 1999b. Olga's Garden: A Testament to Civic Spirit. *New York Times*, March 3, M1.

Gonzalez, Sandy. 1992. Intermarriage and Assimilation: The Beginning or the End? *Wicazo Sa Review* 8(2):48–52.

Good, Anthony. 2003. Anthropologists as Experts: Asylum Appeals in British Courts. *Anthropology Today* 19(5):3–7.

Goode, Judith, and Jo Anne Schneider. 1994. *Reshaping Ethnic and Racial Relations in Philadelphia: Immigrants in a Divided City*. Philadelphia: Temple University Press.

Goodfriend, Joyce. 1992. *Before the Melting Pot: Society and Culture in Colonial New York, 1664–1730*. Princeton, N.J.: Princeton University Press.

Goody, Jack. 1957. Anomie in Ashanti? *Africa* 27:356–363.

———. 1983. *The Development of Family and Marriage in Europe*. Cambridge: Cambridge University Press.

———. 1986. *The Logic of Writing and the Organization of Society*. Cambridge: Cambridge University Press.

Gordon, Milton. 1964. *Assimilation in American Life: The Role of Race, Religion, and National Origin*. New York: Oxford University Press.

Gough, Kathleen. 1968a. Anthropology and Imperialism. *Monthly Review* 19(11): 12–27.

———. 1968b. New Proposals for Anthropologists. *Current Anthropology* 9:403–407.

Green, Jesse, ed. 1990. *Cushing at Zuni: The Correspondence and Journals of Frank Hamilton Cushing, 1879–1884*. Albuquerque: University of New Mexico Press.

Greenberg, Joseph. 1987. CA Book Review of Language in the Americas. *Current Anthropology* 28:647–667.

Gregory, Steven. 1992. The Changing Significance of Race and Class in an African American Community. *American Ethnologist* 19:255–274.

———. 1994. "We've Been Down This Road Already." In Gregory and Sanjek eds., 18–38.

———. 1998. *Black Corona: Race and the Politics of Place in an Urban Community*. Princeton, N.J.: Princeton University Press.

———, and Roger Sanjek, eds. 1994. *Race*. New Brunswick, N.J.: Rutgers University Press.

Grimes, Ronald. 1976. *Symbol and Conquest: Public Ritual and Drama in Santa Fe, New Mexico*. Ithaca, N.Y.: Cornell University Press.

Guinier, Lani. 1994. *The Tyranny of the Majority: Fundamental Fairness in American Democracy*. New York: Free Press.

Gulliver, P. H. 1955. *Labour Migration in a Rural Economy*. Kampala: East African Institute of Social Research.

———. 1985. An Applied Anthropologist in East Africa During the Colonial Era. In *Social Anthropology and Development Policy*, ed. Ralph Grillo and Alan Rew, 37–57. London: Tavistock.

Guo, Zibin. 2000. *Ginseng and Aspirin: Health Care Alternatives for Aging Chinese in New York*. Ithaca, N.Y.: Cornell University Press.

Gupta, Akhil, and James Ferguson, eds. 1997. *Anthropological Locations: Boundaries and Grounds of a Field Science*. Berkeley: University of California Press.

Haekel, Josef. 1970. Source Criticism in Anthropology. In *A Handbook of Method in Cultural Anthropology*, ed. Raoul Naroll and Ronald Cohen, 147–164. New York: Columbia University Press.

Hagan, Jacqueline. 1994. *Deciding to Be Legal: A Maya Community in Houston*. Philadelphia: Temple University Press.

Hall, Chris Iijima. 1992. Coloring Outside the Line. In Root ed., 326–329.

Halpern, Joel. 1958. *A Serbian Village*. New York: Columbia University Press.

Halstead, Narmala, Eric Hirsch, and Judith Okely, eds. 2008. *Knowing How to Know: Fieldwork and the Ethnographic Present*. Oxford: Berghahn.

Handlin, Oscar. 1959. *The Newcomers: Negroes and Puerto Ricans in a Changing Metropolis*. New York: Anchor.

Hannerz, Ulf. 1969. *Soulside: Inquiries into Ghetto Culture and Community*. Stockholm: Almqvist and Wiksell.

———. 1976. Methods in an Urban African Study. *Ethnos* 4:68–98.

———. 1980. *Exploring the City: Inquiries toward an Urban Anthropology*. New York: Columbia University Press.

———. 1987a. American Culture: Creolized, Creolizing. In *American Culture: Creolized, Creolizing*, ed. Erik Åsard, 7–30. Uppsala: The Swedish Institute for North American Studies.

———. 1987b. The World in Creolization. *Africa* 57:546–559.

———. 1989. Culture between Center and Periphery: Toward a Macroanthropology. *Ethnos* 54:200–216.

———. 1990. The Cultural Shaping of Agency. *Antropologiska Studier* 45:28–44.

———. 1992. The Global Ecumene as a Network of Networks. In *Conceptualizing Society*, ed. Adam Kuper, 34–56. London: Routledge.

———. 1993. The Withering Away of the National? An Afterword. *Ethnos* 58:377–391.

———. 1996. *Transnational Connections: Culture, People, Places*. New York: Routledge.

———. 1998. Transnational Research. In Bernard ed., 235–256.

———. 2010. *Anthropology's World: Life in a Twenty-First-Century Discipline*. New York: Pluto Press.

Hansen, Karen Tranberg. 2000. *Salaula: The World of Secondhand Clothing and Zambia*. Chicago: University of Chicago Press.

Hardy-Fanta, Carol. 1993. *Latina Politics, Latino Politics: Gender, Culture, and Political Participation in Boston*. Philadelphia: Temple University Press.

Harries-Jones, Peter. 1985. From Cultural Translator to Advocate: Changing Circles of Interpretation. In Paine ed., 224–248.

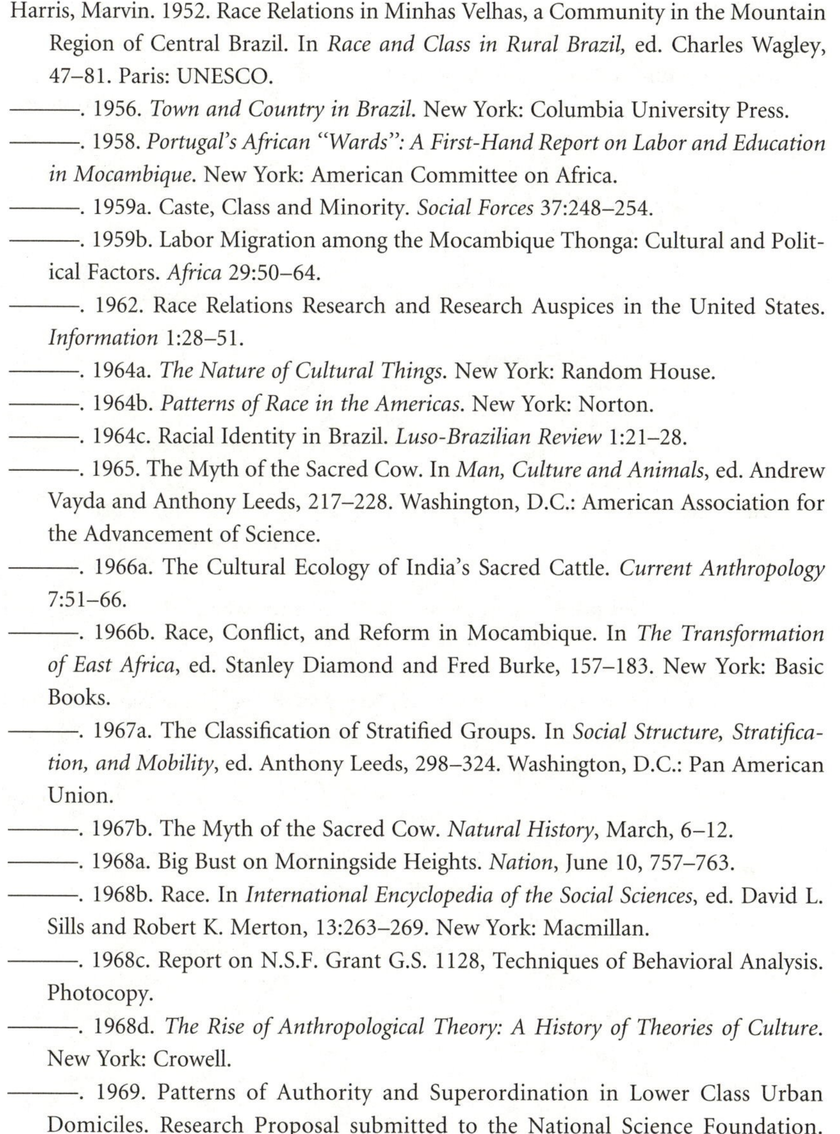

Harris, Marvin. 1952. Race Relations in Minhas Velhas, a Community in the Mountain Region of Central Brazil. In *Race and Class in Rural Brazil*, ed. Charles Wagley, 47–81. Paris: UNESCO.

———. 1956. *Town and Country in Brazil.* New York: Columbia University Press.

———. 1958. *Portugal's African "Wards": A First-Hand Report on Labor and Education in Mocambique.* New York: American Committee on Africa.

———. 1959a. Caste, Class and Minority. *Social Forces* 37:248–254.

———. 1959b. Labor Migration among the Mocambique Thonga: Cultural and Political Factors. *Africa* 29:50–64.

———. 1962. Race Relations Research and Research Auspices in the United States. *Information* 1:28–51.

———. 1964a. *The Nature of Cultural Things.* New York: Random House.

———. 1964b. *Patterns of Race in the Americas.* New York: Norton.

———. 1964c. Racial Identity in Brazil. *Luso-Brazilian Review* 1:21–28.

———. 1965. The Myth of the Sacred Cow. In *Man, Culture and Animals*, ed. Andrew Vayda and Anthony Leeds, 217–228. Washington, D.C.: American Association for the Advancement of Science.

———. 1966a. The Cultural Ecology of India's Sacred Cattle. *Current Anthropology* 7:51–66.

———. 1966b. Race, Conflict, and Reform in Mocambique. In *The Transformation of East Africa*, ed. Stanley Diamond and Fred Burke, 157–183. New York: Basic Books.

———. 1967a. The Classification of Stratified Groups. In *Social Structure, Stratification, and Mobility*, ed. Anthony Leeds, 298–324. Washington, D.C.: Pan American Union.

———. 1967b. The Myth of the Sacred Cow. *Natural History*, March, 6–12.

———. 1968a. Big Bust on Morningside Heights. *Nation*, June 10, 757–763.

———. 1968b. Race. In *International Encyclopedia of the Social Sciences*, ed. David L. Sills and Robert K. Merton, 13:263–269. New York: Macmillan.

———. 1968c. Report on N.S.F. Grant G.S. 1128, Techniques of Behavioral Analysis. Photocopy.

———. 1968d. *The Rise of Anthropological Theory: A History of Theories of Culture.* New York: Crowell.

———. 1969. Patterns of Authority and Superordination in Lower Class Urban Domiciles. Research Proposal submitted to the National Science Foundation. Photocopy.

———. 1970. Referential Ambiguity in the Calculus of Brazilian Racial Identity. *Southwestern Journal of Anthropology* 26:1–14.

———. 1971. Patterns of Authority and Superordination in Lower Class Urban Domiciles. Research Proposal submitted to the National Science Foundation (Renewal). Mimeo.

———. 1974. *Cows, Pigs, Wars, and Witches: The Riddles of Culture*. New York: Random House.

———. 1975. Why a Perfect Knowledge of All the Rules One Must Know to Act like a Native Cannot Lead to the Knowledge of How Natives Act. *Journal of Anthropological Research* 30:242–251.

———. 1976. History and Significance of the Emic/Etic Distinction. *Annual Review of Anthropology* 5:329–350.

———. 1977. *Cannibals and Kings: The Origins of Cultures*. New York: Random House.

———. 1979. *Cultural Materialism: The Struggle for a Science of Culture*. New York: Random House.

———. 1980. History and Ideological Significance of the Separation of Social and Cultural Anthropology. In *Beyond the Myths of Culture: Essays in Cultural Materialism*, ed. Eric Ross, 391–407. New York: Academic Press.

———. 1989. *Our Kind: Who We Are, Where We Came from, Where We Are Going*. New York: Harper & Row.

———. 1990a. Emics and Etics Revisited. In *Emics and Etics: The Insider/Outsider Debate*, ed. Thomas Headland, Kenneth Pike, and Marvin Harris, 48–61. Newbury Park, Calif.: Sage.

———. 1990b. Harris's Final Response. In *Emics and Etics: The Insider/Outsider Debate*, ed. Thomas Headland, Kenneth Pike, and Marvin Harris, 202–216. Newbury Park, Calif.: Sage.

———. 1990c. Harris's Reply to Pike. In *Emics and Etics: The Insider/Outsider Debate*, ed. Thomas Headland, Kenneth Pike, and Marvin Harris, 75–83. Newbury Park, Calif.: Sage.

———. 1999. *Theories of Culture in Postmodern Times*. Walnut Creek, Calif.: AltaMira.

———, and Conrad Kottak. 1963. The Structural Significance of Brazilian Racial Categories. *Sociologia* 25:203–208.

Harrison, Ira, and Faye Harrison, eds. 1998. *African-American Pioneers in Anthropology*. Urbana: University of Illinois Press.

Hart, Keith. 1982. *The Political Economy of West African Agriculture*. Cambridge: Cambridge University Press.

———. 2008. Africa on My Mind. The Memory Bank. Retrieved January 28, 2013 (http://thememorybank.co.uk/2008/01/14/africa-on-my-mind/).

Hayford, J. E. Casely. 1903. *Gold Coast Native Institutions*. London: Frank Cass.

Heer, David. 1980. Intermarriage. In *The Harvard Encyclopedia of American Ethnic Groups*, ed. Stephen Thernstrom, 513–521. Cambridge, Mass.: Harvard University Press.

Henderson, Richard N. 1972. *The King in Every Man: Evolutionary Trends in Onitsha Ibo Society and Culture*. New Haven: Yale University Press.

———. 1976. Onitsha, Nigeria: An African Urban Community. In *The Study of Anthropology*, ed. David Hunter and Phillip Whitten, 524–545. New York: Harper and Row.

Hendricks, Glenn. 1974. *The Dominican Diaspora: From the Dominican Republic to New York City—Villagers in Transition*. New York: Teachers College Press.

Henige, David. 1973. The Problem of Feedback in Oral Tradition: Four Examples from the Fanti Coastlands. *Journal of African History* 14:223–235.

———. 1974. Reflections of Early Interlacustrine History: An Essay in Source Criticism. *Journal of African History* 15:27–46.

———. 1982. Truths Yet Unborn? Oral Traditions as a Casualty of Culture Contact. *Journal of African History* 23:395–412.

Hill, Jane. 1978. Language Contact Systems and Human Adaptation. *Journal of Anthropological Research* 34:1–26.

———. 2001. Proto-Uto-Aztecan: A Community of Cultivators in Central Mexico? *American Anthropologist* 103:913–934.

Hill, Polly. 1966. Landlords and Brokers: A West African Trading System. *Cahiers d'Etudes Africaine* 6:349–366.

———. 1970a. *The Occupations of Migrants in Ghana*. Ann Arbor: Museum of Anthropology, University of Michigan.

———. 1970b. *Studies in Rural Capitalism in West Africa*. Cambridge: Cambridge University Press.

Hirabayashi, Lane Ryo. 1999. *The Politics of Fieldwork: Research in an American Concentration Camp*. Tucson: University of Arizona Press.

Hirschman, Charles. 1983. America's Melting Pot Reconsidered. *Annual Review of Sociology* 9:397–423.

Hodder, Ian, and Mark Hassall. 1971. The Non-random Spacing of Romano-British Walled Towns. *Man* 6:391–407.

Holtzman, Jon. 2000. *Nuer Journeys, Nuer Lives: Sudanese Refugees in Minnesota*. Needham Heights, Mass.: Allyn & Bacon.

Holy, Ladislav, and Milan Stuchlik. 1983. *Actions, Norms and Representations: Foundations of Anthropological Inquiry*. Cambridge: Cambridge University Press.

Hopper, Kim. 1988. More than Passing Strange: Homelessness and Mental Illness in New York City. *American Ethnologist* 15:155–167.

Horowitz, David, ed. 1967a. *Containment and Revolution*. Boston: Beacon Press.

———. 1967b. *From Yalta to Vietnam: American Foreign Policy in the Cold War*. Harmondsworth: Penguin.

———. 1969. *Imperialism and Revolution*. London: Allen Lane.

Horton, John. 1995. *The Politics of Diversity: Immigration, Resistance, and Change in Monterey Park, California*. Philadelphia: Temple University Press.

Howells, William. 1959. *Mankind in the Making: The Story of Human Evolution*. Garden City, N.Y.: Doubleday.

Hu-DeHart, Evelyn. 1994. P.C. and the Politics of Multiculturalism in Higher Education. In Gregory and Sanjek eds., 243–256.

Hudson, Charles. 1973. The Historical Approach in Anthropology. In *Handbook of Social and Cultural Anthropology*, ed. John Honigmann, 111–141. Chicago: Rand McNally.

Hunter, Monica. 1936. *Reaction to Conquest: Effects of Contact with Europeans on the Pondo of South Africa.* London: Oxford University Press.

Hyatt, Marshall. 1990. *Franz Boas, Social Activist: The Dynamics of Ethnicity.* Westport, Conn.: Greenwood Press.

Hymes, Dell, ed. 1972a. *Reinventing Anthropology.* New York: Random House.

———. 1972b. The Use of Anthropology: Critical, Political, Personal. In Hymes ed., 3–79.

Ichioka, Yuji. 1988. *The Issei: The World of the First Generation Japanese American Immigrants, 1885–1924.* New York: Free Press.

———, ed. 1989. *Views from Within: The Japanese American Evacuation and Resettlement Study.* Los Angeles: Asian American Studies Center, University of California, Los Angeles.

Ikeda, Keiko. 1998. *A Room Full of Mirrors: High School Reunions in Middle America.* Stanford, Calif.: Stanford University Press.

Ingold, Tim, ed. 1989. *Social Anthropology Is a Generalizing Science or It Is Nothing.* Manchester, U.K.: Group for Debates in Anthropological Theory.

—. 1990. *The Concept of Society Is Theoretically Obsolete.* Manchester, U.K.: Group for Debates in Anthropological Theory.

Irvine, Judith. 1979. Formality and Informality in Communicative Events. *American Anthropologist* 81:773–790.

Jabavu, D. D. T. 1920. *The Black Problem.* New York: Negro Universities Press.

———. 1934. Bantu Grievances. In *Western Civilization and the Natives of South Africa: Studies in Culture Contact*, ed. I. Schapera, 285–299. London: Routledge.

Jablonski, Nina, ed. 2002. *The First Americans: The Pleistocene Colonization of North America.* San Francisco: California Academy of Sciences.

Jacknis, Ira. 2002a. The First Boasian: Alfred Kroeber and Franz Boas, 1896–1905. *American Anthropologist* 104:520–532.

———. 2002b. *The Storage Box of Tradition: Kwakiutl Art, Anthropologists, and Museums, 1881–1981.* Washington, D.C.: Smithsonian Institution Press.

Jackson, Anthony, ed. 1987. *Anthropology at Home.* New York: Tavistock.

Jackson, Jean. 1997a. Fieldnotes. In *The Dictionary of Anthropology*, ed. Thomas Barfield, 188. Malden, Mass.: Blackwell Publishers.

———. 1997b. Fieldwork. In *The Dictionary of Anthropology*, ed. Thomas Barfield, 188–190. Malden, Mass.: Blackwell Publishers.

———. 1997c. Informants. In *The Dictionary of Anthropology*, ed. Thomas Barfield, 262. Malden, Mass.: Blackwell Publishers.

———. 1997d. Participant-observation. In *The Dictionary of Anthropology*, ed. Thomas Barfield, 348. Malden, Mass.: Blackwell Publishers.

Jacobs, Jane. 1961. *The Death and Life of Great American Cities.* New York: Vintage.

Jacobs, Sue-Ellen. 1974a. Action and Advocacy Anthropology. *Human Organization* 33:209–215.

———. 1974b. Doing It Our Way and Mostly for Our Own. *Human Organization* 33:380–382.

———. 1979. "Our Babies Shall Not Die": A Community's Response to Medical Neglect. *Human Organization* 38:120–133.

———. 1996. Afterword. In Lewin and Leap, eds., 287–308.

Jaimes, Annette, ed. 1992. *The State of Native America: Genocide, Colonization, and Resistance*. Boston: South End Press.

James, Allison, Jenny Hockey, and Andrew Dawson, eds. 1997. *After Writing Culture: Epistemology and Praxis in Contemporary Anthropology*. London: Routledge.

James, Wendy. 1990. Kings, Commoners, and the Ethnographic Imagination in Sudan and Ethiopia. In Fardon ed., 96–136.

Jayawardena, Chandra. 1963. *Conflict and Solidarity in a Guianese Plantation*. London: Athlone Press.

Jensen, Gordon, and Luh Ketut Suryani. 1992. *The Balinese People: A Reinvestigation of Character*. Singapore: Oxford University Press.

Johnson, Allen. 1975. Time Allocation in a Machiguenga Community. *Ethnology* 14:301–310.

———. 1977. The Energy Costs of Technology in a Changing Environment: A Machiguenga Case. In *Material Culture: Styles, Organization, and Dynamics of Technology*, ed. Heather Lechtman and Robert Merrill, 155–167. St. Paul, Minn.: West Publishing Company.

———. 1978. *Quantification in Cultural Anthropology: An Introduction to Research Design*. Stanford: Stanford University Press.

———. 1987. The Death of Ethnography: Has Anthropology Betrayed Its Mission? *The Sciences* 27(2):24–31.

———. 2003. *Families of the Forest: The Matsigenka Indians of the Peruvian Amazon*. Berkeley: University of California Press.

———, and Orna Johnson. 1990. Quality into Quantity: On the Measurement Potential of Ethnographic Fieldnotes. In Sanjek ed., 161–186.

Johnson, Dirk. March 5, 1991. Census Finds Many Claiming New Identity: Indian. *New York Times*, A1.

Johnson, Marion. 1966. Ashanti East of the Volta. *Transactions of the Historical Society of Ghana* 8:3–59.

Johnson, Orna. 1980. The Social Context of Intimacy and Avoidance: A Videotape Analysis of Machiguenga Meals. *Ethnology* 19:353–366.

———, and Allen Johnson. 1975. Male/Female Relations and the Organization of Work in a Machiguenga Community. *American Ethnologist* 2:634–648.

Jordan, Winthrop. 1968. *White over Black: American Attitudes Toward the Negro, 1550–1812*. Baltimore: Penguin.

Kapferer, Bruce. 1988. The Anthropologist as Hero: Three Exponents of Postmodernist Anthropology. *Critique of Anthropology* 8(2):77–104.

———. 1990. From the Periphery to the Centre: Ethnography and the Critique of Anthropology in Sri Lanka. In Fardon ed., 280–302.

Kaplan, Temma. 1982. Female Consciousness and Collective Action: The Case of Barcelona, 1910–1918. *Signs* 7:545–566.

Kasinitz, Philip. 1999. A Tree Grows in Queens. *Lingua Franca*, Spring, B23–B24.

———, and Judith Freidenberg-Herbstein. 1987. The Puerto Rican Parade and the West Indian Carnival: Public Celebrations in New York City. In *Caribbean Life in New York City: Sociocultural Dimensions*, ed. Constance Sutton and Elsa Chaney, 329–349. Staten Island, N.Y.: Center for Migration Studies.

Katznelson, Ira. 1981. *City Trenches: Urban Politics and the Patterning of Class in the United States*. Chicago: University of Chicago Press.

Kautsky, Karl. 1925. *Foundations of Christianity: A Study in Christian Origins*. New York: Monthly Review Press.

Kearney, Michael. 1986. From the Invisible Hand to Visible Feet: Anthropological Studies of Migration and Development. *Annual Review of Anthropology* 15:331–361.

Keesing, Roger. 1974. Theories of Culture. *Annual Review of Anthropology* 1:73–97.

———, ed. 1978. *'Elota's Story: The Life and Times of a Solomon Islands Big Man*. Fort Worth, Tex.: Holt, Rinehart & Winston.

———. 1987. Anthropology as Interpretive Quest. *Current Anthropology* 28:161–176.

Keil, Charles. 1966. *Urban Blues*. Chicago: University of Chicago Press.

———. 1979. *Tiv Song: The Sociology of Art in a Classless Society*. Chicago: University of Chicago Press.

———, and Steven Feld. 1994. *Music Grooves: Essays and Dialogues*. Chicago: University of Chicago Press.

———, Angeliki Keil, and Dick Blau. 1992. *Polka Happiness*. Philadelphia: Temple University Press.

Kelly, Lawrence C. 1985. Why Applied Anthropology Developed When It Did: A Commentary on People, Money, and Changing Times, 1930–1945. In *Social Contexts of American Ethnology, 1840–1984*, ed. June Helm, 122–138. Washington, D.C.: American Ethnological Society.

Kent, R. K. 1965. Palmares: An African State in Brazil. *Journal of African History* 6:161–175.

Kenyatta, Jomo. 1938. *Facing Mount Kenya*. New York: Vintage.

Kerr, Peter. 1991. Cosmetics Makers Read the Census. *New York Times*, August 29, D1, D15.

Kertzer, David. 1988. *Ritual, Politics, and Power*. New Haven: Yale University Press.

Khandelwal, Madhulika. 2002. *Becoming American, Being Indian: An Immigrant Community in New York City*. Ithaca, N.Y.: Cornell University Press.

Khosravi, Shahram. 2010. *"Illegal" Traveller: An Auto-Ethnography of Borders*. New York: Palgrave Macmillan.

Kich, George Kitahara. 1992. The Developmental Process of Asserting a Biracial, Bicultural Identity. In Root ed., 304–317.

Kideckel, David. 1993. *The Solitude of Collectivism: Romanian Villagers to the Revolution and Beyond.* Ithaca, N.Y.: Cornell University Press.

Kikumura, Akemi, and Harry Kitano. 1973: Interracial Marriage: A Picture of the Japanese Americans. *Journal of Social Issues* 29:67–81.

Kilson, Martin. 1975. Blacks and Neo-Ethnicity in American Political Life. In *Ethnicity: Theory and Experience*, ed. Nathan Glazer and Daniel P. Moynihan, 236–266. Cambridge, Mass.: Harvard University Press.

Kirch, Patrick. 2000. *On the Road of the Winds: An Archaeological History of the Pacific Islands before European Contact.* Berkeley: University of California Press.

Kiser, Clyde V. 1932. *Sea Island to City: St. Helena Islanders in Harlem.* New York: Columbia University Press.

Kiste, Robert. 1976. The People of Enewetak Atoll versus the U.S. Department of Defense. In *Ethics and Anthropology: Dilemmas in Fieldwork*, ed. Michael Rynkiewich and James Spradley, 61–80. New York: Wiley.

Kitano, Harry, Wai-tsang Yeung, Lynn Chai, and Herbert Hatanaka. 1984. Asian-American Intermarriage. *Journal of Marriage and the Family* 46:179–190.

Klass, Morton. 1961. *East Indians in Trinidad: A Study in Cultural Persistence.* New York: Columbia University Press.

Kopytoff, Igor. 1987. The Internal African Frontier: The Making of African Political Culture. In *The African Frontier: The Reproduction of Traditional African Societies*, ed. Igor Kopytoff, 2–84. Bloomington: Indiana University Press.

Kristol, Irving. 1966. The Negro Today Is like the Immigrant Yesterday. *New York Times Magazine*, September 11, 50–51, 124–142.

Kroeber, Alfred. 1946. The Ancient Oikoumene as a Historic Cultural Aggregate. *Journal of the Royal Anthropological Institute* 75:9–20.

Kuhn, Maggie, with Christina Long and Laura Quinn. 1991. *No Stone Unturned: The Life and Times of Maggie Kuhn.* New York: Ballantine.

Kuper, Hilda. 1960. *Indian People in Natal.* Pietermaritzburg: University of Natal Press.

Laguerre, Michel. 1984. *American Odyssey: Haitians in New York City.* Ithaca, N.Y.: Cornell University Press.

Lamley, Harry. 1981. Subethnic Rivalry in the Ch'ing Period. In *The Anthropology of Taiwan Society*, ed. Emily Ahern and Hill Gates, 282–318. Stanford, Calif.: Stanford University Press.

Lamphere, Louise. 1987. *From Working Daughters to Working Mothers: Immigrant Women in a New England Industrial Community.* Ithaca, N.Y.: Cornell University Press.

———, ed. 1992. *Structuring Diversity: Ethnographic Perspectives on the New Immigration.* Chicago: University of Chicago Press.

———. 2004. The Convergence of Applied, Practicing and Public Anthropology in the 21st Century. *Human Organization* 63:431–443.

———, Alex Stepick, and Guillermo Grenier, eds. 1994. *Newcomers in the Workplace: Immigrants and the Restructuring of the U.S. Economy*. Philadelphia: Temple University Press.

Landes, Ruth. 1970. A Woman Anthropologist in Brazil. In *Women in the Field: Anthropological Experiences*, ed. Peggy Golde, 119–139. Chicago: Aldine.

Langness, L. L., and Gelya Frank. 1978. Fact, Fiction and the Ethnographic Novel. *Anthropology and Humanism Quarterly* 3:18–22.

Lassiter, Luke Eric. 2005. *The Chicago Guide to Collaborative Ethnography*. Chicago: University of Chicago Press.

Law, Robin. 1977. *The Oyo Empire c. 1600–c. 1836: A West African Imperialism in the Era of the Atlantic Slave Trade*. Oxford: Oxford University Press.

Layton, Robert. 1985. Anthropology and the Australian Aboriginal Land Rights Act in Northern Australia. In *Social Anthropology and Development Policy*, ed. Ralph Grillo and Alan Rew, 148–167. London: Tavistock.

Leach, Edmund. 1961. *Pul Eliya, a Village in Ceylon: A Study in Land Tenure and Kinship*. Cambridge: Cambridge University Press.

———. 1984. Glimpses of the Unmentionable in the History of British Social Anthropology. *Annual Review of Anthropology* 13:1–23.

———. 1989. Writing Anthropology. *American Ethnologist* 16:137–141.

Leacock, Eleanor. 1969. *Teaching and Learning in City Schools: A Comparative Study*. New York: Basic Books.

Lederman, Rena. 1990. Pretexts for Ethnography: On Reading Fieldnotes. In Sanjek ed., 71–91.

———. 2005. Unchosen Grounds: Cultivating Cross-Subfield Accents for a Public Voice. In *Unwrapping the Sacred Bundle: Reflections on the Disciplining of Anthropology*, ed. Daniel Segal and Sylvia Yanagisako, 49–77. Durham, N.C.: Duke University Press.

Lee, Sharon, and Barry Edmonston. 2005. *New Marriages, New Families: U.S. Racial and Hispanic Intermarriage*. Washington, D.C.: Population Reference Bureau.

Lee, Sharon, and Keiko Yamanaka. 1990. Patterns of Asian American Intermarriage and Marital Assimilation. *Journal of Comparative Family Studies* 21:287–305.

Leeds, Anthony. 1964. Brazilian Careers and Social Structure: An Evolutionary Model and Case Study. *American Anthropologist* 66:1321–1347.

———. 1976. Urban Society Subsumes Rural: Specialties, Nucleations, Countryside, and Networks—Metatheory, Theory, and Method. *Atti del XL Congresso Internazionale degli Americanisti* 4:171–182. Genoa: Tilgher.

———. 1994. *Cities, Classes, and the Social Order*. Ed. Roger Sanjek. Ithaca, N.Y.: Cornell University Press.

Legassick, Martin. 1996. The Will of Abraham and Elizabeth September: The Struggle for Land in Gordonia, 1898–1995. *Journal of African History* 37:351–418.

Leis, Philip. 1977. Ethnicity and the Fourth of July Committee. In *Ethnic Encounters: Identities and Contexts*, ed. George Hicks and Philip Leis, 239–258. North Scituate, Mass.: Duxbury Press.

Leonard, Karen. 1992. *Making Ethnic Choices: California's Punjabi Mexican Americans.* Philadelphia: Temple University Press.

Leonetti, Donna, and Laura Newell-Morris. 1982. Exogamy and Change in the Biosocial Structure of a Modern Urban Population. *American Anthropologist* 84:19–36.

Lessinger, Johanna. 1992. Investing or Going Home? A Transnational Strategy Among Indian Immigrants in the United States. In Glick Schiller, Basch, and Blanc-Szanton eds., 53–80.

Leuchtenberg, William E. 2000. Queens. In *American Places: Encounters with History*, ed. William E. Leuchtenberg, 241–259. New York: Oxford University Press.

———. 2001. Riding the Trail of the New Pioneers. *Newsweek* (Atlantic edition), August 6, 52.

Lewin, Ellen, and William Leap, eds. 1996. *Out in the Field: Reflections of Lesbian and Gay Anthropologists.* Urbana: University of Illinois Press.

Lewis, Herbert. 2001. The Passion of Franz Boas. *American Anthropologist* 103:447–467.

Lewis, Oscar. 1950. An Anthropological Approach to Family Studies. *American Journal of Sociology* 55:468–475.

———. 1951. *Life in a Mexican Village: Tepotzlan Revisited.* Urbana: University of Illinois Press.

———. 1964. *Pedro Martinez: A Mexican Peasant and His Family.* New York: Random House.

Liberty, Margot. 1976. Native American "Informants": The Contribution of Francis La Flesche. In *American Anthropology: The Early Years*, ed. John Murra, 99–110. Washington, D.C.: American Ethnological Society.

———, ed. 1978a *American Indian Intellectuals.* St. Paul, Minn.: West Publishing Company.

———. 1978b. Francis La Flesche: The Osage Odyssey. In Liberty ed., 45–59.

Lieberson, Stanley. 1980. *A Piece of the Pie: Blacks and White Immigrants since 1880.* Berkeley: University of California Press.

———. 1985. Unhyphenated Whites in the United States. *Ethnic and Racial Studies* 8:159–180.

———, and Mary Waters. 1988. *From Many Strands: Ethnic and Racial Groups in Contemporary America.* New York: Russell Sage.

Liebow, Elliot. 1967. *Tally's Corner: A Study of Negro Streetcorner Men.* Boston: Little, Brown.

Light, Ivan. 1981. Ethnic Succession. In *Ethnic Change*, ed. Charles Keyes, 53–86. Seattle: University of Washington Press.

Linton, Adelin, and Charles Wagley. 1971. *Ralph Linton.* New York: Columbia University Press.

Linton, Ralph. 1923. *Purification of the Sacred Bundles, a Ceremony of the Pawnee.* Leaflet 7. Chicago: Field Museum of Natural History.

———. 1926. Origin of the Skidi Pawnee Sacrifice to the Morning Star. *American Anthropologist* 28:457–466.

Logan, John, and Brian Stults. 2011. The Persistence of Segregation in the Metropolis: New Findings from the 2010 Census. S4: Spatial Structures in the Social Sciences, Brown University. Retrieved January 28, 2013 (http://www.s4.brown.edu/us2010/Data/Report/report2.pdf).

Logan, John, and Charles Zhang. 2010. Global Neighborhoods: New Pathways to Diversity and Separation. *American Journal of Sociology* 115:1069–1109.

Lovejoy, Paul. 1978. The Role of the Wangarawa in the Economic Transformation of the Central Sudan in the 15th and 16th Centuries. *Journal of African History* 19:173–193.

———. 1980. *Caravans of Kola: The Hausa Kola Trade 1700–1900.* Zaria: Ahmadu Bello University Press.

———. 1982. The Volume of the African Slave Trade: A Synthesis. *Journal of African History* 23:473–501.

———, and Stephen Baier. 1975. The Desert-side Economy of the Central Sudan. *International Journal of African Historical Studies* 8:551–581.

Lowie, Robert. 1937. *The History of Ethnological Theory.* New York: Holt, Rinehart & Winston.

Lozano, Beverly. 1984. The Andalucia-Hawaii-California Migration: A Study in Macrostructure and Microhistory. *Comparative Studies in Society and History* 26:305–334.

Lutkehaus, Nancy. 1990. Refractions of Reality: On the Use of Other Ethnographers' Fieldnotes. In Sanjek ed., 303–323.

Lynd, Robert, and Helen Lynd. 1929. *Middletown: A Study in Contemporary American Culture.* New York: Harcourt Brace.

Lynn, Martin. 1984. Commerce, Christianity and the Origins of the "Creoles" of Fernando Po. *Journal of African History* 25:257–278.

———. 1992. Technology, Trade and "A Race of Native Capitalists": The Krio Diaspora of West Africa and the Steamship, 1852–95. *Journal of African History* 33:421–440.

MacClancy, Jeremy, and Chris McDonaugh, eds. 1996. *Popularizing Anthropology.* New York: Routledge.

Madge, John. 1962. *The Origins of Scientific Sociology.* London: Tavistock.

Mafeje, Archie. 1971. The Ideology of "Tribalism." *Journal of Modern African Studies* 9:253–261.

———. 1975. Religion, Class and Ideology in South Africa. In *Religion and Social Change in Southern Africa*, ed. Michael G. Whisson and Martin West, 164–184. Cape Town: David Philip.

———. 1976. Agrarian Revolution and the Land Question in Buganda. In *A Century of Change in Eastern Africa*, ed. W. Arens, 23–46. The Hague: Mouton.

———. 1978. Soweto and Its Aftermath. *Review of African Political Economy* 11:17–30.

Magdoff, Harry. 1969. *The Age of Imperialism: The Economics of U.S. Imperialism*. New York: Monthly Review Press.

Mahler, Sarah. 1995. *American Dreaming: Immigrant Life on the Margins*. Princeton, N.J.: Princeton University Press.

———. 1998. Theoretical and Empirical Contributions Toward a Research Agenda for Transnationalism. In *Transnationalism from Below*, ed. Peter M. Smith and Luis Guarnizo, 64–100. New Brunswick, N.J.: Transaction.

———. 1999. Constructing International Relations: The Role of Transnational Migrants and other Non-state Actors. *Identities* 7:197–232.

Mahoney, Roger. 2001. Charting a Course for Participation in Mission. The Catholic University of America, March 20. Retrieved February 17, 2013 (http://publicaffairs.cua.edu/RDSpeeches/01Mahony.cfm).

Malinowski, Bronislaw. 1922. *Argonauts of the Western Pacific*. New York: Dutton.

———. 1935 [1978]. *Coral Gardens and Their Magic*. New York: Dover.

———. 1967. *A Diary in the Strict Sense of the Term*. New York: Harcourt, Brace & World.

Malkki, Liisa. 1995. Refugees and Exiles: From "Refugee Studies" to the National Order of Things. *Annual Review of Anthropology* 24:495–523.

———. 1997. News and Culture: Transitory Phenomena and the Fieldwork Tradition. In Gupta and Ferguson eds., 86–101.

Manners, Robert. 1956. Functionalism, Realpolitik, and Anthropology in Underdeveloped Areas. *America Indigena* 16:7–33.

———. 1965. Remittances and the Unit of Analysis in Anthropological Research. *Southwestern Journal of Anthropology* 21:179–195.

Marable, Manning. 1990. A New Black Politics. *The Progressive*, August, 8–23.

Marcus, George. 1995. Ethnography in/of the World System: The Emergence of Multi-sited Ethnography. *Annual Review of Anthropology* 24:95–117.

———. 2006. Where Have All the Tales of Fieldwork Gone? *Ethnos* 7:113–122.

———. 2009. Introduction: Notes Toward an Ethnographic Memoir of Supervising Graduate Research Through Anthropology's Decades of Transformation. In *Fieldwork Is Not What It Used to Be: Learning Anthropology's Method in a Time of Transition*, ed. James Faubion and George Marcus, 1–34. Ithaca, N.Y.: Cornell University Press.

———. 2010. Notes from Within a Laboratory for the Reinvention of Anthropological Method. In Melhuus, Mitchell, and Wulff eds., 69–79.

———, and Dick Cushman. 1982. Ethnographies as Texts. *Annual Review of Anthropology* 11:25–69.

———, and Michael Fischer. 1986. *Anthropology as Cultural Critique: An Experimental Moment in the Human Sciences*. Chicago: University of Chicago Press.

Margolis, Maxine, and Conrad Kottak. 2003. Marvin Harris (1927–2001). *American Anthropologist* 105:685–688.

Mark, Joan. 1982. Francis La Flesche: The American Indian as Anthropologist. *Isis* 73:496–510.

———. 1988. *A Stranger in Her Native Land: Alice Fletcher and the American Indians.* Lincoln: University of Nebraska Press.

Marks, Morton. 1974. Recovering Ritual Structures in Afro-American Music. In *Religious Movements in Contemporary America,* ed. Irving Zaretsky and Mark Leone, 60–134. Princeton, N.J.: Princeton University Press.

Mascia-Lees, Frances, Patricia Sharpe, and Colleen Ballerino Cohen. 1989. The Postmodernist Turn in Anthropology: Cautions from a Feminist Perspective. *Signs* 15:7–33.

Massey, Douglas, and Nancy Denton. 1993. *American Apartheid: Segregation and the Making of the Underclass.* Cambridge, Mass.: Harvard University Press.

Matisoff, James. 1991. Sino-Tibetan Linguistics: Present State and Future Prospects. *Annual Review of Anthropology* 20:469–504.

Matory, J. Lorand. 2005. *Black Atlantic Religion: Tradition, Transnationalism, and Matriarchy in the Afro-Brazilian Candomble.* Princeton, N.J.: Princeton University Press.

Matthews, Z. K., and Monica Wilson. 1981. *Freedom for My People: The Autobiography of Z. K. Matthews: South Africa 1901 to 1968.* Cape Town: David Philip.

Mayer, Adrian. 1961. *Peasants in the Pacific: A Study of Fiji Indian Rural Society.* Berkeley: University of California Press.

McCabe, James. 1872. *Lights and Shadows of New York Life: Or, the Sights and Sensations of the Great City.* New York: Farrar, Straus and Giroux.

McKnight, David. 1990. The Australian Aborigines in Anthropology. In Fardon ed., 42–70.

McLaurin, Irma, ed. 2001. *Black Feminist Anthropology: Theory, Praxis, and Poetics.* New Brunswick, N.J.: Rutgers University Press.

McLeod, W. C. 1967. Celt and Indian: Britain's Old World Frontier in Relation to the New. In *Beyond the Frontier: Social Process and Cultural Change,* ed. Paul Bohannan and Fred Plog, 25–41. Garden City, N.Y.: Natural History Press.

McNeill, William. 1976. *Plagues and Peoples.* Garden City, N.Y.: Anchor.

———. 1979. Historical Patterns of Migration. *Current Anthropology* 20:95–102.

Mead, Margaret. 1938. *The Mountain Arapesh. I. An Importing Culture.* New York: American Museum of Natural History.

———. 1959. *An Anthropologist at Work: Writings of Ruth Benedict.* Boston: Houghton Mifflin.

———. 1969. Introduction to the 1969 Edition. In Margaret Mead, *Social Organization of Manu'a,* xi–xxiii. Honolulu: Bishop Museum Press.

———. 1972. *Blackberry Winter: My Earlier Years.* New York: Morrow.

———. 1976. Introduction. In *Margaret Mead: The Complete Bibliography 1925–1975*, ed. Joan Gordan, 1–21. The Hague: Mouton.

———. 1977. *Letters from the Field, 1925–1975*. New York: Harper & Row.

Meggitt, Mervyn. 1977. *Blood Is Their Argument: Warfare Among the Mae Enga Tribesmen of the New Guinea Highlands*. Palo Alto, Calif.: Mayfield.

Melhuus, Marit, Jon Mitchell, and Helena Wulff, eds. 2010. *Ethnographic Practice in the Present*. Oxford: Berghahn.

Mellars, Paul, Katie Boyle, Ofer Bar-Yosef, and Chris Stringer, eds. 2007. *Rethinking the Human Revolution: New Behavioural and Biological Perspectives on the Origin and Dispersal of Modern Humans*. Cambridge, U.K.: McDonald Institute for Archaeological Research.

Meltzer, David. 2009. *First Peoples in a New World: Colonizing Ice Age America*. Berkeley: University of California Press.

Merriam, Alan. 1965. Music and the Dance. In *The African World: A Survey of Social Research*, ed. Robert Lystad, 452–468. New York: Praeger.

———. 1973. The Bala Musician. In *The Traditional Artist in African Societies*, ed. Warren d'Azevedo, 250–281. Bloomington: Indiana University Press.

Merton, Robert. 1941 [1976]. Intermarriage and the Social Structure. In *Sociological Ambivalence and Other Essays*, 217–250. New York: Free Press.

Miller, Daniel. 1995. Introduction: Anthropology, Modernity and Consumption. In *Worlds Apart: Modernity Through the Prism of the Local*, ed. Daniel Miller, 1–22. London: Routledge.

———, and Don Slater. 2000. *The Internet: An Ethnographic Approach*. London: Berg.

Mintz, Sidney. 1977. The So-called World System: Local Initiative and Local Response. *Dialectical Anthropology* 2:253–270.

———. 1985. *Sweetness and Power: The Place of Sugar in Modern History*. New York: Viking.

Mitchell, J. Clyde. 1956. *The Kalela Dance: Aspects of Social Relationships Among Urban Africans in Northern Rhodesia*. Manchester, U.K.: Manchester University Press.

———. 1965. The Meaning of Misfortune for Urban Africans. In *African Systems of Thought*, ed. Meyer Fortes and Germaine Dieterlen, 192–202. London: Oxford University Press.

———. 1966. Theoretical Orientations in African Urban Studies. In *The Social Anthropology of Complex Societies*, ed. Michael Banton, 37–68. New York: Praeger.

Mittelback, F. G., and Joan Moore. 1968. Ethnic Endogamy: The Case of Mexican Americans. *American Journal of Sociology* 74:50–62.

Miyakawa, Edward. 1979. *Tule Lake*. Waldport, Or.: House by the Sea Publishing Company.

Mondlane, Eduardo. 1969. *The Struggle for Mozambique*. Baltimore: Penguin.

Montejano, David. 1987. *Anglos and Mexicans in the Making of Texas, 1836–1986*. Austin: University of Texas Press.

Moore, Sally Falk. 1987. Explaining the Present: Theoretical Dilemmas in Processual Ethnography. *American Ethnologist* 14:727–736.

———, and Barbara Myerhoff. 1977. Secular Ritual: Forms and Meanings. In *Secular Ritual*, ed. Sally Falk Moore and Barbara Myerhoff, 3–24. Assen, Netherlands: Van Gorcum.

Morgan, Lewis Henry. 1851 [1962]. *League of the Ho-de-no-sau-nee, or Iroquois*. New York: Corinth.

Morris, H. S. 1968. *The Indians in Uganda: A Study of Caste and Sect in a Plural Society*. Chicago: University of Chicago Press.

Murguia, Edward, and Phyllis Cancilla Martinelli, eds. 1991. Special issue: Latino/Hispanic Ethnic Identity. *Latino Studies Journal* 2(3):5–83.

Murguia, Edward, and W. Parker Frisbie. 1979. Trends in Mexican American Intermarriage. *Social Science Quarterly* 58:374–389.

Murie, James R. 1981a. *Ceremonies of the Pawnee. Part I. The Skiri*. Ed. Douglas R. Parks. Washington, D.C.: Smithsonian Institution Press.

———. 1981b. *Ceremonies of the Pawnee. Part II. The South Bands*. Ed. Douglas R. Parks. Washington, D.C.: Smithsonian Institution Press.

Murphy, Robert. 1991. Anthropology at Columbia: A Reminiscence. *Dialectical Anthropology* 16:65–81.

———, and Julian Steward. 1956. Tappers and Trappers: Parallel Process in Acculturation. *Economic Development and Cultural Change* 4:335–355.

Myerhoff, Barbara, and Stephen Mongulla. 1986. The Los Angeles Jews' "Walk for Solidarity": Parade, Festival, Pilgrimage. In *Symbolizing America*, ed. Herve Varenne, 119–135. Lincoln: University of Nebraska Press.

Myrdal, Gunnar. 1957. *Rich Lands and Poor*. New York: Harper & Row.

Nader, Laura. 1972. Up the Anthropologist: Perspectives Gained by Studying Up. In Hymes ed., 284–311.

Nagengast, Carol. 1994. Violence, Terror, and the Crisis of the State. *Annual Review of Anthropology* 23:109–136.

Nakashima, Cynthia. 1992. An Invisible Monster: The Creation and Denial of Mixed-Race People in America. In Root ed., 162–178.

Naroll, Raoul. 1970. Data Quality Control in Cross-cultural Surveys. In *A Handbook of Method in Cultural Anthropology*, ed. Raoul Naroll and Ronald Cohen, 927–945. New York: Columbia University Press.

Nee, Victor, and Brett deBary Nee. 1973. *Longtime Californ': A Documentary Study of an American Chinatown*. New York: Pantheon.

Newfield, Jack, and Paul DuBrul. 1977. *The Abuse of Power: The Permanent Government and the Fall of New York*. New York: Viking Press.

Nichols, Johanna. 1997. Modeling Ancient Population Structures and Movement in Linguistics. *Annual Review of Anthropology* 26:359–384.

Nishimoto, Richard. 1995. *Inside an American Concentration Camp: Japanese American Resistance at Poston, Arizona*. Ed. Lane Hirabayashi. Tucson: University of Arizona Press.

Obbo, Christine. 1980. *African Women: Their Struggle for Economic Independence.* London: Zed.

———. 1990. Adventures with Fieldnotes. In Sanjek ed., 290–302.

O'Hare, William. 1992. *America's Minorities: The Demographics of Diversity.* Washington, D.C.: Population Reference Bureau.

———, and Judy Felt. 1991. *Asian Americans: America's Fastest Growing Minority Group.* Washington, D.C.: Population Reference Bureau.

———, Kelvin Pollard, Taynia Mann, and Mary Kent. 1991. *African Americans in the 1990s.* Washington, D.C.: Population Reference Bureau.

Okely, Judith. 1987. Fieldwork up the M1: Policy and Political Aspects. In Jackson ed., 55–73.

———. 1992. Anthropology and Autobiography: Participatory Experience and Embodied Knowledge. In Okely and Callaway eds., 1–28.

———. 2008. Knowing Without Notes. In Halstead, Hirsch, and Okely eds., 55–74.

———. 2012. *Anthropological Practice: Fieldwork and the Ethnographic Method.* Oxford: Berg.

———, and Helen Callaway, eds. 1992. *Anthropology and Autobiography.* London: Routledge.

Okubo, Mine. 1946. *Citizen 13660.* New York: Columbia University Press.

Olwig, Karen Fog, and Kirsten Hastrup, eds. 1997. *Siting Culture: The Shifting Anthropological Object.* London: Routledge.

Omer-Cooper, J. D. 1966. *The Zulu Aftermath: A Nineteenth-Century Revolution in Bantu Africa.* London: Longmans.

Omi, Michael, and Howard Winant. 1986. *Racial Formation in the United States: From the 1960s to the 1980s.* New York: Routledge and Kegan Paul.

Ong, Aihwa. 1992. Limits to Cultural Accumulation: Chinese Capitalists on the American Pacific Rim. In Glick Schiller, Basch, and Blanc-Szanton eds., 125–143.

Onwuachi, P. Chike, and Alvin Wolfe. 1966. The Place of Anthropology in the Future of Africa. *Human Organization* 25:93–95.

Ortner, Sherry. 1984. Theory in Anthropology Since the Sixties. *Comparative Studies in Society and History* 26:126–166.

———. 2006. *Anthropology and Social Theory: Culture, Power, and the Acting Subject.* Durham, N.C.: Duke University Press.

Osgood, Cornelius. 1940. *Ingalik Material Culture.* New Haven, Conn.: Yale University Publications in Anthropology.

———. 1958. *Ingalik Social Culture.* New Haven, Conn.: Yale University Publications in Anthropology.

———. 1959. *Ingalik Mental Culture.* New Haven, Conn.: Yale University Publications in Anthropology.

O'Shaughnessy, Patrice, Shirley Wong, and Kevin McCoy. 1999. Melting Pot Ave.: City's Most Racially Mixed Block Shows Face of N.Y. in Year 2000. *Daily News,* November 22–26.

Ottenberg, Simon. 1955. Improvement Associations Among the Afikpo Ibo. *Africa* 25:1–27.

———. 1958. Ibo Oracles and Intergroup Relations. *Southwestern Journal of Anthropology* 14:295–317.

———. 1975. *Masked Rituals of Afikpo: The Context of an African Art*. Seattle: University of Washington Press.

———. 1990. Thirty Years of Fieldnotes: Changing Relationships to the Text. In Sanjek 1990a, 139–160.

———. 1996. *Seeing with Music: The Lives of Three Blind African Musicians*. Seattle: University of Washington Press.

Ova, Ahuia. 1925. Motu Feasts and Dances. Trans. Rev. J. B. Clark. In *Territory of Papua Annual Report for the Year 1922–23*, 37–40. Melbourne, Australia: Government Printer.

Owen, Roger. 1965. The Patrilocal Band: A Linguistically and Culturally Hybrid Social Unit. *American Anthropologist* 67:675–690.

Owusu, Maxwell. 1970. *Uses and Abuses of Political Power: A Case Study in Continuity and Change in the Politics of Ghana*. Chicago: University of Chicago Press.

———. 1976. Colonial and Postcolonial Anthropology of Africa: Scholarship or Sentiment? In *A Century of Change in Eastern Africa*, ed. W. Arens, 7–22. The Hague: Mouton.

———. 1978. Ethnography of Africa: The Usefulness of the Useless. *American Anthropologist* 80:10–34.

Oxfeld, Ellen. 1993. *Blood, Sweat, and Mahjong: Family and Enterprise in an Overseas Chinese Community*. Ithaca, N.Y.: Cornell University Press.

Padilla, Elena. 1958. *Up from Puerto Rico*. New York: Columbia University Press.

Paine, Robert, ed. 1985a. *Advocacy and Anthropology, First Encounters*. St. John's, Canada: Institute of Social and Economic Research, Memorial University of Newfoundland.

———. 1985b. Preface. In Paine ed., xiii–xvii.

Palmer, Robin. 1977. The Italians: Patterns of Migration to London. In Watson ed., 242–268.

Pardo, Mary. 1998. *Mexican American Women Activists: Identity and Resistance in Two Los Angeles Communities*. Philadelphia: Temple University Press.

Park, Kyeyoung. 1989. "Born Again": What Does It Mean to Korean Americans in New York City? *Journal of Ritual Studies* 3:289–303.

———. 1997. *The Korean American Dream: Immigrants and Small Business in New York City*. Ithaca, N.Y.: Cornell University Press.

Parkin, David. 1990. Eastern Africa: The View from the Office and the Voice from the Field. In Fardon ed., 182–203.

Parks, Douglas R. 1978. James R. Murie: Pawnee Ethnographer. In Liberty ed., 75–89.

———. 1981. Editors' Introduction. In James R. Murie, *Ceremonies of the Pawnee. Part 1*, 1–28. Washington, D.C.: Smithsonian Institution Press.

Passel, Jeffrey, Wendy Wang, and Paul Taylor. 2010. *One-in-Seven New U.S. Marriages Is Interracial or Interethnic: Marrying Out*. Pew Research Social and Demographic Trends. Retrieved January 28, 2013 (http://www.pewsocialtrends.org/2010/06/04/marrying-out/).

Peacock, James. 1997. The Future of Anthropology. *American Anthropologist* 99:9–17.

Pecorella, Robert. 1994. *Community Power in a Post Reform City: Politics in New York City*. Armonk, N.Y.: M. E. Sharpe.

Peel, J. D. Y. 1984. Making History: The Past in the Ijesha Present. *Man* 19:111–132.

———. 1987. History, Culture and the Comparative Method: A West African Puzzle. In *Comparative Anthropology*, ed. Ladislav Holy, 88–118. New York: Basil Blackwell.

Pelto, Pertti. 1970. *Anthropological Research: The Structure of Inquiry*. New York: Harper & Row.

Penny, Thomas. 2008. U.S. White Population Will Be Minority by 2042, Government Says. Bloomberg.com, August 14. Retrieved January 31, 2013 (http://www.-bloomberg.com/apps/news?pid = newsarchive&sid = afLRFXgzpFoY).

Peregrine, Peter, Ilia Peiros, and Marcus Feldman, eds. 2009. *Ancient Human Migrations: A Multidisciplinary Approach*. Salt Lake City: University of Utah Press.

Peterson, Mark Allen. 2000. The Long Walk II: "For as Long as I Can Remember Anthropology Has Been Reinventing Itself": An Interview with Donald Powell Cole. *Nomadic Peoples* 4(2):7–20.

Phillipson, D. W. 1977. The Spread of the Bantu Language. *Scientific American* 236(4): 106–115.

Philpott, Stuart. 1977. The Montserratians: Migration Dependency and the Maintenance of Island Ties in England. In Watson ed., 90–119.

Pierpont, Claudia Roth. 2004. The Measure of America: How a Rebel Anthropologist Waged War on Racism. *New Yorker*, March 8, 48–63.

Piot, Charles. 1999. *Remotely Global: Village Modernity in West Africa*. Chicago: University of Chicago Press.

Plaatje, Sol T. 1916. *Native Life in South Africa*. Athens: Ohio University Press.

Plath, David. 1990. Fieldnotes, Filed Notes, and the Conferring of Note. In Sanjek ed., 371–384.

Porter, Arthur. 1963. *Creoledom: A Study of the Development of Freetown Society*. London: Oxford University Press.

Posadas, Barbara. 1981. Crossed Boundaries in Interracial Chicago: Filipino American Families since 1925. *Amerasia Journal* 8(2):31–52.

Powdermaker, Hortense. 1939. *After Freedom: A Cultural Study in the Deep South*. New York: Atheneum.

———. 1962. *Copper Town: Changing Africa*. New York: Harper & Row.

———. 1967. *Stranger and Friend: The Way of an Anthropologist*. New York: Norton.

Price, Richard. 1983. *First-time: The Historical Vision of an Afro-American People*. Baltimore: Johns Hopkins University Press.

Pringle, Heather. 2011. The First Americans. *Scientific American*, November, 33–45.

Quartey-Papafio, A. B. 1910. Law of Succession Among the Akras or the Gã Tribes Proper of the Gold Coast. *Journal of the African Society* 10:64–72.

———. 1911. The Native Tribunals of the Akras of the Gold Coast. *Journal of the African Society* 10:320–330, 434–446; 11:75–94.

———. 1913. The Use of Names Among the Gãs or Accra People of the Gold Coast. *Journal of the African Society* 13:167–182.

———. 1914. Apprenticeship Among the Gãs. *Journal of the African Society* 13:415–422.

———. 1920. The Gã Homowo Festival. *Journal of the African Society* 19:126–134, 227–232.

Quigley, Declan. 1997. Deconstructing Colonial Fictions? Some Conjuring Tricks in the Recent Sociology of India. In James, Hockey, and Dawson eds., 103–121.

Racial Segregation. 1991. *Newsday*, April 10, 16.

Radin, Paul. 1920 [1963]. *The Autobiography of a Winnebago Indian*. New York: Dover.

Ralston, Richard. 1969. The Return of Brazilian Freedmen to West Africa in the 18th and 19th Centuries. *Canadian Journal of African Studies* 3:577–592.

Rapport, Nigel, and T. M. Luhrmann. 1989. Anthropology and Autobiography: Two Accounts of the 1989 ASA Conference at York. *Anthropology Today* 5(4):25–28.

Redfield, Robert. 1930. *Tepotzlan, a Mexican Village: A Study of Folk Life*. Chicago: University of Chicago Press.

———. 1950. *A Village That Chose Progress: Chan Kom Revisited*. Chicago: University of Chicago Press.

———, and Alfonso Villa Rojas. 1934. *Chan Kom: A Maya Village*. Chicago: University of Chicago Press.

Reinicke, John. 1938. Trade Jargons and Creole Dialects as Marginal Languages. *Social Forces* 17:107–118.

Renfrew, Colin. 1992. Archaeology, Genetics and Linguistic Diversity. *Man* 27:445–478.

Resek, Carl. 1960. *Lewis Henry Morgan: American Scholar*. Chicago: University of Chicago Press.

Rhoades, Robert. 1980. European Cyclical Migration and Economic Development: The Case of Southern Spain. In *Urban Life: Readings in Urban Anthropology*, ed. George Gmelch and William Zenner, 110–119. New York: St. Martin's.

Richards, Audrey. 1939a. The Development of Field Work Methods in Social Anthropology. In *The Study of Society: Methods and Problems*, ed. Frederic Barlett, Morris Ginsberg, E. J. Lindgren, and R. H. Thouless, 272–316. London: Routledge and Kegan Paul.

———. 1939b. *Land, Labour and Diet in Northern Rhodesia: An Economic Study of the Bemba Tribe*. London: Oxford University Press.

Richards, Martin. 2003. The Neolithic Invasion of Europe. *Annual Review of Anthropology* 32:135–162.

Ricourt, Milagros, and Ruby Danta. 2003. *Hispanas de Queens: Latino Panethnicity in a New York City Neighborhood.* Ithaca, N.Y.: Cornell University Press.

Riker, James, Jr. 1852. *The Annals of Newtown in Queens County, New-York.* New York: Fanshaw.

Ringer, Benjamin. 1983. *"We the People" and Others: Duality and America's Treatment of Its Racial Minorities.* New York: Tavistock.

Rink, Oliver. 1986. *Holland on the Hudson: An Economic and Social History of Dutch New York.* Ithaca, N.Y.: Cornell University Press.

Rivera, Edward. 1982. *Family Installments: Memories of Growing Up Hispanic.* New York: Penguin.

Rivers, W. H. R. 1906. *The Todas.* Cambridge: Cambridge University Press.

Roberts, John Storm. 1972. *Black Music of Two Worlds.* Tivoli, N.Y.: Original Music.

Robinson, Randall. 2000. *The Debt: What America Owes to Blacks.* New York: Penguin.

Rodman, Margaret. 1992. Empowering Place: Multilocality and Multivocality. *American Anthropologist* 94:640–656.

Rodriguez, Clara. 1989. *Puerto Ricans: Born in the U.S.A.* Boston: Unwin Hyman.

Rodriguez, Sylvia. 2006. *Acequia: Water Sharing, Sanctity, and Place.* Santa Fe, N.M.: School for Advanced Research Press.

Root, Maria. 1992a. From Shortcuts to Solutions. In Root ed., 342–347.

———, ed. 1992b. *Racially Mixed People in America.* Newbury Park, Calif.: Sage.

Rosaldo, Renato. 1989. *Culture and Truth: The Remaking of Social Analysis.* Boston, Mass.: Beacon.

———. 1994. Cultural Citizenship and Educational Democracy. *Cultural Anthropology* 9:402–411.

Roseberry, William. 1988. Political Economy. *Annual Review of Anthropology* 17:161–185.

———. 1989. *Anthropologies and Histories: Essays in Culture, History and Political Economy.* New Brunswick, N.J.: Rutgers University Press.

Rothschild, Rose. 1993. District Needs Statement. In *Community District Needs*, 61–80. New York: Department of City Planning.

———. 1996. District Needs Statement. In *Community District Needs*, 67–86. New York: Department of City Planning.

Rowe, John. 1946. Inca Culture at the Time of the Spanish Conquest. In *Handbook of South American Indians.* Vol. 2. *The Andean Civilizations*, ed. Julian Steward, 183–330. Washington, D.C.: Government Printing Office.

Rubinstein, Robert, ed. 1991. *Fieldwork: The Correspondence of Robert Redfield and Sol Tax.* Boulder: Westview.

Sabloff, Jeremy. 1998. Distinguished Lecture in Archeology: Communication and the Future of American Archeology. *American Anthropologist* 100:869–875.

Sacks, Karen Brodkin. 1988. *Caring by the Hour: Women, Work, and Organizing at Duke Medical Center.* Urbana: University of Illinois Press.

Sahlins, Marshall. 1961. The Segmentary Lineage: An Organization of Predatory Expansion. *American Anthropologist* 63:322–345.

———. 1978. The Apotheosis of Captain Cook. *Kroeber Anthropological Society Papers* 53/54:1–31.

———. 1985. *Islands of History.* Chicago: University of Chicago Press.

———. 1992. *Anahulu: The Anthropology of History in the Kingdom of Hawaii.* Vol. 1. *Historical Ethnography.* Chicago: University of Chicago Press.

———. 2000. *Culture in Practice: Selected Essays.* New York: Zone.

Saito, Leland. 1998. *Race and Politics: Asian Americans, Latinos, and Whites in a Los Angeles Suburb.* Urbana: University of Illinois Press.

Salgado de Snyder, Nelly, and Amado Padilla. 1982. Cultural and Ethnic Maintenance of Interethnically Married Mexican Americans. *Human Organization* 41:359–362.

Salins, Peter. 1993. Zoning for Growth and Change. In *Planning and Zoning New York City,* ed. Todd Bressi, 164–184. New Brunswick, N.J.: Center for Urban Policy Research.

Salvo, Joseph, Ronald Ortiz, and Francis Vardy. 1992. *The Newest New Yorkers: An Analysis of Immigration into New York City During the 1980s.* New York: Department of City Planning.

Salzman, Philip. 1994. The Lone Stranger in the Heart of Darkness. In Borofsky ed., 29–39.

Sanday, Peggy. 2003. Public Interest Anthropology: A Model for Engaged Social Science. Paper prepared for School of American Research Workshop on Public Interest Anthropology. Retrieved January 28, 2013 (http://www.sas.upenn.edu/~psanday/SARdiscussion%20paper.65.html).

Sangren, P. Steven. 1988. Rhetoric and the Authority of Ethnography. *Current Anthropology* 29:405–427.

Sanjek, Roger. 1969a. Radical Anthropology: Values, Theory and Content. *Anthropology U.C.L.A.* 1:21–32.

———. 1969b. Some Aspects of Authority in a Black Family. Unpublished term paper, Columbia University.

———. 1971. Brazilian Racial Terms: Some Aspects of Meaning and Learning. *American Anthropologist* 73:1126–1143. Reprinted in Darnell ed., 2002, 65–92.

———. 1972. *Ghanaian Networks: An Analysis of Interethnic Relations in Urban Situations.* PhD dissertation, Department of Anthropology, Columbia University.

———. 1974. What Is Network Analysis, and What Is It Good For? *Reviews in Anthropology* 1:588–597.

———. 1977. Cognitive Maps of the Ethnic Domain in Urban Ghana: Reflections on Variability and Change. *American Ethnologist* 4:603–622.

———. 1978. A Network Method and Its Uses in Urban Ethnography. *Human Organization* 37:257–268.

———. 1982a. The American Anthropological Association Resolution on the Employment of Women: Genesis, Implementation, Disavowal and Resurrection. *Signs* 7:845–868.

———. 1982b. *Federal Housing Programs and Their Impact on Homelessness.* New York: Coalition for the Homeless. Reprinted in *Housing the Homeless*, ed. John Erickson and Charles Wilhelm, 315–321. New Brunswick, N.J.: Center for Urban Policy Research, 1986.

———. 1982c. The Organization of Households in Adabraka: Toward a Wider Comparative Perspective. *Comparative Studies in Society and History* 23:57–103.

———. 1983. Female and Male Domestic Cycles in Urban Africa: The Adabraka Case. In *Female and Male in West Africa*, ed. Christine Oppong, 330–343. London: Allen & Unwin.

———. 1984. *Crowded Out: Homelessness and the Elderly Poor in New York City.* New York: Coalition for the Homeless & Gray Panthers of New York City. Reprinted in *Homeless Older Americans: Hearing Before the Subcommittee on Housing and Consumer Interests of the Select Committee on Aging, House of Representatives, 98th Congress*, Comm. Pub. No. 98–461, pp. 119–184. Washington, D.C.: U.S. Government Printing Office, 1984.

———. 1987a. Anthropological Work at a Gray Panther Health Clinic: Academic, Applied, and Advocacy Goals. In *Cities of the United States: Studies in Urban Anthropology*, ed. Leith Mullings, 148–175. New York: Columbia University Press.

———. 1987b. County and College: The World in Queens. *Queens College Report* 3(3):2.

———. 1987c. Elmhurst Businesses Surveyed. *Newtown Crier* 17(4):16, 20.

———. 1987d. Local Houses of Worship Overview. *Newtown Crier* 17(6):8, 20, 22.

———. 1988. *The People of Queens from Now to Then.* Asian/American Center Working Paper. Flushing: Queens College, City University of New York.

———. 1989a. The World in Woodside. In *Inside Woodside: A Multi-Cultural Festival.* Festival booklet. Woodside, N.Y.: Woodside on the Move.

———, ed. 1989b. *Worship and Community: Christianity and Hinduism in Contemporary Queens.* Asian/American Center Working Paper. Flushing: Queens College, City University of New York.

———, ed. 1990a. *Fieldnotes: The Makings of Anthropology.* Ithaca, N.Y.: Cornell University Press.

———. 1990b. Fire, Loss, and the Sorcerer's Apprentice. In Sanjek ed., 34–44.

———. 1990c. Maid Servants and Market Women's Apprentices in Adabraka. In Sanjek and Colen eds., 35–62.

———. 1990d. On Ethnographic Validity. In Sanjek ed., 385–418.

———. 1990e. The Secret Life of Fieldnotes. In Sanjek ed., 187–270.

———. 1991. The Ethnographic Present. *Man* 26:609–628.

———. 1993. Anthropology's Hidden Colonialism: Assistants and Their Ethnographers. *Anthropology Today* 9(2):13–18.

———. 1994a. The Enduring Inequalities of Race. In Gregory and Sanjek eds., 1–17.

———. 1994b. Intermarriage and the Future of Races in the United States. In Gregory and Sanjek eds., 103–130.

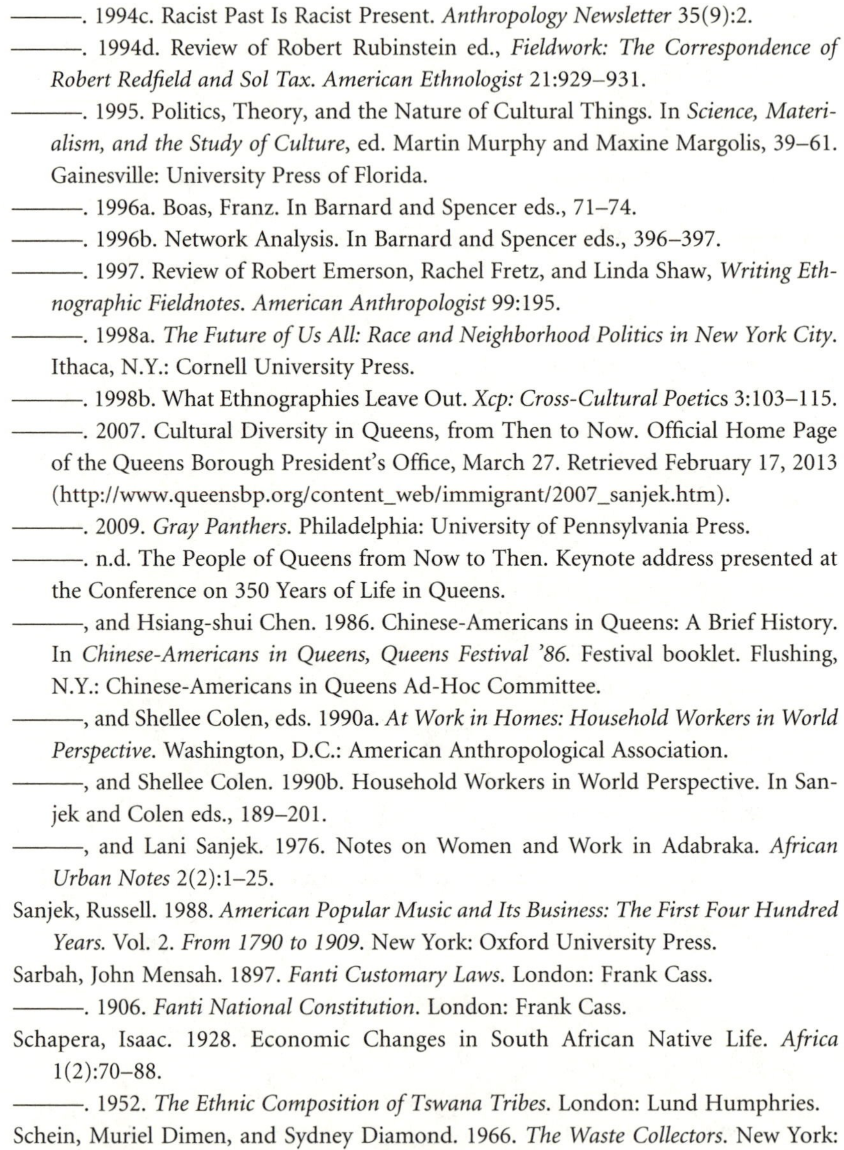

———. 1994c. Racist Past Is Racist Present. *Anthropology Newsletter* 35(9):2.

———. 1994d. Review of Robert Rubinstein ed., *Fieldwork: The Correspondence of Robert Redfield and Sol Tax. American Ethnologist* 21:929–931.

———. 1995. Politics, Theory, and the Nature of Cultural Things. In *Science, Materialism, and the Study of Culture*, ed. Martin Murphy and Maxine Margolis, 39–61. Gainesville: University Press of Florida.

———. 1996a. Boas, Franz. In Barnard and Spencer eds., 71–74.

———. 1996b. Network Analysis. In Barnard and Spencer eds., 396–397.

———. 1997. Review of Robert Emerson, Rachel Fretz, and Linda Shaw, *Writing Ethnographic Fieldnotes. American Anthropologist* 99:195.

———. 1998a. *The Future of Us All: Race and Neighborhood Politics in New York City.* Ithaca, N.Y.: Cornell University Press.

———. 1998b. What Ethnographies Leave Out. *Xcp: Cross-Cultural Poetics* 3:103–115.

———. 2007. Cultural Diversity in Queens, from Then to Now. Official Home Page of the Queens Borough President's Office, March 27. Retrieved February 17, 2013 (http://www.queensbp.org/content_web/immigrant/2007_sanjek.htm).

———. 2009. *Gray Panthers.* Philadelphia: University of Pennsylvania Press.

———. n.d. The People of Queens from Now to Then. Keynote address presented at the Conference on 350 Years of Life in Queens.

———, and Hsiang-shui Chen. 1986. Chinese-Americans in Queens: A Brief History. In *Chinese-Americans in Queens, Queens Festival '86.* Festival booklet. Flushing, N.Y.: Chinese-Americans in Queens Ad-Hoc Committee.

———, and Shellee Colen, eds. 1990a. *At Work in Homes: Household Workers in World Perspective.* Washington, D.C.: American Anthropological Association.

———, and Shellee Colen. 1990b. Household Workers in World Perspective. In Sanjek and Colen eds., 189–201.

———, and Lani Sanjek. 1976. Notes on Women and Work in Adabraka. *African Urban Notes* 2(2):1–25.

Sanjek, Russell. 1988. *American Popular Music and Its Business: The First Four Hundred Years.* Vol. 2. *From 1790 to 1909.* New York: Oxford University Press.

Sarbah, John Mensah. 1897. *Fanti Customary Laws.* London: Frank Cass.

———. 1906. *Fanti National Constitution.* London: Frank Cass.

Schapera, Isaac. 1928. Economic Changes in South African Native Life. *Africa* 1(2):70–88.

———. 1952. *The Ethnic Composition of Tswana Tribes.* London: Lund Humphries.

Schein, Muriel Dimen, and Sydney Diamond. 1966. *The Waste Collectors.* New York: Department of Anthropology, Columbia University.

Schensul, Stephen. 1973. Action Research: The Applied Anthropologist in a Community Mental Health Program. In *Anthropology Beyond the University*, ed. Alden Redfield, 106–119. Athens: University of Georgia Press.

———. 1974. Skills Needed in Action Anthropology: Lessons from El Centro de la Causa. *Human Organization* 33:203–209.

———, and Jean Schensul. 1978. Advocacy and Applied Anthropology. In *Social Scientists as Advocates: Views from the Applied Disciplines*, ed. George Weber and George McCall, 121–165. Beverly Hills, Calif.: Sage.

Schieffelin, Edward. 1993. Performance and the Cultural Construction of Reality: A New Guinea Example. In *Creativity/Anthropology*, ed. Smadar Lavie, Kirin Narayan, and Renato Rosaldo, 270–295. Ithaca, N.Y.: Cornell University Press.

Schoen, Robert, Verne Nelson, and Marion Collins. 1978. Intermarriage Among Spanish Surnamed Californians, 1962–1974. *International Migration Review* 12:359–369.

Schumaker, Lyn. 2001. *Africanizing Anthropology: Fieldwork, Networks, and the Making of Cultural Knowledge in Central Africa*. Durham: Duke University Press.

Schurr, Theodore. 2004. The Peopling of the New World: Perspectives from Molecular Anthropology. *Annual Review of Anthropology* 33:551–583.

Schwartz, Shepard. 1951. Mate Selection Among New York City's Chinese Males, 1931–38. *American Journal of Sociology* 56:562–568.

Seligman, C. G. 1910. *The Melanesians of British New Guinea*. Cambridge: Cambridge University Press.

Sexton, James. 1981. *Son of Tecun Uman: A Maya Indian Tells His Story*. Tucson: University of Arizona Press.

———. 1985. *Campesino: The Diary of a Guatemalan Indian*. Tucson: University of Arizona Press.

———. 1992. *lgnacio: The Diary of a Maya Indian of Guatemala*. Philadelphia: University of Pennsylvania Press.

Sharpe, Barrie. 1984. Marriage Rules on the Plateau: An Exchange. *Africa* 54(4):24–30.

Shelley, Reg. 1978. Ahuia Ova: New Insights into the Life of a Prominent Papuan. *Oceania* 48: 202–206.

Sherzer, Joel, and Richard Bauman 1972. Areal Studies and Culture History: Language as a Key to the Historical Study of Culture Contact. *Southwestern Journal of Anthropology* 28:131–152.

Shokeid, Moshe. 1971. *The Dual Heritage: Immigrants from the Atlas Mountains in an Israeli Village*. Manchester, U.K.: University of Manchester Press.

———. 1988. Anthropologists and Their Informants: Marginality Reconsidered. *European Journal of Sociology* 29:31–47.

———. 2001. Fieldwork in Social and Cultural Anthropology. *International Encyclopedia of the Social and Behavioral Sciences*, ed. Neil Smelser and Paul Baltes, 8:5628–5632. Amsterdam: Elsevier.

———. 2007. From the Tikopia to Polymorphous Engagements: Ethnographic Writing under Changing Fieldwork Circumstances. *Social Anthropology* 15:305–319.

———. 2009. *Three Jewish Journeys Through an Anthropologist's Lens: From Morocco to the Negev, Zion to the Big Apple, the Closet to the Bimah*. Brighton, Mass.: Academic Studies Press.

Sieber, R. Timothy. 1994. The Life of Anthony Leeds: Unity in Diversity. In Leeds, 1–26.

Silverman, Sydel. 1965. Patronage and Community-Nation Relationships in Central Italy. *Ethnology* 4:172–189.

Simmons, Leo. 1942. *Sun Chief: The Autobiography of a Hopi Indian.* New Haven, Conn.: Yale University Press.

Singer, Merrill. 1990. Another Perspective on Advocacy. *Current Anthropology* 31:548–550.

———. 2000. Why I Am Not a Public Anthropologist. *Anthropology News* 41(6):6–7.

Siu, Paul. 1987. *The Chinese Laundryman: A Study in Social Isolation.* New York: Columbia University Press.

Skinner, George W. 1957. *Chinese Society in Thailand: An Analytic History.* Ithaca, N.Y.: Cornell University Press.

———. 1964. Marketing and Social Structure in Rural China, Part I. *Journal of Asian Studies* 24:3–43.

Smith, Marian. 1959. Boas' "Natural History" Approach to Field Method. In *The Anthropology of Franz Boas*, ed. Walter Goldschmidt, 46–60. San Francisco: Chandler.

Smith, Robert C. 1998a. Reflections on Migration, the State and the Construction, Durability and Newness of Transnational Life. In *Soziale welt*, ed. L. Pries, 197–217. Baden-Baden: Nomos Verlagsgesellschaft.

———. 1998b. Transnational Localities: Community, Technology and the Politics of Membership within the Context of Mexico and U.S. Migration. In *Transnationalism from Below*, ed. Peter M. Smith and Luis Guarnizo, 196–238. New Brunswick, N.J.: Transaction.

Smith, Robert J. 1989. Presidential Address: Something Old, Something New—Tradition and Culture in the Study of Japan. *Journal of Asian Studies* 48:715–723.

———. 1990. Hearing Voices, Joining the Chorus: Appropriating Someone Else's Fieldnotes. In Sanjek ed., 356–370.

Snow, Dean. 2009. The Multidisciplinary Study of Human Migration: Problems and Principles. In Peregrine, Peiros, and Feldman eds., 6–20.

Society for Applied Anthropology. n.d. Ethical and Professional Responsibilities. Retrieved February 15, 2013 (http://sfaa.net/sfaaethic.html).

Sone, Monica. 1953. *Nisei Daughter*. Seattle: University of Washington Press.

Southall, Aidan. 1969. Spirit Possession and Mediumship Among the Alur. In *Spirit Mediumship and Society in Africa*, ed. John Beattie and John Middleton, 232–272. New York: Africana.

———. 1970. The Illusion of Tribe. In *The Passing of Tribal Man in Africa*, ed. Peter Gutkind, 28–50. The Hague: Mouton.

———. 1971. Cross Cultural Meanings and Multilingualism. In *Language Use and Social Change: Problems of Multilingualism with Special Reference to Eastern Africa*, ed. W. H. Whitely, 376–396. London: Oxford University Press.

———. 1988. The Segmentary State in Africa and Asia. *Comparative Studies in Society and History* 30:52–82.

Southworth, Bruce. 1998–1999. *The Future of Us All.* The Community Pulpit 8. New York: Community Church of New York.

Spencer, Baldwin, and Frank Gillen. 1899 [1968]. *The Native Tribes of Central Australia.* New York: Dover.

Spencer, Jonathan. 1989. Anthropology as a Kind of Writing. *Man* 24:145–164.

Spicer, Edward, Asael Hansen, Katherine Luomala, and Marvin Opler. 1969. *Impounded People: Japanese-Americans in the Relocation Centers.* Tucson: University of Arizona Press.

Spickard, Paul. 1989. *Mixed Blood: Intermarriage and Ethnic Identity in Twentieth-Century America.* Madison: University of Wisconsin Press.

Spier, Leslie. 1928 [1979]. *Havasupai Ethnography.* New York: AMS.

Spigner, Clarence. 1990. Black/White Interracial Marriages: A Brief Overview of U.S. Census Data, 1980–1987. *Western Journal of Black Studies* 14:214–216.

Spradley, James. 1976. Trouble in the Tank. In *Ethics and Anthropology: Dilemmas in Fieldwork,* ed. Michael Rynkiewich and James Spradley, 17–31. New York: Wiley.

Srinivas, M. N. 1976. *The Remembered Village.* Berkeley: University of California Press.

———, and Andre Beteille. 1964. Networks in Indian Social Structure. *Man* 64:165–168.

———, A. M. Shah, and E. A. Ramaswamy. 1979. Introduction. In *The Fieldworker and the Field: Problems and Challenges in Sociological Investigation,* ed. M. N. Srinivas, A. M. Shah, and E. A. Ramaswamy, 1–15. Delhi: Oxford University Press.

Stafford, Walter. 1985. *Closed Labor Markets: Underrepresentation of Blacks, Hispanics, and Women in New York City's Core Industries and Jobs.* New York: Community Service Society.

Stannard, D. E. 1989. *Before the Horror: The Population of Hawai'i on the Eve of Western Contact.* Honolulu: University of Hawaii Press.

———. 1992. *American Holocaust: Columbus and the Conquest of the New World.* New York: Oxford University Press.

Starn, Orin. 1986. Engineering Internment: Anthropologists and the War Relocation Authority. *American Ethnologist* 13:700–720.

Stauder, Jack. 1974. The Relevance of Anthropology to Colonialism and Imperialism. *Race* 16:29–51.

Stenning, Derrick. 1957. Transhumance, Migratory Drift, Migration: Patterns of Pastoral Fulani Nomadism. *Journal of the Royal Anthropological Institute* 87:57–73.

Stepick, Alex. 1998. *Pride Against Prejudice: Haitians in the United States.* Needham Heights, Mass.: Allyn & Bacon.

Stocking, George, Jr. 1966. Franz Boas and the Culture Concept in Historical Perspective. *American Anthropologist* 68:867–882.

———, ed. 1974. *The Shaping of American Anthropology, 1883–1911: A Franz Boas Reader.* New York: Basic.

———. 1979. Anthropology as Kulturkampf: Science and Politics in the Career of Franz Boas. In *The Uses of Anthropology*, ed. Walter Goldschmidt, 33–50. Washington, D.C.: American Anthropological Association.

———. 1985. Philanthropoids and Vanishing Cultures: Rockefeller Funding and the End of the Museum Era in Anglo-American Anthropology. *History of Anthropology* 3:112–145.

———. 1989. The Ethnographic Sensibility of the 1920s and the Dualism of the Anthropological Tradition. *History of Anthropology* 6:208–276.

———. 1991. Colonial Situations. *History of Anthropology* 7:3–8.

Strathern, Andrew. 1979. *Ongka: A Self-Account by a New Guinea Big-Man*. New York: St. Martin's Press.

Strathern, Marilyn. 1987a. An Awkward Relationship: The Case of Feminism and Anthropology. *Signs* 12:276–292.

———. 1987b. Out of Context: The Persuasive Fictions of Anthropology [and Comments and Reply]. *Current Anthropology* 28:251–281.

Strauss, Claudia, and Naomi Quinn. 1994. A Cognitive/Cultural Anthropology. In Borofsky ed., 284–300.

Stuckert, Robert. 1964. Race Mixture: The African Ancestry of White Americans. In *Physical Anthropology and Archaeology: Selected Readings*, ed. Peter Hammond, 192–197. New York: Macmillan.

Stull, Donald, ed. 1990. When the Packers Came to Town: Changing Ethnic Relations in Garden City, Kansas. *Urban Anthropology* 19:303–427.

———. 1994. Knock 'Em Dead: Work on the Killfloor of a Modern Beefpacking Plant. In Lamphere, Stepick, and Grenier eds., 44–77.

———, Janet Benson, Michael Broadway, Arthur Campa, Ken Erickson, and Mark Grey. 1990. *Changing Relations: Newcomers and Established Residents in Garden City, Kansas*. Lawrence: Institute for Public Policy and Business, University of Kansas.

———, and Michael Broadway. 2004. *Slaughterhouse Blues: The Meat and Poultry Industry in North America*. Belmont, Calif.: Wadsworth.

Sturtevant, William. 1968. Anthropology, History, and Ethnohistory. In *Introduction to Cultural Anthropology*, ed. James Clifton, 451–475. Boston: Houghton Mifflin.

Suarez-Orozco, Marcelo. 2000. Everything You Ever Wanted to Know About Assimilation But Were Afraid to Ask. *Daedalus* 129(4):1–30.

Sullivan, Gerald. 1999. *Margaret Mead, Gregory Bateson, and Highland Bali: Fieldwork Photographs of Bayung Gede, 1936–1939*. Chicago: University of Chicago Press.

Sung, Betty Lee. 1990. *Chinese American Intermarriage*. New York: Center for Migration Studies.

Sussman, Robert, ed. 1993. Contemporary Issues Forum: A Current Controversy in Human Evolution. *American Anthropologist* 95:9–96.

Suttles, Wayne. 1991. Streams of Property, Armor of Wealth: The Traditional Kwakiutl Potlatch. In *Chiefly Feasts: The Enduring Kwakiutl Potlatch*, ed. Aldona Jonaitis, 71–133. Seattle: University of Washington Press.

Sutton, J .E. S. 1974. The Aquatic Civilization of Middle Africa. *Journal of African History* 15:527–546.

———. 1979. Toward a Less Orthodox History of Hausaland. *Journal of African History* 20: 179–201.

Suzuki, Peter. 1981. Anthropologists in the Wartime Camps for Japanese Americans: A Documentary Study. *Dialectical Anthropology* 6: 23–60.

Swartz, Marc. 1968. Introduction. In *Local-Level Politics*, ed. Marc Swartz, 1–46. Chicago: Aldine.

Takakura, Shinichiro. 1960. *The Ainu of Northern Japan: A Study in Conquest and Acculturation*. Philadelphia: American Philosophical Society.

Tambiah, Stanley Jeyaraja. 1970. *Buddhism and the Spirit Cults in Northeast Thailand*. Cambridge: Cambridge University Press.

———. 1985. *Culture, Thought, and Social Action: An Anthropological Perspective*. Cambridge, Mass.: Harvard University Press.

Tanenbaum, Susie. 1995. *Underground Harmonies: Music and Politics in the Subways of New York*. Ithaca, N.Y.: Cornell University Press.

Tannen, Deborah. 1990. *You Just Don't Understand: Women and Men in Conversation*. New York: Ballantine.

Tarmann, Allison. January 2003. International Adoption Rate in U.S. Doubled in the 1990s. *Population Reference Bureau*. http://www.prb.org/Articles/2003/InternationalAdoptionRateinUSDoubledinthe1990s.aspx

Tax, Sol. 1951 [1963]. *Penny Capitalism: A Guatemalan Indian Economy*. Chicago: University of Chicago Press.

———. 1979. Autobiography of Santiago Yach. In *Currents in Anthropology*, ed. Robert Hinshaw, 1–68. The Hague: Mouton.

Tchen, Jack Kuo Wei. 1984. *Genthe's Photographs of San Francisco's Old Chinatown*. New York: Dover.

———. 1990. New York Chinese: The Nineteenth-Century Pre-Chinatown Settlement. *Chinese America: History and Perspectives* 4:157–192.

Tedlock, Barbara. 1995. Works and Wives: On the Sexual Division of Textual Labor. In Behar and Gordon eds., 267–286.

Telsch, Kathleen. 1988. Amerasian Influx Expected by U.S. *New York Times*, October 9.

Tenzer, Heather. 1999. Queens Author Looks at Changes in Elmhurst-Corona and Sees "Future." *Queens Chronicle*, January 28, 4.

Terrell, John. 1986. *Prehistory in the Pacific Islands: A Study of Variation in Language, Customs, and Human Biology*. New York: Cambridge University Press.

TeSelle, Gene. 2000. A Serious Look at Real Diversity. Presbyterian Voices for Justice, April 19. Retrieved February 17, 2013 (http://presbyvoicesforjustice.org/2004/future_of_us_all.htm).

Thomas, David Hurst. 2000. *Skull Wars: Kennewick Man, Archaeology, and the Battle for Native American Identity*. New York: Basic.

Thomas, Piri. 1967. *Down These Mean Streets.* New York: Vintage.

Thomas, William I., and Florian Znaniecki. 1984. *The Polish Peasant in Europe and America.* Ed. Eli Zaretsky. Urbana: University of Illinois Press.

Thompson, Robert Farris. 1974. *African Art in Motion: Icon and Act.* Berkeley: University of California Press.

Thornton, Robert. 1983. Narrative Ethnography in Africa, 1850–1920: The Creation and Capture of an Appropriate Domain for Anthropology. *Man* 18:502–520.

Thornton, Russell. 1987. *American Indian Holocaust and Survival: A Population History since 1492.* Norman: University of Oklahoma Press.

Thottam, Jyoti. 1999. Queens' Changing Face Is Professor's Laboratory. *Flushing Times,* March 4, 20, 22.

T'ien, Ju–K'ang. 1953. *The Chinese of Sarawak: A Study of Social Structure.* London: London School of Economics and Political Science.

Tinker, John. 1973. Intermarriage and Ethnic Boundaries: The Japanese American Case. *Journal of Social Issues* 29:49–65.

Trask, Haunani-Kay. 1996. Feminism and Indigenous Hawaiian Nationalism. *Signs* 21:906–916.

Turnbull, Colin. 1963. The Lesson of the Pygmies. *Scientific American* 208(1):2–11.

Turner, Victor. 1967. *The Forest of Symbols: Aspects of Ndembu Ritual.* Ithaca, N.Y.: Cornell University Press.

———. 1974. *Dramas, Fields, and Metaphors: Symbolic Action in Human Society.* Ithaca, N.Y.: Cornell University Press.

Uchida, Yoshiko. 1982. *Desert Exile: The Uprooting of a Japanese American Family.* Seattle: University of Washington Press.

Valentine, Charles. 1968. *Culture and Poverty: Critique and Counter-proposals.* Chicago: University of Chicago Press.

Valle, Maria Eva. 1991. The Quest for Ethnic Solidarity and a New Public Identity Among Chicanos and Latinos. *Latino Studies Journal* 2(3):72–83.

Van Esterik, Penny. 1985. Confronting Advocacy Confronting Anthropology. In Paine ed., 59–77.

Van Maanen, John. 1988. *Tales of the Field: On Writing Ethnography.* Chicago: University of Chicago Press.

Vansina, Jan. 1990. *Paths in the Rainforests: Toward a History of Political Tradition in Equatorial Africa.* Madison: University of Wisconsin Press.

van Velsen, Jaap. 1961. Labour Migration as a Positive Factor in the Continuity of Tonga Tribal Society. In *Social Change in Modern Africa,* ed. Aidan Southall, 230–241. London: Oxford University Press.

———. 1964. *The Politics of Kinship: A Study of Social Manipulation Among the Lakeside Tonga of Nyasaland.* Manchester, U.K.: University of Manchester Press.

———. 1967. The Extended Case Study Method and Situational Analysis. In *The Craft of Social Anthropology,* ed. A. L. Epstein, 129–149. London: Tavistock.

van Willigen, John. 1986. *Applied Anthropology: An Introduction.* South Hadley, Mass.: Bergin & Garvey.

Villa Rojas, Alfonso. 1945. *The Maya of East Central Quintana Roo.* Washington, D.C.: Carnegie Institution.

Vincent, Joan. 1986. System and Process, 1974–1985. *Annual Review of Anthropology* 15:99–119.

———. 1991. Engaging Historicism. In *Recapturing Anthropology: Working in the Present,* ed. Richard Fox, 45–58. Santa Fe, N.M.: School of American Research Press.

Vogt, Evon. 1965. Review of William Holland, *Medicina Maya en Los Altos de Chiapas. American Anthropologist* 67:524–526.

———. 1994. *Fieldwork Among the Maya: Reflections on the Harvard Chiapas Project.* Albuquerque: University of New Mexico Press.

Wagley, Charles. 1949. *The Social and Religious Life of a Guatemalan Village.* Washington, D.C.: American Anthropological Association.

———. 1983. Learning Fieldwork: Guatemala. In *Fieldwork: The Human Experience,* ed. Robert Lawless, Vinson H. Sutlive, Jr., and Mario Zamora, 1–17. New York: Gordon & Breach.

———, and Marvin Harris. 1958. *Minorities in the New World: Six Case Studies.* New York: Columbia University Press.

Wallerstein, Immanuel. 1961. *Africa, the Politics of Independence: An Interpretation of Modern African History.* New York: Vintage.

———. 1974. The Rise and Future Demise of the World Capitalist System: Concepts for Comparative Analysis. *Comparative Studies in Society and History* 16:387–415.

Wallman, Sandra. 1985a. Discussion 3. In Paine ed., 80–81.

———. 1985b. Discussion 6. In Paine ed., 219.

———. 1997. Appropriate Anthropology and the Risky Inspiration of "Capability" Brown: Representations of What, by Whom, and to What End? In James, Hockey, and Dawson eds., 244–263.

Walt, Vivienne. 1988. Foreign Adoptions Open New World of Love. *Newsday,* November 6, 19.

Warner, Margaret Hall. 1988. *W. Lloyd Warner, Social Anthropologist.* New York: Publishing Center for Cultural Resources.

Warner, W. Lloyd. 1962. *American Life: Dream and Reality.* Chicago: University of Chicago Press.

———, ed. 1963. *Yankee City.* New Haven, Conn.: Yale University Press.

Washington, Joseph R., Jr. 1970. *Marriage in Black and White.* Boston: Beacon.

Waters, Mary. 1990. *Ethnic Options: Choosing Identities in America.* Berkeley: University of California Press.

Watson, James. 1975. *Emigration and the Chinese Lineage: The Mans in Hong Kong and London.* Berkeley: University of California Press.

———, ed. 1977a. *Between Two Cultures: Migrants and Minorities in Britain.* Oxford: Basil Blackwell.

———. 1977b. The Chinese: Hong Kong Villagers in the British Catering Trade. In Watson ed., 181–213.

———, ed. 1997. *Golden Arches East: McDonald's in East Asia*. Stanford, Calif.: Stanford University Press.

Watson, William. 1958. *Tribal Cohesion in a Money Economy: A Study of the Mambwe People of Northern Rhodesia*. Manchester, U.K.: University of Manchester Press.

Wax, Emily. 1998. In Elmhurst and Corona, It's Tomorrow Already. *Newsday*, September 27, G1.

———. 1999. Providing a Haven for the Roma. *Newsday*, March 10, G1.

Weglyn, Michi. 1976. *Years of Infamy: The Untold Story of America's Concentration Camps*. New York: Morrow.

Weingrod, Alex. 1990. *The Saint of Beersheba*. Albany: State University of New York Press.

Wells, Spencer. 2002. *The Journey of Man: A Genetic Odyssey*. New York: Random House.

West, Cornel. 1993. Audacious Hope and a Sense of History. *Crossroads* 35:2–6.

Wheatley, Paul. 1975. Satyanrta in Suvarnadvipa: From Reciprocity to Redistribution in Ancient Southeast Asia. In *Ancient Civilization and Trade*, ed. Jeremy Sabloff and C. C. Lamberg-Karlovsky, 227–283. Albuquerque: University of New Mexico Press.

Wheeler, David. 1993. Black Children, White Parents: The Difficult Issue of Transracial Adoption. *Chronicle of Higher Education*, September 15, A16.

White, Ann Terry. 1951. *Prehistoric America*. New York: Random House.

———. 1953. *The First Men in the World*. New York: Random House.

Whitten, Norman E., Jr. 1988. Toward a Critical Anthropology. *American Ethnologist* 15:732–742.

Whyte, William Foote. 1943. *Street Corner Society: The Social Structure of an Italian Slum*. Chicago: University of Chicago Press.

———. 1955. Appendix: On the Evolution of "Street Corner Society." In *Street Corner Society*, enlarged ed., 279–358. Chicago: University of Chicago Press.

———. 1993. *Street Corner Society: The Social Structure of an Italian Slum*. 4th ed. Chicago: University of Chicago Press.

———. 1997. *Creative Problem Solving in the Field: Reflections on a Career*. Walnut Creek, Calif.: AltaMira Press.

Wiest, Raymond. 1973. Wage-Labor Migration and the Household in a Mexican Town. *Journal of Anthropological Research* 29:180–209.

Wilkerson, Isabel. 1991. Black-White Marriages Rise, But Couples Still Face Scorn. *New York Times*, December 2, A1, B6.

Wilks, Ivor. 1968. The Transmission of Islamic Learning in the Western Sudan. In *Literacy in Traditional Societies*, ed. Jack Goody, 161–197. Cambridge: Cambridge University Press.

———. 1975. *Asante in the Nineteenth Century: The Structure and Evolution of a Political Order.* Cambridge: Cambridge University Press.

———. 1982. Wangara, Akan and the Portuguese in the 15th and 16th Centuries. *Journal of African History* 23:333–349, 463–472.

Williams, Brett. 1988. *Upscaling Downtown: Stalled Gentrification in Washington D.C.* Ithaca, N.Y.: Cornell University Press.

Williams, Eric. 1944. *Capitalism and Slavery.* Chapel Hill, N.C.: Capricorn.

Williams, F. E. 1939. The Reminiscences of Ahuia Ova. *Journal of the Royal Anthropological Institute* 69:11–44.

Williams, Patricia. 1997. *Seeing a Color-Blind Future: The Paradox of Race.* New York: Noonday.

Williamson, Joel. 1980. *New People: Miscegenation and Mulattoes in the United States.* New York: New York University Press.

Willmott, W. E. 1970. *The Political Structure of the Chinese Community in Cambodia.* London: Athlone Press.

Wilson, Godfrey. 1941. *An Essay on the Economics of Detribalization in Northern Rhodesia, Part I.* Lusaka: Rhodes-Livingstone Institute.

———. 1942. *An Essay on the Economics of Detribalization in Northern Rhodesia, Part II.* Lusaka: Rhodes-Livingstone Institute.

———, and Monica Wilson. 1945. *The Analysis of Social Change: Based on Observations in Central Africa.* Cambridge: Cambridge University Press.

Wilson, Monica. 1977. The First Three Years, 1938–41. *African Social Research* 24:279–283.

———, and Archie Mafeje. 1963. *Langa: A Study of Social Groups in an African Township.* Cape Town: Oxford University Press.

Wirth, Louis. 1928. *The Ghetto.* Chicago: University of Chicago Press.

Wolcott, Harry. 1990. *Writing Up Qualitative Research.* Newbury Park, Calif.: Sage.

———. 1995. *The Art of Fieldwork.* Walnut Creek, Calif.: AltaMira,

Wolf, Eric. 1969. *Peasant Wars of the Twentieth Century.* New York: Harper and Row.

———. 1982. *Europe and the People Without History.* Berkeley: University of California Press.

———. 1988. Inventing Society. *American Ethnologist* 15:752–761.

———. 1990. Distinguished Lecture: Facing Power—Old Insights, New Questions. *American Anthropologist* 92:586–596.

———, and Joseph Jorgensen. 1970. Anthropology on the Warpath in Thailand. *New York Review of Books,* November 19, 26–35.

———, and Sidney Mintz. 1957. Haciendas and Plantations in Middle America and the Antilles. *Social and Economic Studies* 6:380–412.

Wolf, Margery. 1990. Chinanotes: Engendering Anthropology. In Sanjek ed., 343–355.

Wolfe, Alvin. 1963. The African Mineral Industry: Evolution of a Supranational Level of Integration. *Social Forces* 11:153–164.

Wong, Bernard. 1982. *Chinatown: Economic Adaptation and Ethnic Identity of the Chinese.* New York: Holt, Rinehart and Winston

Worsley, Peter. 1964. *The Third World.* Chicago: University of Chicago Press.

Wright, Susan. 1995. Anthropology: Still the Uncomfortable Discipline? In *The Future of Anthropology: Its Relevance to the Contemporary World*, ed. Ahmed Akbar and Cris Shore, 65–93. London: Athlone Press.

Wu, David. 1982. *The Chinese in Papua New Guinea: 1880–1980.* Hong Kong: Chinese University Press.

Yanagisako, Sylvia Junko. 1985. *Transforming the Past: Tradition and Kinship Among Japanese Americans.* Stanford, Calif.: Stanford University Press.

———. 2002. *Producing Culture and Capital: Family Firms in Italy.* Princeton, N.J.: Princeton University Press.

Yang, Martin. 1945. *A Chinese Village: Taitou, Shantung Province.* New York: Columbia University Press.

Yatsushiro, Toshio. 1953. *Political and Socio-cultural Issues at Poston and Manzanar Relocation Centers.* PhD dissertation, Department of Anthropology, Cornell University.

———. 1978. *Politics and Cultural Values: The World War II Japanese Relocation Centers, United States Government.* New York: Arno Press.

A Year of Crises: UNHCR Global Trends 2011. 2012. UNHCR: The UN Refugee Agency. Retrieved January 29, 2013 (http://www.unhcr.org/4fd6f87f9.html).

Yengoyan, Aram. 1986. Theory in Anthropology: On the Demise of the Concept of Culture. *Comparative Studies in Society and History* 28:368–374.

Yinger, John. 1995. *Closed Doors, Opportunities Lost: The Continuing Crisis of Housing Discrimination.* New York: Russell Sage.

Young, Michael W. 1984. The Intensive Study of a Restricted Area, or, Why Did Malinowski Go to the Trobriand Islands? *Oceania* 55:1–26.

———. 2004. *Malinowski: Odyssey of an Anthropologist, 1884–1920.* New Haven, Conn.: Yale University Press.

Yuan, D. Y. 1980. Significant Demographic Characteristics of Chinese Who Intermarry in the United States. *California Sociologist* 3:184–196.

Zavella, Patricia. 1994. Reflections on Diversity Among Chicanas. In Gregory and Sanjek eds., 199–212.

Zorbaugh, Harvey. 1929. *The Gold Coast and the Slum: A Sociological Study of Chicago's Near North Side.* Chicago: University of Chicago Press.

Index

Acknowledgments

Gerontologists distinguish *cohort effects* on historically specific generations—in my case, I am part of a cohort that entered anthropology and adulthood in the 1960s.[1] They also identify *life-cycle influences*—for me, notably, fieldwork in Brazil when I was nineteen, Ghana in my middle and late twenties, Gray Panther experiences in my early thirties to early forties, Elmhurst-Corona through my forties and into my fifties, and Gray Panthers again in my sixties. How differently, I have wondered, might I see the world, and anthropology's world, had these fieldwork engagements been shuffled in different order or occurred in different decades? How then might I have understood and written about these places, people, and issues?

The "color full before color blind" thread of this book, the focus on race in my work across five decades, combines cohort and life cycle impacts: my interests as a young reader; Anne Schwerner and the 1950s–1960s civil rights movement; Marvin Harris; people I met in Brazil, then Ghana, then Berkeley, then Queens; and reengaging in the 2000s with writings on "anatomically modern human" global dispersals.

The feminist movement emerging in the late 1960s and 1970s deeply affected Lani Sanjek and me, then in our later twenties (cohort and life-cycle effects intersecting here again). As mentioned in the Preface, it undoubtedly contributed to foregrounding women as much as men in my fieldwork and writings about Ghana and Queens and with the Gray Panthers. Yet how could it have been otherwise? These were very impressive women I met in each place, certainly as much as the men, frequently more so than the men. My work in the 1970s with other colleagues, mainly women, on the AAA Committee on the Status of Women and then in pressing the AAA to enforce its adopted position on gender equity in employment—including Carol Kramer, Carole Vance, Rayna Rapp, Louise Lamphere, Naomi Quinn—translated feminist consciousness into action.[2]

Coediting and writing overview sections with Shellee Colen for *At Work in Homes: Household Workers in World Perspective* in the later 1980s also deepened my feminist, as well as political economic, orientations.[3]

These personal, fieldwork, and professional life episodes no doubt led me to view other theoretical "movements" between the 1960s and now as less momentous or compelling. Yet working alongside or even countering this were the wide-ranging theoretical and ethnographic interests of the scores of anthropologists I worked closely with as authors in the Anthropology of Contemporary Issues series during the 1980s and 1990s, as Queens fieldwork team members, and as contributors to *Fieldnotes*, *At Work in Homes*, and *Race*. Often their ideas and work challenged me to read more widely, to engage other and new theoretical perspectives. They provided me with "continuing education" in a welcome way at the time, and I have enjoyed following later work by many of these colleagues.

While Brazilian, Ghanaian, and Elmhurst-Corona fieldwork informants and friends left indelible traces on me, my most profound acknowledgment is to the Gray Panthers and Over 60 Clinic clients and volunteers in Berkeley, California, whom I met during 1976–1978.[4] Then in my early thirties, I became a political compatriot and friend to people in their sixties, seventies, and eighties, many of them veterans of the struggles of the 1930s. They gave me a new and unexpected outlook on what the human life cycle could be—indeed, on what I could be. I thank Lani for pulling me, a novice applied and advocacy anthropologist, into this and for its impact thereafter on my research and writing and on our lives together. We became old young, something we were privileged to share with a cohort of other young Gray Panthers. Now in our sixties ourselves, we understand and benefit from this even more. Lani has also read and helped improve each of the essays in this book over the years, as well as the preface and acknowledgments.

In revising the essays for this volume, I have updated, streamlined, clarified, and eliminated some redundant or unneeded passages and phrases. In this effort, I have heeded advice from Queens College students, including that I remove strings of references from the text and transfer points I think important from endnotes into the body of the chapters. ("We don't read endnotes," they let me know.) They also provided a sounding board about which essays to include and in what order. In addition to thanking them collectively, I thank Luis Caridad for his responses to several revised chapters. I appreciate as well Ulf Hannerz and Moshe Shokeid's comments on the preface.

Last, I thank colleagues who encouraged individual chapters: Alan Barnard, George Bond, Thomas Cook, Gudrun Dahl, Chen Hsiang-shui, Robert Hackenberg, Ulf Hannerz, Tim Ingold, the late Carol Kramer, Maxine Margolis, Martin Murphy, Mark Nowak, Kyeyoung Park, Charles Ragin, Jonathan Spencer, Ronald Stade, and Donald Stull.